81

ECONOMICS OF FUTURES TRADING

FOR COMMERCIAL AND PERSONAL PROFIT

**A PUBLICATION OF
COMMODITY RESEARCH BUREAU, INC.**

*Established in 1934 for research in
price movements, production, distribution
and consumption of commodities*

Other Publications
- *Commodity Year Book*
- *Modern Commodity Futures Trading*
✓ *Forecasting Commodity Prices*
- *The Fastest Game in Town*
- *Techniques of a Professional Commodity Chart Analyst*
- COMMODITY CHART SERVICE®
- FUTURES MARKET SERVICE®
- CRB EASY-UPDATE CHARTS
- ELECTRONIC FUTURES TREND ANALYZER
- CRB COMMODITY INDEX REPORT
- Other specialized commodity publications

A complete listing of publications can be obtained by writing directly to
Commodity Research Bureau, Inc.

Economics of Futures Trading

FOR COMMERCIAL
AND PERSONAL PROFIT

By THOMAS A. HIERONYMUS

publishers

 Commodity Research Bureau, Inc.

ONE LIBERTY PLAZA, NEW YORK, N.Y. 10006

DEDICATION

To My Teacher

The late L. J. Norton

Contents

Preface

This book is designed to serve several purposes—probably more than can be reasonably expected. It is, in the first instance, a college level textbook for a course in commodity futures markets and trading. The subject matter is in an area almost totally neglected in college curricula, particularly in business and finance schools. There is a great deal of student interest but limited satisfactory literature and teaching expertise. Hopefully, a textbook will serve as the catalyst that will get greater inclusion and generate enough teacher confidence that more courses are offered. The manuscript has been tried on students and seems to have at least one thing going: they read it with minimum coercion. It begins at the beginning, includes the economic results of trading, and does not shy away from the complexities that are a part of the subject matter.

It is a "how it is done" and a "how to do it" book designed to be used by commercial people in the commodity trades and by investors in futures contracts. The combination of what markets are about and how to use them is compatible because one cannot *really* know what markets are about unless he knows how they are used, nor can one succeed in the use of futures markets if he does not understand the economics behind the trading. So, I have put them together and, hopefully, made them interdependent.

It is an appraisal of the adequacy and effectiveness of the system in the performance of its economic functions. Having put together the economics and the use of futures trading, it was but a short step to looking for things the matter with the system as it exists. Over the years, I have developed some notions about how markets ought to be run and regulated that differ from standard doctrine and procedure. Either much that is known about futures trading is not true or much that I think I know is in error. So, the book is a forum, and conflict is to be expected.

At the start I thought that the preparation of a manuscript would be fairly simple. Having knocked about the field of futures trading for twenty years and written fairly extensively, I thought that I could link together much that I had written with only a moderate amount of new work. Such was not the case. I found that much that I had done was in too much depth and detail or too applied and, more importantly, I found that many standard concepts—including some of my own—were difficult to reconcile and could not be fitted together into a coherent whole. I hope that enough concepts were modified that the material is internally consistent.

In looking back on the experience, some central points stand out. A statement of these before the beginning is useful in setting the reader straight about the biases of the author and, in a measure, describing what the book is about.

First, futures trading is a zero sum game. For every buyer there is a seller; for every long there is a short; the clearing house breaks even so that for every dollar made there is a dollar lost; the market is a balance of judgments so that for every good judgment there is a poor judgment. The markets are remarkably symmetrical. The symmetry turns up repeatedly as different aspects of trading are examined. The net hedged positions are a mirror image of the net speculative positions. Class interval tabulations of winners and losers among speculators form a nearly perfect normal curve. The amounts of money made and lost form the convex of the curve. Price variations are random so that the next price change is as apt to be up as down. There is a balance of competitive power in the market so that the game is remarkably fair to all of the players.

Futures trading is an exciting game, the score of which is kept with money. There are important amounts of money involved so that the game is taken seriously. But a game it is. The people who participate, including the commercials—the hedgers—appear to be first interested in the game itself and second in the money.

Second, futures trading is a remarkably close approximation to the classical economic concept of pure competition. The established, high volume markets, nearly meet the tests for perfect markets. They are not planned with the economic concept of pure competition in the fore but evolved into this form out of the crucible of market forces. They can serve as models for the further development of less sophisticated sister markets.

Third, the markets are mainly about the pricing of commodities, which is speculative. And so the markets are about speculation. Hedging, in its standard context, is a nonsense term. Equal and opposite is still speculative. In addition, a high proportion of "hedged" positions are taken with a "view of the market." If this book makes only one contribution, it is the thorough lousing up of a standard doctrine of hedging.

Fourth, futures markets are investment media. They are financial markets and futures contracts are financial instruments. The markets generate equity capital

from the speculators and, as furnishers of capital, the speculators play a significant role in the direction of the economic processes. Speculators form judgments, back them with capital, and, in part, order the system. Thus, commodity
speculation is, indeed, investment.

Fifth, much of the regulation of markets is misdirected: a) much of the
alleged manipulation and price distortion hasn't really happened, b) when
prices have been distorted, the guilt has usually been misplaced, c) market
dominance is more apt to be accomplished by hedgers than by speculators, and
d) regulation has generally restricted speculation and decreased competition.
The markets are relatively free of monopolistic influences but a preoccupation
with price distortion has hampered market growth and development.

Sixth, the futures markets that work, work well indeed. These are the visible
ones. But rather more markets do not work than do. The rate of failure among
newly established futures markets is high. When compared to the total risk
shifting—financing problems, the amount of futures trading is quite small.
Thus, the institution has great growth potential. There is need for much more
speculation of a higher quality than now exists.

The book is a tribute to the people who trade commodities, both commercials
and speculators. For twenty years I have had the somewhat unique experience
of being continuously associated with the operation, regulation, and trading of
futures while, at the same time, being continuously concerned with forecasting
the prices of a major group of actively traded commodities (feed, grains, soybeans, and soybean products). This duality of interest has not only resulted in
insights that either of the areas alone would not have produced but has also
brought me into continuous association with the players. They are a fascinating
group of sportsmen who try to run a good game and who play to win. This is
the story of their activities as I have observed them for a long time. The
activities are theirs but the generalizations and implications are mine, and I can
do naught but accept responsibility for the mistakes that I have doubtless made.
I am deeply grateful to the people of the markets for the long association. To
start naming names is tempting, but it would be a mistake for there are so many
who have contributed to my education.

In a broader sense, the book is a tribute to a competitive economic system that
is not only highly productive of goods and services, but more importantly,
contributes so much to liberty and the excitement of a life style. These markets
are such a system at its best, open to all, and where men are bounded only by
their capacity. Unfortunately, where there is capacity there is also incapacity and
where there are winners there must also be losers. But the game is fair and the
people who play it are free.

Preface to the Second Edition

I like the preface that I wrote in 1971 and so it remains unchanged. Events of the intervening years have reinforced rather than changed my biases. The looking forward that I did then was enough correct that I am not embarrassed.

Writing a second edition of a successful book is dangerous. It is tempting to turn a readable volume into a demonstration of scholarship and in the process limit both readability and usefulness. In contemplating revision the omissions and incompletely documented parts of the volume were readily apparent. New studies have been made and there have been changes in futures markets. I have tried to add the new without adding bulk or tediousness.

The book is accomplishing its purpose. It is a text in the increasing numbers of college level courses in commodity markets and trading. It is flattering that few copies come on the used book market when the course is completed. It is a text in training programs of companies in the commodity trades and appears to be useful to people starting work for firms in the field. It has been accepted by traders so that a sense of comradeship has developed. As every trader knows, Murphy's Law is operative—"That which can go wrong will"—as is its companion—"Some of our greatest successes are fashioned from lucky mistakes." ✓

In the main, the second edition is a modernization job, changing prices to new levels in illustration and selecting more recent examples of principles. In spite of the turmoil of commodities in the 1970's there has been relatively little fundamental change. Volume of trade and open interest have increased dramatically. The number and kinds of commodities have increased. But the underlying principles are unchanged.

Survival and growth in these troubled times is a tribute to the merit of the market form of futures trading. The markets have grown as uncertainty has increased. Understanding of markets has increased.

A new and comprehensive regulatory law—The Commodity Futures Trading Act of 1974—grew out of the commodity turmoil of 1972 and 1973. Numerous punitive bills were introduced but the Act is favorably disposed toward market growth and development. These things lead me to be even more optimistic about the future, not only the future of futures trading but about the future of an economic system directed by competitive prices.

Part I

DESCRIPTION

It is difficult to imagine a duller way to start a book than with a section titled "Description." The term has the least possible sex appeal. Yet, description is what the first part must be about. The first objective of description is to put everyone on an equal footing of knowledge about terms and processes; to develop a sufficient familiarity with the events that are taking place on the trading floors of exchanges, in the customer rooms of commission houses, and in the offices of merchants and processors that the reader can see past the actions to their purposes, to their relationships to the commerce of commodities, and to their economic meaning.

A second objective is to put the reader in a participant role. Trading in commodities is a great and exciting game. To fully appreciate it one must cast oneself in the role of a player; this is a subject ideally suited to a world of Walter Mittys. It is well and good to philosophize about the social and econmic implications of football but it is more fun to imagine that one is a Galloping Ghost in Memorial Stadium or a Bart Starr on a sub zero day in Green Bay.

To play you must know the rules; so describe we must.

CHAPTER 1

Introduction

Interest in Futures Trading. The institution of futures trading is old and big. Organized trading in commodity futures dates back more than 100 years and in some years the dollar value of the volume of trading on the Chicago Board of Trade alone has exceeded that of trading on the New York Stock Exchange. There are fifteen supervised exchanges in the United States and a larger number abroad, scattered from Canada to the Argentine, Japan, India, Australia, and the principal European nations. There is a long list of commodities that are or have been traded on organized exchanges.

Futures trading is little known and less understood. Only a small percentage of people know what futures markets are or have seen one in operation. More people have heard of futures markets. But people who have seen markets are even more mystified, if this is possible, than the people who have not even heard of the markets. There is a mystery about these markets that seems difficult to penetrate.

The largest of the markets is the Chicago Board of Trade. One need only stand on the visitors' balcony, watching the trading and the expressions on the faces of the other visitors to gain a sense of mystery and confusion. The trading floor is two stories high and the size of a football field. On an ordinary day some six hundred people are present, a few are sitting at telephones but most are on their feet and in motion, some walking and some running. There are several dense concentrations of people standing on steps that form hexagonal pits. Here, the action is frantic with as many as 300 men shouting, waving their arms, and signaling with their fingers simultaneously. In isolation, as on a television camera, one trader bellows at the man next to him with such vigor that his face turns red, and waves both hands, a trading card, and a pencil in his face. The other reciprocates, both write quickly on cards, and turn to repeat the

3

whole process to other traders or to the pit in general. A few feet away messengers run from telephones and other communications machines to the pits and back. Incongruously, there are other people, apparently participants who stroll about chatting with other people similarly engaged or quietly watching, oblivious to the din surrounding them. High on the end walls there are huge electronic scoreboards with flashing numbers that seem to relate to a multiplicity of scores somehow ascertained from the action in the pits. But nothing is shown about which team has the ball. The visitor is told that the players do know what they are doing and the action somehow relates to a real world of commerce in grains, oilseeds, cattle, and chickens. The visitors shakes his head and walks away. It *is* possible for one who has seen and heard to be more mystified than one who has not.

The mystery is not lessened as the casual observer learns a bit more. Next he discovers that the players are trading in wheat, corn, etc. for delivery in various months in the future as March, May, or December. Ah, so; this helps. But then he learns that only a very few of the trades are ever consummated by actual delivery, say one or two percent, and that the total quantity traded far exceeds the quantity that moves to and through the market where the trading takes place and even exceeds the total produced and used in the United States.

Then the trading must be in paper, a veritable blizzard thereof. But the paper is for real because our friend has heard that his family physician paid for a vacation trip to Hawaii from profits made in cocoa. Perhaps he also knows that his grandfather got done out of the family farm by the LaSalle street gamblers who conned him into buying wheat options.

A final thing contributing to this mystery is that the game is of complete fascination to the relatively few people who understand and play it. The people of the markets defend futures trading with an almost religious fervor. To them, it is a major contribution to the economic productivity of the nation and the epitome of sophistication in economic development. What is there here that makes working for a living at this thing such great sport?

Why the Interest? The size of the institution of futures trading and the mystery surrounding it by no means explains the breadth of interest in futures trading. It has been the subject of public controversy throughout most of its life. On Oct. 5, 1947, while discussing the high and rising price of wheat, the President of the United States said, "The cost of living in this country must not be a football to be kicked about by gamblers in grain." A few days later his Attorney General alluded to traders in grain as "greedy men blinded by the lust for money, trafficking in human misery." The legislatures of the various states passed numerous bills limiting futures trading during the latter part of the 19th century. A law prohibiting futures trading was passed in Germany in 1896 and repealed four years later. The first national U.S. law regulating grain futures trading was passed in 1921 and immediately declared unconstitutional. The Grain Futures Act was passed in 1922. This law was extensively amended in

1936 and renamed the Commodity Exchange Act. This law was amended extensively through 1968.

The extreme fluctuations in commodity prices, and rapid increases in food prices beginning in mid-1972, resulted in numerous legislative proposals in the Congress. These culminated in the passage of The Commodity Futures Trading Act of 1974. The Act is a complete revision of over 50 years of federal regulation. It brings all exchanges and commodities under regulation and establishes an independent five member Commodity Futures Trading Commission.[1]

The justification of legislation is "that the transactions and prices of commodities on such boards of trade are susceptible to speculation, manipulation, and control, and sudden or unreasonable fluctuations in the price thereof frequently occur as the result of such speculation, manipulation, or control, which are detrimental to the producer or the consumer and the persons handling commodities and the products and byproducts thereof in interstate commerce . . ." Until the 1974 Act, the focus of legislation was on the price effects of futures trading. The new legislation has a broader focus, including positive aims of growth and development of markets.

It is said that every golf shot makes someone happy, either the hitter or his opponent. And so it is with prices except that the appropriate word seems to be unhappy. Every price change either reduces revenue to the seller or increases cost to the buyer. Widely fluctuating prices appear to be offensive to many people with orderly minds whether they be businessmen, government employees, legislators, or the public. A price that changes frequently is automatically suspect. It is also annoying and troublesome to processors and many merchants. Futures trading is blamed for all three price changes; too low, too high, and too swinging. The focus of futures trading is on prices and prices are always misbehaving for someone.

A second source of interest in futures trading stems from businessmen who use futures markets in their production, warehousing, merchandising, and processing activities. These people trade in futures contracts as an adjunct to their ordinary business activities. Skill in commodity futures trading is essential to the successful operation of many kinds of businesses. In addition, skillful use of futures markets enables some firms to make larger earnings than their competitors who do not use this tool. Unskillful or misguided use of futures markets is often the root cause of the failure of firms who use commodities traded in futures markets in their businesses. The use of futures markets can be a major source of unsuccess as well as a tool for achieving success.

Skill in the use of futures markets in connection with commodity businesses requires relatively rare talents and is difficult to develop. Futures trading activities become the nerve centers of many businesses and receive a large amount of attention. The people who do the trading are highly paid, the importance and

[1] Because of the length of the name and the frequency with which it is used, we adopt the letters CFTC when referring to the commission.

rarity of their skills gaining the most meaningful kind of recognition—money. A processing plant may cover a city block and be several stories tall; an impressive collection of equipment, housing hundreds of people performing complicated tasks making exotic products. Deep in the bowels, in a single room, a handful of traders make some of the most important decisions affecting the profit of the company. These are the people who work under the greatest uncertainty and stress and are among the highest paid employees.

Third, futures markets are of academic interest as a form of commerce and market organization. A part of the academic interest stems from the controversy that has always surrounded the institution; academicians are attracted to and like controversy. More importantly, futures markets are a highly developed, sophisticated system of exchange that is open to close observation. The competitive condition of openness to observation is more closely met in these markets than in other exchange processes. In view of these characteristics of sophistication and openness it is surprising that the academic attention is as limited as it is.

Fourth, futures trading is a direct source of income to a large number of people. The operation of the mechanics, the plant so to speak, is big business. The facilities must be provided and the rules must be written and enforced. Trading and prices must be reported and recorded. Exchanges have numerous employees, large capital assets, and substantial operating budgets.

The actual trading is done by professional speculators, scalpers, pit traders, and brokers. The brokers act, in large measure, on instructions from commission futures merchants. The commission houses act on behalf of non-members principals—the trade and the public—for commissions. They take and execute orders, handle funds, keep records, consult with customers, analyze markets, and assemble and disseminate information. They employ a lot of people.

Finally, markets are of interest to the public. People are drawn to markets by the mystery, glamour, and excitement and many stay to play the game. The largest number of people interested in commodity futures trading are speculators. In their breasts, as in most of us, beat hearts that contain, as well as love and compassion, a substantial amount of avarice. Commodity futures markets are a last frontier of large earnings from a small stake. There is ease of entry. Commission houses are readily available and interested in new business. Units of trading are small so that a position can be financed with a small amount of money—a few hundred dollars puts the beginner in business. Price variations are large in relation to the equity capital required. Price moves in excess of initial margins occur frequently so that if the speculator does the right thing he doubles his money quickly. That he is unlikely to do this very many times in succession so that he makes a lot of money is neither here nor there. It is possible, some people have done it, he has a shot, hence the enticement.

This cynical attitude toward the greed of speculators looks to a second cynical view; that markets are in the business of holding out an unattainable will-of-the wisp so that they can draw in and gobble up the public money. Neither attitude is fair or accurate. Speculators are made of better stuff. For avarice let us substitute ambition and add venture and competition. As an hypothesis let us say that the speculators will venture all to gain a lot; that they will accept the long odds against them in exchange for a shot at the top. And further, that they will play the game for its own sake.

Commodity trading is a great competitive game. There is abundant information available to all; there are no effective inside secrets. There are no dominating power positions; each man is as good as the next. The players who are right win and those who are wrong lose. The name of the game is skill; skill in forecasting prices, skill in trading, and skill in capital management.

Cheap Expertise. By way of incentive to study, the thought that knowledge about commodity futures markets is a short cut to becoming an expert is offered. As noted, futures trading is a mystery to most people and relatively little academic attention has been paid to the system. There are many people knowledgeable about pieces and parts of the institution and about various phases of trading, but there are not many who are broadly knowledgeable about the market. One who masters the jargon that is a part of the mystery and masters some rudimentary concepts of being long, short, and spread, open interest, hedging, basis, bearish and bullish, leverage, margin requirements, position and trading limits, and the like has penetrated deeper than most and can make quite an impression.

This is easy to do. The development of skills with which to effectively operate in futures markets is not simple because the level of skill possessed by people active in markets is high. But the concepts are simple. The mystery is a façade and the rewards for penetrating it are satisfying.

The Plan of the Book. The book is structured into four major parts: Description, Economics, Use, and Market Operation. This seems to be the most workable order for starting from scratch and working through to changes that need to be made in the markets so that they can better fulfil their missions. There is no "best way" to approach the subject. It is desirable to know about all parts before one studies each part but this is, of course, impossible. A beginning must be made somewhere. One might start with the regulation of markets and work toward the economics, or with market activities of trade firms and work toward the reasons for success and failure, or proceed from a speculation orientation.

The reasons for starting with description were noted above. But to be complete, one more reason should be mentioned: It is desirable to avoid incorporating mistaken concepts as well as to describe the markets accurately. A major fault in much that has been said on this subject is a tendency to place trading in a vacuum; to fail to relate activities back to their commercial and economic roots. The markets are not a world unto themselves but a part of the commercial world of commodity production, marketing, processing, and use. They are financial institutions that serve as a means of raising capital and as investment media. The high level of development and the stylization and formalization of the trading processes have all too often obscured this relation to the real world. At the beginning of study there is an Alice in Wonderland feeling about futures markets that is difficult for the student to shake. In much that has been written it is apparent that the authors failed to get out of the land of Oz. Perhaps we shan't either.

The purpose of the second part; the economics of futures trading is to describe the economic functions so that users can put their own operations in perspective relative to the total process. The persistence of the markets for more than a century and the recent growth in futures trading makes it clear that these markets play significant roles in the economic processes. Had they not, they would have long since disappeared. This is particularly convincing in the light of the strenuous political opposition that they have encountered.

This section includes a brief discussion of the history and development of futures markets, the competitive characteristics of the markets, the risk shifting and equity financing functions, the role that markets play in price establishment, and the forces establishing price relationships between cash and futures and among futures prices.

The third part relates to "how to make a buck." The objective is to outline the problems of people in relation to market use, develop guidelines for problem solution, and put the solutions in a context of the economics of futures trading. Effective use of markets can only be made by people who understand the economic background of the trading processes.

This section includes hedging, arbitrage activities of warehousemen, merchants, and processors, pricing procedures of primary producers and commodity users, and a discussion of how to speculate in commodity futures. All of this is rather more than can be accomplished in a single volume. Thus, discussion is limited to principles with some illustrations. The most pretentious part of the whole volume is the "how to speculate" section. The presumption is that what is meant is how to speculate successfully and this is quite another matter. Pitfalls in speculation are emphasized because ways to "louse up" seem to be the things that are most widely known.

The objective of the fourth part is to call attention to some of the things that might be done to improve the way that markets work. Futures markets are increasing in number and in size. This is true because the functions to be performed are increasing. There is a vast potential for further growth and it is by no means certain that markets are optimally organized, governed, and regulated to exploit this potential.

This section includes evaluation of market performance, evaluation of market regulation with particular regard to protection of the public, price distortion, manipulation, position limits, and margin requirements, and some recommendations for accelerating market growth.

CHAPTER 2

Exchanges and Commodities

The current scope of futures trading can best be seen by reading the commodity pages of leading financial newspapers. One section lists the exchanges and the prices of the various delivery months of the commodities traded. The breadth and diversity is immediately apparent; there are numerous exchanges, a large number of commodities, and several delivery months are listed for each commodity. Prices are indicated for the open, high, low, close, previous close or change in price from the preceding day, and usually the life of the contract high and low. On focusing in on a section one notes:

CHICAGO MERCANTILE EXCHANGE
Frozen Pork Bellies

	Open	High	Low	Close	Prev. Close	Life of Contr. High	Low
Feb.	70.05	70.77	68.02	68.10	70.02	104.10	55.25
Mar.	69.00	69.50	66.60	66.70	68.50	100.15	58.20
May	68.50	69.10	66.15	66.25	68.20	96.50	63.30
July	67.75	68.45	65.70	65.80	67.70	94.95	64.50
Aug.	64.85	65.45	62.70	63.00	64.90	92.45	62.25

(On a typical day, in a newspaper offering the most complete coverage available, there are about 50 such items regarding North American markets and a dozen or more regarding European markets.)

What does this mean? Contracts for the delivery of pork bellies in the several months listed were traded on the Chicago Mercantile Exchange at the prices and within the price ranges shown. These are futures contracts in contrast to forward contracts. The distinguishing difference between the two kinds of contracts is that futures contracts are traded under the rules and subject to the regulations of the exchange which is chartered, designated and licensed for the purpose of trading in futures contracts. They are not prices of trades in physical

9

bellies but rather prices at which contracts for the eventual exchange of bellies will be made. Futures contracts are standardized agreements made on organized exchanges.

A pork belly is a piece of flesh peeled from the lower central section of a hog's anatomy—one from either side. Nearly all bellies are eventually sliced into the familiar product, bacon. A contract consists of 36,000 pounds of 10 to 14 pound bellies of standard grade. On the day that the quotation was taken from, there were 4,860 contracts traded. There were 2,667 for February delivery, 1,045 for March, 499 for May, 488 for July, and 161 for August. The prices shown are cents per pound. The trading is in increments of .025 cents per pound so that the quotations shown that end in 7 or 2 as 70.02 should have a 5 added to 70.025. Price fluctuations represent substantial changes in contract value. One cent per pound on 36,000 pounds is $360 and .025 cents is $9.00. The change in the February belly price from the close to close shown is $693.00 per contract. The range for the season until the day quoted was $17,586. The range to date was a fluctuation of 61 percent of the median value. The range in money value was a substantial amount, but 36,000 pounds of bacon is a substantial amount, too.

A focus on each of the other items yields similar results. Wheat is traded on several exchanges in contracts of 5,000 bushels for delivery in July, September, December, March, and May. The price is dollars per bushel, and fluctuations are quoted in $1/4$ cent per bushel. A contract of soybean oil is 60,000 pounds, the price is quoted in cents per pound, the minimum fluctuation is .01 cents, and the exchange is the Chicago Board of Trade. All of the quotations have some elements in common. They are about prices of commodities. The trade is in contracts of standardized size and quality. The contracts involve substantial quantities, and price fluctuate.

Exchanges

A commodity exchange is a voluntary association of people whose business involves, often times among other things, trading in commodity futures contracts. The older exchanges were chartered by special acts of the legislatures of the various states in which they were located. The exchanges of more recent origin are organized under membership corporation laws. Most of the exchanges, the older ones in particular, developed out of organizations for trading in cash or spot commodities. They were associations of merchants, organized to formulate rules and supervise trading practices, hence the names, "Board of Trade," "Association of Commerce," "Produce Exchange," etc.

The oldest commodity exchange in the United States is the Chicago Board of Trade. It started operations in 1848 as a spot market and received its charter in 1859. Futures trading was developed at the Chicago Board of Trade in 1865.

The New York Produce Exchange was incorporated in 1862 and operated as a spot market. The New York Cotton Exchange was organized in 1870 and incorporated in 1871. The New Orleans Cotton Exchange was formed in 1870.

The Chicago Board of Trade served as the pattern and pace maker for the numerous grain exchanges that were established during the second half of the 19th century. There was futures trading on some of these. In 1920[1] the following cities were listed as having cereal futures markets: Chicago, Minneapolis, Duluth, Milwaukee, Omaha, Kansas City, St. Louis, Toledo, Baltimore, San Francisco, and New York. The cereals traded were wheat, corn, oats, rye, and barley.

The same report described other futures trading: "There is also at Duluth a futures market for the special variety of wheat known as durum. There is similarly a market in kaffir corn (including milo maize and feterita) at Kansas City. In addition to the food grains, flax futures are traded at Duluth. Toledo has a futures market for the several important kinds of hayseed—clover, alsike, and timothy. The New York Produce Exchange has a futures market in cotton-seed oil. At New York, also, and at New Orleans are important markets in cotton futures. Butter and eggs, prior to the entrance of the United States into the World War, were traded in through a call for futures on the New York Mercantile Exchange, the New York Butter and Eggs Exchange, and the Chicago Butter and Egg Board. Provisions futures (pork products) are traded in at Chicago. This enumeration probably exhausts the list of futures markets in the United States for this country's agricultural products."

Several exchanges for trading in rubber, cocoa, silk, hides and metals were organized in the 1920's, mainly in New York. The number of these was somewhat reduced in 1933 when the Rubber Exchange of New York, The National Silk Exchange, The National Metal Exchange, and The New York Hide Exchange merged to form the Commodity Exchange, Inc.

The exchanges in the United States at which there was futures trading in 1975 were: Board of trade of the City of Chicago, Chicago Mercantile Exchange, MidAmerica Commodity Exchange, International Monetary Market (Chicago), Kansas City Board of Trade, Minneapolis Grain Exchange, Pacific Commodities Exchange, Inc. (San Francisco), New York Cotton Exchange, Citrus Associates of the New York Cotton Exchange, Inc., Wool Associates of the New York Cotton Exchange, Inc., Petroleum Associates of the New York Cotton Exchange, Inc., New York Mercantile Exchange, Commodity Exchange, Inc. (New York), New York Cocoa Exchange, Inc., New York Coffee and Sugar Exchange, Inc.

In addition to the active exchanges there are several organized exchanges on which futures trading has existed in the past. These are: Duluth Board of Trade, Memphis Board of Trade, Milwaukee Grain Exchange, New Orleans Cotton

---

[1] Federal Trade Commission, The Grain Trade, Vol. V, Sept., 1920.

Exchange, Portland Grain Exchange, Northern California Grain Exchange, Seattle Grain Exchange, and Merchants' Exchange of St. Louis. Some of these exchanges have been inactive for quite some time while others have only recently dropped from the active list. Trading on some of the active exchanges has declined to nearly inactive status. Trading is not something that an exchange decides to have or not to have. There is trading when someone shows up to trade and not when the members don't.

There are commodity futures exchanges in other countries but it is difficult to identify and describe them because they operate with different degrees of formality and under various kinds of charters. At some point in the course of commerce forward contracts become futures contracts and the line between them is fuzzy. Formalized futures trading as it is conducted on United States exchanges is not singularly an American product but it is nearly so. This has not always been the case. For many years the Liverpool wheat futures market was very active and was the dominant pricing influence in the world wheat trade. Futures trading in Germany became so active and attracted so much attention that it was banned by law in 1896. Four years later it was clear that the ban did not cure the evils ascribed to futures trading and the ban was removed.

The Winnipeg Commodity Exchange in Canada is an old and significant futures market. Currently there is trading in oats, barley, rye, flaxseed, rapeseed, and feed wheat futures, the last being a quite recent addition. Prior to World War II, Winnipeg was one of the most important wheat futures markets in the world. But since World War II a governmental agency, the Canadian Wheat Board, has become the sole wheat marketing organization so that there is no basis for futures trading in Canada's high quality spring wheat.

There are nine separate organizations in London that can be identified as futures markets although the volume of trading on most of them is small. The two of greatest significance to U.S. trade interests are the United Terminal Sugar Market Association and the London Cocoa Terminal Market Association. Business on these two exchanges is now about as large as on their counterparts in New York.

The two markets in Liverpool are the Liverpool Cotton Futures Market Ltd., and the Liverpool Corn Trade Association.

The Bourse de Commerce in Paris conducts futures trading in cocoa, sugar, corn, and soybean meal.

Cocoa is a popular commodity for futures trading. In addition to the markets noted above, it is traded on Stichting Cocatermijnmarkt in Amsterdam.

There are several futures markets in Japan, the most important of which is Tokyo Grain and Commodity Exchange. Commodities traded in Japanese futures markets are various kinds of textile yarn, rubber, sugar, and various kinds of edible beans. The most important of these commodities is the Azuki bean—not so important in a commercial sense but trading is in large volume and widespread among the public. In pre-war years rice was the star player on the Japanese futures markets but with the advent of strict government control on distribution of rice, this commodity has long been absent from trading.

The activities of exchanges typically involve things in addition to futures trading. First in importance among these is the operation of cash markets for trading in spot or actual commodities. The various grain exchanges operate cash markets where samples of cash grain are brought to the trading floor and buyers and sellers negotiate on exchange of title. Other nonfutures function include establishments of rules and commission rates for trading in cash commodities, weighing of commodities moving through the terminal and, inspection and establishment of grades. At some exchanges, as Minneapolis Grain Exchange, the nonfutures trading roles are dominant while others are concerned almost exclusively with futures trading. Our concern here is with futures market operations.

The various exchanges are separate and independent organizations, each with its own history, tradition, and identity. This separateness is jealously guarded; each is vain about its operation and importance and there are instances of rivalry almost to the point of conflict. This is true even though there are people who are members of more than one exchange and there are many companies who have members of all of the U.S. exchanges in their employ. That is, the larger commission houses must have employees who have trading privileges on all exchanges if they are to adequately serve their customers. Commodity exchanges have common problems with regard to rules, regulation, and procedures as well as relationships with the federal government; they have common cause and there is basis for close cooperation and not great basis for intensive competition because the different exchanges generally trade in different commodities. Yet cooperation is only slowly evolving. This independence stems from personality traits of people who trade commodities and are members of commodity exchanges. As a general matter they are independent, competitive, and egotistical. There is a definite pecking order among the exchanges. The problem is that membership of each exchange thinks its exchange is at the head of the line.

In spite of the independence of the exchanges their organization and operation is more notable for similarities than differences. Their rules and procedures vary in detail, but not in essentials. It is thus possible to present a composite of exchange organization and operation.

Objectives. The primary aim of a commodity exchange is to provide and regulate a market place so that its members, and through them trade interests, including the public, have facilities for trading in futures contracts for specific commodities. The objectives are: (1) To establish equitable principles of business conduct by members, (2) To provide an organized market place and establish the time of trading, (3) To provide uniform rules and standards for the conduct of trading, (4) To establish uniformity of contract size and trade customs regarding quality and its establishment, time and place of delivery, and terms of payment, (5) To collect and disseminate price and market information to members and the public, (6) To provide a mechanism for the adjustment of disputes among members, and (7) To provide machinery to guarantee the settlement of contracts and the payment of financial obligations in connection with trading among members. In addition there is an unstated but nevertheless generally recognized objective and obligation to guarantee the financial and business conduct integrity of members in their commodity contract dealings with nonmembers. In short, the exchanges provide the playing field and equipment, write the rules, and act as referee, head linesman, and field judge but do not handle the football. They do not trade and neither win nor lose although, as football officials, sometimes get written up (or down) in the newspapers.

Governance. Commodity exchanges are great democratic bodies, governed and operated by the members. Government is vested in a Board called Board of Directors, Board of Governors, or Board of Managers. The Board is elected by the membership and its officers are either elected by the members of the Board or the membership. Directors, governors, or managers typically serve three year terms with annual elections so that there is continuity of Board composition.

The number of Board members is large, typically 15 to 21. Some exchanges have two or three non-member or public directors appointed by the Board. Boards are selected in the best democratic tradition so that they are representative of the various facets of the membership. Some exchange by-laws require a diversity of occupations as merchants, processors, commission houses, and independent traders, or a minimum of directors from outside of the city where the exchange is located. But the balance of the Board is usually taken care of by the election process. Officers and directors are typically slated by a nominating committee. Sometimes the slate is not opposed, but more often it is. The process results in a balanced representation of interest groups. There is no formal organization of interest groups that would parallel a precinct or ward structure, but there are informal cliques so that Board members are often representative of a constituency.

A high proportion of the work of the Board is done by committees that are appointed by the Board from its own members and the exchange membership at large and elected, in some cases, by the exchange membership. The number of committees is large. In 1974, there were 27 committees of the Chicago Board of Trade, 30 of the Chicago Mercantile Exchange, 26 of the Kansas City Board of Trade and 19 of the New York Cocoa Exchange.

Names of committees and specific duties vary by exchange. Typically, there are committees that deal with matters pertaining to: (1) Floor Trading Practices, (2) Price Reporting, (3) Business Conduct, (4) Arbitration, (5)

Appeals, (6) Nomination, (7) Membership, (8) Amendments to the Rules, (9) Commodities [several] (10) New Commodities, (11) Weighing, Warehousing, and Delivery, (12) Physical Facilities Management, (13) Supervision of Finances and Properties, and (14) Public Relations and Education.

Day to day administration of each exchange is accomplished by executive officers and staff. They are responsible for carrying out the policies and decisions of the Board and the various committees. Departmental organization of the staff typically parallels the committee structure. The size of the staff varies with the size of the exchange and is more or less proportionate to the volume of business done on the exchange. In 1974, there were 210 on the staff of the Chicago Board of Trade, 90 on that of the Chicago Mercantile Exchange, and 20 on the Kansas City Board of Trade.

The development of the staff function is fairly recent. It was not until 1948 that the Chicago Board of Trade had its first paid executive officer. By-laws of exchanges are quite detailed and involve specific limitations on the powers delegated to the Boards. Seemingly minor matters must go to the vote of the membership. Members of the Boards take their responsibilities quite seriously and delegate limited responsibility to the staff and closely review the work of the committees.

A high proportion of the committee members take their jobs seriously, attend committee meetings frequently and regularly, and remain on committes for extended periods. They work closely with the paid staff whose jobs are in the area of the responsibilities of the committee.

Financing. The North American exchanges are nonprofit organizations. They provide the facilities through which members may attempt to operate for profit but their objectives do not include making money. As a general proposition, one of their objectives necessarily includes staying solvent and paying the help. Almost without exception they lack the funds to do the things that their paid staffs and many members would like them to do.

The exchanges are financed in three principal ways: investments, dues, and fees. Some exchanges own the buildings in which they are housed and rent space and some have substantial investments in other businesses and securities. Members of most exchanges pay annual dues that are levied to cover operating deficits. These dues are not very large but even so members tend to resist increases. The assessment of the Chicago Board of Trade, the largest of the markets, was $600 per member in 1975. Income from fees include forwarding price quotations and price quotation equipment, weighing and inspection of commodities, rental of communication equipment, tables and booths on the exchange floor, and the sale of literature prepared by the exchange. Some exchanges charge a transaction fee instead of levying dues so that the cost of exchange operation is paid in direct proportion to the use made of the exchange.

Membership. The membership in U.S. exchanges is limited to individuals—

there are no memberships held by companies. Only members of exchanges are allowed to trade in future contracts. The typical commodity exchange has a fixed, limited number of memberships but some, for example the Winnipeg Commodity Exchange, have no limitation on the number of people who may be admitted to memberships. The U.S. exchanges, where futures trading is active, have limited membership.

The number of exchange members is sometimes fixed by the charter and sometimes may be adjusted by the board of directors. The number of members at the various exchanges varies over time. There were 82 original members of the Chicago Board of Trade. In the 1920's the number exceeded 3000 before falling off sharply in the 1930's. A limit was fixed at 1422 where it remained until 20 memberships were retired in the 1950's and a new limit established.

Memberships on active exchanges are generally of value and have a price, the price varying with the activity of the exchange. In addition to trading privileges, there are often property values involved. The Chicago Board of Trade, for example, owns the large office building in which it is housed. During much of the post–World War II period the real property value per member was worth more than the going market price of memberships. The value of memberships on that exchange fell to $3,500 before the action to retire 20 memberships was taken. The price ranged from $90,000 to $125,000 in 1975.

Membership in The Chicago Mercantile Exchange was limited to 500 through 1974. This was too small a number to accommodate the increasing volume of trade as had been apparent for several years. In 1964, the memberships traded for as little as $3,000. With the growth of the markets values rose rapidly so that a membership traded for $84,000 in October, 1969. The situation presented the exchange with an interesting problem: A general feeling that a larger membership was needed to handle the large volume of business, but also a knowledge that an increase in the number of members would reduce the value of memberships (or cause them to increase less than they otherwise would). Nothing was done. By 1975, the price range was $77,000 to $129,500. In late 1975 they decided to make trading privileges in non-livestock commodities available at $20,000. They authorized 150 of these with the expectation that when they were all taken up that another 150 would be offered. The action was designed to serve two purposes. First, to increase the number of people to carry the increased volume, and second, to stimulate trading in commodities that the Exchange thought needed increased attention.

The Chicago Board of Trade had a similar problem and took similar action. In 1975, when trading in mortgage futures—GNMA—was started, they authorized the sale of 100 trading privileges at $5,000 per year for the first year.

There are less active exchanges in which the authorized membership has not been fully taken up and in which members would be hard pressed to sell at any price.

Memberships in the major exchanges are broadly held, both occupationally and geographically. Membership lists include every facet of the industry in the commodities traded: producers, warehousemen, exporters, importers, processors, merchants, brokers, futures commission merchants, and speculators. The geographical spread of memberships is as broad as the geography of the commodity with numerous memberships held by non-U.S. citizens.

There are two reasons for owning a membership; to get on the floor and trade, and to obtain the reduced commission rates extended to members who are not present at the market but trade through agents. Usually, member commission rates are one half of nonmember rates. A varying proportion of the membership is on the trading floor at any given time. Typically, about 40 percent of the membership is on the floor of the more active exchanges. The proportion is less on the less active exchanges.

While memberships are held by individuals many of them are effectively controlled by companies. Many members are employees of firms whose business involves futures trading. The companies loan the individuals money to purchase memberships, get agreements for surrender when the employee leaves the company, and sponsor the applicant.

The principal requirements for membership are that the applicants be of good character and financially responsible. Generally, applicants are endorsed by two members. Financial requirements vary by exchanges and by the purpose of the membership. If the applicant is going to use the membership for himself the requirements are fairly high but if it is to be a "company membership" the applicant's personal financial position is not a significant determinant. Applicants names are posted with an invitation to the membership to comment. After an applicant has passed a membership committee he is recommended to the board of directors which may elect him. The newly elected member must subscribe to the by-laws and rules and agree to abide by all existing regulations and subsequent amendments. He, in effect, submits to the law of the exchange with regard to contract trading.

Once elected the applicant may negotiate a purchase from a member (in N.Y. exchanges, a seat is usually bought first in the name of a member). He bids until he persuades a member to sell or becomes discouraged by competitive bids and asking prices. He has a limited time for negotiation; if he does not make a purchase within the time limit his election is voided.

Obtaining a membership is not all that complicated or difficult. The exchanges are relatively open; a bit more net worth than the price of the membership and the absence of a bad reputation appears to be all that is required.

Settlement of disputes. Disputes in trading occur on all exchanges. They involve identity of trades, prices, quantities, and trading rules and have a common element—money, large sums and small. Exchange rules provide for arbitration without recourse to courts of law. Some exchange rules require that disputants submit to arbitration on the complaint of one party while others simply provide machinery for voluntary arbitration when requested. As a practical matter, disputes that cannot be reconciled between the individuals concerned go to the arbitration committees.

The arbitration procedure is comparable to an action at law but is stripped of legal formalities, rigidity, and is private except as the disputants request open sessions. The arbitration committees have extensive powers, including the production of papers and subpoena of members to attend and give testimony. The findings of the arbitration committee may be taken to a board of appeals but the awards of this group are final and conclusive and have the full force of law. Once the arbitration proceedings have been agreed on, either voluntarily or by the terms of membership, the courts refuse to intervene until the arbitration process has been exhausted. Appeal can then be made to the courts only on the most narrow grounds of violation of constitutional rights or of the charter and by-laws of the exchange. In short, the exchanges settle disputes and discipline their members. There have been legal actions regarding monetary awards and disciplinary actions, including expulsion, but these are rare and nearly always unsuccessful.

Commodities Traded

The list of commodities *actively* traded in North American futures markets is impressive for its length and diversity. Some classification is possible and perhaps even useful. The list is:

Grains: Wheat, corn, oats, barley, grain sorghums
Oilseeds and Products: soybeans, rapeseed, flaxseed, soybean meal, soybean oil, coconut oil, palm oil
Livestock and Products: Cattle, feeder cattle, hogs, broilers, turkeys, pork-bellies, skinned hams, boneless beef, eggs
Foods: Potatoes, orange juice, sugar, coffee, cocoa
Fibers: Cotton, wool
Forest Products: Plywood, lumber
Metals: Gold, silver, platinum, palladium, copper, U.S. silver coins
Petroleum: Propane, crude oil, industrial fuel oil, heating oil
Currencies and financial instruments: British Pound, Canadian Dollar, Deutschemark, Japanese Yen, Mexican Peso, Swiss Franc, French Franc, Dutch Guilder, Federal guaranteed Mortgages (GNMA), U.S. Treasury bills.

There is a tendency toward specialization in groups of commodities by the various exchanges. The Kansas City and Minneapolis markets trade in only grains and most of the trading on The Chicago Board of Trade is in grains, soybeans, and soybean products. The Chicago Mercantile Exchange is primarily a livestock and livestock product market, while the Commodity Exchange, Inc. is primarily a futures market in the metals. On the New York Cocoa Exchange, trading is in cocoa futures exclusively. But specialization is not complete. Silver, gold, broilers, cattle, and plywood futures are traded on the Chicago Board of Trade, and the New York Mercantile Exchange trades in the interesting combination of palladium, platinum, plywood, potatoes, industrial fuel oil, heating oil, boneless beef, silver coins, gold, and eight foreign currencies. Some commodities are traded on more than one exchange: wheat at Chicago, Minneapolis, and Kansas City, silver on the Chicago Board of Trade, the MidAmerica Commodity Exchange and the Commodity Exchange, Inc., and potatoes on the New York Mercantile and the Chicago Mercantile.

The list of the commodities above was one point in time, late 1975. The makeup was different in earlier times and will doubtless be different in the future. In the 19th century there was a futures market in petroleum at Oil City, Pa. Lard futures trading was formerly of major importance on the Chicago Board of Trade but was last traded in 1963. Cottonseed oil was actively traded on the New York Produce Exchange. Commodities previously traded but not now active on the Chicago Mercantile Exchange include: onions, scrap iron, frozen shrimp, frozen broilers, butter, hides, and apples.

The list becomes more interesting as the blanks are filled in. Other important oilseeds in world commerce include sunflowerseed, peanuts, and cottonseed. Other edible fats and oils include lard, cottonseed oil, butter, and fish oil. Orange juice makes the list but not pears, peaches, and grapefruit juice. In addition to the above, livestock by-product feeds include wheat millfeeds, corn gluten feed, linseed meal, meatscraps, etc. Interesting and surprising commodities are in the list but the list is by no means complete.

As we shall see, the volume of trading varies greatly within commodities at different times and among commodities. A couple of examples are sufficient at this point: 1) There were 60,000 contracts of oats futures traded on the Chicago Board of Trade in 1967 and 123,259 contracts in 1968, more than double, while the contracts of rye traded decreased from 45,770 to 28,143 between the same two years. The total value of all commodity contracts traded on the Chicago Board of Trade was estimated at $50.1 billion in 1967 but only $35.0 billion in 1968. 2) In 1968 there were 1,398,200 contracts of pork bellies traded on the Chicago Mercantile Exchange but only 204 contracts of hams. Now, each belly is attached to a ham and each hog has two of each. A ham is worth a little more than a belly, and the prices of hams vary quite as much as bellies. An anomaly; very interesting.

Common Characteristics. Why are some commodities traded on futures markets while others of similar characteristics and equal importance are not? What common characteristics do commodities traded have? The answer to the first of these questions is quite involved and must await further development of our subject. Some characteristics of commodities prerequisite to their being traded in futures markets have been enumerated. The Federal Trade Commission[2] listed (1) homogeneity such that commercial units are interchangeable, (2) durability, or minimum degree of perishability, and (3) an adequate supply of the actual commodity flowing to or through the terminal market where the futures market is established. They added that a large volume of trade is obviously not a prerequisite, but is essential to the highest efficiency of a futures market.

Baer and Saxon[3] developed a rather exacting list:

1. Units must be homogeneous. It is a condition precedent for all futures trading that units of the commodity be interchangeable. The trader does not buy or sell a contract for a specific or identified grade or specific lot but buys or sells according to established grades and descriptions. The commodity need not be tangible but must be describable.

2. The commodity must be susceptible of standardization and grades. Differences make it impossible for every unit of a commodity to be regarded commercially as the equivalent of every other. If standards can be established so that by inspection and classification the commodity may be divided into a definite number of well defined, uniform grades the units of each grade become homogeneous, the commodity is suitable for futures trading.

3. Supply and demand must be large. The authors use alligator pears as an example of a commodity for which a satisfactory futures market could not be maintained. Both the supply and demand are small, consequently speculators with large financial resources might gain control so that it would cease to be a natural and free market and become merely a battleground for contending speculative factions.

4. The supply must flow naturally to market. Not only must a supply of a commodity be large, but its flow to world markets must also be substantially free and unhampered by artificial restraint, whether by government or private agencies. They cite several examples of commodities whose supply has been substantially affected by individual governmental actions and marketing agreements.

5. Supply and demand must be uncertain. If supply and demand are both certain, prices are capable of ready adjustment without the intervention of any organized market machinery. When supply and demand are large, and both uncertain and subject to wide fluctuations from season to season or year to year, a condition exists where the forces of supply and demand on free markets is

---

[2] Ibid., pp. 24–25.

[3] Baer, Julius B. and Saxon, Olin Glenn, Commodity Exchanges and Futures Trading, Harper & Brothers, 1948. Chap. VI.

constantly changing. This interplay of uncertain economic forces produces the constant fluctuations in price which must exist in any successful futures market.

6. The commodity should not be too perishable because the futures contract may call for a delivery of units of the commodity many months into the future. Consequently, the commodity must be capable of being stored at all times and for considerable periods to meet requirements of the market in times of scarcity. A commodity subject to rapid deterioration does not meet this requirement.

The same authors discussed commodities not adaptable to futures trading. Here they list: (1) perishable commodities as uncanned fruits and vegetables, (2) manufactured goods whose supply can be controlled and whose styles change, and goods where the supply is under monopoly control, citing sulphur with the supply controlled by two major producers.

In looking over the list of commodities traded, it is clear that the lists of requirements do not explain why some commodities are traded and others are not nor why the volume of trading ranges so greatly by commodities and over time. Some common characteristics can be identified. First, they are all bulk commodities that can be described and the separate lots of which are more or less interchangeable. Second, none of the commodities has been processed or manufactured to the point of being a product identified with the processes of a particular firm; in general they are bulk commodities but are not, in a strict sense, raw materials. Third, prices are variable and relatively competitively determined.

There are characteristics that are not common to all of the commodities. Most notable is the high degree of perishability of some. Cattle, hogs, iced broilers, and fresh eggs are the most notable examples. For some of the commodities, for example corn, there are many suppliers and many users so that there is no important control of either the supply or use side by a few firms; the condition of atomistic competition is fairly met. But for others, there is a relatively high degree of concentration as in the case of broilers and soybean oil where a few firms control a high proportion of the supply. Some of the commodities flow through a marketing system of country points, subterminals, and terminal markets to and through a distribution system. But for others the flow of actual product is highly decentralized as in the case of fats and oils, potatoes, and livestock. A centralized market is not a prerequisite to futures trading. Several of the commodities, grains in particular, have supply, demand, and price structures that are affected by various kinds of governmental programs.

The institution of futures trading has broadened the definition of the term commodity. The introduction of trading in various foreign currencies in 1972 added a different dimension as did the later addition of federally guaranteed mortgages and U.S. treasury bills. These and other financial instruments are bulk, interchangeable, and have fluctuating values. The possibility of trading in ocean freight has been explored. These developments raise an interesting question about the possible ultimate scope of futures trading. It appears unlikely, but certainly is conceptually possible that labor contracts might one day be included.

From these considerations it appears to be a mistake to impose a very rigorous set of prerequisite characteristics for eligibility for futures trading. It seems that if a commodity is describable, interchangeable with other similarly described lots, and has a variable price, it may be traded on an organized futures market. Perhaps the appropriate question is not why some commodities are traded but rather why so many others are not.

The Dynamics

Futures trading is an unstable activity. The quantities traded vary sharply between days, months, and years. Trading in individual commodities is started and fades out or plods along, going nowhere, or takes hold and grows rapidly. Exchanges come and go. We will explore some of the reasons for the dynamics in later chapters, but at this point some description is useful.

Table 1 is an attempt to take a very long run look at the volume of grains traded. There are no usable records prior to 1884. Trading on all markets was combined in developing the table. The first point of particular interest is that the all time peak of trading in grain probably occurred in the 1880's. The general level of activity held fairly constant through the 1920's. The great depression of the 1930's, the introduction of various farm price support and inventory schemes, and fixed prices of World War II pulled the volume down to about one third of the earlier level. Volume improved by the mid-1960's, and increased rapidly from 1966 through 1974.

The table does not include cotton because of the lack of continuous data but the general pattern appears to have been similar. It does not include soybeans because of the relative recent origin of the crop. There was futures trading in other commodities, particularly from 1920 on.

Table 2 shows the detail of trading volume by exchanges and commodities from 1961 through 1975. Volume is but one measure of the size and importance of trading. It is the most commonly used and most readily available measure. There are several points of interest.

1. Total volume of trading was fairly stable through 1965; there was a rapid increase from 1966 through 1972, and a veritable explosion beginning in mid-1972.

2. Some exchanges declined in importance and disappeared from the list and others were fading throughout most of the period. Milwaukee declined and disappeared just as the New Orleans Cotton Exchange, the Memphis Board of Trade, and the Seattle Grain Exchange had in the 1950's. St. Louis came in and left promptly. This is a very old market that had a large volume of trading at an

Table 1. Volume of Futures Trading in cereal grains,
wheat, corn, oats, barley, rye on U.S. Markets, five
year averages, millions of bushels.

1884–88	23,600
1889–93	18,000
1894–98	21,600
1899–03	19,400
1904–08	18,900
1909–13	16,000
1914–18	19,400
1921–25	21,753
1926–30	20,336
1931–35	13,489
1936–40	10,491
1941–45	6,481
1946–50	9,640
1951–55	8,898
1956–60	7,764
1961–65	10,430
1966–70	17,180
1971–74	25,803

Source: Federal Trade Commission and Commodity Exchange Authority, U.S.D.A.

earlier time and remained an important cash grain market at the end of the period. The New York Produce Exchange, after a rally in the early 1960's declined and disappeared.

3. The number of commodities traded increased. There were 30 different commodities traded in 1961 and 50 in 1975. There was a tendency to add commodities rapidly near the end of the period. Note particularly, increases in the metals and financial instruments and the development of specialized contracts for the same commodity on the various exchanges.

4. Trading in some commodities declined and stopped or nearly stopped (Frozen shrimp, millfeeds, cottonseed oil, wool tops, tomato paste). Volume in others declined gradually and then recovered sharply, such as eggs on the Chicago Mercantile Exchange. Some commodities were introduced and became instantly successful, while others were introduced and flopped. The most striking contrast is pork bellies and skinned hams. Belly trading was started in 1961 and ham trading in 1964. Belly trading was quite successful by 1965, but ham trading had not developed. The two have quite comparable characteristics, but traders in futures contracts responded very differently.

Figure 1 shows graphically the explosive growth in futures trading since 1961.

Table 2(a). Annual Volume of Trading (Contracts in Thous.) in the United States, 1961–75

Exchange and Commodity	Contract Unit	1961	1962	1963	1964	1965	1966	1967	1968	1969	1970	1971	1972	1973	1974	1975
Chicago Board of Trade																
Wheat	5,000 bu.	517	877	824	744	684	1183	1934	1306	756	560	550	856	1567	2377	2263
Corn	5,000 bu.	627	966	823	684	794	2046	1946	1576	1609	2140	2074	1942	4075	4679	4835
Oats	5,000 bu.	224	272	140	101	90	112	60	123	134	92	45	36	183	199	154
Rye	5,000 bu.	192	218	128	91	45	83	46	28	20	4	0	0	0	0	0
Soybeans	5,000 bu.	2410	946	2846	2588	3565	3153	1105	944	1003	2031	3113	4043	2743	2731	3914
Soybean oil	60,000 lbs.	385	320	636	399	594	575	285	301	781	1907	1486	1111	1763	1620	1490
Soybean meal	100 tons	323	335	263	291	325	466	354	367	416	868	475	631	660	878	792
Lard, drummed	40,000 lbs.	16.0	2.86	.02	0	0	.57	0	0	0	0	0	0	0	0	0
Steer carcass beef	30,000 lbs.	—	—	—	—	1.56	0	0	0	0	0	0	0	0	0	0
Live choice steers	27,600 lbs.	—	—	—	—	—	4.19	32.9	23.7	57.4	4.6	.1	0	0	0	0
Iced broilers	28,000 lbs.	—	—	—	—	—	—	—	2.26	93.6	95	55	23	328	221	179
Plywood	69,120 sq. ft.	—	—	—	—	—	—	—	—	.39	47	223	218	274	383	285
Silver	5,000 ounces	—	—	—	—	—	—	—	—	23.9	191	559	813	1632	1462	1953
Cotton	100 bales	0	0	0	0	0	0	0	0	0	0	0	0	0	0	0
MidAmerica Commodity Exchange (Chicago Open Board of Trade)																
Wheat	1,000 bu.	4.12	9.12	6.66	8.78	5.59	9.7	27.6	31.9	24.1	14.2	7.6	15.5	74.7	624.0	363.8
Corn	1,000 bu.	2.01	4.28	1.87	1.37	1.10	5.05	7.06	9.06	13.1	11.3	10.4	12.6	102.6	760.5	802.2
Oats	1,000 bu.	.70	1.48	.33	.16	.20	.22	.36	1.60	3.1	1.2	.7	2.1	9.3	5.2	5.0
Rye	1,000 bu.	2.62	5.66	1.55	.86	.26	.46	.43	.28	.44	.8	—	—	—	—	—
Soybeans	1,000 bu.	27.4	9.55	29.2	35.9	47.9	50.3	12.6	12.3	10.0	25.6	46.1	81.2	56.5	557.3	657.1
Silver	1,000 ounces	—	—	—	—	—	—	—	.48	8.7	4.3	49.8	80.8	400.0	587.3	439.9
Kansas City Board of Trade																
Wheat	5,000 bu.	72	110	112	98	106	186	239	219	148	179	150	293	346	427	609
Corn	5,000 bu.	0	.07	.07	.01	0	6.2	1.8	.09	0	0	0	0	.35	0	0
Grain sorghums	280,000 lbs.	11	.005	.17	.001	0	6.9	7.1	2.0	1.6	4.7	.1	0	0	0	0
Soybeans	5,000 bu.	0	0	.01	0	.16	0	0	0	0	—	—	—	—	—	—
Bran	120 tons	0	0	0	0	0	0	0	0	0	—	—	—	—	—	—
Shorts	120 tons	0	0	0	0	0	0	0	0	0	—	—	—	—	—	—
Middlings	105 tons	0	0	0	0	0	0	0	0	0	—	—	—	—	—	—
Feeder cattle, live	25,000 lbs.	—	—	—	—	—	.47	.18	.48	0	—	—	—	—	—	—

Table 2(b)

Exchange and Commodity	Contract Unit	1961	1962	1963	1964	1965	1966	1967	1968	1969	1970	1971	1972	1973	1974	1975
Minneapolis Grain Exchange																
Wheat	5,000 bu.	43.8	46.5	40.6	31.0	32.3	61.9	67.0	80.5	44.5	49.7	54.2	116.9	171.7	174.6	197.1
Corn	5,000 bu.	0	.07	.07	0	0	0	0	0	0	0	0	0	0	0	0
Oats	5,000 bu.	4.0	1.4	0	0	0	0	.01	.003	0	0	0	0	0	3.9	0
Rye	5,000 bu.	.002	.004	.002	.002	0	0	0	.10	0	0	0	0	0	0	0
Soybeans	5,000 bu.	0	.005	0	0	0	0	0	0	0	0	0	0	0	0	0
Durum wheat	5,000 bu.	0	0	0	0	0	0	0	0	0	0	0	0	.40	.1	2.23
Pork Bellies	36,000 lbs.	0	0	0	0	0	0	0	0	0	0	3.3	2.3	0	0	0
Chicago Mercantile Exchange																
Eggs, shell	18,000 doz.	350	330	166	73.0	96.4	79.5	29.3	165	447	679	380	475	617	361	143
Idaho potatoes	80,000 lbs.	—	—	—	—	—	—	—	24.2	88.5	78.0	23.9	6.1	9.5	9.1	2.0
Pork Bellies	36,000 lbs.	.43	.56	1.7	155	715	728	1047	1399	2159	1778	1695	2057	1155	735	1443
Live cattle, midwest	40,000 lbs.	—	—	—	1.6	59.3	169	299	253	999	579	746	1370	2548	2517	2457
Hogs, live	30,000 lbs.	—	—	—	—	—	8.1	9.4	8.9	63.8	115	261	543	1062	1084	1427
Lumber	100,000 bd. ft.	—	—	—	—	—	—	—	—	.77	85.5	100.1	66.5	194.8	238.4	256.3
Gold	100 oz.	0	0	0	0	0	0	0	0	0	0	0	0	0	2.1	407.0
U.S. Silver Coins	$5,000	0	0	0	0	0	0	0	0	0	0	0	0	18.6	87.0	34.8
Copper	12,500 lbs.	0	0	0	0	0	0	0	0	0	0	8.2	1.4	0	6.1	1.6
Sorghum	400,000 lbs.	0	0	0	0	0	0	0	0	0	0	.5	7.4	2.3	1.3	.7
Feeder cattle	42,000 lbs.	0	0	0	0	0	0	0	0	0	0	0	14.8	22.8	31.0	29.6
British Pound	25,000 BP	0	0	0	0	0	0	0	0	0	0	0	38.8	31.4	14.0	15.0
Canadian Dollar	100,000 CD	0	0	0	0	0	0	0	0	0	0	0	19.3	29.2	3.7	2.7
Deutschemark	125,000 DM	0	0	0	0	0	0	0	0	0	0	0	9.7	77.3	49.4	54.8
Mexican Peso	1,000,000 MP	0	0	0	0	0	0	0	0	0	0	0	44.0	120.3	90.9	48.5
Japanese Yen	12,500,000 JY	0	0	0	0	0	0	0	0	0	0	0	17.7	125.7	7.2	1.8
Swiss Franc	125,000 SF	0	0	0	0	0	0	0	0	0	0	0	0	22.0	42.5	69.9
Dutch Gilder	125,000 DG	0	0	0	0	0	0	0	0	0	0	0	0	11.3	1.5	.9
French Franc	250,000 FF	0	0	0	0	0	0	0	0	0	0	0	0	0	11.4	6.2

Table 2(c)

Exchange and Commodity	Contract Unit	1961	1962	1963	1964	1965	1966	1967	1968	1969	1970	1971	1972	1973	1974	1975
St. Louis Merchants Exchange																
Millfeeds	210,000 lbs.	—	32	.003	0	0	0	0	0	0	—	—	—	—	—	—
New York Cotton Exchange and Wool Associates and Citrus Associates																
Cotton	100 bales	35.0	32.4	19.1	5.8	.90	.73	70.5	240	64.4	33.7	358.8	365.4	450.3	396.4	525.1
Wool	6,000 lbs.	95.0	43.8	29.2	35.0	35.9	33.9	17.9	10.9	6.4	3.7	3.6	3.8	4.7	2.4	.9
Orange Juice, fzn. conc.	15,000 lbs.	—	—	—	—	—	1.3	22.9	149	130	.73	158	124	152	97	66
Propane	100,000 gal.	—	—	—	—	—	—	—	—	—	—	1.5	.9	7.0	8.3	4.8
Petroleum	5,000 bbl.	—	—	—	—	—	—	—	—	—	—	—	—	—	14.4	34.3
New York Mercantile Exchange																
Potatoes, Maine	50,000 lbs.	209	215	120	393	531	590	547	455	366	317	151	247	674	771	796
Palladium	100 ounces	—	—	—	—	—	—	—	42.6	10.9	.8	.1	.5	1.9	2.3	1.3
Platinum	50 ounces	.02	0	.01	2.2	1.7	1.0	16.3	97.0	84.0	98.9	112.4	159.3	147.8	199.6	90.3
Frozen Beef	30,000 lbs.	—	—	—	—	—	—	—	—	—	—	.6	1.0	2.6	4.8	3.4
Silver Coins (U.S.)	$10,000	—	—	—	—	—	—	—	—	—	—	180	26.4	90.0	90.9	50.7
Gold	32.151 oz.	—	—	—	—	—	—	—	—	—	—	—	—	—	1.2	36.7

Table 2(d)

Exchange and Commodity	Contract Unit	1961	1962	1963	1964	1965	1966	1967	1968	1969	1970	1971	1972	1973	1974	1975
New York Coffee and Sugar Exchange																
Coffee	32,500 lbs.	17.1	4.4	5.5	32.9	15.1	3.2	.45	.07	.07	.1	.2	7.7	182.6	151.9	71.1
Sugar, World	112,000 lbs.	13.3	63.2	345	235	188	261	624	526	536	76	455	875	1030	737	791
Sugar, Domestic	112,000 lbs.	35.0	65.7	144	111	42.7	38.1	16.0	13.0	14.3	11.2	7.7	19.6	21.8	43.5	11.3
New York Cocoa Exchange																
Cocoa	30,000 lbs.	125	116	206	116	222	510	408	397	406	313	213	278	431	345	314
Rubber	33,000 lbs.	—	—	—	—	—	—	—	—	—	—	—	—	—	—	4.2
Commodity Exchange, Inc.																
Copper	25,000 lbs.	56.9	35.6	8.5	126	164	43.7	51.0	40.9	86.2	117.5	235.4	251.2	564.6	411.1	494.0
Mercury	10 flasks	—	—	—	—	—	—	3.9	2.5	1.3	4.7	1.8	1.1	.2	.8	.1
Rubber	22,400 lbs.	8.5	2.0	2.1	1.1	.69	.17	.14	.05	.06	.01	0	0	0	.18	.07
Silver	5,000 ounces	—	—	3.9	10.4	15.5	10.0	15.5	480	585	—	—	—	—	—	—
Total All Exchanges (Approximated in Thous. contracts)		6060	5180	7144	6428	8423	10,460	9454	9332	11,207	13,623	14,563	18,332	25,827	27,733	32,200

Source: Association of Commodity Exchange Firms, Inc. (Futures Industry Association).

27

FIGURE 1. Volume of Futures Trading on all Markets Combined, 1961–1975, in millions of contracts

FIGURE 1. Volume of Futures Trading on all Markets Combined, 1961-1975, in millions of contracts

(millions)

35

30

25

20

15

10

5

1961 1962 1963 1964 1965 1966 1967 1968 1969 1970 1971 1972 1973 1974 1975

28

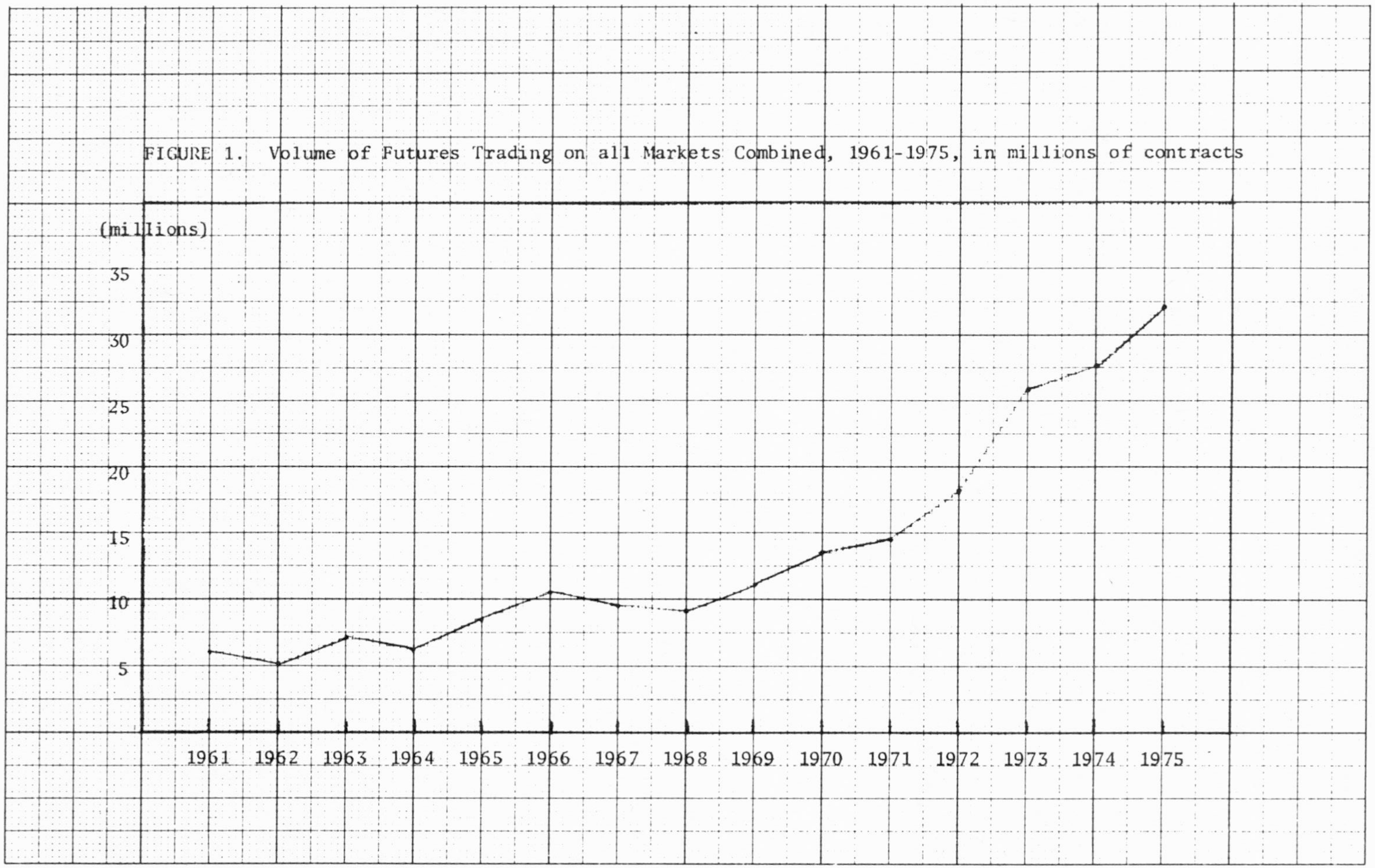

Table 3 shows the share of total volume on each of the exchanges. The comparisons are less than perfectly accurate because of differences in commodity value per unit (soybeans are worth approximately 2.5 times as much as corn, but the contracts are 5,000 bushels for both commodities) and differences in contract size. (Grain contracts on the MidAmerica Commodity Exchange are 1,000 bushels each, but are 5,000 bushels on other exchanges. In 1974, the 426,686 wheat contracts traded on the Kansas City Board of Trade represented 2.1 billion bushels, while the 623,939 wheat contracts traded on MidAmerica represented only 624 million.)

The Chicago Board of Trade is the largest exchange, but its position of dominance decreased rapidly in the 1960's before leveling off in the first half of the 1970's. The rapid growth of the Chicago Mercantile Exchange is associated with the introduction of Pork Belly trading in 1961, Live Cattle in 1964, and Live Hogs in 1966. All three markets have been very successful. The rapid growth of the Commodity Exchange, Inc. is associated with silver futures trading which started in 1963, but which was of small consequence until 1968.

The most rapidly growing exchange is MidAmerica, where volume increased from 57 thousand contracts in 1970 to 2.6 million in 1974. The key to this growth was the small contracts of 1,000 bushels of wheat, corn, oats, and soybeans and 1,000 ounces of silver. Formerly the Chicago Board of Trade permitted trading in 1,000 bushel lots, but when this practice was stopped small unit traders went to MidAmerica. The smaller contracts are better suited to the purposes of many grain producers and the direct participation of grain producers in futures markets has increased. The tremendous increase in price volatility of commodities beginning in mid-1972 made the smaller contracts a better vehicle for many people.

A point that should be especially noted is that in 1974, seventy percent of all futures trading was in the grains, soybeans and products, cattle, hogs, and pork

Table 3. Proportion of Total Trading on Each Exchange

Exchange	1962	1966	1969	1972	1974	1975
			(percent)			
Chicago Board of Trade	76.01	72.85	43.67	52.20	52.56	49.51
Chicago Mercantile Exchange and International Monetary Market	8.01	9.55	33.54	25.20	19.09	19.88
Kansas City Board of Trade	2.13	1.91	1.33	1.60	1.54	1.89
MidAmerica Commodity Exchange	.58	.63	.53	12.9	9.28	7.50
Minneapolis Grain Exchange	1.17	.59	.40	1.05	.64	.62
New York Coffee and Sugar Exchange	1.98	2.89	4.92	4.93	3.36	2.71
New York Cotton Exchange and Associates	1.49	.04	1.79	2.70	1.84	1.96
New York Mercantile Exchange	4.15	5.65	4.16	2.39	3.92	3.13
New York Cocoa Exchange	2.23	4.87	5.63	1.52	1.24	.99
Commodity Exchange, Inc.	.85	.61	6.02	5.83	6.42	11.8
Pacific Commodities Exchange	.00	.00	.00	.01	.07	.00
Total	100.00	100.00	100.00	100.00	100.00	100.00
Total contracts (000's)	5,180	10,460	11,207	18,175	27,733	32,200

bellies. In spite of the proliferation of commodities traded that has taken place since 1960, the bulk of futures trading is in primary agricultural commodities. It may be that this market form will become of major importance for an even larger list of commodities than now listed, but only time will tell.

The major changes of exchanges disappearing and commodities coming and going tend to obscure the large changes that take place in the more stable areas. The area of greatest stability appears to be grain, soybean, and soybean product trading on the Chicago Board of Trade. But it is also unstable. In the 15 years (1961–75) the volume of trading in wheat ranged from 517 thousand contracts (2.6 billion bushels) to 2.4 million contracts (12.0 billion bushels). The others had comparable ranges.

What all of this does is raise the question of why some commodities are traded and others not and why the volume varies as it does. Obviously, the exchanges don't know for sure, else there would not be such a record of failures.

CHAPTER **3**

Mechanics of Futures Trading

The Futures Contract

A futures contract is an agreement to later buy and sell a commodity. In these thirteen words lies the first and most important key to understanding futures trading. Trading is in contracts for later consummation. Trades are exercises in futurity. They are not purchases and sales of actual or cash commodities. Title does not change hands; money does not change hands. The unit of the commodity that the contract pertains to may but need not exist at the time that the contract is made.

Second only to this fundamental is the fact that very few—one or two percent—of the contracts made ever mature and are consummated. Trading in futures contracts is for purposes other than the exchange of title. The purposes are what the study of futures trading is about. They relate to the real world of trading in actual commodities. The contracts are for real and may be consummated if the buyer or the seller elects to hold the contract to maturity. Futures trading is not a game played in a commercial vacuum—it just seems like it at first glance.

Contracts calling for later performance are quite usual in the economic system and are familiar to everyone. Occasionally a customer goes into an automobile agency, selects a car, pays for it, and drives it away. But this is not the way most purchases and sales are made. Usually a contract is made and signed describing the car to be purchased, the time of delivery, and outlining the financial terms. The actual automobile may be at the agency, the factory, or may not even exist. It may be necessary to make up the combination of colors, accessories, etc. that the customer wants. Usually the customer posts some money to guarantee the contract with the understanding that the money posted

31

will eventually be applied to the purchase. Another example is a contract calling for the purchase and sale of a house that has not yet been built. The builder and the buyer make an agreement accurately describing the house, its location, time of completion, terms of payment, the price, and the penalties to be exacted in the event of default on the contract. Usually a monetary guarantee of performance is posted by one or both parties to the contract.

In the businesses relating to trading in cash commodities, contracts calling for deferred delivery are also a quite common, if not the usual way of doing business. For example, corn is sold by farmers to country elevators, to interior merchants, and to processors or exporters. These are lots of actual corn that move through the marketing channels from production to consumption. Change of title takes place at each point and payment is made. Physical movement and exchange of title may take place at essentially the time that the agreements are made but this is not always the case. The farmer may, and often does, sell corn in October or November for delivery at the local elevator in January or March or May. The elevator may sell for prompt shipment or shipment by Dec. 15 or March 15. The exporter may sell a loaded cargo or a cargo for delivery at a foreign port several weeks or months later, etc. These are cash forward contracts involving physical and ownership transfer. They may involve specific lots but usually relate to a described quality.

These contracts calling for deferred performance and exchange of title are both like and unlike futures contracts. The same basic terms relating to price, quantity, quality, time and place of delivery, terms of payment, and recourse in the event of default are present. But we should distinguish three principal differences. First, futures contracts are traded on organized exchanges while cash forward contracts are traded in informal, decentralized markets. There is a legal difference for commodities traded on United States futures markets. According to the Commodity Futures Trading Commission Act of 1974, all goods, articles, services, rights and interests traded for future delivery are under regulation of the Commodity Futures Trading Commission. Futures trading is prohibited except on designated (those licenced and supervised) exchanges. It is illegal to trade in corn futures contracts except on designated exchanges for which corn futures trading has been approved. Any other trading in corn that relates to deferred consummation is not futures trading and, for purposes of completeness of classification, should be called forward contracting.

This fine line of distinction is more interesting as we consider onions. Onions are a commodity so that futures trading in onions can be conducted only on a designated exchange. But a separate piece of legislation prohibits futures trading in onions on any designated exchange. Thus, there is no futures trading in onions. Yet, onions are grown extensively under contractual arrangements between producers and marketing agents and forward contracts are made between marketing agents and users of onions. The distinction seems to be in the degree of formalization. Just how organized the forward contracting in cash onions could get to be without becoming illegal is a subject to which no attention has been paid but is intriguing.

2. Second, futures trading is in standardized contracts. The contracts are identical with regard to all terms (quantity, quality, etc.) except the month of delivery and the price. The months of maturity are designated and the time of delivery within the month is standardized. Thus, contract negotiation involves only the number of contracts and the price. The hubbub on the floor of an active exchange is only about price and number of contracts.

3. Third, trading in futures contracts is highly formalized. The rules of trading are detailed and strictly enforced. The objective of this formalization is to assure open, competitive trading in which all traders have an equal opportunity to do business. Futures trading is done in market places modeled after the oldest concepts of open markets. The rules are similar to those of the medieval fairs of France and England during the Middle Ages. The rules of the ancient fairs provided that trading be confined to the designated market place and the times that were agreed upon for trading, that all bids and offers be made publicly before witnesses, and that every person in the market have equal opportunity to accept bids and offers. The rules prohibited merchants from going out from the market place and engrossing the supply so that they might become the sole or controlling seller. Private negotiations behind closed doors were prohibited. Disputes arose that related to such things as merchants who went into the countryside, bought all of the geese and brought to the market only the number that would maximize their total revenue. It appears that the demand for geese was inelastic and the principle of profiting from monopoly control of the supply of a commodity having an inelastic demand schedule was recognized at least a thousand years ago. More significantly, it was disapproved and prohibited.

The Trading

The detail of the trading processes varies among exchanges according to the volume of business and the customs of the exchanges. But the rules of the exchanges are quite similar and the differences in procedures are of minor significance. The trading is in pits or rings with, generally, one pit or ring for each commodity. Where volume is small or commodities are closely related more than one commodity may be traded in the same pit or ring.

The pit is a structure of wood, usually hexagonal in shape, with three or four steps up the outside and a similar number down the inside. Some pits are as much as 75 feet across. The whole thing is quite horizontal and the bottom of the pit is at the exterior floor level. The term pit is not very descriptive; it is a series of raised steps designed so that the traders can see each other better.

Various areas of the pit are designated by a pit committee for trading in the various delivery months with trading in the most active month usually taking place on the top steps where there is the greatest access to messages and phones. Trading is not restricted by area; anyone can trade in any delivery month with anyone else.

The ring is a circular or oval piece of brass that may be as much as 20 feet in diameter raised some 3½ feet—a comfortable leaning height—above the floor by posts. The traders stand behind the ring and trade across the ring with each other.

In some markets trading starts and ends simultaneously in all deliveries of all commodities and in all pits or rings. In others, trading starts at different times in the different commodities and for the different delivery months of each commodity. At some markets trading is a continuous auction from opening to closing bell while others open with a call. In a call market opening bids and offers are posted and each delivery month is called separately. The initial trades—amounts and prices—are posted and continuous auction trading follows.

In all markets the times of trading are established by the rules and trading is started with a loud bell. There are usually warning bells rung just before trading starts and ends. Trading before the opening bell and after the closing bell is prohibited and the rules are strictly enforced. The occasional violations that occur are usually detected and the offenders disciplined. This rule results in quite hectic activity at times, particularly in the expiring delivery months. Orders flow into the pit for execution near or at the close of trading and sometimes the volume of this business is quite large. Each principal behind the order wants execution at the last traded price which cannot always be accomplished. Some markets, notably the Chicago Board of Trade, close trading in the expiring delivery month at a time other than the general closing time. At Chicago the general closing time is 1:15 P.M. but trading in expiring contracts ceases at high noon. This gives a clearer field for the traders interested in the expiring month.

The rules require that all bids and offers be cried out in a loud, clear voice so that all can hear and that each trader have equal opportunity of acceptance. This is done with such vigor that the noise makes it virtually impossible in active markets for anyone to hear what is being said. As a result, the traders resort to hand signals. A palm held out is an offer to sell and a palm in is a bid to buy. Fingers held vertically indicate the quantity in bushels or in contracts. Fingers are then turned horizontally to indicate the price at which the bid or offer is being made.

When a bid or offer is made the trade must be made with the first person to accept. If more than two people accept simultaneously the business is split between them if more than one contract is involved.

At each pit there is a raised pulpit in which observers are placed. They overlook the trading and note the prices at which traders are made. The traders are obligated to see that the observers are informed of the prices at which trades are made. The observers record the prices, time stamp them and feed them into a communication system.

The communication system is extensive and nearly instantaneous. The prices are communicated by telephone to board markers or to a computer which activates price display boards on the trading floor. At the same time the prices are put on ticker tape that feeds out of receiving machines located in brokerage offices and the offices of commodity firms. In 1975 there were 770 Chicago Board of Trade ticker receiving points, scattered over the U.S., Canada, and in Europe. The ticker coverage of other exchanges is smaller but none-the-less great.

In addition, the quotations from all of the exchanges are fed into central computer operated reporting systems and transmitted to subscribers where they activate electrically operated display boards or desk top units. The number of these units is large and increasing rapidly. At the end of 1975 Chicago Board of Trade quotations were received in 90 countries.

Time is of the essence in reporting prices. The time lag from trader to pulpit is measured in seconds—say one or two. From that point the time lag is measured in milliseconds. Prices are registered on the trading floor and at ticker outlets at the same time. There is a further time lag between the ticker and the central reporting services but it, too, is measured in split seconds. Thus one can sit in a brokerage office or at one's desk in the office of a processing firm or grain exporter in Decatur, Ill., London, or Hong Kong and know the prices at which trades are made quite as soon as can the people on the exchange floors.

When a trade is made each of the traders makes a note on a card of the price, the quantity, the delivery month, and the person with whom the trade was made. Thus the trade is recorded twice. This record is submitted to the Clearing House for reconciliation after the close of the trading session. It is interesting to note that many of the trades are quite large and price changes are frequent so that the gains or losses from trades are often substantial by the close of the session. Yet agreements are reached quickly with a shout or a hand signal and without the signing of documents or even exchange of memoranda. Often as much as 100 million bushels of soybeans, worth $600 million, are traded in a day by these verbal contracts without any disputes arising.

This detail of trading rules and procedures is worth noting because it demonstrates the open competition of the markets. All traders, large and small, have equal access to all other traders. All bids, offers, and transactions are public, and all prices become public information instantly.

Contract Terms

As we have noted, very few futures contracts ever reach maturity and are consummated. But some do and are. They are valid, enforceable contracts. If the seller elects to make delivery he may do so and will receive payment at the price at which he made the contract. If the buyer wishes to hold his contract to maturity he will receive delivery and in effect will pay the price at which he made the contract. As noted, futures contracts are standardized and interchangeable. The specific terms of the contracts vary by commodities and by exchanges. The terms of the contracts are precise and closely specified. One gets the impression in reading them that every conceivable loophole has been tried, discovered, and plugged. The exchange officials have done a remarkable job of anticipating every devious thought of the sellers. For example the pork belly futures contract on the Chicago Mercantile Exchange requires three and one half pages of relatively small type for description. The original futures contracts for grains as they evolved in the 19th century followed existing trade practices. As the contracts of more recent origin were written, careful attempts were made to precisely describe existing practices in trading the cash commodity. These contracts, then, are interchangeable with and as close substitutes as possible for transactions in cash commodities. Because they must be uniform, that is, cannot vary by individual lots, they cannot be perfect substitutes for cash contracts which can and do vary individually. But when futures contracts have been written that failed to accurately represent existing trade practices, active trading has failed to develop. The terms of some futures contracts are fairly frequently revised as the conditions of the cash commodity trading changes. For others, contract terms remain constant over long periods of time.

It is important that each person who trades in futures contracts know the general terms of contracts in which he trades. There is sufficient uniformity among contracts that an example is adequate for our purposes here.

Suppose that on January 10 one buys a contract of May soybeans futures for $5.87. What does this mean? It means that he has made a contract, an agreement, to buy some soybeans to be delivered in May and pay $5.87 per bushel for them. What are the terms of the contract?

1. The commodity is soybeans.
2. The price is $5.87 per bushel.
3. The quantity is 5000 bushels.
4. The quality is No. 2 yellow as determined on the basis U.S. Department of Agriculture grain standards. But the seller, if he elects may substitute No. 1 yellow and be paid a premium of 3 cents per bushel or No. 3 yellow (14% or less moisture) and be paid a discount of 3 cents per bushel. In addition, the seller must furnish live transit rail billing.

5. The time of delivery is some day in May, whichever day the seller elects—from first to last.

6. The place of delivery is in store in a public warehouse that has been designated as regular for delivery by the Chicago Board of Trade. The elevators designated regular for delivery must be licensed, located within the rail switching district of the City of Chicago, and be located on both rail and water. An exception to this is that delivery may be made during the last three business days of the delivery month in rail cars located in the switching district of Chicago. In fact, delivery is made by the seller furnishing an endorsed warehouse receipt. (This latter note should dispel the old wives' tale of the man who took delivery and woke up one morning to find several carloads of a commodity dumped in his front yard.)

7. The terms of payment are cash on delivery of the warehouse receipt. There are no credit transactions in the making and taking of delivery on futures contracts. It should be kept in mind, however, that the warehouse receipt is a negotiable instrument so that a high proportion of the value of the soybeans can be borrowed to make payment.

8. In the matter of default, should the buyer of a contract fail to take delivery on a contract, the deliverer shall promptly sell the commodity on the open market for the account of the delinquent. The rules governing failure to make delivery are not as simple because the solution is not as simple. It is easy to sell something in hand but it is not easy to buy something to replace a defaulted delivery; the seller would not default if the commodity were available at the delivery point. The general principle is that the holder of the contract to buy takes whatever measures are necessary to fulfill his own obligations and takes recourse upon the seller. But these things do not happen; the sellers make delivery "or else," and the buyers take delivery "or else." The "or else" is easier if the trader does it himself rather than leave it to the exchange. Anything can be negotiated at a price and there is an old saw common in futures trading circles that goes "He who sells what isn't his'n must pay the price or go to prison." Exchanges have broad emergency powers under which they can suspend trading and fix settlement prices when delivery cannot be made. But these powers are almost never used. The posture of the exchanges is that these are valid contracts and will damned well be honored. There are no contract defaults or fixed settlement prices on record in the modern history of the Chicago Board of Trade or the Chicago Mercantile Exchange and these two do some 75% of all the commodity futures business.

In addition to the terms of the contracts there are additional regulations of trading that should be noted. First, price quotations and minimum price fluctuations are established by the exchanges. Soybeans, as most grains, are quoted in cents and quarters of a cent per bushel, with $\frac{1}{4}$¢ per bushel ($12.50 per contract) as the minimum change. Frozen orange concentrate is quoted on a pound price, showing as 50.15 or 50 and 15/100 cents per pound. Fluctuations are recorded in multiples of 5/100 cents per pound, with 5/100 cent fluctuation representing $7.50 on each contract of 15,000 pounds.

Second, the exchanges generally establish maximum daily permissible price changes. For soybeans the permissible change is 30 cents per bushel above or below the previous day's close. For orange juice the regulation is: No limit is imposed on or after the 8th day of the current delivery month. In others, prices may move no more than 3 cents ($450.00 per contact) above or below the lowest price in the closing range of the previous market session. During any session, trades may not be made at prices more than 3 cents per pound above the lowest price for that session, or more than 3 cents per pound below the highest price. (For nearly all commodities on all exchanges there are limits on possible daily price ranges but it is not at all unusual for these limits to be suspended during the delivery month as in the case of frozen orange concentrate.)

The purpose of the daily limits is to prevent a major price change from carrying too far from its own momentum; a chance for the traders to consider the matter overnight (not to suggest that they could sleep on it) and for the losers to regroup their forces. Setting the limits is a delicate matter. They are kept narrow in the interest of orderly movements in prices. But if they are set too narrow they hamper the normal movement of prices and, more importantly, they act as a magnet. Holders of contracts to buy do not want to be caught in a market that is down the limit so that they can't sell. Conversely, holders of contracts to sell do not want to be caught in a market that is up the limit. In either case liquidity is lost and the trader has lost control of his own destiny. Thus, as a market moves up or down sharply and approaches the daily permissible limit, traders about to be caught, get out, which forces the price farther in the direction it is already moving, thereby aggravating the move. The fact remains, though, that the loss that can occur on a single day is limited.

The increased volatility of prices beginning in 1972 created extensive problems in setting daily variation limits. For some commodities, as cattle in 1973, there were extensive periods of continuous limit moves. In 1975, coffee futures rose the limit on seven successive days. In the main, the problems were solved by increasing limits, as from 1 to 1½ cents per pound for cattle. The Chicago Board of Trade adopted a system of variable limits. If the price changes the limit for three successive days, the limit is increased by 50 percent until the problem is solved. When limit moves cease, limits revert to earlier levels.

A limit move on a major exchange is interesting to watch. Limit moves nearly always occur as the result of a major change in one or more of the factors affecting prices and usually happen when market participation is at a high level. An example: In the summer of 1966 the weather was unfavorable for grain production and prices rose. The soybean price, in particular, was quite strong. The August 1st crop report made it clear that there would be a shortage and that high prices would be required to ration the supply during the ensuing 12 months, and the price continued to rise. Market participation was broad and the volume of trading large. Huge sums of money were made and lost. The government report estimating production on Sept. 1, to be released after the market close on Friday, September 9, was anxiously awaited. The price ran up eight cents near the close of trading on Friday. The report showed a marked improvement in the crop during August—from 859 million bushels indicated August 1 to 925 million indicated on September 1. This report dramatically changed the thinking of the traders. The holders of contracts to buy were discouraged and wanted out and the holders of contracts to sell were gleeful, anticipating that they could buy supplies for delivery at much lower prices. It was a long, anxious weekend and the tension was tremendous as the opening bell on Monday approached. The bell rang and there was great noise and congestion in the pit with people pushing, shouting, and frantically waving arms and hands. But nothing happened. The price was down the 10 cent limit offered and there were no buyers. An eerie quiet settled with only an occasional plaintive cry to sell made. And so the day went with almost no trading. Occasionally an offer to sell was quietly accepted. On Tuesday the market opened down the limit and there was very little trading until mid-session when the sellers decided the break might be over and started to buy. For a time the volume of trading was huge. The price strengthened one and one half cents but more sales came in so that it closed down the limit with no trading. Prices stabilized on Wednesday with a large volume of trading in a narrow range. The total volume of trading by days in bushels was:

September	9	67,312,000
September	12	3,655,000
September	13	66,335,000
September	14	54,159,000

Third, there are usually volume of trading and position limits imposed on ✓ some classes of traders. For the principal grains these limits are established by the government. The limits vary by exchanges and commodity. For example no person may own more than 3 million bushels of corn futures nor trade more than 3 million bushels in a single day. The rule applies only to speculators—bona fide hedgers are excepted. The rule does not affect very many people but it is noted because it is a significant difference between futures trading and cash forward trading where there are no limits.

Fourth, trading in the delivery month is stopped prior to the end of the month. The length of time before the end varies by commodities and exchanges with five or seven business days the most usual. For example, trading in grains is stopped so that seven business days remain which is, roughly, the 20th. After the suspension of trading all outstanding contracts must be settled by delivery. The purpose of the early cessation of trading is to allow time for moving commodities into position for delivery and an orderly exchange of title.

It is obvious from the large number of contracts traded in the several exchanges that there are a lot of specific contract terms with which traders need be familiar. Such familiarity is not as difficult as it might seem at first glance. Most people trade in but a few commodities. It is not necessary to know all of the technical detail of the commodity contract but rather the general provision and the relative values of the commodity on delivery and the cash commodity in ordinary commercial transactions. Most exchanges publish and distribute brief leaflets that describe the commodity, the general terms of the futures contract, and the rules of trading for each commodity. These are available on request from exchanges and brokers.

Delivery Months

Several delivery months for each commodity are established by the exchanges. There are three bases for selection of months: natural climactic months relating to the season of the year, concentration of volume of trading for liquidity, and inertia. In the beginning, a century ago, the months for grain futures trading evolved from existing trade practices and related to the times of growing, harvesting, and marketing of crops. For wheat, July was the first month of harvest and availability of winter wheat. September is the month of harvest of wheat planted in the spring. By December the size of the harvest was known and much information about use for the year was available. Also December was the last month for shipment via the Great Lakes before the winter freeze. The Great Lakes were and are an important channel in the flow of wheat to market. March is the first month of shipment via the Lakes after the spring thaw. May is a "clean up" month—the last full month before the new crop is available. In May, the old crop influences of supply dominate the price-making factors, while the prospects for the new crop harvest dominate the July price. For corn, December is the first month of availability of new crop corn at the terminal markets. March is the opening of navigation on the Lakes. By May, careful appraisals can be made of the carry-over of old crop corn at the beginning of harvest in the fall and the first indications of planting and weather are guides to the need to save corn for use the following year. In earlier times, July reflected the summer weather and the rate of use and September was the last old crop month. More recently July tends to be the last purely old crop month and September a transition to new crop. There are distinct seasonal years for the crop commodities and certain months are climactic in bringing price making forces into focus and are thus natural delivery months for future contracts.

Some non-crop commodities have seasonal patterns of production and storage. This was true of eggs until recently when the seasonal pattern of production was smoothed out by improved technology. There is a seasonal pattern of stocks of pork bellies with a low in September–October and a high in May–June. The winter is a season of accumulation and the summer a season of liquidation. February is a natural first month and August a last.

Many commodities do not have pronounced seasonal patterns of production, inventory, and use so that there is not a logical crop year and one month is the same as another for delivery purposes. Some of these commodities as cattle or iced broilers are not storable. It would be desirable to have every month a delivery month but to do so would scatter the volume of trading to such an extent that the markets would not be liquid and liquidity—ease of getting in and out without disturbing the price—is important. Thus, there is a tendency to designate every other month for trading with the expectation that as volume permits, all months can be traded.

There is no way to explain the existence of the delivery month pattern for some commodities except that exchanges are great democratic institutions that change slowly. Soybeans is a case in point. At one time November was the month of harvest and September ended the season but technology changed so that new crop soybeans are nearly always available in moderate volume in September and are always available in large volume in October. When September became neither fish nor fowl the climactic old crop trading was concentrated in July. But July was too long before the end of the season so August was added without dropping the others. A more logical pattern could be worked out than the current September, November, January, March, May, July, and August but there is a great reluctance to drop a month that some people want to use.

The time that futures contracts extend forward is generally one year. As one contract reaches maturity and expires it is replaced by the same month of the next year. There is a tendency to extend the life of contracts. Corn has been extended from one year to about 14 months. Contracts for some commodities do not run a full year while others extend much more than a year; in 1975 silver had a 15 month time span.

Settlement of Contracts

Futures contracts may be settled by delivery or by making an opposite or offsetting transaction in futures. The holder of a contract to buy will receive delivery of the cash commodity if he waits until maturity and the seller of a contract must make delivery if he waits until contract maturity. There are some, but not many, deliveries on every maturing delivery of every commodity traded. When delivery is made and taken, title passes and the futures contract becomes a cash transaction. It has matured, is fulfilled, and ceases to exist. The delivery provision and the fact that deliveries are made and taken forces the trade in, and the prices of futures contracts to conform to the real world of cash commodity transactions.

Most futures contracts are offset by making opposite transactions. The owner of a futures contract to buy, say, December corn may elect at any time before he receives delivery to make a contract to sell December corn. He now both owns a contract to buy and a contract to sell which is a nonsense position. As the price goes up he makes on the one hand and loses on the other. Were the contracts to exist until maturity he would receive delivery from the person he made the purchase contract with at the agreed price and make delivery to the person with whom he made the contract to sell at the different agreed price, all of which would obviously be a cumbersome process and is not permitted. No person may hold both a contract to buy and a contract to sell the same maturity of the same commodity on the same exchange. As soon as the second transaction is made it is matched against the first and both are canceled and cease to exist. If the buying price of the original contract is lower than the selling price of the second contract a profit has been made and the trader receives money from the settlement system but if the price agreed in making the original contract is higher than the price agreed in the second transaction, the trader has lost and must pay money in. Contracts are settled by the payment of value differences when the contracts are offset.

Long, Short, and the Open Interest. When a trader, in his first transaction, makes a contract to buy he is long; he has commodity coming. And when a trader, in first transaction, makes a contract to sell he is short; he owes commodity. This is the long and the short of it. When a trader who is long makes a contract to sell the two are offset and he is out of the game; is neither long nor short. All that is left is to count the winnings and losings. The same is true, of course, of an original short who makes a contract to buy. The terminology as it is used here—"makes a contract to buy," and "makes a contract to sell" is clumsy and in actual usage is shortened to "buy" and "sell." One buys to become long or one buys to offset an existing short position and become even.

An open contract is an outstanding agreement that has been neither settled by delivery or offset. It remains to be reckoned with. Someone is long and someone else is short. If A sells to B, A is short, B is long, and there is one open contract. If subsequently C sells to B, A is short one contract, B is long two contracts, C is short one contract, and the open interest is two contracts. If then D sells to A, A is even, C is short one, B long two, D is short one, and the open interest is still two. Next, C buys a contract from B; now C is even, B is long one, D is short one and the open interest is one. For every buyer there is a seller and for every seller there is a buyer. For every long position there is a short position and vice versa. One long plus one short equals one open contract.

The significance of volume of trading and open interest will be considered in later chapters but one quantitative fact is worth noting here: It takes a lot of volume of trading to change the open interest appreciably. Volume of trading, open interest at the close and change in open interest in all corn futures on five consecutive days were:

Corn

Date	Vol. of Trade 000 bu.	Open Interest 000 bu.	Change in Open Int.
1	21,095	263,490	—
2	21,535	264,320	+ 830
3	28,205	265,955	+1,635
4	37,900	272,060	+6,105
5	25,695	270,230	−1,830

Some casual observations may be made: 1) The volume of trading varies greatly from day to day. 2) Size of the change in open interest is somewhat but not closely related to the volume of trading. Note that the ratios of volume to change in open interest were 26:1, 17:1, 6:1, and 14:1. 3) The volume of trading is much greater than the minimum required to increase or decrease the open interest. From these it follows that there are a lot of positions taken and offset within a trading day and that the identiy of who is long and who is short may change rapidly.

Clearing House. The complexity of settling monetary differences is readily apparent when the volume of trading and the year or longer life of individual contracts is considered. A may buy from B in January and hold the position until December and stand for delivery. In the meantime, B may buy from C offsetting his contract, C buy from D, etc. a thousand times over. For A to find out who owes him the commodity would be quite a stunt. There is another problem: There would be a marked tendency for the losers to disappear from the scene and the winners to show up promptly.

In cash forward markets, contracts for deferred shipment often change hands several times. They are endorsed from person to person and settlement often becomes complicated. In the early days of futures trading clerks went from office to office each day to collect and pay out money. The system was advanced when the clerks met in a single room and settled up differences. Then came settlement by offset with the meaningless contract canceled. Finally came the Clearing House. The Clearing House is a party to all trades and guarantor of all contracts.

The exchanges have developed corporations charged with the functions of 1) reconciliation of all futures transactions, and 2) assuring the financial integrity of these transactions. With two exceptions, the clearing houses of the several exchanges are separate corporations. Membership in the clearing corporation is limited to but does not include all members of the exchange; membership in the clearing corporation is much smaller than exchange membership and requirements for entry are much more difficult to meet. The clearing corporations are stock companies and each member is required to purchase stock, the amount of stock depending on the volume of business cleared. In addition, members are required to deposit a substantial sum of money in the guarantee fund of the corporation. Members of the exchange who are not clearing members must clear through a clearing member.

The clearing corporation has a board of governors who are elected and represent all segments of the membership. It has paid staff officers who cannot be associated with member firms. The clearing corporation is operated not-for-profit. Its income is derived chiefly from service fees from members for clearing trades and from interest earned on invested capital.

The clearing corporation becomes a party to all trades; a buyer to all sellers and a seller to all buyers as soon as each days' trading is reconciled and accepted. Each day, each clearing member receives cards from the trading floor that carry the details of each transaction in the pits. The clearing member enters this information on trade confirmation cards and forwards them to the Clearing House. Thus, for each transaction there is a "buy" card and a "sell" card. After all trade confirmation cards are received from every clearing member, the buy records are matched to the sell records. The data for each trade must match exactly as to the clearing member buying, clearing member selling, commodity, delivery month, quantity, and price.

If a trade confirmation record cannot be matched to one for the opposite side of the trade a duplicate unmatched trade notice is made. These trades are known, as "out trades." One copy of the notice is returned to the clearing member buying and one copy to the clearing member selling. These two must then reconcile the differences between the reports whether the trades are for the clearing member's accounts or non-clearing member's accounts cleared through them. The number of "out trades" is quite small and the differences are nearly always small and quickly reconciled. If differences cannot be reconciled by a meeting of the two parties the trades are rejected by the clearing house and the dispute then goes to the arbitration of the exchange. Thus, each day's business is balanced before the next day's trading begins. The volume of business handled is large—as many as 20,000 transactions per day—and fully automated and computerized on the large exchanges.

There have been occasions when, with a large volume of business, the work of the clearing house could not be completed before time to open the market the next day and the opening was delayed. The root cause of the delay was not with the method or with difficulty in reconciling out trades but rather with difficulty in locating traders whose cards did not match. After such hectic days the boys hied themselves off to local watering holes where they could not be found or reasoned with if found. Disciplinary action quickly corrected the problem.

An essential part of settling all accounts daily is establishing a settlement price for each delivery month of each commodity traded. This settlement price is based on the closing price or closing range. It becomes the official basis for paying money into and taking money out of the clearing house.

In addition to owning stock and making a guarantee deposit, each clearing member must make a margin deposit as a performance bond to assure settlement of the contracts. Margin is deposited by both buyers and sellers. The amount of the margin deposit is determined by the number of open contracts held by the clearing member. The standing margins per contract are fixed by the governors of the clearing corporation.

Margins are usually the same for all clearing members, although the governors may depart from the rule of uniformity in emergencies or where particular risks are deemed hazardous. Hazardous conditions exist when one clearing member holds a large share of either the long or short side of the open interest. This rarely occurs. The size of the standing margin is kept as low as is consistent with security of the contracts. Excessive margins add to marketing costs through interest costs and loss of liquidity. The clearing corporation closely watches margin requirements in relation to market conditions.

When the clearing house has reconciled and accepted all trades at the end of the day, the clearing house computes the "pay or collect" amounts for all accounts, both the clearing members and non-member accounts cleared through the members. On most exchanges, the collect and pay amounts are offset to obtain a net pay or collect amount. If a net payment to restore the full standing margin is due the clearing house it must be made before the opening of the next day's trading. The clearing house provides checks for members with net collect balances. Many clearing members maintain surplus margins so that when their net positions grow they already have enough margin on deposit.

Standing margins are usually large enough to cover daily maximum price fluctuations. However, when market prices move against a member's position his standing margin is impaired to the extent of the price change. The clearing house can call for additional margin at any time to cover these price changes. This is known as a variation margin call, and the member must pay the amount called for by certified check within one hour.

There is no record of any buyer or seller ever having financial loss through default on a transaction cleared through the clearing house of a U.S. exchange. This is much more of a tribute to the meticulous operation of clearing houses than it is to the integrity of members. How can they lose? They get their money first. The system does speak for the integrity of the contracts and to the rigor with which all trades are backed by sufficient financial resources to accept losses.

It should be noted here that this system of financial guarantee applies only to the relationship of the clearing house to its members. A different system governs the financial relationship of clearing members and exchange members who clear through them and clearing members and their non-exchange member customers.

A final note on the clearing house is that it breaks even. Except for the small clearance fee it pays out quite as much money as it takes in and takes in quite as must as it pays out. It is a party to all trades; short to all longs and long to all shorts. Thus, the total of all futures trading is a gross zero. Futures trading is a zero sum game. This is a fact that should be tucked away for later reference.

Making Delivery. Delivery on futures contracts is made by the seller furnishing a negotiable instrument to the buyer. This may be a warehouse receipt for a stored commodity, a shipping certificate for a commodity that is furnished out of current production, or an inspection certificate for a commodity not in storage. The essence of the matter is that the seller furnishes and transfers a document of title and receives payment. The specific procedures and documents vary by commodity and by exchange.

In general, the contract terms call for "delivery within the contract month to be at the seller's option upon notice to the buyer as prescribed by the rules." That is, the seller must furnish advance notice of delivery. Notice time extends from the end of the current day up to as much as eight days depending on the commodity and the exchange. In the case of a one notice day commodity such as the grains, the first notice day is the last business day of the month preceding the delivery month—for December contracts it is November 30 unless it falls on a holiday or weekend, etc. The buyer is warned, "Tomorrow it is yours; be prepared."

There is provision made for retendering. If the notice of delivery the next day is received before a specific hour in the trading session—say 11:30—the person receiving the notice may go into the pit and sell a like amount and retender the notice. This ends his obligation to accept delivery. If the notice is received too late in the day to sell and retender, he may furnish notice and deliver the following day in which case he incurs storage, insurance, and interest costs for his overnite ownership. For some commodities there are additional commission charges and reinspection fees that must be paid. For example, in pork bellies and eggs, you must accept delivery, sell and deliver, incurring an extra commission.

From this process two things should be noted. First, the documents of delivery can circulate rapidly so that one lot of a commodity can satisfy quite a lot of open contracts. Delivery may lodge with a buyer who wants, will take, ship, or use the commodity or it may lodge with a buyer who treats it like a hot potato and quickly flips it back into the system. Thus, the quantity of a commodity in delivery position is not necessarily a measure of the liquidation that may take place even if only a small number of delivery notices circulate. Second, getting rid of an unwanted delivery is simple and not very expensive so long as trading in the delivery month is still in progress. Once trading ceases, only the longs and shorts who really mean it remain, but until the last bell, both longs and shorts have their options open.

The clearing house, a party to all trades, is the instrument through which delivery is made. It receives or makes payments on deliveries and passes delivery notices to the longs and either clears their offsetting trades or collects from them. Thus, the full financial resources of the clearing house are behind the delivery integrity of all contracts.

The clearing house passes delivery notices to the oldest long—the clearing member who has been long for the greatest period of time. The clearing member, in turn, passes the notice to the non-clearing member or the customer who has been long the longest; the first shall be served.

The Traders

We have pictured the floor and the pits of an exchange as a crowded and busy place. This is true for the active commodities traded on the high volume exchanges. There are regularly 200 to 250 of the 500 members of the Chicago Mercantile Exchange on the floor actively trading. The norm on the Chicago Board of Trade is 400 to 500 of the 1402 members. On the other hand not more than a dozen of the 400 members of the Minneapolis Grain Exchange may be seen in the wheat pit on a given day. The primary business of the membership of the Minneapolis Exchange is cash grain trading and the volume of futures trading is small. There are all gradations of attendance and activity, from a small pit with one, two, or perhaps five people standing or sitting idly about to a large pit containing 200 wildly active traders. Yet on all exchanges there are present, if not in the pits on the floor, the same general types of traders. The description here relates to relatively active trading.

Who are the traders? With our academic penchant we can classify them but it should be kept in mind that the classifications are not discreet and distinct. Some members belong exclusively to one classification, others mostly to one, and the activities of others are scattered over the several classifications. The list includes four types: scalpers, pit traders, floor traders, and brokers.

Scalpers. The scalper is a busy type, interjecting himself into as many trades as possible. He stands ready to buy one trading unit—$1/4$ cent per bushel—below the last traded price and ready to sell one trading unit up from the last price. The operating principle is that an incoming order to buy will raise the price slightly, after which it will sink to its old level and an incoming order to sell will depress the price slightly and then the price will return to its equilibrium level. In this case the scalper bridges a time gap in the flow of orders to the pit. He adds to the liquidity of the market and enables orders to be filled without delay at very small price concessions. A second activity of the scalper is to spread orders. A spread is the simultaneous purchase of one delivery month and the sale of another for the same commodity. A broker may receive an order to buy December and sell March. He knows that the two months have been trading at a difference of 4 cents so he tries it at that difference. If there are no takers a scalper may offer to sell December and buy March at 3¾. If it is the best that the broker can do, he will accept. The scalper then tries to reverse his position by buying December and selling March at the old difference of 4 cents. He may do it on opposite spread orders or he may do it one leg at a time, buying the December if the next move of the market is down and expecting to get out even on the March on the next upsurge. Or the sale of the December side may fit and make profitable a purchase that the scalper has just made on our first kind of scalp so that he has only to break even on the March purchase. Or the spread may fit two scalps that he has just made, evening him up at a profit (or letting him out of a losing position before the losses get large). A third kind of scalp is geographical within a pit. Pits get phsyically congested and when prices are fluctuating sharply the quick execution of market orders is imperative. A scalper may hear a broker on one side bid a higher price than another broker on the other side offers. The scalper says "done" to one and "done" to the other. It seems improbable but it can and does happen.

The scalper deals in small fluctuations in price, quarters of a cent as described here. In active markets he may try for a half or a cent. These seem small amounts but a quarter of a cent on one contract of 5000 bushels is $12.50. It is a small accommodation price to a broker in a hurry or with a large order to fill instantly but if done enough times successfully it adds up to enough to make a living.

The crux of the matter is doing it successfully; a high proportion of the scalps turn out to be losses instead of profits. The scalper may buy ¼ below the last trade and then find several orders to sell. He must then make a quick decision. Should he accommodate the decreasing offers for another ¼ and still another or should he take his loss and start over? If he is a true scalper he admits his error and gets out as best he can—quickly. Scalping is a journeyman type of operation, involving a highly specialized skill. The scalper trys to anticipate the direction of the next change in price and profit from it. His basic posture is that a stable price will continue stable, that a down trending price will continue down, and that an uptrending will continue up. In a market that he judges to be stable he initiates trades from both the buy and the sell sides. In uptrending markets he initiates from the buy side and in downtrending markets from the sell side. Judging the very short run trends in prices is difficult, requiring a high degree of skill. The other traders in the pit are not in the business of giving away multiples of $12.50. There are other scalpers to contend with, each trying for small profits on a liveable percentage of a lot of trades. When a broker makes a price concession to a scalper in filling an order he has, in some degree, been defeated. The essential scalping skills are lightning fast judgment in initiating trades and quickness in admitting and coping with errors. The service that scalpers perform is furnishing liquidity in filling orders; they bridge short time gaps in the flow of orders. Scalpers limit their activities to a single pit or ring and infrequently move from one pit to another.

Pit Traders. One characterization of a pit trader is that he is a grown up scalper with more money and intestinal fortitude. This is hardly fair to scalpers because scalpers possess skills that pit traders lack and so are more "grown up" in one sense, but it does describe what pit traders do in the sense that they take bigger positions and stay with them for longer periods of time and larger price changes; they bridge bigger time gaps in the flow of orders. Pit traders enter the ✓ pits each day with no position and leave at the close with no position. They try to make money from intra-day price changes. They buy when they think the price is going up and sell when they think it is going down.

There are as many methods of operation as there are pit traders, and each pit trader tries them all at different times. They match wits with each other, with scalpers, brokers, and floor traders. One method of operation is to trade against the flow of orders from the outside. If the initial flow of orders for the day seems to be predominantly selling, the pit trader buys on a scale down, assuming that the selling will soon be exhausted and will be followed by a flow of orders to buy that he can sell to on a scale up, taking profits. All day long the pit trader watches the other traders, brokers in particular, trying to anticipate the trades that they will make before the end of the session and get in position to accommodate them—profitably. If the pit trader anticipates large selling orders near the close he sells short during the session as the opportunity to do so presents itself with small bulges in the market. He is thus set to buy when the price declines under the weight of selling late in the session. If he anticipates all of this correctly he makes some money. If, on the other hand, the selling orders do not come, he is caught in the position of having to extricate himself from his short position rather quickly so that he can end the day even, and, the chances are, this will cost him some money. This is particularly true if other pit traders have made the same mistake and compete with him for the limited sell orders or if a floor trader who will take an overnight position catches him short and frantic and will only sell to him on a rising scale of prices. This method of operation against the market is that of a skeptic or a cynic; one who says, "This move is false. The price will end the day where it started."

A second method of operation is to trade with the market; to sense the development of a price move and either buy or sell quickly as is appropriate. The key consideration in this game is to know whether a given move in price foretells a further move in the same direction or whether the move will quickly be reversed. This type is a believer, trying to ride on the coattails of the flow of orders.

Pit traders rely on different kinds of information in forming their expectations about the next move in price. Some close their ears to all news about factors affecting the cash prices of the commodity and rely only on what they see, hear, and sense in the pit itself. Others have substantial disdain for the technical position of the pit and rely on news of the commercial world: whether primary producers are selling or holding, processors are ready buyers or not, the amount of export business done, and speculator buying. The underlying philosophy of the first is that the pit will read itself and tells its own story and, if they can read the pit fast and accurately, they will make money. The basic philosophy of the second is that commercial factors determine the flow of orders and the game is to be right with the flow. This categorization is fine for illustrative purposes and pit traders typically identify themselves in one direction or the other. But when one is asked why he did what he did at that time, the answer may flow from one kind of information at one time and from the opposite at another. Doubtless there are pit traders who know nothing and care nothing about the outside world but they are not numerous. They know which is trade of outside origin and which is trade of inside origin and the forces behind the flow of orders from the outside.

Pit traders are quick to take advantage of conditions of unexecuted orders in the pits. Sometimes there are resting orders of substantial size a bit above or a bit below the current price. There may be orders to buy substantial amounts moderately below the trading level; that is, the price may be trading around $2.75 with orders to buy if the price declines to, say, $2.74 and more at $2.73 and/or orders to sell at, say $2.76 and $2.77. It is to the advantage of the holders of these orders to conceal their existence and they are skillful at concealment, but pit traders are skillful readers. When such orders exist and are accurately read they make an excellent backstop for pit traders. With resting orders at $2.74 the pit trader can buy with impunity at 2.74\frac{1}{4}$; he can't lose much and may make a lot—even from just above resting orders to buy to just below other resting orders to sell. This does not have quite the character of shooting fish in a barrel that it seems. The resting orders may be a figment of the trader's imagination or they may be pulled out as the price approaches, leaving our hero dangling. Or some competing pit trader will sense the resting order and take a bigger risk, buying at 2.74\frac{1}{2}$, cutting our hero out.

In addition to resting orders, there are unactivated stop loss orders in the pits. The stop loss order says, "If the price goes so low as $2.74 I give up. Sell me out." A stop loss order becomes a market order to be executed as best the broker can when a trade is made or an offer to sell made at $2.74 or below. If this happens the price may skid sharply. If the pit traders sense an abundance of stop loss orders close under (or above) the market they can profit by selling (or buying) vigorously to touch off the stops and then catching the market in a basket when the stop selling (or buying) is exhausted. This maneuver has its offsets, too. Other pit traders may catch them at it and buy aggressively at 2.74\frac{1}{4}$ in the expectation that the price will move back up to $2.75 making a profit and leaving our heroes poorer and wiser. Rarely will a pit trader admit to taking a shot at a stop. But how many football players will admit to a forearm shiver?

Pit traders also scalp when the opportunity is presented but generally they are preoccupied with other games and the scalpers are quicker. There is not a firm distinction between the two activities nor are individuals exclusively identified with one or the other. In addition, pit traders occasionally take overnight positions when they like the looks of the situation or when they cannot handily get loose from an existing position. But, when they do this they put on another tag and join our next category—the floor trader.

Floor traders. Floor traders are more difficult to categorize than scalpers and pit traders. They are professional speculators whose positions are quite flexible, who trade in more than one commodity, who usually go into the pits only to observe, and who take relatively large positions. They wander about the floor pensively, listening to comments, nodding, and occasionally commenting. They are the oracles, the students, and are at the front of the pecking order. Their reputations vary widely with some being spoofed as unimportant and others held in awe, regarded as quite successful, and major market factors. The hard facts about their success or failure and size of operations are nearly nonexistent. They are almost all quite secretive and there is widespread interest in where they stand in the market. Their number is quite small.

The methods of operation of floor traders are as diverse as they are numerous. Some trade predominantly with the market and others against, but almost none do either exclusively. Some are basically spreaders, long some delivery months and short others; long some commodities and short others while others tend to be long or short nearly all commodities at a given time. They are all sometimes long and sometimes short and generally do not have a strong bias toward either long or short. As a group they are short run opportunists and long run position traders. They often build up rather large basic positions, adding to them as they sense strength or weakness. Above all else they are flexible; their opinions and positions are good for the moment only even though they often hold opinions and positions for protracted periods of time.

Comments of floor traders about the course of prices ahead are a mixture of the discussion of underlying commercial forces affecting cash commodity prices and the technical position of the other traders and the speculating public. Some appear to be more aware of and responsive to commercial factors while the thinking of others seems to be dominated by technical considerations and current price behavior.

The greatest difference among floor traders is in their time horizons. The behavior of some is much like pit traders with a lot of trading in and out each day and a frequent reversal of position. The positions of others appear to be much more stable, remaining unchanged, in broad outline, for weeks or months.

Occasionally, the behavior of a floor trader is quite spectacular, conspicuously buying, selling, and taking delivery. Such actions may or may not indicate what he is actually doing. He may appear to be doing one thing while he actually is doing the opposite through orders placed with brokers. Or he may be attempting to encourage a following to help the anticipated move along. Or he may simply feel that quite as many people will move against him as with him and not really care what anyone knows.

Brokers. In most markets the largest group is the brokers. These men execute the orders that flow in from the outside and that are placed with them by floor traders. They act as agents for principals. They are paid a fee for each contract traded and the regulations of most exchanges provide that they be paid in this way rather than on a salaried basis.

Brokers can and do trade for their own accounts although there is a marked tendency to specialize. Some trade exclusively for single firms such as futures commission merchants, processors, exporters, merchants, and warehouse companies while others get business from a multiplicity of sources. Some firms may have two or three brokers in a single active pit as wheat, soybeans, or pork bellies and, at times, use independent brokers. In pits in which there is little activity independent brokers predominate.

The positions that brokers take come about in three main ways. First, they inherit their own mistakes. When a broker executes an order in a different way than instructed the trade is his rather than the customer's. He may buy 20,000 bushels to fill an order that read 10,000 bushels in which case he is long 10,000 for his own account. Or he may try to execute a spread order one leg at a time and miss, in which case the one leg is his. Some brokers do a huge volume of business under great pressure and mistakes are easily made. Some mistakes are profitable and others are unprofitable.

Second, some brokers make trades for their own accounts to supplement brokerage earnings while they are getting established or to simply supplement brokerage income in low volume markets. Getting established as a broker is a slow process and a supplemental source of income is often necessary.

Third, some brokers continue to accept brokerage business while getting established as traders for their own accounts. In this case, the brokerage business is on the descendency.

One reason for specialization in brokerage rather than trading for one's own account is that a broker is a highly skilled technician who must concentrate all of his attention on his specialty. A second reason is that the two activities are often in conflict. Under the regulations, an order to a broker for the account of someone else takes precedence over any trades for his own account. Suppose that a broker has sold 25,000 bushels for his own account expecting a fractional price decline and a few extra dollars for his day's work and then receives an order to buy 250,000 bushels at the market. He must execute the second order before he can offset his own position, even though the order tells him he has made a mistake. The conflict may cost him money on his own trade and cause him to do a poor job of executing the order. Brokers know when they have resting orders and stop loss order in hand and can often accurately anticipate the inflow of orders from their own sources. If they trade for themselves they are tempted to use their special information to their advantage as traders. This in-evitably reduces their effectiveness as brokers. The two functions, brokerage and pit trading are in fundamental conflict and only rarely can one man wear the two hats successfully.

There is a great range in the amount of business done by different brokers. It varies, of course, by exchanges and by commodities. If the trading in a com-modity goes flat the brokers lose income. Brokers who specialize in commercial business have more stable incomes than brokers who specialize in speculative business because speculative volume is more variable. But there is a wide range in the amount of business done by the different brokers in the same pit. They are all paid the same per contract. Their stock in trade is their skill in execution of orders. They must decide, instantly, the tactics that will be most effective in filling a given order; whether to wait for bids or offers, or whether to hold with the current price, or to bid up or offer down promptly. To be effective they must know the pit; who will do how much at what price. They must read the inten-tions of scalpers, pit traders, and other brokers while concealing their own intentions.

There is no objective way to measure the effectiveness of brokers and they are judged on the basis of impressions of customers. They gain reputation for being good or not so good and business flows to them or away from them. Some brokers have incomes ranging into six figures, while others make a meager living.

One of the skills of a broker is in knowing his deck. The deck is a stack of orders that are to be executed away from the current price. Some are to buy and some are to sell as the price rises while others are to buy and sell as the price declines. Some are at specific prices while others are for immediate execution as soon as a price is reached, and some involve a scale of quantities and prices. The orders are typically on pieces of paper about five by seven inches. The broker arranges them in the order of execution that will take place as the price moves up or down. He then folds them lengthwise for concealment and puts them in his pocket so that his hands will be free to handle his trading card and pencil, and to signal with. Occasionally, the decks are as much as an inch thick and require great memory skill and anticipatory planning.

The Contest. The activities of the traders in the pits are a contest in which the rewards are trading profits and brokerage fees. They are all adversaries, each against all of the others. There are winners and losers and there are great ranges in the size of the winnings. People come, try their hands, stay if they win, and go away if they lose. Very little is known about who wins and who loses or how much. Brokerage fees flow into the pit in relation to the volume of outside trade.

Scalpers and pit traders have two sources of income, each other and the difference between prices paid by outside buyers and received by outside sellers. In exchange for this difference the outside principals receive liquidity in making trades. The cost is not known. Presumably the scalpers and pit traders do, in the aggregate, make money but this is not absolutely certain. The traders in the pits make money from the outside traders and collect it from the brokers. The brokers keep the collection as small as they can and are paid on the basis of their skill in doing so.

The game in the pits is an intensively competitive one, the name of which is skill in anticipating movements of price and quickness in execution of trades. The hours from bell to bell are great but so is the pressure and the outcome is uncertain with disaster always in the wings.

The Futures Commission Merchant

To this point we have been concerned with the trade on the exchange floor but this is not what futures trading is mainly about. It mainly has to do with the activities of the people that the brokers represent—the outside trade. Brokers represent three general classes of principals: individual members who do not want to execute their own trades, commercial firms such as merchants, exporters, and processors who are members of the exchange and members of the Clearing House, and Futures Commission Merchants. The first two of these are principals in their own right rather than intermediaries.

The Futures Commission Merchants are intermediaries who stand in between the brokers in the pits (and subsequently the clearing house) and their customers who are the real principals in a high proportion of all trades. The legal definition is: "The words 'futures commission merchant' shall mean and include individuals, associations, partnerships, corporations, and trusts engaged in soliciting or in accepting orders for the purchase or sale of any commodity for future delivery on or subject to the rules of any contract market and that, in or in connection with such solicitation or acceptance of orders, accepts any money, securities, or property (or extends credit in lieu thereof) to margin, guarantee, or secure any trades or contracts that result or may result therefrom." The usual trade term for the Futures Commission Merchant is, "Commission House." They are members of the exchanges who act as agents for their customers.

In 1969 there were 420 futures commission merchants registered under the Act. They had 2,554 principal and branch offices and agents in 467 offices. There are commission house offices located within reasonable proximity of nearly every potential customer in the United States, Canada, Europe, and Japan and throughout much of the rest of the world.

Kinds of Commission Houses. There is a multiplicity of kinds of commission houses. Some are large firms with a primary emphasis on securities who maintain commodity departments. They own memberships or have working relationships with members of all of the active commodity exchanges. They vary in the degree of emphasis that they place on commodity business with commodity trade ranging from minor to major importance. Firms of this type are the largest in commodity commission business.

A second type of commission house is one that specializes in commodity futures business. Some, but not many, of these have expanded into the securities business. These may be quite large, holding memberships on all of the commodity exchanges or they may specialize in commodities traded on only one exchange. It is fairly usual for two or three members of an exchange to form a commission house and start soliciting business. Their scale of operation may remain small and specialized in the commodities of one exchange or they may expand to include membership in other exchanges and do business in many or all commodities. For most, the degree of expansion depends upon the degree of success but some remain small and specialized by choice. The commodity commission business is one of relatively easy entry.

A third type of futures commission business is the cash commodity firm that more or less incidentally does some futures commission business. These are merchants, processors, exporters, etc. who own memberships in exchanges and who have found it profitable in the conduct of their principal business to become clearing members. There is little else involved in becoming a futures commission merchant so that they can gain some income from commissions at little cost. In addition, their business of buying cash commodities may be aided by offering a futures trading service. An example is the cash grain merchant at a terminal whose primary business is originating grain from independent country elevator firms. The country elevators have occasion to use futures markets and the terminal merchant is in a stronger position to originate grain if he can offer a full line of services.

Agreements with Customers. Commission houses enter into agreements with their customers, with the customer signing a Customers Agreement Card. The agreement forms used by the various companies are different, some being quite long and detailed. Generally speaking, the longer a company has been in business the longer is the form, as it has a longer record of problems in dealing with customers. The customer agreements provide: (1) All orders and transactions shall be subject to the constitution, rules, regulations, customs, and usages of the pertinent exchange and its clearing house. (2) The commission house is directed, required, and authorized as agent and for the customers account to (a) execute or cause to be executed all orders for contracts for the purchase or sale of commodities for future delivery and (b) to accept or make deliveries on any maturing contracts. (3) The commission house has the right to refuse to accept orders or to cancel open orders. (4) That the customer shall, at all times, maintain, without call or notice, the minimum margins required by the commission house or by the exchange or its clearing house. The commission house is authorized to liquidate inadequately margined positions. The liability of the customer is not limited to the amount of margin posted but rather he is liable for all losses that may occur. (5) The customer agrees to pay commissions, delivery and inspection fees and interest on debit balances as provided by the rules of the exchange. (6) Any indulgences granted by the commission house shall not constitute a waiver of any right of the commission house. (7) That the customer (if a natural person) represents himself to be over 21 years of age. These are the key provisions and all of the others relate to the use of funds and securities and enforcement. *The agreement is a limited power of attorney in which the commission house is authorized to execute the orders placed, the customer agrees to abide by the rules of the exchange, maintain margins as required, be financially responsible for the trades he makes, and the commission house is empowered to refuse orders or make offsetting transactions if the customer is in violation of the agreement.* There are special agreements for partnerships and corporations, husbands and wives, and trading for minors.

In addition, there are discretionary agreements in which the commission house may be authorized to initiate trades for the account of the customer.

Still further, there are management agreements in which some person other than the customer is authorized to place orders with the commission house for the account of the customer. Management agreements take many forms and are subject to special rules and regulations, by both the exchanges and the Commodity Futures Trading Commission.

The agreements are written by the commission houses and so deal primarily with the performance of the customer. However, the houses are responsible for a workmanlike job of execution of the orders that they accept, proper accounting, and the security of funds and financial instruments placed in their trust. Commission houses are liable for the mistakes that they make when the mistakes work to the disadvantage of the customer but when the mistakes work to the advantage of the customer the results are credited to the customer's account. Suppose a customer places an order to buy five contracts and the house executes ten. If the price is higher when the error is discovered and the five contracts offset, the profit is credited to the customer's account but if the price has gone down the house has to assume the loss.

Services Provided. Commission houses provide four general kinds of services for customers. All are designed for his care and success; once a house has him it wants to keep him. First, they offer the best order execution of which they are capable. The first factor in order execution is speed. Commission houses must maintain extensive communication networks to direct orders to the proper exchanges and to the pits at the exchanges. Every effort is made to minimize the time from order placement to execution in the pit. The system is so well oiled that there are instances on record in which the time lapse from customer's verbal order to pit execution was less than 10 seconds. The customer is typically not only in a hurry to get orders executed but also anxious to know the price so that the route back to central office to branch office needs to be nearly as fast. The second element of execution is the skill of the broker. The commission houses try to employ the services of the best brokers in each of the pits. Some brokers are more skilled in filling some kinds and sizes of orders than others and the houses try to use the best brokers for the particular orders involved. A third facet of order execution is in knowing the price at which an order can be filled. A customer may have in mind the sale of 100,000 bushels and want to know the price at which it can be done before deciding how to place the order. The house needs to be able to form an accurate judgment and advise the customer. Success in this depends upon a flow of good information.

Second, the commission house acts as the agent of the customer in several ways in addition to the execution of trades; it guarantees the contracts to the clearing house, it makes and takes delivery, collects and pays money on delivery or offset, serves as the custodian of funds of the customer, and keeps and renders accounting of profits, losses, and balances. With the recent mechanization and computerization of accounting many of the reports have gotten to be quite elaborate, showing the result of each transaction, the credit balance, the profit and loss position of each existing position, an equity balance, the margin required, and the free balance available for new positions. Accounting is usually made after each new transaction and at the end of each month.

Third, the commission houses provide information for customers. This service takes many forms and varies widely among houses. In former times there were numerous advisory services that provided, for a fee, publications recommending positions and making themselves available for telephonic or telegraphic advice. Most of these have disappeared. The advice job for which they were paid has been taken over by the commission houses. Some houses spend large amounts of money assembling information, analyzing it, and advising customers. They hire commodity analysts who are responsible for small groups of commodities as grains, livestock products, precious metals, etc. They pay well enough that they employ a substantial proportion of the best analysts in the business.

Information is transmitted to customers through market letters and through registered representatives. The letters take several forms and different letters go to different customers. This is not to suggest that houses give different advice to different customers, rather they treat different customers with different degrees of thoroughness and in the way that each customer wants to be treated. As a general proposition the larger customers get the more elaborate and frequent analyses and the more sophisticated customers the more specific advice. Some houses furnish daily letters to customers, others weekly. Some wire market reviews to their branch offices each day that are available to customers on request. Some houses furnish periodic, in depth studies, of the situation and outlook for individual commodities.

Many firms also distribute information provided by independent advisory firms such as Commodity Research Bureau, Inc.

Houses vary widely in the degree to which they make specific recommendations about positions. Most houses do form and hold opinions but most are restrained in the extent to which they make these available. Few make their opinions public. Some have a policy of providing background information only so that the customer is expected to weigh the facts and make up his own mind. Others are quite specific about saying be long this, short that, and leave this one alone. Most houses try to guide customers away from what the house thinks are bad positions.

In addition to information affecting the future course of prices some houses develop and publish reference materials regarding specific commodities such as soybeans, cocoa, and silver, general descriptions of markets and trading methods, and how to use markets for specialized purposes such as hedging stored commodities.

Fourth, the commission houses furnish registered representatives. Every customer is a customer of someone. The registered representative is the contact point of the customer. He accepts and transmits orders and reports filling prices. He calls the customer to inform him of new developments in markets and answers questions when the customer calls him. He calls the customer when interesting market situations develop, usually called to his attention by the analytical staff of the home office. He helps the customer in formulating trading objectives and procedures, trying to take into account the individual circumstances involved.

There is some specialization among registered representatives. Many are general, concerned with all of the trading activity of their customers, both securities and commodities. They get their information from the home office specialists, both verbally and from the various publications. There is a wide range in their interest in and attention to commodity trading. Primary interest is in security investors who occasionally make a commodity trade.

The large integrated houses employ specialized commodity registered representatives who handle a limited number of commodities each. They handle the large commodity accounts, especially the trade accounts. One, for example, may be a specialist in the soybean complex—soybeans, soybean oil, and soybean meal. They are prepared to take the problems of commercial firms in hand and advise customers about positions. The kinds of firms handled by such a specialist include soybean processors, mixed feed manufacturers, oil refiners, margarine manufacturers, and such other firms as buy and sell soybeans and soybean products. These people have access to the analytical work of the research department but they are also analysts in their own right. Thus firms with specialized problems and whose accounts are fairly large have access to the results of a comprehensive analytical system.

In the smaller firms that specialize in commodities, the registered representatives generally handle all of the trading activities of each of their individual customers. In some instances, the house maintains a research staff that the account executive can turn to for information and analysis so that they concentrate on servicing accounts and acquiring new customers. In others, the account executives are both analysts and responsible for servicing accounts. In these cases the account executives tend to specialize in groups of commodities and trade information with each other.

Registered representatives are paid in different ways by the different companies. Some are salaried, some paid a share of the commissions generated, and some are paid by a combination of the two. Policy varies among companies and within companies. With relatively few exceptions the compensation of registered representatives is importantly related to the volume of trading done by their customers. Registered representatives cultivate customers, develop close working relationships with them, and closely guard the identity of their customers. Registered representatives change jobs from time to time, taking some of their customers with them. Customers are capricious, changing registered representatives and firms fairly frequently. There is a wide range in the earnings of registered representatives as is to be expected in any activity paid extensively on a production basis. Some barely make a living while others do quite well, some do so well that they decline opportunities to move into managerial positions when they arise.

Some firms prohibit registered representatives and analysts from trading for their own accounts while others permit trading and still others encourage trading almost to the point of making it mandatory. One school of thought is that analysts and registered representatives who trade are better motivated, more thorough in their work, and that customers have more confidence in advice from people who have their money where their advice is. Another thought is that employees who trade are primarily concerned with their own activities to the neglect of customers and tend to let their market judgment become biased by their own positions. There is a third influencing factor. Some analysts and registered representatives develop large customer following and can fairly well write their own tickets.

Operational Objectives. The primary objective of the commission house is to maximize commissions. The fulfillment of this objective requires three principal secondary objectives: effective execution of orders, location of new customers, and keeping existing customers alive. The key test of commission house operation is how effectively the house can accept, transmit, and fill customers' orders. Nothing alienates customers faster than for the house to return a report of "unable" when the market has traded at the price ordered subsequent to the order placement. It means that the house couldn't get the job done even though someone else did. Nor do customers like to see a price bid up when they are buying only to see the price recede as soon as the orders are filled.

The search for customers is a delicate matter with regard to speculative business. Speculation, particularly commodity futures speculation, has long since been under a pall of public question. It offends some concepts of morality, is linked with a gambling image, and is widely regarded as a fast way to lose money. Regardless of the merit or demerit of this image the result of its existence has been a soft sell approach to potential speculators. There has been little aggressive search for new business and about as far as houses go is to point out the potential of commodity trading to some securities customers. On the other hand, the use of commodity futures by trade interests for "hedging" has a favorable image so that commission houses aggressively advertise for new business.

Keeping existing customers alive is important in maximizing commissions; a customer who loses money trades in ever decreasing amounts until he ceases entirely while a customer who makes money spends ever increasing amounts on commissions. Money paid into the clearing house because of customer losses is money that cannot be spent on commissions.

The houses place primary emphasis on "suicide prevention" in the preservation of customers. It is generally thought that the worst mistake that speculators make is in letting small losses grow into disastrous losses. Registered representatives watch accounts carefully and try to get customers to close losing positions while losses are small.

The Customers

Number and Identity. The number of people who are customers of commission houses is not known but is thought to be large. It is known that many commission houses have several thousand customers each. The Commodity Exchange Authority made occasional cross section studies of the composition of the market for specific commodities on single days. One was a study of the soybean futures market on November 30, 1959. They required all clearing members who reported positions to furnish information about each of their customers. This information included the size of the position, whether long, short, or spread, whether hedging or speculation and the occupation and address of the customer. There were 8,075 individual positions of which 7,311 were speculative and 754 were hedging. The occupations covered the complete range of occupations found in the U.S. For example, there were 252 grain merchandisers and exporters, 99 livestock feeders and dealers, 1,617 farmers, 103 professional speculators, 235 physicians, 117 lawyers, 252 salesmen, 46 housemaids and private detectives, 56 brokers, 408 housewives, 34 students, 648 retired and 22 unemployed. The geographic distribution was world wide. A similar study of corn futures on Sept. 30, 1961 revealed 4,456 speculators and 381 hedgers; one made of wheat futures August 31, 1964 showed 6,717 speculators and 522 hedgers, and another for corn on Jan. 27, 1967 showed 11,709 speculators and 1,509 hedgers. The occupational and geographical distributions were comparable to those of the soybean study. Traders in commodities are numerous and diverse. The term, "Speculating Public" is frequently used and is accurately descriptive.

Getting to be a Customer. In this complicated world some things are simple and getting to be a customer of a commission house is one of them. It is somewhat like buying an automobile or television set; the problem is more how not to than how to. If one shows some interest he will be offered an agreement to sign, asked for money, and promised a large amount of service and careful supervision. This is the way that the economy works in general and we should expect it to apply to commission house customers but it only applies with limits. Different houses have different policies in accepting customers so that some are more selective than others. In part, selectivity is based on the expected profitability of the account but it is also based on whether the house thinks that the potential customer really has any business trading in commodity futures.

A first distinction made is between trade and speculative accounts. Trade accounts are those who "legitimately" use futures markets in their ordinary business activities. Farmers, warehousemen, merchants, processors, etc. can and should use futures contracts as a tool in business. These are the "hedgers" and "hedging" has a favorable image. Hedging accounts are sought and welcomed without question. But, as we shall see, hedgers speculate, both as a part of their hedging activities and in addition to hedging. Rarely is an account of a business related to commodities refused.

Speculative accounts are more closely examined. Some houses fail to make their services available to potential customers if they judge the account will trade in such small volume, complain so much, and require so much service as to be more bother than it is worth. Nearly all houses apply some minimum criteria before signing on a new customer. The basic assumption is that the speculating customer will lose money; and the houses have qualms about whose money they will be a party to taking. One almost gets the impression that even the commission houses have doubts about the advisability of commodity speculation.

The first question the house asks is whether the customer can afford and is willing to lose the money deposited. If the answer isn't pretty clearly "yes" the account is declined. Some houses require registered representatives to apply a "know your customer" rule, that they inquire into the general financial status, reputation, and credit rating of the customer. Some require financial statements and place upper limits on the size of margin deposits, size of positions, and total losses that they will permit in an attempt to prevent serious losses.

A universal rule is that the customer be 21 years of age. Some houses refuse to accept accounts of women. Whether this is because women complain so much when they lose that the business isn't worthwhile or whether they think that women are psychologically incapable of accepting the risks of commodity speculation is uncertain.

Some houses require a minimum initial deposit of $5,000, $10,000 or more. This is partly to assure that the account is large enough to cover its cost but it also is a means of establishing the customer's ability to absorb losses and of assuming that he can absorb losses from more than one trade without being forced to quit. Both of these contribute to the chances of success.

None of this should dismay the potential trader who has only a little money that he can't afford to lose—he can find a house that will accept him. Some houses take the position that everyone who wants to trade will find a way and go no farther than to caution the customer that he may lose.

Kinds of Orders. When a customer has signed an agreement and deposited some money he is ready to trade and must instruct the registered representative. When he has decided which commodity, whether to buy or sell, how much,[2] and which delivery month, he must indicate any price reservations that he may wish to make. There are several common kinds of orders:

Market. The market order is to be filled promptly at the best price that the broker can obtain. If he has to bid up to buy or offer down to sell he does so. In active markets with a large volume of trading, market orders can be filled with little or no price concession but large orders may result in paying more or receiving less than would be the case if more time were allowed, and market orders in low volume markets may require substantial price concession.

Limit. The customer may say "buy but pay no more than" or "sell but take no less than" and thus be assured that he will get at least the price he wants if the order is filled but he also runs the risk of not getting the order filled.

Stop. A "buy stop" instructs the broker to buy when the price (or a bid) rises to the specified level and a "sell stop" instructs him to sell when the price (or an offer) declines to the specified level. A stop order becomes a market order when the commodity is traded at the specified price. Once the price is ticked the broker promptly executes as best he can. Stop orders may be used to either initiate or to offset positions. The most common use is the "stop loss" order in which the customer says, in effect, if the price goes against my position (down if long or up if short) by a specified amount, I want out. They may be used to protect existing profits or limit losses. Stop loss orders are often placed immediately after positions are initiated. They are not complete protection because some price concession may have to be made after the specified price is reached.

Stop Limit. The stop order may be modified by placing a limit on the conces-

---

[2] There is a peculiarity in terminology that should be noted. The amount is stated in terms of the numbers of contracts for all commodities except grain. One pork belly is one contract of 36,000 pounds, one soybean meal is 100 tons, etc., but the grains are stated in the number of bushels. An order for one contract of 5,000 bushels of wheat is stated as 5,000 bushels, or an order for 10 contracts as 50,000 bushels, etc. instead of 1 wheat or 10 wheat.

sion that the broker may make after the stop is reached. The customer may say, "Sell if the price declines to $2.48½ but do not take less than $2.48¼." He runs the risk of not getting the stop order filled.

Trailing Stop. A trailing stop is a variable rather than a specified stop price. If the customer is long he may place a two cent trailing stop which becomes a market order anytime the price declines two cents from the highest level reached.

Scale Orders. This is a series of limit orders. The customer may want to buy one contract at 9.80, a second at 9.70, etc. until he has accumulated a total of five. He may buy on a scale down or a scale up or he may sell on a scale down or up.

Contingent Orders. These require the broker to fill an order when something happens in another delivery month or in a different commodity. He may be instructed to buy May soybeans at the market if January soybean oil trades at 20.20 or to buy July corn at the market if December trades at $2.75, etc.

Spread. These are entered at differences rather than specific prices. The order may say "Buy one February bellies and sell one May bellies at 40 points difference or more, premium May." The broker must make the two transactions at a difference of no less than 40 points.

Time. Orders may be placed for execution at a specific time such as 10:05 A.M. More often time orders are placed for execution at the open or close of the market. In this case the broker must execute the order within the opening or closing range of prices. This is not difficult because he may make one or the other side of the range in filling the order.

Discretionary. The broker may be instructed to exercise some judgment in filling the order in which case he can not be held responsible for the outcome. The amount of discretion offered or accepted is limited. These generally take the form of "take your time" (Marked T.Y. T. or Not Held) the import of which is that the broker should act promptly but not so fast as to force the market.

In addition to the several kinds of orders placed there are various time limitations placed on the period to which the order applies. Market orders apply, by definition, to the current moment. But the limit orders have expiration times. At one extreme is "fill or kill" which says to execute immediately at the specified price if possible but if it cannot be done to cancel the order. The order may be good until a specified time such as 11:00 A.M. or good today only, or good this week or "Open." An open order lasts until filled or expiration of trading in the delivery month.

Problems are sometimes created by open orders because they may be forgotten. A trader may be long broilers at 38¢ anticipating that the price will go to 41¢ and so places a limit order to sell at 41 or better. Time passes without much change taking place until the price starts to sag. The trader tires of his loss and sells at 37, forgetting the existence of the open order. Suppose, then, that the price increases to 41¢, at which time the open order becomes effective. The trader thus becomes short without intending to. One of the jobs of a registered representative is to prevent this kind of thing. A device used is to make the notation "One offsets the other" when a trader has two offsetting orders in the market at one time. A trader may see that July corn is trading at about $2.76 and decide to become short because he expects a price decline. He could enter an order to sell at the market with a three cent stop loss, and a limit order to buy at $2.71, one cancels the other, good until cancelled. The order is executed promptly at the best price the broker can obtain, say $2.75\frac{3}{4}$. Should the price go up to $2.78\frac{3}{4}$ the stop becomes a market order to be executed at the best price possible but should the price go down to $2.71 the short position is bought in. In either case the opposite order is cancelled. The bracketing orders remain in effect until one or the other prices is reached or until trading in the July delivery ends.

This last example is not the end of the complexity that can be obtained by combining the various kinds of orders listed above. What all of this says is that the commission house and the broker can usually be given any instructions that can be understood and kept track of.

Houses vary in the degree of complexity and difficulty of the orders that they will accept. Some are reluctant to accept intermarket spreads at fixed differences such as buy Kansas City May wheat and sell Chicago May wheat at 3 cent premium Chicago, while others accept such orders readily. Some houses refuse to accept orders to trade at the close of exipiring deliveries, insisting that offsetting orders become effective five or two minutes before the final bell while others accept such orders readily. But most houses will try anything that they can understand.

Margin Requirements. In addition to the margins required by the clearing house of its members, the exchanges establish margin requirements that all clearing members must require of their customers. On some exchanges, these requirements are different for members and nonmembers. The comments here relate to the nonmember customers of commission houses. In addition, on some exchanges, margins are different for intra-day and inter-day positions with a smaller margin required for in and out trades within one trading session. In some cases margins vary with the classification of the trade with the margins of "hedging" accounts being less than for speculative accounts.

The margin requirements are minimum; the individual houses may require larger margins for different customers. There are original and maintenance margins, the latter being the equity value below which the position value may not fall. Should the equity value fall below the maintenance level the customer must post additional margin to restore the account to the original margin value.

As we have seen, the purpose of the margin requirement of the clearing house is to guarantee contract performance. The requirement that commission houses require margins of their customers serves this same purpose and assures commission house solvency; the houses are not permitted to extend credit to customers, because it might thus jeopardize their own solvency. The law requires that customers' margin money be kept in segregated accounts so that it is not available for the use of the commission houses. These accounts are audited frequently. Thus, commission houses cannot accept customer deposits and use them to margin their own speculative activity. The rules of the exchanges and the law are remarkably tight. They have become that way more as a matter of plugging holes after unfortunate occurrences than as a matter of foresight. But laws and rules are broken and there have been instances when commission houses did use customers' money to speculate, lost, and went bankrupt. Restitution was made by other houses and the exchanges involved. From an exchange point of view there are some open questions about the regulation of commission houses but from a customer's point of view the money on deposit is as safe as the banking system. The customer should keep this security in mind when he receives a margin call.

Margins are established in dollars per contract. There is a tendency for them to be on the general order of five to ten percent of the value of the contract. The general principle in setting margins is that they be kept as low as is judged to be consistent with contract security. This judgment is reached on the basis of observation of the ordinary fluctuations in the price of the commodity and on the basis of specific situations that arise from time to time that might lead to erratic price fluctuations. While there is no formula, margins appear to be a function of the value of the commodity represented by the contract and price volatility. Margins are changed infrequently, often remaining constant for a commodity for one or more years. There is a tendency for the maintenance margin to be on the order of 80 percent of the original margin although it may be as high as 85 percent or as low as 60 percent.

All of this becomes simpler with some illustrations. A table of margin accounting may be established:

Day	Transaction	Price	Original Margin	Maintenance Margin	Position Value	Capital	Equity
1.	B 10 JLY Corn	2.80	$2000.00	$1500.00	0	$2000.00	$2000.00
2.		2.79	"	"	− 100.00	2000.00	1900.00
3.		2.78½	"	"	− 150.00	2000.00	1850.00
4.		2.74½	"	"	− 550.00	2000.00	1450.00
5.		2.74½	"	"	− 550.00	2550.00	2000.00
6.	B 10 JLY Corn	2.74½	4000.00	3000.00	− 550.00	4550.00	4000.00
7.		2.78	"	"	+ 150.00	4550.00	4700.00
8.		2.80	"	"	+ 550.00	4000.00	4550.00
9.		2.85	"	"	+1550.00	2450.00	4000.00
10.	S 20 JLY Corn	2.84	0	0	0	3660.00	3660.00

On day 1 a customer goes to the wire office with the thought that the price of corn should rise. He signs a customer agreement, learns that the margin requirement is $1000.00 per contract of $5,000 bushels or 20 cents per bushel and that he must maintain a minimum equity of $750 per contract or 15 cents per bushel, deposits $2000, and buys 10,000 bushels of July corn at $2.80. He has made a contract to buy and pay for 10,000 bushels of number two yellow corn in store in a public warehouse in Chicago on which any day the following July the seller may elect to deliver, the additional details of the transaction to be governed by the rules and regulations of the Chicago Board of Trade. He is on his way to fame and fortune, particularly the latter. The next day he notes that something has gone wrong with the system and the price has gone down to 2.79. His position is worth a negative $100. He still has a credit balance and his equity is $1900, more than the minimum $1500 required. Perhaps tomorrow will be better. But it wasn't, the price declining to 2.78½. He now has a position value of negative $150 (1½ × 10,000 bushels) a credit balance of $2000, and an equity of $1850 which he notes is only $350 away from a margin call. The next day is worse with the price down 4¢ which he now instantly translates to $400 for a total loss of $550. He now lacks the minimum equity of $1500 and his registered representative requests that he restore the original margin by depositing $550. If he does not make the deposit the position will be closed and he will have lost $550 and have to pay $70 in commission, leaving a credit balance of $1380. It might be even worse if the selling order is filled at less than $2.74½ the next day. On day 5 he deposits $550, the price is unchanged so that his position value is still negative $550, his capital is $2550 and his equity $2000. On day 6 he decides that if a purchase of corn at $2.80 was a good thing, $2.74½ is even better, he digs up another $2000 for original margin, and buys 10 more July corn. He now has a capital of $4550 and an equity of $4000. Fortune shines on day 7 and the price goes up to $2.78 so that his equity is $4700. On day 8 the price goes up two cents, making him look very good indeed. He has a position value of plus $550 (nothing on the first purchase and 4½¢ × 10,000 on the second), capital of $4550 an an equity of $5100. This is all so good that he requests a check for the additional margin deposit of $550, reducing his capital and equity accordingly. The price continues to rise reaching $2.85. He has 5¢ profit on the first purchase and 10½¢ on the second for a total position value of $1550. This plus the capital of $4000 is a total of $5550. Noting that he needs only $4000 margin he withdraws his $1550 profit leaving only $2450 capital and a total equity of $4000. He could have left the money in and bought more, using the profit as margin. He might try to take out an additional $1000 to reduce the equity to the maintenance margin of $3000 but the house would probably refuse. On day 10 the price goes down to $2.84 reducing his position value to $1350 and his equity to $3800. He decides to quit, selling 20 July corn for $2.84. He has no margin requirement, no position value, his account is credited for $1210 (1350–140 commission) so that he has a credit balance of $3660 which he may leave or withdraw.

For our purposes here we need not attempt to guess at the reasoning of our customer at the points of decision nor comment on the wisdom of his action—they were obviously wise because he won just as they would have been obviously stupid had the price continued down—but some points are worth noting. Commission did not enter into the calcuation until the positions were closed although they were in mind. Changes in equity were a large percentage of the capital investment even though the price did not change greatly.

In addition to illustrating the mechanics, this table serves to underscore the reality of the profits and losses associated with changes in price even though trades remain open. He had to put money in when he got behind. He could have used equity gains to margin additional trades. He took money out when he got ahead. These were not paper profits and losses; they were for real. A contract is not worth the original purchase or sale price but today's price regardless of when the capital account is debited or credited.

This discussion of margin requirements and the earlier comment on the margin agreement leave a somewhat delicate question open: Just how exacting are the houses in requiring margins? Under the agreement the customer is responsible for margin maintenance without notice and the house may close an inadequately margined trade. But this does not mean it will automatically offset inadequately margined trades; in practice, they don't. Exchange rules provide that the houses require maintenance of minimum margins. Accounts must be checked continually and customers requested to deposit additional margin when the account equity is below the minimum margin requirement. They do not require that houses automatically offset deficiently margined positions. The customer may have a "reasonable" period in which to make the deposit. There is flexibility in being "reasonable." Margin calls antagonize customers, a thing to be avoided whenever possible.

Any deficiency will draw a routine notice by mail. When the deficiency is small, the market quiet, and the account one of substantial size that has been with the company for some time, the company can be very reasonable. The company will let the process take place at the leisurely pace of the U.S. mail, or be content with "I will put a check in the mail if the price does not change favorably enough tomorrow." If the deficiency is large the customer is contacted by telephone and the "reasonableness" is less. At the other extreme, if the account is small and there has been a history of margin calls that have been hard to get—to the point that the house doesn't care whether it keeps the account—"reasonableness" may be reduced to a certified check in one hour. There are all gradations in between.

Two additional factors enter into the interpretation of reasonableness. First, the houses try to act in the best interest of the customer. If a customer gets frequent margin calls he is probably overtrading and losing more money than he should or holds a losing position that will probably get worse and should be terminated. The house tries to nudge him in the right direction. Second, the house doesn't intend to let the account run into a total deficit so that it loses money. This can happen and technically the customer is liable for any deficiency existing when the account is closed but these are difficult and expensive to collect. Typically, the registered representative is responsible should the customer lose more money than he has on deposit and the reasonableness of registered representatives runs out before their own money is involved.

Part II

THE ECONOMICS
OF FUTURES TRADING

In Part I we discussed what futures markets are. The next subject is what futures markets are about. Claims and counter-claims about their utility and disutility in the economic processes have been made throughout their history. Two facts are extant; they are a major activity, having to do with the use and transfer of large sums of money and they have persisted and grown for a long time in a competitive economic, and a generally negative, social-political world. From these it can well be argued that they are productive else they would not have lasted; that a competitive economic system tests activities and keeps those that add to total product while rejecting those that do not. The argument may or may not be valid. At some point it becomes desirable to do some evaluation but first we should examine the relationships of the activity to the world (one is tempted to say *real* world) of commodity production, trading, and use.

Futures markets are about several things and they are about different things to different people. This is somewhat analogous to the old story of the four blind men who felt different parts of an elephant—trunk, tusk, leg, and tail—and reached quite different conclusions about the nature of the beast. To merchants the markets are about price differences, to speculators they are about price changes and gains and losses, to producers they are about revenue guarantee and credit availability, to government agencies they are about price aberrations and security of customer funds, and to commission futures merchants they are about volume of trading. Economists try to put the elephant together by making lists of the functions of futures markets.

Each of us must make his own list—it is the nature of economists to reshuffle each other's list, looking for something to criticize in other economists' work while attempting to achieve distinction. The list of things that futures markets are about offered here is: 1) competitive markets, 2) risk shifting, 3) equity financing, and 4) speculation. No order of importance is suggested; the several things are an interlocking package.

CHAPTER **4**

Historical Development

Futures markets were not invented and imposed on the existing marketing system but evolved out of the need for the performance of marketing functions that the then existing marketing system was not doing adequately. They did not start as a separate or alternative way of doing business but as an extension and refinement of existing practices. They have been in a continuous state of change, development, and refinement throughout their history. The focus of futures trading has changed as the commercial setting has changed. The commercial setting has changed rapidly in recent decades and will likely change at a greater speed in the decades ahead.

A look at the evolutionary process is useful in identifying the functions performed, determining what futures trading is about, and in forming opinions about changes in the system that need be made to adjust to changes to come. Perhaps more to the point, putting futures trading into historical perspective is helpful in making effective use of the markets. That is, knowing how we got here is useful in understanding the present situation which is essential to making profits rather than sustaining losses.

The roots of futures trading are as deep as commerce itself. Nearly all authors find it impossible to resist going back into ancient history to find the beginning.[1] The concept of futurity in contractual arrangements is as old as commerce. The rules of futures trading certainly date back to the medieval fairs of France and England which were large and complex by the 12th century. Time dealings in the products of whole fisheries existed in Holland in the early

[1] See especially Emery, Henry Crosby, *Speculation on the Stock and Produce Exchanges of the United States,* Studies in History, Economics and Public Law, Vol. VII, No. 2, Columbia University, 1896; Bakken, Henry, *Theory of Markets and Marketing,* Mimir, Madison, Wis., 1952; and Baer & Saxon, *Commodity Exchanges and Futures Markets and Trading,* Harper, N.Y., 1948.

1600's. There was a famous speculative bubble in Dutch tulips in 1634–37 that has been repeatedly used in illustrating the ridiculousness and evil of rampant commodity speculation. One favorite point of beginning is in the trade in warrants, particularly in pig iron in England, in the early 18th century. There are accounts of highly developed trading systems in Japan in the early 1600's.

All of this is interesting and is especially useful in developing concepts of competitive markets but as a practical matter we need look no farther back than the frontier of the U.S. in the mid-19th century for the origin of modern commodity futures trading. The essential ingredients of mercantile law, warrants for interchangable units, futurity of contracts, and price speculation were already developed and present in U.S. commerce. The circumstances of the frontier, particularly in the grain trade, were the catalyzing agent out of which futures trading grew. Emery[2] put it thus, "Untrammeled by business traditions of past centuries, or by the tendency to fit new conditions to old methods, the trade of this country has unconsciously adopted new and direct means for attaining its ends. There has been little 'history' or 'evolution' about the process, for the practical mind of the business man has simply seized the most direct method of 'facilitating' business, a course forced on him by the constantly increasing size of his transactions."

The history of modern commodity futures trading is closely associated with the development of the commerce of the city of Chicago. In 1833, Chicago was incorporated as a village, having grown up adjacent to Fort Dearborn. It grew rapidly and became a city in 1837 with a population of 4,107. The strategic location of Chicago at the lower terminus of the Great Lakes and close to the fertile lands of northern Illinois resulted in rapid growth. The opening of the midwest was dependent upon water transportation; the land was fertile but muddy and nonwater transportation was limited to oxcart and horse.

The grain requirements of Chicago were produced nearby. As farmers spread over the fertile plains, market outlets became difficult to obtain and did not exist at all at the perimeters. Similarly, as Chicago requirements increased, the procurement of supplies became a problem. Transportation was expensive and its development received high priority. In the 1840's it cost about the full value of wheat to haul it sixty miles by oxcart. Corn was less valuable so that its point of origin price reached zero at a lesser distance. Plank roads were laid for substantial distances on the approaches to the city. After more than a decade of financial difficulty the Illinois-Michigan canal was opened in 1848. Railroads quickly radiated in all directions.

Chicago, the lake terminus, tapped the heartland of this opening agricultural area. It began early to supply commodities to the more populous east and for export. As early as 1832 export shipments of beef and pork were made. In 1839

[2] Op. cit. p. 37 Emery, H. C., *Speculation on the Stock and Produce Exchanges of the United States,* Studies in History, Economics, and Public Law. Vol. VII No. 2, Columbia, 1896.

arrangements were made to ship 1678 bushels of wheat by boat to Black Rock, N.Y.

The rapid development of Chicago as a grain terminal took place following the opening of the Canal. By the time of the Crimean War in the 1850's, Chicago, with its rich outlying agriculture area, was in an excellent position to supply the disrupted world grain trade. During the Civil War Chicago served as the chief grain concentration point of the Union armies.

With a rapidly expanding population and eastbound commerce, processing facilities developed. Thus, there were three principal demands for grain at Chicago: reshipment east, processing, and to support the livestock population of the city itself. This latter was of large size, consisting of horses, pigs, chickens, and cows including, finally, the notorious one belonging to Mrs. O'Leary.

The Board of Trade of the City of Chicago was organized in 1848 with 82 members. Its primary objective was to promote the commerce of the city. One of its most notable early accomplishments was the development of a system of standards for wheat and the starting of a system of inspection and weighing grain. In 1859 The Board of Trade was authorized by the State of Illinois to hire and instruct personnel to measure, gauge, weigh, and inspect grain.

The development of quality standards and an inspection process and the substitution of weighing for the measurement of grain greatly facilitated trade. The substitution of weight for volume measures made the development of advanced grain handling machinery possible. Increase in physical efficiency was important in the development of Chicago as a great grain terminal market. The fungibility of grain resulted in increased physical efficiency in handling and enabled the issuance of warehouse receipts. These documents of ownership were useful in exchange of title and as collateral in financing trade.

The making of grain fungible was a key step in the development of impersonal, transferable contracts that eventually became futures contracts.

As traffic in grain increased rapidly following the opening of the Canal, problems of spot exchange increased. Trading in commodities at Chicago followed the old world custom of public trading, taking place in squares and on street curbs. Grain trading moved about from curb to curb with merchants often meeting in several places in one day. Such confusion finally became intolerable and a convenient meeting place was provided by The Board of Trade. Facilities for the display of grain were provided and regular hours of trading were prescribed.

Corn and Wheat

To fix a precise time for the beginning of futures trading requires a tighter distinction between forward contracts and futures contracts than can be made. The most likely story has to do with the corn trade.

As soon as the Illinois-Michigan canal opened, a brisk trade in grain developed along the river. Farmers produced grain close to the river and hauled it to local elevators by oxcart and sleds. Merchants built corn cribs for subsequent shipment to Chicago. Farmers hauled corn in during the late fall and winter when the roads were frozen and passable. The merchants held it until it reached a low enough moisture to ship safely and the river and canal were free of ice. This practice of holding corn necessitated building up substantial inventories.

Merchants generally extended their capital resources as far as possible in building facilities and farmers wanted payment as soon as the grain was delivered. There was a great deal of price risk involved in holding corn from fall and winter to spring so that bankers were reluctant to make large loans on unsold grain. As a result the river merchants quickly developed the practice of going to Chicago and making contracts, at firm prices, for the delivery of grain in the spring.

These were time, or forward, contracts calling for delivery of a standard quality at an agreed price and substantially deferred delivery. The length of time until delivery set the time contracts apart from "to arrive" contracts which usually called for immediate delivery. The first time contract on record was made on March 13, 1851.[3] It called for delivery of 3000 bushels of corn in June at a price one cent per bushel under the March 13 price.

In some instances the Chicago merchants advanced funds with which to pay farmers, and in others, bankers judged the firm contracts desirable collateral and made loans. Merchants were able to bid more rationally for farmers' grain when they held firm sales contracts. This doubtless worked to the advantage of farmers. The forward contracts materially lessened the pricing and financing problems of the river merchants.

The time contracts business developed rapidly and became a usual practice. The Crimean War and subsequently the Civil War resulted in sharply fluctuating prices. Chicago merchants were reluctant to bid vigorously for deferred delivery. They tended to keep the forward bids below prices that they thought would prevail at the time of delivery because of the danger of a price decline. There were other, more venturesome people who would bid up to or above current prices. Many of these were not connected with the grain trade; they were merchants in other lines, land speculators, lawyers, physicians, and the like. With a mental picture of Chicago in the 1850's in mind, we can readily visualize the scene. A country merchant rides into town in January and proceeds to the place of business of the terminal merchant to whom he regularly sells. On offering 20,000 bushels for June delivery at the current price he hears, "I would like to bid that much but with the large stocks in Chicago and a large crop coming in I can only pay 15 cents below today's price." Our friend mentions the high price that he has already paid farmers, comments on the ancestry

[3] Irwin, H. S., *Evolution of Futures Trading*, Mimir, Madison, Wis., 1954.

of terminal grain merchants in general, and takes himself to the nearest saloon to find solace. There he comments to all and sundry regarding the greed and cowardice of grain merchants in general and one in particular. On hearing this one stalwart soul says, "I know nothing of corn, being a builder of houses myself, but it occurs to me that the price of corn will be quite as high in June as it is now." Being true to his occupation, just as we know country merchants today, our man asks, "Is that a firm offer?" "I shouldn't want to go quite that far but I will bid five cents below today's price. That will take you off of the hook and out of your cups and leave room for a bit of a profit for me." "Done," replies the country merchant and they sign a contract. Some weeks later the builder of houses, who has now become interested in these matters, notes that the price of corn for June delivery is five cents above the price that he has paid. He figures that $1000 in his pocket is better than 20,000 bushels of corn in his lap in June so he peddles his contract to the nearest terminal merchant and wonders why he had not discovered this easy road to riches sooner.

Others made the great discovery. By the mid 1850's contracts frequently changed hands several times before coming to rest with a merchant who was seriously interested in receiving the corn in question. The speed with which trading in forward contracts grew is not known. It appears that the increased grain trade during the Civil War and the fluctuating prices of that period stimulated activity so that trading in time contracts received major attention by 1863.

Forward contracts, as distinctly different from "to arrive" contracts, in wheat made their appearance slightly later than those in corn. Some notice of time contracts in wheat was taken in the newspapers of 1852. The problems of wheat accumulation were different than corn because wheat could move to Chicago readily at harvest. Before the spread of the railroads it was teamed in while the roads were in good condition. Because it was higher in value than corn it could be hauled greater distances. Thus, the interior buyers of wheat did not have the same risk and financial problems.

Wheat accumulated rapidly at Chicago during and after harvest. Substantial stocks were built up and moved out gradually to satisfy local milling requirements, the export market, and eastern millers. These stocks were owned by eastern export and milling interests, Chicago merchants, and, in a small amount, by country shippers. In the case of corn, Chicago merchants were the original buyers of forward contracts but they became sellers of wheat forward contracts. They were the ones who had the problem of price risk and financing. They sold forward to eastern millers and exporters.

Millers and exporters also had price risk and financing problems. During the 1850's and 60's prices were erratic. There was a rapid increase in production and shipment so that there were frequent market gluts and price declines. As the eastern interests saw large stocks build up at Chicago they were reluctant buyers except at sharply discounted prices. The Chicago merchants found non-grain interests to buy forward contracts. Doubtless, O'Learys' saloon did a thriving business.

Forward contracts were originally made between country merchants and terminal receivers with the parties intending to make and take delivery. They involved an eventual change of title to grain. When our builder of houses entered, this changed; he did not intend to take or make delivery and as the forward contracts changed hands numerous times, a relatively small proportion of the participants intended to fullfil the contracts. This use of contracts for purposes other than exchange of title is one of the key differences between forward and futures contracts.

The first cognizance the Chicago Board of Trade took of the developing trade in time contracts was in a rule adopted March 27, 1863. It provided for the suspension of the privileges of membership of any person who failed to comply with the terms of contracts that he made. It seems that when time for settlement arrived some of the contracting parties were difficult to locate. The rule applied only to the contracts made on the exchange. An earlier rule (1858) had been adopted restricting trade to members of the Board. There was doubtless extensive time contracting outside of the Board and its members.

The 1863 rule apparently did not solve the problem of contract settlement. In May, 1865 the first rule dealing specifically with time contracts was adopted. It provided for the deposit of a margin, not to exceed 10 percent of the value of the commodity, when demanded by either party.

The General Rules of the Board of Trade were adopted Oct. 13, 1865 and the margin rule was included in them. Rules relating to time contracts set forth the procedure to be followed in event of failure to deliver, provided for standardization of delivery procedures, and prescribed terms of payment.

By this time all of the essential elements of futures trading were present: contracts made for purposes other than exchange of title (although not clearly recognized), deposit of funds to guarantee performance, restriction of trade to members, and standardized contract terms. We could date the origin of modern commodity futures trading as October 13, 1865 if it is, indeed, desirable to attach a single date to what was actually an evolutionary process.

The initial rules of 1865 were followed by others as the Board gradually extended its control over trading in time contracts. The process of the extension of control was gradual and it appears that rules were adopted in response to disputes that arose. The Board took little initiative or leadership in the development of futures trading. There was resistance on the part of grain handlers to the increasing use of time contracts. Further, it was totally new territory in terms of a market so that the anticipation of problems was difficult. Trading rules were fairly complete, there was a substantial volume of trading, and merchants used futures to hedge inventories to earn carrying charges by 1875.

Cotton

The development of futures trading in cotton occurred at about the same time as that in corn and wheat although there is no evidence indicating that either was affected by the other. On the contrary, the evidence is that they evolved separately out of comparable circumstances.

The cotton trade in the U.S. was closely connected with that of England for a long period of time prior to the Civil War. Development of futures trading in the two countries was parallel. Time contracts were reported in New York in 1851, about 20 years prior to the organization of the New York Cotton Exchange. Time contracts were mentioned in Liverpool in 1857 and their volume increased rapidly during the Civil War. Cox[4] made reference to professional speculation in cotton in Liverpool early in the 18th century. Contracts for forward delivery of cotton were traded from one buyer to another, probably passing through several hands before the time of actual delivery. They were not made to cover specific shipments but were filled from any cotton available.

The rules of the New York Cotton Exchange written in 1872 indicate that there was organized trading in futures at that time. It appears to have developed immediately after the organization of the Exchange in 1870. Rules were based on existing forward contracting practices. They provided for a standardized contract, margin deposit, transfer of contracts, described deliverable grades, delivery procedure, and payment. In addition, the rules governed the trading practices of brokers.

Trading in cotton futures at Liverpool developed slower than in New York, taking about a decade after 1871. Members of the two markets did business so that there was full knowledge on both sides of the nature of trading. Liverpool probably developed slower because it was a more important spot market and because it was bound by long standing custom. The New Orleans Cotton Exchange was organized in 1871 but trading in time contracts was not important until ten years later.

Forward contracts in cotton developed out of the financial arrangements between principal New York exporters and English importers on the one hand and between the same exporters and interior cotton merchants on the other. The interior merchants guaranteed the credit of producers at local banks. As the producers agreed to sell their cotton to the merchants, the merchants, in turn assured the banks of loan repayment. To protect themselves against a fall in the price of cotton during the season, they made time contracts with the New York and, later, the New Orleans merchants. The terminal merchants were then in a position to offer cotton for export at firm prices. The export price of cotton was effectively established prior to the start of the planting season. The

---

[4] Cox, A. B. "Evolution of Cotton Marketing," Mimeo, B.A.E., USDA, 1925.

interior merchants dominated the outlets and the credit system to such an extent that they were able to relate the purchase price to their original sales prices.

Eggs

Futures trading in eggs had a peculiarly long evolutionary history, extending from about 1880 to 1919. The development of forward contracting in eggs was the result of the seasonality of egg production.

The production of eggs following the Civil War was decentralized and quite inefficient. Most farms had small flocks to provide for the household. The surplus eggs were generally sold at the local general stores. The farm flock was the basis of the farmer's wife's liberty. She set the hens, raised the chickens, slaughtered the males, and kept the pullets to lay eggs. She traded the eggs for food and typically came away with some money, "egg money," which she secreted away. It was a 100 percent profit operation. Such feed as the chickens couldn't scrounge in the barnyard, she pilfered from her husband's corn crib.

Production of surplus eggs was highly seasonal. In the spring the hens became amorous, the feed improved, and the lay increased. As hot weather arrived, lethargy set in and by winter, production fell to only the family's needs.

The storekeepers handled the eggs to accommodate their farm customers and paid little attention to quality. Most of the stores that bought eggs were within moderate distance of Chicago and could ship to commission merchants there. Some of the larger volume buyers developed connections in eastern markets. As the volume of production and shipment grew, a system of interior egg packers and shippers developed. They bought from the larger volume producers and the general stores and shipped to Chicago and to the eastern markets. Some of the eggs shipped to Chicago were forwarded east.

The demand for eggs in the cities was fairly uniform throughout the year leading to a need to accumulate during the flush production season for winter consumption. Eggs are perishable, particularly during hot weather. Various attempts were made to preserve eggs. Some were packed in salt and some in lime but the largest quantities were kept in various pickling solutions. A pickled egg is vastly inferior to a fresh egg but is better than no egg at all. The pickling business suffered a blow when ice houses were built. The first ice house was probably erected about 1868. Irwin[5] lists egg quotations Dec. 30, 1878 as Fresh, 20¢; Icehouse, 14–18¢; and pickled, 5–12¢. By the 1880's icehouses were numerous in Chicago and large storage stocks were built up. It was not until the 1960's that the seasonal variation in egg production was essentially eliminated by changed technology.

The seasonal accumulation and liquidation of inventories resulted, not only in physical problems of storage and grading, but in financing, risk assumption,

[5] Ibid., p. 19 (Irwin).

and price determination. Large sums of money were tied up in inventories and most of it had to be borrowed from banks. Decisions had to be made about how many eggs to withdraw from immediate consumption during the flush production season and how high prices would have to be to bid to obtain storage stocks. Later in the year decisions related to how rapidly to move eggs out of storage and the prices at which refrigerator eggs could be sold. If prices were bid too high during the flush period of production the resultant storage stocks could not be sold later at prices high enough to show a profit over storage costs. But if the prices were not bid up enough the dealers would lose business to other dealers whose judgment was better.

During the early part of the period the principal risks related to quality deterioration. Risks of price declines were small as the eggs could be purchased at very low prices in the spring. As storage technology improved, quality risks were reduced but as business grew and competition for eggs increased, the risks associated with price change increased. Sometimes competition for eggs forced prices high enough in the spring to cause losses for the storage season.

Fluctuations in prices sometimes resulted in increased profits but the danger of losses was of more concern to dealers because a large loss could force a dealer out of business. The dealers established moderate proportions of their total working capital that they would put in inventory operations. This was often the limiting factor in the size of their operations; they could store more eggs than they had funds that they were willing to hazard.

The dealers solved the problem by selling eggs to their friends. It was something of a status symbol to own a car or two of storage eggs. The dealers were responsible for quality and the actual purchases and sales. In 1895 a trade paper said "at the present the indications are that there will be active speculation in eggs this season. There are men of moderate means outside the produce business who make a practice of investing in a car or so every year. . . . Nearly all these outside investors have friends among the produce houses who act as their agents. Not a great deal of money is required to carry a car of eggs."

The next developmental step was time contracts. These called for delivery of refrigerated eggs in the fall or early winter. The dealers accumulated storage eggs and sold contracts for delivery. Some were sold to egg distributors in the city and in the east but most were sold to the acquaintances of the egg dealers. The contracts had the additional advantage of being negotiable. There was usually an understanding that when the buyer of the contract wanted to take his profits or losses the dealer would pay the current price of contracts for deferred delivery and sell to someone else. In 1899 the Egg Reporter said, "The tendency to buy and sell futures in eggs is increasing alarmingly. A few years ago it was done to some extent by a few speculators, but this year we find many old, established firms doing it."

By 1917 the contracts were highly developed and standardized. The attitude toward them was quite impersonal and settlement rings were formed. Oftentimes the original seller of a contract bought it back, sometimes from the person he sold it to and sometimes from a third, fourth, or fifth party. When this happened the original seller settled with each contracting party on the basis of price differences. The dealers eventually got most of their own contracts back and merchandised their own eggs. A substantial amount of difficulty was encountered in locating the losers when prices fluctuated sharply.

The Chicago Produce Exchange was organized in 1874 and was composed of dealers in produce of various kinds. In 1895 the Produce Exchange Butter and Egg Board was organized as a group within the Chicago Produce Exchange. A short time later a butter versus oleomargarine dissension developed and in 1898 the butter and egg dealers withdrew and formed the Chicago Butter and Egg Board. This was the trade association most closely related to the development of time contracts in eggs. Its primary purpose was to supply butter and egg price quotations. Prior to 1911 the Board paid little attention to time contracts and most of the trade was done at saloons frequented by egg dealers.

In 1911 the rules of The Board provided for margin deposit on contracts made between members. Trade in time contracts was the subject of much controversy within the Board with a general tone of disapproval tending to dominate. Trade in time contracts was suspended in 1918 because of the rules of the Food Control Act. Trading resumed in 1919 but there was great difficulty in getting contract fulfillment.

In 1919 a complete set of rules for futures trading was written and futures trading was added to the activities of The Butter and Egg Board. The effect was a new organization which was called The Chicago Mercantile Exchange. Futures trading in butter and eggs officially started Dec. 1, 1919.

Thus, futures trading in eggs was born on about its 40th birthday. The long delay in organization and the formalization is the more interesting when the informal trade existed in the same city as the very active futures trade in grain.

Soybeans and Soybean Products

The soybean crop developed in the U.S. immediately following World War I and achieved commercial significance about 1935. Production expanded rapidly and reached 100 million bushels at the beginning of World War II. Wartime shortage of edible fats and oils resulted in an increase to 200 million bushels; the first 300 million bushel crop was produced in 1950. Expansion continued at a rapid rate so that 1975 production was in excess of 1.5 billion bushels. This rapid expansion resulted from growth in the market for the products made from soybeans and was stimulated by various government programs for other crops: corn, wheat, and cotton in particular.

The soybean is an oilseed but its major production area and marketing processes are the same as the grains. Prior to 1960 more than 75 percent of the crop was produced in the corn belt. The same farms that produced soybeans produced corn, wheat, and oats; and soybeans were marketed through the same country elevators and terminal markets as the grains.

Soybeans are used for processing into soybean oil and soybean meal, both in the U.S. and the countries to which soybeans are exported. Soybean oil is a moderate quality edible fat used interchangeably with other fats and oils. Principal competitors of soybean oil include butter, lard, cottonseed, sunflower, groundnut, and palm oils. It goes into a much larger world of total fats and oils. The demand for all fats and oils is highly inelastic. Thus, the factors affecting soybean oil prices are complex and uncertain and prices are inherently volatile.

Some soybean meal is used for human consumption, but nearly all is used as a protein supplement in feeding poultry, hogs, and cattle. Demand for meal has increased rapidly as feeding technology has improved and the livestock population increased. Price elasticity of demand for meal appears to be less inelastic than for oil but the dynamics of demand change have made meal prices difficult to forecast. Prices are volatile and the commodity trades over wide price ranges.

Soybean futures trading was initiated at The Chicago Board of Trade and at The Chicago Open Board of Trade in the fall of 1936. The volume of trade was large (878 million bushels) in 1940–41 but wartime restrictions resulted in the suspension of trading. The postwar volume of trading was quite small until the fall of 1948.

There was a soybean meal futures market at Memphis prior to World War II but the volume of trade was small. Trading was resumed in 1946 but the volume remained small. Soybean oil was traded in New York beginning in 1946 but the volume was very small until 1950.

During World War II there were no price problems associated with the soybean industry. Prices of beans, oil, and meal were fixed by government regulation so handlers and processors were not concerned about possible gains and losses resulting from price changes.

Price ceilings were eliminated in the fall of 1946 and processors found themselves in a whole new world. Farmers were used to and preferred to sell the bulk of the crop—as much as 80 percent—at harvest. Processors had no choice but to buy. If they didn't, the beans moved out of position and became unavailable. They were thus in the position of owning soybeans that would be made into oil and meal over a period of as much as nine months and prices of oil and meal were highly uncertain. Even moderate changes in product prices could result in ruinous losses or huge profits. Their primary concern was with the potential losses that could put them out of business rather than with profits.

A large amount of capital was required to buy the soybeans and most of it had to be borrowed. Bankers were quite aware of the volatility of soybean prices and looked askance at such dangerous loans—they would lose if a processor-customer went broke but did not stand to gain if he profited from price increases. Bankers are not notably venturesome but, had they been, this "heads I lose and tails I break even" kind of proposal would have had no appeal. The processors simply could not finance the inventories even had they been inclined to do so. Such was the general case. It should be noted that some could and did; they bought at harvest and sold products when they made them. This practice was generally quite profitable as both soybeans and products consistently rose from depressed harvest time levels.

Soybean oil was sold to refiners who were generally integrated toward the production of the final products of oil—shortening, margarine, and cooking and salad oils. They were large companies that sold branded products and soybean oil was only one of numerous raw materials they purchased. Thus variations in soybean oil prices were of much less consequence to users than to processors.

Nearly all of the meal was sold to feed manufacturers. It was combined with other ingredients in making the final product. Again, they produced a branded consumer product and operating margins between raw material cost and finished product prices were fairly wide. The consequences of meal price fluctuations were less for feed manufacturers than for soybean processors.

A practice of selling meal and oil for deferred delivery developed. Processors offered discounts to users for forward contracting and the farther forward they agreed to accept delivery the greater was the price discount. In October, 1947 the prices (monthly average) of soybean oil and meal for delivery during the various subsequent months of the crop year were:[6]

Del. Period	Oil ¢1 lb.	Meal $1 ton
Spot	20.50	84.00
Nov.	20.00	81.90
Dec.	19.50	80.50
Jan.	19.25	80.25
Feb.	19.00	80.25
March	18.75	80.25
April	18.25	78.65
May	18.00	78.60
June	17.75	78.50
July	17.67	78.50
Aug.	17.50	78.50
Sept.	17.37	78.50

[6] Hieronymus, T. A. *The Economics of Risk in the Marketing of Soybeans and Soybean Products,* Unpublished Ph.D. Thesis, Univ. of Ill., 1949.

These discounts were large when expressed in terms of value per bushel of soybeans. In October, the product from a bushel of soybeans for spot delivery was $3.66 while the same products for delivery in July, 1948 sold for $3.30. This was a classic case of Keynesian normal backwardation. Processors bid for soybeans on the basis of prices that they could get for the products in the various forward positions.

This discounting practice had not gone on for very long when resellers entered the market. The resellers were broker-dealers who bought products from processors and sold them to users. As they bought products for deferred delivery at discounts they simply held them for a time, expecting the deferred price to rise to the spot price, which it had a tendency to do. As they accumulated more than they felt safe in carrying, they sold to users, and other resellers, and to people not connected with the soybean industry. Some of the contracts changed hands numerous times—one meal contract was found to have been endorsed 30 times.

Jobbers and dealers often overextended themselves and went broke. Some of the endorsers of contracts were difficult to locate and collect from when the contracts matured. Difficulties increased as the trade in deferred contracts broadened. The first reason was that as more people became involved, it was increasingly difficult to check the financial position of the purchaser. Second, as trade broadened the discounts decreased so that the purchase of forward contracts was no longer akin to shooting fish in a barrel. As competition among speculators increased, the profits decreased.

Trading on the Chicago Board of Trade in soybean oil futures contracts was started during the summer of 1950 and trading in soybean meal futures in 1951. Contract terms were virtual copies of existing trade practices. Trade expanded rapidly and forward contracting disappeared in a short time.

It is interesting to note that this instance of transition of forward contracting to futures trading (a) occurred nearly a century after the comparable transition in corn and (b) took several years to complete.

Speculation

These sketchy reviews of the evolution of futures trading in four commodity areas tell only a small part of the story. They serve to make the point that futures trading evolved out of risk, financing, inventory, and pricing problems of handlers and processors of cash commodities. The evolution of the process involved participation of people outside of the commodity businesses—speculators. These people, who made the system work, were not enticed in to fill a necessary role and limit their activity to the minimum level of speculation necessary. Rather, they found out about it, came flocking in, and took the play away. The first fifty years of the history of futures trading in the U.S. is the history of feverish speculative activity, of contests among giants, and of attempts to manipulate prices. These contests resulted in the evolution of a set of competitive rules.

The sources of information for the story are limited and tedious. Further, put in the context of the defense of futures trading that so much of the literature of futures trading has been about, it is a history of futures trading that has been largely swept under the rug and regarded as a chronology of events that belong to a dead past. We shall see as we proceed, the extent to which the events truly belong to the past or are a part of the contemporary scene but some recounting is, if nothing else, interesting. The principal sources are the rules of the Chicago Board of Trade as they evolved, contemporary newspaper stories, and Taylor's[7] three volume chronology of the Chicago Board of Trade. The bulk of this section is excerpted from Taylor. The terms "manipulation" and "corner" occur frequently. They should not be put in a modern context of definitions of the terms nor should it be concluded that markets were actually controlled as described. They were the then contemporary impressions of events as they were generally accepted. It is doubtful that Taylor fully understood the operation of the market. This is not in criticism because his was a chronology of contemporary impressions rather than an analytical work but we do want to reserve judgment of the events to a later point.

The events included here relate to the Chicago Board of Trade. It is clear that they were similar to the events of the other principal grain exchanges of Milwaukee, New York, St. Louis, Kansas City, Toledo, etc. Space does not permit description of the others nor are the records as complete, and, further, Chicago was the largest of the lot.

In 1864 the Secretary of the Chicago Board of Trade reported the most successful year in history despite a decrease in cash grain receipts. The explanation was found in a great development in speculative trade to which the officers of the Board were opposed. "It is time that speculation has been too much the order of the day, and buyers of 'long,' 'short,' and 'spot' have passed through all gradations of fortune, from the lower to the higher round, and in many instances have returned to the starting point, if not a step lower, but it is to be hoped that with the return to peace this fever of speculation will abate, and trade will be conducted on a more thoroughly legitimate basis."

Regarding 1866 Taylor said "In July there was a 'corner' in No. 1 spring wheat and the price went to $1.91. News of great Prussian victories, which meant a speedy end to the war, forced prices down again. Wheat was quoted June 7, at $1.66½, and rose irregularly through the month. By July 9th it had reached the high point, $1.91, and on the 12th it fell to $1.65, and to $1.43 by the 17th. This corner created much adverse newspaper criticism and many

[7] Taylor, Charles H., *History of the Board of Trade of the City of Chicago*, Robert O. Law Company, Chicago, 1917.

charges and countercharges among members of The Board. It was charged that warehousemen aided the corner by false representations concerning the amount and quality of grain in store and fraudulent receipts."

In 1867 an Illinois Elevator bill was passed. Section 17 provided, "All contracts for the sale of grain for future delivery, except in cases where the seller is the owner or agent of the owner of such grain at the time of making of the contract and in actual possession thereof, are hereby declared void and gambling contracts, and all money paid in settlement of differences of any such contracts may be recovered back in the same manner as other money lost in gambling." and Section 18, "All parties to such gambling contracts shall be guilty of a misdemeanor. . . ." On Aug. 10, 1867 arrests were made of nine prominent members of the exchange but the cases never came to trial. The law was later found constitutional but was unenforced by common consent and at the next session of the legislature, sections 17 and 18 were repealed.

An historian, Andreas, called 1868 the year of the corners saying, "There was a corner a month, three on wheat, two on corn, one on oats, one attempted on rye, and the year threatened to go out with a tremendous one on pork products. The corner in No. 2 spring wheat, which succeeded in June, started at $1.77 and culminated June 30 at $2.20. The price in New York at the time was $2.02, and the day after the corner the Chicago price fell to $1.80, and the second of July to $1.75. This corner created much discussion as to restrictive rules, and the agitation was brought to a head by a corner in September corn." The President of The Board, Robbins, was caught short and was unable to pay his losses. He resigned but the directors took note of his character and reputation and retained him in office. A test case went to The Board of Arbitrators who found that the shorts knew well what they were doing and forced them to pay the settlement price in lieu of delivery.

Taylor called 1872 a year of intense activity in speculation and discussed corners, manipulation, and difficulty in making delivery. One of the more outstanding of these had to do with oats and was operated by Mr. Chandler, a prominent merchant. He peddled "puts" about the city, inducing speculation on the part of a large number of people not ordinarily in the market. Chandler and his friends did not count on a large inrush of oats attracted to Chicago by the high prices and the corner failed. Many people lost money and there was much public indignation. One farmer from 35 miles west of the city was said to have sold a contract for 15,000 bushels at 38 cents. He was unable to get his oats into storage and had to pay 41 cents for his contract. When he was later able to move the oats into an elevator he received only 31 cents.

All of this activity resulted in difficulty in settling losses and in charges of fraud. There was a new margin rule passed that called for the right to demand 10 percent margin plus the change that had taken place in the price. Thus the concept of a maintenance margin was introduced. It also developed that there were far more warehouse receipts outstanding than there was grain in the city. Bins were found to contain false bottoms. The Board sought authority to measure warehouses but this was only partially successful. Firms seemed to be going broke frequently and buying each other, only to have the tide flow back with the bought firms buying the buyers. Most of the characters remained on stage. The Board rigorously suspended the members who were in financial difficulty but they came back rather quickly. In 1873 there was a new rule on suspension for failure to fulfill any obligation or contract or for making false or fictitious reports of purchases or sales.

In 1874 the Grange, a powerful farm organization in Illinois, attempted to get a law passed calling all contracts in futures gambling and prohibiting contracts for sale except as the actual commodity was owned. The Board argued that speculators were the best buyers and protected farmers from merchants who attempted to buy as low as possible. While the Grange bill failed, a law was passed prohibiting trade in options to sell or buy (in contrast to futures contracts), forestalling the market by spreading false rumors, cornering the market, or attempting to corner the market.

In July of 1874 there was litigation in the courts regarding settlement of losses in an 1871 "corner." The court found that the 1874 law did not apply but that the 1871 transactions were gambling and could not be enforced because delivery could not be made nor was intended.

The law seemed to be disregarded because there are accounts of two great corners, one in oats and the other in corn, in the latter part of 1874. The position of the Board was that there should be no rule which countenanced or encouraged nonfulfillment saying "No corners can possibly occur when dealers refrain from selling what they have not got, and we recommend this course to those who wish to avoid the usual risks attending transactions of this character." However, a rule was passed fixing responsibility for establishing a settlement price at "commercial value" in the event of default. In 1876, defaults on the 1875 corn "corner" were settled at 48 cents while the market price at the end of the year was 53 cents. The longs were incensed and threatened to take the matter to the courts. They were persuaded to accept the ruling of the arbitration committee by being threatened with disciplinary action for running a corner.

At this point a digression to sample the mood and character of Chicago and the Exchange in 1875 seems worthwhile. We quote Taylor: "On January 13, The Board of Trade was the scene of a demonstration which caused considerable adverse comment in the press and on the part of the more sedate members. King Kalakaus, King of the Hawaiian Islands, was the guest of Chicago and was received on 'Change. He was escorted to the Office of the Directors, where an address of welcome was given by President Armour, to which the King responded. He was then taken to the Exchange room, where he was given a boisterous reception, the younger members joining in singing what was then a popular song, 'The King of the Cannibal Islands.' Order was finally restored and President Armour made a speech, to which the king replied with a bow. Mayor Calvin then spoke, saying: 'I have the honor of escorting into your midst the King of the Can——' This was greeted with a tremendous outburst of laughter and the mayor apologized, but the King was evidently offended and left the chamber. Later, two members attempted a burlesque reception, one representing President Armour, and the other, in a black mask, representing the King. This was too much for the self respect of the Board. The offending members were hooted down, a drum head court martial was held and they were suspended for one week. The following day, J. R. Bensley, C. T. Wheeler, and A. S. Burt were appointed as a committee on decorum."

In 1877 there was an account of the suspension of D. H. Lincoln and Company. Mr. Lincoln was the newly elected President of the Board. He gave as the reason for his suspension the failure of correspondents to make good their margins. Accounts were settled on the basis of 25 cents on the dollar. Lincoln continued in office and in the commission business but in January, 1878 he was forced to suspend although his liabilities were only $2500.

In February, 1879 the resumed tide of speculation set in and Chicago was the scene of the wildest and most general speculation it had ever known. The Arbitration Committee fixed and enforced settlement prices in a wheat situation in which the shorts were unable to deliver. Corn prices were also subject to wild gyrations and there was extensive discussion of corners.

Eighteen hundred and eighty is notable for the failure of Mr. Dow, President of the Board. He paid off at 45 to 50 cents on the dollar. The decade seems to have been one in which presidents were especially vulnerable. Perhaps they paid too much attention to the business of the exchange and too little to trading.

Eighteen hundred and eighty-one was a year of great speculation. Scarcely a month of the year was free from cornering operations in some branch of the trade. The volume of trade was greatly increased and vast sums of money were made and lost. In this year, the Board seems to have grasped its future. Until this time, as we have noted, the general attitude of the exchange was that it was primarily concerned with trade in cash commodities and that the speculative activity was disapproved. The rules had been changed as crises arose. But in 1881 they seemed to see the potential of a large speculative market and to positively adjust rules and the conditions of trade to facilitate speculative activity. The following year was the year of contention in which there was extensive resort to the decisions of committees and to the courts. This might well be identified as the time that systematic commodity speculation came of age. There was a general dissatisfaction with the fixing of settlement prices in the event of default. After much controversy a vote was taken and the rule prohibiting corners was repealed.

By 1884 the list of suspensions was short. The trade appears to have matured to the point of operating with more restraint. More particularly, close attention was paid to margin requirements and the enforcement of margin rules and to placing greater responsibility in the hands of the clearing house. From this time on there is little reference to suspension for lack of funds, defaults on contracts, and settlement prices. The general policy of forcing the longs and shorts to settle in open trade or by delivery was clearly established and the clearing house margin system was the instrument for contract enforcement.

Tightening up of financing rules and practices by no means reduced the speculative enthusiasm nor decreased the growing importance of the market. A contemporary view of the scope of the market and the manipulative problems with which it was beset was presented by H. D. Lloyd writing in *The North American Review* in 1883 "the greatest of these price factories is the Chicago Board of Trade. Thirty years ago its thirty-eight members were scouring the country back of them to persuade the farmers to send their stuff to Chicago for sale. Cheese, crackers and ale were spread out in the Board room to induce the members to attend, but for days in succession, the minutes read: 'None present.' Last year the Board received and paid for $382,000,000 worth of farm products and the total of transactions was not less than $3,000,000,000. It has become not only the chief of the food markets, but the greatest speculative market in the world, as an authority on speculation testified last winter before the New York legislature. It is the only market to which all the world goes to trade. Orders to buy and sell come to it daily from London, Liverpool, Glasgow, Edinburgh, Dublin, Cork, Bordeaux, Marseilles, Zurich, Havre, Antwerp, Amsterdam, Berlin, and Hamburg. It gives the American farmer the best of markets. No other farmer has such a market as this which mobilizes and cashes the crops of The Mississippi valley. Its scores of railways fetch and carry; its banks, stretching from Zuider Zee to the Yellowstone, bring the capital of the Bank of England and of the Hopes of Amsterdam to meet the farmer when he drives up to the country station with a wagonload of grain to sell. Its telegraph wires tell him of the prices, the weather and the supply and demand of the world.

"Corners used to come on The Board of Trade once in a year or two. Now there are corners almost all of the time. The Chicago corner used to be the venture of some local titan and was felt only within the then provincial jurisdiction of the Board. Now it is often the cosmopolitan work of the combined capitalists of half a dozen cities, and its effects, as *The London Times* said of the Pork corner of 1880, are felt in advancing prices all over the world. . . . The corners generally used to fail; but the accumulative experience of many collapses has not been in vain. . . . During the wheat corner of 1879, three out of every four flouring mills in the country were kept idle for over two months. One of the oldest members of the produce exchange prepared for the legislature an estimate that this syndicate, by not selling and not letting others sell and by fleecing those who had been inveigled into dealing with them, and by the injury that had been done to the millers, the shipping interests, the exporters and the consumers of flour, had caused a loss to the country of not less than $300,-000,000."

The greatest speculative era lay ahead and the markets tended to be dominated by towering individuals, each in his own time and his own commodity. We will return at a later point to consider some of the more notable market activities in enough detail to appraise them. For now we should mention a few of the notable events. Eighteen hundred and eighty-eight was the Hutchinson year in which this old, renowned speculator dominated the market. During this activity it was said that the speculative activity was general. In 1889 Hutchinson again dominated the market but ran into increasing opposition and lost money. In 1891 there was a notable corn corner. The price rose from 60 to 80 cents during the third week of November before it declined to 75 cents. Many defaults on delivery were settled at 75 cents. At the close of November delivery, cash corn fell to 46½ cents. In May, 1892 the price of corn rose from 47 cents on the 16th to 71 cents on the 21st, declined to 60 cents on the 22nd. Coster and Martin were said to be the important longs. On the 31st the market opened at $1.00 with Coster and Martin receiving a deluge of offers backed by deliverable corn. One of the longs in the group, Bartlett, offered to sell at 90 cents. The crowd quickly grasped the significance of this and the price fell to 50 cents in thirty seconds.

One of the more notable operations was that of Leiter in 1897 and 1898 in which he opposed Armour and lost. In 1900 Sir Thomas Lipton joined the Chicago Board of Trade, cornered the pork market and lost heavily. Speculative trade in wheat in 1900 was said to be 50 to 100 million bushels per day. In 1901 the talk was of the Phillips activity in corn. In 1902 James A. Patten came on the scene with a major bull activity in oats. He was of growing importance until he managed one of the most notorious of all manipulations in wheat in 1908 and 1909.

Attempts were made from time to time to broaden deliverable grades and generally ease delivery terms to reduce the vulnerability of the market to control. It was argued that hedging trade was being driven from the market by frequent corners. These proposals were generally turned down, sometimes by overwhelming margins. Clearly, the interest and emphasis was on speculative trade.

Bucket Shops

Description of the tone of the era is not complete without mention of bucket shops. To bucket an order is for the receiver of the order to cover it himself without making a contract with someone else or clearing the transaction. No bonafide trade is made. A bucket shop was a business that accepted orders and simply took the other side without the transactions ever actually being made. The prices were those made by actual trading on an exchange. The bucket shop received the quotations of the exchange and "filled" the orders at those prices. It was a system of wagering on price changes.

Bucket shop activity started in the U.S. about 1876 and persisted until about 1915. The bucket shops were disapproved of by the exchanges and various governing bodies—state and federal—as gambling devices and, after a long struggle, were eliminated. The main device in their elimination was control of quotations without which they could not function. This was not easy because, as dissemination of quotations was restricted, so was trade feeding in to the exchanges. Further, a strong claim was made that information about prices on exchanges was public property and could not be restricted.

The bucket shops were not back-alley operations. Some set themselves up as exchanges who formed sub-exchanges where they actually traded or had the appearance of trading. Others advertised themselves as commission houses and had all of the appearances of legitimate houses. There were bucket shops in all major cities in central and eastern United States. To the participating public speculators there was no real difference; whether they bet on the prices generated by other peoples' actual trades or made real contracts was neither here nor there. The outcome in terms of gains and losses was the same. The fact seems to be that a high proportion of bucket shop customers did not know the difference between a bucket shop and a commission house.

The beginning of the long bucket shop battle was an advertisement in the Chicago newspapers in 1876:

RUMBLE and COMPANY
"My $1,000 was made from $20 and $100 invested in grain by Rumble & Co., grain and privilege brokers, 132 LaSalle St., Chicago. Weekly reports free. Circular tells of puts & calls."

The advertisement was noted at the Board and inquiries were made. It was publicly announced that Rumble and Company were not known at The Board but the matter did not seem to cause much consternation at the time.

In 1878 Taylor[8] commented: "The bucket shop was gaining a foothold in Chicago, and several mentions of this nefarious industry were made during the year. The evil had not grown to such an extent, however, that any action was taken, or perhaps thought of by The Board of Trade. Chicago papers of January 27 contained the announcement of the 'Free Board of Trade.' The announcement ran: 'Every man is his own broker; middlemen abolished and each operator to conduct his own transactions on accurate information. Established by

8 Op. Cit. p. 565.

W. C. Lincoln, on the model of The New York Public Produce Exchange Hall just behind Board of Trade in old Toledo building. Telegraphic connections with Board of Trade. No deal over 5000 bushels. Commission $\frac{1}{8}$ of 1 percent.' In February the Tribune said: 'It is reported that Bucket Shops, as they are called in New York, are about to be opened in Milwaukee and St. Louis. Of course the proprieters of these think that no family is complete without one.' In March it was stated that The Free Board of Trade, which was dubbed 'The Pool Box Board,' had increased its commissions to $\frac{1}{4}$ of 1 percent with 1 cent margins. W. C. Lincoln was given as the manager, and Clem Periolat, Billie Clapp, Dan Loring, and Lawrence and Martin are mentioned among the owners. It was stated that the concern had been losing money. The fact that there were few other mentions of the 'Bucket Shops' during the year is proof that they were not viewed with particular alarm."

The most vivid account of bucket shopping appeared in the Chicago Tribune on September 28, 1879. "In July last, the great corner in wheat closed up, the price holding as high as $1.05 per bushel until the settlement was made, when it reached 93 cents, and still later to 87 cents and to 83 cents. Since the first ten days in September, the tendency of the price has been upward, and on one day last week it touched $1.08. At the first sign of advance the gambling began. In all previous years the excitement of this kind of operations was confined to The Board of Trade, that is, the operations have been carried on by members, for, and on account of outsiders. But this year has witnessed the success of institutions which bear the euphonious and expressive title of 'bucket shops.' To do business on 'Change an outsider has to hand over his $100 or $1,000 to a broker, who, for a commission, invests that amount either in a purchase or a sale, putting up the money as a margin. At the bucket shops no broker is necessary; any person, man or woman, boy or girl, white, black, yellow or bronze can deal directly. That is, by putting in $1.00 or $3.00 or $5.00 or $50.00, at the rate of 1 cent per bushel, he or she, becomes the owner of the risk in 100 or 300 or 500 or 5,000 bushels of wheat. If wheat advances 1 cent per bushel, the investor doubles his stake, if the price falls the loss is proportionate. As a general rule the winnings are few—so few and exceptional that it may be said that 99 or even a greater percent of the money deposited in the bucket shops remains there. The fraud, cheat and swindle are so transparent that it seems to be a libel on common intelligence to admit that these establishments do an immense business every day. The most surprising thing is the general character of the customers who patronize these establishments. First—there are the boys— lads from 12 to 16 years of age, school boys, cash boys in retail stores, boot-blacks and newsboys, messenger boys, boys of all degree and occupations, who singly, or by combinations of two or more, can raise $1.00 or $2.00 or $5.00. These rush to the Board of Trade alley, where the shops are in operation, and by the hundreds pour in their money. The occasional profit of $\frac{1}{4}$ or $\frac{1}{2}$ or 1 cent a bushel, serves to whet the avarice and inspire the appetite for new ventures. Sometimes these lads, also represent school girls and sisters, whose small savings are also sent to be emptied into the bucket hops. Boys of larger growth and men, clerks, salesmen, bookkeepers, men in business, hackmen, teamsters, men on salaries, and men employed at days' work, stone cutters, blacksmiths and workmen of all wages and occupations; students and professors of colleges, reverend divines, dealers in theology, members of Christian Associations, members of societies for the prevention of cruelty to animals, and for the suppression of vice, gentlemen who war on saloons which allow minors to play pool, and teachers of Sunday Schools, hard drinkers and temperate men, old men and young men—as well as those of all classes who live in the cities and towns of the state, and of Indiana, Wisconsin, and Michigan, and even occasionally an Ohio man, as those who live in Chicago—all, in person or by agent, purchase their 500 or 1,000 or 5,000 or 10,000 bushels, depositing their margins, and confidently hope to have their money back with 100 or even 500 percent profit.

"These unfortunates do not include the most daring and reckless of all gamblers who do business in the bucket shops. There is not an average woman who thinks her means are more scant than she would like to have them, who does not in her heart despise the caution, or, as she calls it, the cowardice, of the average man, nor is there one who does not insist to herself that, if she were only a man, instead of being cruelly condemned to be a woman, she would go on that Board of Trade and just sweep The Board, making enough money in thirty days to render herself and her husband and family independent for life. Confidence in her own courage and the belief that men fail because they won't succeed, make her chafe under the conventionalities which exclude her from money-making walks of life, and the bucket shop opens to her imagination the longed-for opportunity to show what she might do if she had only a chance. To these shops, women come with their tens, twenties, and fifties, and boldly stake their money. They are not women of desperate or questionable condition, they are the wives and mothers of families in comfortable financial condition. To a woman of this kind, the bucket shop, which holds out a chance to win 200 percent in 24 hours, overcomes all other considerations, and she boldly stakes her cash and with her ticket under her pillow, dreams of the time when with plethoric purse she will be recognized as a first-class customer in every dry goods house in Chicago. The ventures of these women are not confined to the bucket shops; they venture their money through brokers on 'Change, in deals not only in grain, but in pork and lard, and everything else in which any other person has at any time ever made money by bold, daring, reckless and furious gambling. But, while this is the case to some extent, the great part of these dealings by women is in the bucket shops; there the deal is direct and the result soon known, and, as all these operations are made unknown to husbands, the facilities for secrecy are much greater than in the higher grade of business. A lady can pay her $50 at the bucket shop and take her ticket in any name she may select, or even without any name at all, and in the case of loss, no one is the wiser. In case of gain she can, as she invariably will do, reinvest both stake and gain, and lose all at one fell swoop."[9]

Bucket shop operations were generally quite profitable. The customer traded on such thin margins that they were quickly taken out until they could raise a new stake. When they won they were encouraged to put back the profits until they lost. In addition, some commission was charged and the cost of doing business was small. But there are accounts of the frequent bankruptcies of the shops. The patrons knew only to buy and this put the operators in a chronic short position. When prices rose they lost money and when they did too much business in relation to their reserve funds they went out of business. The obvious solution was to lay off the net open positions that they did not want to assume by trades on the exchange. There is no record of the extent to which this was done. The exchange prevented it to the best of its ability.

Conclusions

The foregoing selective sketching of some bits of the history of futures trading suggests several general conclusions regarding what futures are about. The first point that should be recognized is that the markets evolved, over a long period of time, out of the surrounding commercial circumstances. They are a product of their own long history and the story of futures trading is closely related to that of trade in cash commodities.

The basic impetus for futures markets related to inventory risks, and financing and pricing problems. As commerce developed and required the accumulation of inventories, particularly of seasonally produced crops, merchants and processors found themselves with problems that were best managed by forward contracting. This forward contracting developed into standard procedures that were eventually codified and formalized into futures trading.

Forward contracting quickly moved away from commercial interests into the hands of speculators. Relatively little was gained by passing risks from people who did not want them and could not carry them to people who didn't want them or couldn't afford them either. Forward contracts could be made with other commercial people only by the payments of substantial risk premiums which partly compensated the buyers for risk but in addition reduced prices enough to eliminate a high proportion of the risk. These lower prices were reflected back through the marketing system to producers who bore the brunt of the cost. Thus, early in the development, speculators became an essential part of

---

[9] As an aside, one wonders whether Journalism lost some of its character between the 19th and 20th centuries.

the process. They were better able to assume the risks of price change than were the commercial interests.

Speculators did not step nobly forward to assume their necessary place; they rushed in with enthusiasm and abandon to participate in an exciting game that held out the promise of possible huge profits. They cared not at all about their place in the economic world but were motivated by avarice and excitement. In large measure, they took the play away from the commercial trade. Speculation, then, is an activity in itself.

Markets were beset with problems of rigging, manipulation, power plays, financial failures, and technical problems of delivery. And, for a very long time, there was a limited desire or inclination to correct the procedures. For every bit of new speculative blood that flowed in there was someone waiting to lap it up. The exchange members recognized that they had a good thing going when they could control and work the technicalities of the game. This is likely too harsh a judgment; they were by nature opposed to rules that circumscribed their behavior, a fiercely independent bunch of swingers. They not only stood ready to devour the outside participants but fought great battles among themselves. The readiness with which they forgave defaults on indebtedness and restored culprits to good standing makes one wonder if they were not more interested in the game itself than in making money.

As time passed and the size of the market increased, the amount of disputing also increased, and increasing recourse was taken to the law. There was increasing public concern about problems that beset markets. One source was the effectiveness of the markets in filling their underlying roles as risk shifting and financing institutions. Some of the members were primarily concerned with this aspect of the trade. Producers recognized that markets free of problems of control were more useful to them than markets as they existed, although understanding was far from sophisticated and most of their criticism was misplaced if not completely in error. A second source of public concern stemmed from concepts of morality-immorality that related to the then prevailing ethics regarding gambling.

These stresses from both within and without the markets led to the development of rules promulgated by the exchanges and to increased governmental influence. Thus, futures trading came to be much about how to make the markets work efficiently and fairly.

Finally, we note that there was a superstructure of activity built up that related to the incomes of people and firms from sources other than price changes. Commission houses, brokers, and exchange employees were the core of this group. They were responsible for bringing in new money, new players, looking after them as best they could, and running the game. They developed a large stake in the game itself without regard to its outcome or the functions that it performed.

CHAPTER **5**

Competitive Markets

The proposition advanced by this chapter is that futures markets closely approach the conditions of pure competition. If this is the case, the markets are a noteworthy contribution to the economic processes and a means to a better understanding of them. In this connection, one observer noted, "Here again it is somewhat curious that the futures markets have not been cast into the competitive equilibrium model, as a close approximation to the theoretical no-profit equilibrium, given the competitive conditions. But economists have tended to explain them either in terms of risk-transfer or as a game of chance, instead of receiving them as true markets. Price determination as such is curiously treated as a free gift of nature in the competitive model, instead of the economic activity that it really is."[1]

If the proposition is true, the study of futures markets is worthwhile in understanding how the total of the economic processes work. This, however, is but a by-product of testing of the proposition because, if it is true, an appreciation of the competitive nature of the markets is essential to successful operations in futures markets.

A Note on Competition

In most twentieth century industrial nations there has been a trend, for three centuries or so, toward less direct governmental control of economic activity. Feudal and pre-industrial conditions were replaced by what is generally characterized as "free private enterprise" or "competitive capitalism." But it has been observed that the system is neither free, private, nor enterprising and that the owners of capital are often not competitive. A better term might be "competi-

---

[1] Gray, Roger W., "Fundamental Price Behaviour Characteristics in Commodity Futures," *Futures Trading Seminar,* Vol. III Mimir Publishers Inc., 1965.

tive price ordered system." This more accurately describes, not only the system as it has evolved, but characterizes one widely accepted concept of the optimum system. In addition, it helps in delineating an appropriate role for government to play. But for more than a century the downtrend has reversed and governments of the industrial nations have played an increasing role in economic activity and their appropriate role is in public debate. They own and operate productive resources, redistribute income, and establish the rules within which private enterprise functions. Some enterprises are better operated by government, as the highway and educational systems. A strong case is made for some redistribution of income from the more productive to the less fortunate; only the amount is at issue. Governments have widely accepted regulatory functions relating to health, safety, and violations of competition. These several things touch on the pricing system and affect its operation. The generally accepted proposition is that where the competitive system works to provide essential services, protect the well being of individuals from incursion from others, and equitably distribute the fruits of production it should be allowed to operate freely. The superior productivity of a freely operating private enterprise system is recognized. The right to compete, to be more productive, and to receive greater rewards is almost universally recognized as an essential part of liberty. Thus, a competitive economic system is an optimum.

Perhaps the most articulate statement of the way a competitive system works was made by Adam Smith in *The Wealth of Nations* in 1776, "Every individual endeavors to employ his capital so that its produce may be of greatest value. He generally neither intends to promote the public interest, nor knows how much he is promoting it. He intends only his own security, his own gain. And he is led in this by an INVISIBLE HAND to promote an end which was no part of his intention. By pursuing his own interest he frequently promotes that of society more effectively than when he really intends to promote it." As each of us does his own thing in pursuit of his own selfish ends he unwittingly and inevitably maximizes productivity and, hence, social welfare. As each of us chooses the job that pays the best we choose the ones that contribute to the satisfaction of the wants of others. To choose a lesser paying job in the interest of doing good in the world is to waste human resources. We should note that Smith's statement is somewhat qualified by including the word frequently. For the statement to be totally true three conditions must exist: pure or perfect competition, greed, and fear.

The statement assumes that every individual endeavors to employ his capital so that its produce may be of greatest value. It is generally true in the employment of inanimate resources as land, factories, and machinery but is not so true in the employment of human resources. People elect to work and consume at varying proportions of capacity. Somewhat less than a maximum effort is not only tolerated by society but is approved—but indolence is not. There is still a strong work ethic that rests on a concept of obligation to further the general welfare by being productive.

But to make the system work at full tilt requires greed. It is the greedy people who are the great producers. A college placement officer submitted three students to an employer for interviews and the employer chose the one that seemed least likely to the placement officer. When asked why, the employer answered, "I asked each how much money he wanted to make in a lifetime and the winner replied, 'They haven't printed that much yet—I want it all'—well motivated."

The corollary motivating characteristic is fear—fear of not getting rewarded and not having anything to consume or of having too little. If the system pays off on the basis of productivity, fear of loss of income is an important contributor to total output, hence the general welfare. The cowards, as well as the greedy, are the nobility of a competitive economic system.

We almost universally approve of competition in economic activity as a general proposition. We extol a competitive system as an intricate mechanism of great beauty. But at the same time we seek to avoid competition for ourselves. We form conglomerates that will give us dominating market positions from which we can reap monopoly revenues. We seek to enact fair price laws that will protect us from competition. We form teacher and labor unions to negate the full impact of competitive forces. We seek licenses that will give us exclusive rights to operate television stations, bus lines, and electric utilities in restricted geographic areas. College professors and civil servants work out tenurial arrangements so that they cannot be fired except for the worst of performances. These arrangements are worked out under the most laudable banners of the public interest but one must wonder about the roles played by greed, fear, and indolence. One must wonder, too, about how valuable these protective backwashers are. Could it be that they stifle productivity and prevent individuals from rising to the top and force the more productive to share with the less?

The point of this is that it is a mistake to talk about the beauties of competition. It both rewards and punishes. It is a hard taskmaster, mean and ruthless. It has only two things going for it. First, it is inordinately productive. No other system yet devised has resulted in such rapid increases in productivity. It is often criticized for producing the wrong things as by Galbraith in *The Affluent Society*. But it produces the things that people want as measured by how they spend money. Galbraith's tailfins and Nader's safety notwithstanding, the automobile companies either produce automobiles that people want or go broke. Henry Ford once thought that consumers should have only black automobiles and so lost sales leadership to Chevrolet.

Second, it offers the reward of succeeding; the exhilarance of winning. It affords an opportunity for individuals to climb from one economic level to

another; to be more productive and to be rewarded for it. Perhaps more importantly, it offers an opportunity to compete. And competition is a basic drive in
the psychological make-up of many people. The proposition is that winning is
better than losing but losing beats not playing.

The key to a competitive economic system is the pricing mechanism. In the
system no individual or organization is charged with the responsibility of what,
how, or for whom to produce; yet the things that satisfy consumer demand get
produced in the right amounts and get to the right places at the right time. A
competitive system is coordinated by an elaborate mechanism of prices and
markets. Everything has a price, both commodities and services. As too much of
one thing is produced, or too much of a service is offered, prices decline and
factors of production move to other products and services just as a shortage
draws factors of production. Always the migration is from the less profitable to
the more profitable; from the low priced to the high priced.

There are sometimes discussions of planned versus unplanned economies
which is the purest of nonsense; all that is at issue is how planned. There is no
such thing as unplanning. A competitive system is said to be without a central
intelligence but this is not so. Fluctuating prices, reflecting the ebbs and flows of
supplies, factors of production, wants, and purchasing power, form into a
market that is the central intelligence that orders the processes. In this context,
market is an elusive concept, being many transactions in many places at a multitude of prices. The market is the omniscient invisible hand.

The system works perfectly in a situation of pure competition. But pure
competition is an economic ideal that never exists in the real world. Perfect
competition is a technical term; describing a case where no producer—farmer,
businessman, or worker—has any individual influence on price; when his
produce, merchandise, or service is of large enough size to influence price some
degree of monopolistic imperfection is present. The conditions of perfect
competition may be listed as: (1) a large number of buyers and sellers so that
no individual one has an influence on price, (2) homogeneous product, the
characteristics of which can be objectively measured and described, (3) free
entry and exit, (4) full information about production, stocks, price, and distribution, and, (5) independence and impersonality of decisions and operations.

As we have noted, nearly everyone tries to prevent the existence of perfect
competition in his own area. In addition, industrial development into an efficient market structure requires large scale operations that violate the conditions
of perfect competition. It is impossible to have an efficient steel industry that
even remotely meets the conditions. Perfect competition in the railroads or
public utilities would result in duplication and waste; perfect competition in
radio and television would result in chaos.

The existence of perfect competition leads to its demise. To the victors
belong the spoils and because some competitors are better than others they grow
and achieve monopolistic dimensions. If the system permits individuals and

firms to excel, the excellence tends to result in growth to sizes large enough to exert market influence.

Thus, the model of perfect competition is more honored in the breach than the observance. It nevertheless, remains the design ideal of the private enterprise system, particularly in the U.S. As the model is breached, rules are devised to establish a simulation of competition in which no one is allowed to achieve a position of market dominance. Outstanding among these are the antitrust laws. A second kind of rule making is exemplified by labor legislation, to maintain equality of bargaining power. Both kinds of rules are designed to make the pricing system work as though perfect competition existed.

Futures Markets and the Competitive Model

Operations of futures markets can now be viewed against requirements of pure competition. The requirements come remarkably close to being fulfilled. There are a large number of participants in active futures markets. Cross section studies of the composition of markets on specific days reveal the presence of a high proportion of the processors, merchants, and distributors of the commodity, a substantial number of trade associated and professional speculators, and a large number of public speculators. One such analysis of the structure of the corn futures open interest on January 27, 1967[2] revealed the presence of 13,224 individual accounts, of which 2,002 were trade associated such as merchandisers, warehousemen, processors, and feed manufacturers. The other 11,022 accounts were held by people of every imaginable occupation. The geographic distribution was world-wide, involving all states of the U.S. and 25 foreign countries—even one in Liechtenstein.

The ownership was widely diffused; 5,006 accounts had positions of 5,000 bushels each, 4,382 had 10–15,000 bushels, 2,397 had 20–45,000 bushels while only 138 had positions of 500,000 bushels or more. This is not to suggest that there are not influential or dominating individual positions in some markets at some times but rather that, in major, mature markets, ownership is so widely diffused that no single position can have an appreciable influence on price behavior.

In addition, the rule requiring that all trading occur in one pit or ring assures the maximization of the number trading in a given market, preventing fragmentation into several separate monopolistic markets. The rules of futures trading have evolved in a way that minimizes the influence that any one individual can have. The face to face trading, open outcry, specified hours of trading, and equal access to all bids and offers contribute to the prevention of significant individual influence.

Product homogeneity is closely approached by rigid contract specifications.

---

[2] *Trading in Corn Futures, September 1966–March 1967,* Commodity Exchange Authority, USDA, August 1967.

Cash trading ranges over wide grade and quality characteristics but futures trading prices identical lots of a commodity. As we have noted, an essential characteristic of a futures contract is that individual lots be interchangeable and that quality characteristics be precisely identifiable. In this regard, futures trading can only exist when the homogeneity condition of pure competition is met.

Free entry and exit cannot, of course, be met but it is closely approximated. The system of the clearing house, which guarantees the integrity of all contracts, makes it possible to buy and sell on small margins. The contract size generally involves a relatively small quantity of the commodity—while 36,000 pounds of pork bellies or a truck load of eggs may seem like a lot from a consumption point of view, its value, from an investment point of view is not large. Small margins times small contracts equals low capital requirements for entry. It doesn't take much money to start the game. Contract size and margin requirements are deliberately kept small to attract players. Ease of entry exists—staying may be quite another matter.

Successful futures markets are liquid; liquidity is essential to success. Trading tends to be in large volume. As we have noted, there is a lot of trading involved in relatively small changes in open interest. Investment and disinvestment by individuals can be made almost instantaneously.

The full information requirement of pure competition has two aspects, one having to do with trading and the other with information about the commodity. In all futures markets the trades must be public and the traders are obligated to see that the prices at which trades are made are recorded. These prices are given world-wide, instantaneous dissemination. In some markets, the quantities traded and the identities of the traders are also made of record. There are no secret deals at prices away from the market or quantity discounts or special price concessions to established customers, etc. The recorded price is the price to all and sundry.

As noted below, the existence of futures markets results in the generation of a vast amount of information about commodities that would not otherwise exist. For purposes having to do with the conditions of competition it is sufficient to note that the markets themselves collect and make available a large amount of information about production, stocks, movement, and use of the commodities traded. The integrity of this information is not questioned and has the status of official information.

Our final condition of independence and impersonality of operations is forced on the participants by the organization and regulation of the markets. All contracts are made with the Clearing House, the extension of credit is prohibited, all buyers and sellers must have equal access to bids and offers, and most traders do not know which principal they may be dealing with because the actual trade is with a broker. In fact, the identity of principals is closely guarded by registered representatives because their accounts are their stock-in-trade. All accounts are identified by number in the trading processes. The rules of the exchanges prohibit favoritism—a broker can't give even his best friend a break.

As we later explore the matter of manipulation we will find that there have been instances of concerted action and trading by groups that violate the requirement of independence. But we shall find that these don't work in mature markets. There is no honor among thieves and invariably at least one tries to secretly desert the combine first or trade in opposition to it. The breadth of the markets, their impersonality and competitiveness make concerted actions exceedingly difficult. That is to say, competition tends to beget competition.

The Generation of Information

A spin-off result of futures trading is an increase in the amount of information relevant to commodity prices and pricing. The collection and dissemination of information is a major economic function that must be performed if commodity markets are to operate efficiently. The ordering of production, storage, processing, and distribution of commodities on a world-wide scale is extremely complex. It is done by prices and price relationships. The quality of the job that gets done is affected by the completeness and accuracy of information that goes into price determination. Anything that contributes to the completeness and accuracy of information contributes to the efficiency of the economic processes.

He who would control must first conceal. If a merchant possesses information that is not available to the people from whom he buys or to whom he sells he is in a position to reap monopolistic profits. In the cash commodity trades, some firms are very much larger than others and the large ones can afford the expense of collecting market information while the small ones cannot. The most outstanding example is the position of farmers vis-à-vis terminal grain merchants, meat packers, citrus fruit processors, potato merchants, etc. Without comprehensive information they are not in a position to form intelligent ideas about real market value and can be taken advantage of. The need for better information for farmers and country merchants has long been recognized and a large information gathering and analysis activity has been developed by the U.S. Department of Agriculture. This extensive service has been stimulated and expanded as the result of requests from commission futures merchants and their customers, those in the trades, and speculators. For example, the USDA decided to discontinue several of the quarterly reports of grains in all positions, beginning January 1, 1969. They thought that they did not have sufficient funds to compile reports accurately enough to be better than not making reports at all; that reports of questionable accuracy were worse than none at all. The complaints were so numerous and emphatic that the reports were resumed after the single omission.

Baer and Saxon[3] illustrate the importance of the existence and publicity of futures price quotations with the description of an incident: "Some time ago the project of organizing a new exchange market in an agricultural commodity was under consideration. In order to sound out opinion in the trade and industry, a questionnaire was sent out to producers, merchants, and manufacturers in the field. The preponderance of sentiment on the part of operators in the commodity was adverse to the establishment of futures trading. One dealer returned his questionnaire with a 'NO' inscribed across the face of the document, and in order to discover the reasons for his opposition a member of the group responsible for the questionnaire visited the center of the adverse sentiment and interviewed the merchant whose emphatic negative had impressed itself upon him. There was no doubt in the mind of the caller that the merchants' reply had been dictated by a genuine self interest, but the same self interest was more eloquent of the outstanding value of the publication of prices by commodity exchanges than any abstract summary could possibly be. The merchant said: 'I have many buyers traveling throughout the producing areas to purchase directly from growers. They pay cash. When they go to a grower and offer him a definite price per pound in spot cash, the grower is tempted to sell without investigating prevailing prices. He often does so. But, if there were an exchange in existence, its prices would be telegraphed all over the country and would appear in every newspaper of any size and circulation. The seller would know just how closely the price he was offered approached the prevailing market price. Our buyers work to purchase the commodity under the prevailing market, and they make excellent purchases below the market. If the exchange were established, I would probably have to pay current market prices for all I buy.' " It is not suggested that the actions of the buyer are typical of the behavior of merchants generally or the buyers could long be successful with this kind of larceny but it does illustrate the importance of price publicity and the importance attributed to futures price quotations by members of the trade. They equate such publicity with increased competition. The illustration demonstrates the point that everyone approves of competition—for the other guy.

Kinds of Information. The kinds of information surrounding futures trading activity can be somewhat separated by source. We should first list the exchanges themselves. They own, control, and are responsible for the collection and dissemination of price quotations. It is to the best interests of the members of the exchanges that price quotations receive the widest possible coverage. In addition to the ticker quotations systems previously described, prices are broadcast by many radio and television stations and published in most metropolitan and many smaller newspapers. Part of this coverage is instigated by the exchanges and part is in response to the requests of listeners and readers who trade in futures contracts.

Some exchanges prepare daily and weekly summaries of the trading activity,

[3] Ibid., p. 100–101.

changes in prices, and a description of the factors affecting trading and prices. This kind of activity is designed to stimulate interest and business.

Most exchanges tabulate and distribute trading and market information to their members. Much of this is prominently posted on the trading floor. It relates to weather, planting, receipts, shipments, stocks, volume of trading and open interest, and to government reports. Pressure to do this was generated during the 19th century when there was so much false information available. There was a demand for accurate information made equally available to members. The result is that exchange information is given status equal to official information. In addition to this regular flow of information on a daily and weekly basis, many exchanges publish annual yearbooks of futures prices, trading, and commodity commerce for the commodities traded. These yearbooks are among the best sources of long term commodity statistics.

A second major source of market information is the federal government. The information collected, analyzed, and distributed by The Statistical Reporting Service and the Economic Research Service of the USDA is huge and comprehensive. How much of the existence of this is the result of demand stimulated by futures trading activity is conjectural. Some, but not much, is probably the correct answer. It exists for commodities not traded in futures markets. It existed for others before they were traded in futures. It is prepared for producers, merchants, processors, and distributors. No one would suggest in requesting appropriations from Congress in support of market information work that commodity speculators need it. But trade interests are vitally interested in futures markets, doubtless request the development of information useful in their futures operations, and are listened to by government.

The quality of governmental information is probably improved as the result of widespread interest in futures trading. Traders closely scrutinize information for error, generally with the benefit of hindsight, and are quick to point out errors. In April, 1965 soybeans were in short supply and the report showing stocks in all positions on April 1 was considered of major importance in indicating the direction that prices would need to take for the last six months of the crop year. If the report was small prices would have to go up, while, if large, they would decline. The report was issued after the close of trading on the third Friday in April. It was quite small. But close examination by trade analysts revealed that the stocks in Minnesota could not possibly be as small as reported. The error was called to the attention of the USDA and corrected prior to the start of trading on Monday. In the absence of futures trading, the error might have gone undetected or if detected, uncorrected, forever. Nearly certainly, it would not have been detected and corrected over the weekend. Such alert and competent critics have doubtless played a role in stimulating USDA employees to achieve their present level of excellence.

There are private surveys made of crop conditions, cattle and hog numbers, poultry production, etc. They try to anticipate the official government information or improve on its accuracy. The basic attempt is to get information faster. Surveys are made of producers' intentions and their sales attitudes. Some of these are comprehensive while others are cursory. Some are released publicly ahead of government estimates while others are held for the private use of the compilers and their customers. How much of this activity exists is not known but it is likely that the reports that come to general attention are but the tip of an iceberg. How much would exist in the absence of futures trading is not known, but, likely, substantially less.

There are commodity news services in the business of collecting and distributing commodity information to subscribers. The subscribers are commission futures merchants, merchants, processors, distributors, and a few large scale speculators. The machines run somewhat noisily and print out information on rolls of paper. Every conceivable kind of commodity and general economic information from all over the world is gathered, fed in on the one end, and printed out on the other. It is an insidiously compulsive arrangement. To justify the subscription price the feeders must keep the machine clacking noisily away. To get their monies worth, the subscribers must read everything that comes out. Information is reported as it becomes available and thus lacks classification or organization so that the subscriber who takes his eyes away may miss something pertinent to his operation. The system is certainly conducive to the completeness of market information. Again, much of this would exist without futures markets but there would be less and it would be less widely distributed.

The commission house letters that are sent to customers, some daily and some weekly, contribute to the generation of market information and its analysis. There is a compulsion about these, too. Customers expect them on schedule so that they must be written whether the analyst has anything to say or not. The analysts are held accountable by the customers for completeness of information and its interpretation. As a result they seek complete and accurate information.

As a result of all of this one may begin to worry lest the world of commodity trading drown in a flood of information. Perhaps it shall. Just how much of this really contributes to the efficiency of the operation of the economic system may be argued. But it is all deemed essential by someone. It is all taken into account in price formulation. If completeness of information contributes to economic efficiency then we must judge that futures markets also contribute.

Regulation to the Competitive Model

Futures trading is a closely regulated activity. The terms of trade and trading are specified and the means of enforcement and punishment of violations are established. Nearly all of the regulation is aimed toward enforcement of the conditions of pure competition. The regulation has not developed in a deliberate attempt to identify and fulfill classical economists concepts of pure competition but rather has been in response to pressure to correct trading abuses. As practices developed that gave "unfair" advantage to one party versus another or resulted in price behavior that appeared to be caused by the conditions of futures trading rather than the conditions of cash supply and demand factors, demand for regulation arose. The kinds of cornering, manipulation, concealed trading, and dissemination of false information that appeared to exist so extensively in the 1870 to 1900 period was disapproved by the exchange members and the public. They were "unfair" and were corrected by rules, regulations, and punishments. "Unfair" appears to mean unequal. If our look at the history of futures trading in the previous chapter is accurate, the guiding philosophy of regulation is that all men should be free to act as they want, so long as their actions do not deny the same opportunity to others. This implies equality of access to the marketplace and to information. The goal of regulation has been to make all men equal in their opportunity to compete—there is no implication of equality in their ability. The essential point is that the goals of regulation, as they developed, are precisely consistent with goals of establishment of the conditions of pure competition.

The rules and regulations of the exchanges are designed to govern: (1) The relations of the exchanges to the public and to State and Federal regulatory bodies. (2) The conditions under which a commodity may be traded on the exchange, (3) the relation of individual members to the exchange, (4) The relation of members to customers, and (5) The relation of members to members. One measure of the underlying philosophy of regulation is the list of offenses for which a member may be suspended or expelled. The specifics vary by exchanges but a general list is:

1. Making a false or fictitious transaction in which no change of ownership is involved.
2. Making of purchases or sales, or making bids or offers when such action is designed to bring about a condition of demoralization or otherwise register a price that does not fairly reflect true market values.
3. Engaging in reckless or unbusinesslike dealings.
4. Trading systematically opposite to the orders or market positions of customers.
5. Manipulating prices or attempting to corner the market.
6. Dissemination of false or misleading information.
7. Defaulting intentionally on the delivery of futures contract sales.
8. Engaging in any course of conduct which, aside from the violation of any rules or regulations for which other penalty is provided, a majority of the Board of Directors judge is dishonorable or detrimental to the welfare of the exchange.

The Commodity Futures Trading Commission Act is administered by the Commodity Futures Trading Commission. The demand for legislation and regulation came from producers and their organizations who protested sudden and unreasonable fluctuations in prices thought to be caused by traders in futures contracts and from customers of commission houses—the speculating public, especially farmers—who were or thought they had been defrauded by members of the exchanges. In broadest outline public regulation of futures trading is designed to: (1) assure that exchanges make and enforce rules and regulations appropriate to the maintenance of competitive trading, (2) prevent manipulation and distortion of prices, and (3) protect the public from fraud resulting from misappropriation of funds or from non-competitive trading practices.

It is illegal to manipulate a futures price or to take advantage of the ignorance of a customer in establishing the prices on his transactions. It is in violation of the rules and regulations of exchanges to make transactions and take positions for which the principal does not have sufficient money to guarantee the financial integrity of the contracts. This is in sharp contrast to the world of cash commodities. It is perfectly legal for any firm to engross the supply of cash corn and hold it for whatever monopolistic price he sees fit or for a firm to divert physical oranges into secondary channels to force the price of frozen orange juice up but let these things be done in conjunction with futures market operations and the full weight of the exchanges and the federal law descend upon the culprit. In cash transactions it is legal to bid a lower than prevailing price to the seller or quote a high price to the buyer in the hope that he doesn't know any better but the agent of the principal in a futures contract is required to make the best possible transaction. Overextension of credit is a normal business risk in cash commodity transactions but it is in violation of the rules and regulations of exchanges when done in futures.

It should not be concluded from this discussion that the kind and amount of regulation is optimum; some evaluation of regulation is reserved to a later stage. The point to be made here is that regulation is substantial and is designed to force futures trading to conform to the competitive model.

It is easy to look at the history of futures trading and the development of such extensive regulation and conclude that traders in trading must be inherently evil to require so much supervision. It is apparent that everything noncompetitive has been tried. It also may well be that some violations of competition are more imagined than real and that less regulation is desirable. But the extensive regulation that has developed in the fish bowl atmosphere of futures trading serves to underscore our point that competition is mean and ruthless. In a sense competition is evil. Futures trading is no more or less evil than pure competition. The appropriate conclusion seems to be that futures trading is a rough game but is competitive and as fair as regulation can make it.

CHAPTER 6

Risk Shifting

We concluded from our look at the history of the origin and development of futures trading that the basic impetus for forward contracting and, subsequently, futures trading was the need on the part of merchants to shift ownership risks. The risks arose out of a combination of ownership of inventories and variable and uncertain prices. The merchants were both financially unable and unwilling to accept these risks; their bankers would not finance them and one major loss could destroy the entire business so tediously built up. During the 1870's and 1880's the process of hedging was developed.

One key to understanding the risk shifting process is that a futures contract is a temporary substitute for a cash transaction; it stands, for a time, in the place of a cash commodity, finally being consummated by making delivery in only a small number of cases.

Risks are shifted by the process of hedging. To hedge is to take a position in futures equal and opposite to an existing cash position. If a merchant has a stock of 100,000 bushels of corn in his elevator, he is long cash corn. If the price goes up, he makes money. If it goes down, he loses money. He is subject to the risk of a price decline. He can offset this risk by selling 100,000 bushels of futures contracts. As he sells he becomes short futures. He is long cash and short futures; thus he is hedged. So long as cash and futures move up and down together, what the hedger makes on the one position he will lose on the other; consequently he will neither gain nor lose from a change in price.

In the ordinary course of events of being a merchant, the cash corn is sold to a processor, exporter, or feeder. As this happens the merchant is no longer long cash corn, he is only short futures and thus subject to the risk of a price increase. He buys his short futures and completes the whole of the transaction. The short futures contracts have stood, for a time, in the place of a sale of the cash corn.

Gains and losses resulting from changes in the price of cash corn between the times of purchase and sale are equal and opposite to and offset by gains and losses resulting from changes in the price of the futures contracts so that the sale of the cash corn that ends the merchandising transaction is made on the basis of the same price level as the purchase of the cash corn.

The hedger shifts the price risk of ownership to the purchasers of the futures contracts. Thus, the process of hedging is the shifting of risks from the holders of inventory positions (which may be short as well as long) in cash commodities to those who take the opposite position in futures markets. This is generally from hedger to speculator.

Open Interest and Position Information

We can best see the nature of the risk shifting process by looking at the structure of the open interest. Some, but not complete, information about the size and structure of open interest is available. The exchanges and the CFTC make daily reports of the open interest in each delivery of each commodity. But these only indicate the totals and tell us nothing about who is long and who is short.

We noted earlier that the C.E.A., from time to time, made cross section studies of the structure of the open interest on specific days that show, in detail, who is long and who is short by occupation and location and whether they are hedgers or speculators. These have covered only a few commodities at infrequent intervals.

The CFTC Act requires that holders of positions exceeding certain minimum levels report daily to the CFTC the long and short positions held by delivery months and whether the positions are hedging or speculation. The people who must report are designated "large traders." Their positions are classified, by long and short, as Speculative, Spreading, and Hedging. People whose positions are smaller than reporting levels are designated "small traders." Their open contracts include both hedging and speculative positions and are derived by subtracting large traders' commitments from total open contracts. The reports are summarized and published each month and are released about the 12th of the following month. Reporting levels are:

Wheat	500 thousand bushels
Corn	500 thousand bushels
Oats	200 thousand bushels
Soybeans	500 thousand bushels
Soybean Oil	50 contracts (1.5 million pounds)
Soybean Meal	50 contracts (25 hundred tons)
Live Beef Cattle	50 contracts (1 million pounds)
Shell Eggs	25 contracts (525 thousand dozen)
Frozen Pork Bellies	25 contracts (900 thousand pounds)

Live Hogs	50 contracts (750 thousand pounds)
Cotton	50 contracts (5000 bales)
Frozen Orange Juice	25 contracts (375 thousand pounds)
Potatoes	25 carlots

Comparable information is not available for the nonregulated commodities which include the metals and import commodities (cocoa, sugar, coffee, rubber).[1]

Anatomy of the Corn Futures Market on January 27, 1967

A special survey of the corn futures market was made on January 27, 1967.[2] In the survey, all futures commission merchants and exchange clearing members reported every account having open contracts in corn futures at the close of business. These survey reports gave the amount of positions and showed the type of account, whether hedging or speculative. Reporters on the survey also gave the name of each account on their records, city and state in which located, and the occupation of the account owner. The market was thoroughly dissected and thus we are afforded an opportunity to inspect its anatomy.

The number of accounts and positions reported were:

| | | Positions | (1,000 Bu.) |
Classification	*Number*	*Long*	*Short*
Speculative	11,709	240,835	139,680
Hedging	1,509	126,435	227,965
Unclassified	6	55	85

The unclassified were residents of foreign countries and were dropped from the following analysis.

The positions of the members of the Chicago Board of Trade and the proportion of the total open inteerst they represented were:

| | *Million Bushels* | | | *Percent of Market* | | |
| | | *Positions* | | | *Positions* | |
	Number	*Long*	*Short*	*Number*	*Long*	*Short*
Speculative	312	68.2	60.3	2.4	18.6	16.4
Hedging	155	65.8	180.1	1.2	17.9	49.0

This tabulation indicates that members represented a very small percentage of the number of accounts reported but their combined positions represented a substantial share of the total positions—36 percent of the total long and 65 percent of the total short positions. Members trade in very much larger volume than do commission house customers, which is hardly a startling discovery.

[1] All of this is being changed as CFTC becomes operative (1976).
[2] *Trading in Corn Futures, September 1966–March 1967*, CEA, USDA, August 1967.

Occupations. Table 4 shows positions by occupation. The occupational grouping obscures part of the diversity of kinds of people that make up the market. Other in the Corn Trade includes feed and seed dealers, livestock feeders and dealers, and producer cooperatives. In the business category, the Manufacturers included wholesale trade proprietors, food brokers, meat packers, vegetable canners, etc. Retailers were food, grocery, apparel, furniture, hardware, jewelry, automobiles and all of the rest of the kinds of businesses with which consumers are familiar. In the professional classification "other" was made up of accountants and auditors, architects, artists, social workers, chemists and engineers. There were 400 chemists and engineers, even more than physicians. Skilled workers' occupations were aviators, draftsmen, radio and television operators, electricians, plumbers, machinists, brick masons, and barbers. Clerical included bookkeepers, cashiers, stenographers, office machine operators, etc. Service included such as housemaids and private detectives. The final "other" under Miscellaneous would seem unnecessary in view of the completeness of the list but covered ministers, unemployed, and military. The point of this is that to list the occupations of traders in a major futures market is to list all of the occupations in an industrial society.

The grouping other than the corn and commodity trades was not planned to come out even—it just happened that way. The grouping was done on the basis of general income level with the thought in mind that people with higher incomes would take larger positions but this was the case to a limited extent only. Business proprietors held larger positions than the others but physicians' positions were no larger than teachers and skilled workers no larger than unskilled. Housewives were fairly numerous and held positions comparable to the professions, insurance agents, and others. But we must mistrust the housewife classification. It may be that some men carried accounts in wives' names to avoid being caught trading commodities.

Hedgers and Speculators. There were a lot of speculative and relatively few hedging accounts, the speculators outnumbering hedgers by nearly eight to one. In addition, one must have some reservation about whether some accounts identified as hedging truly were. To hedge is to be equal and opposite. What were some of the hedges opposite to? The opposite position of an inventory of cash corn is a short futures position but except for merchants, exporters and warehousemen, nearly every hedging category was net long. For a hedged futures position to be long requires either that there be a sale of cash corn for which no purchase has been made or that a consumption requirement exist as in the case of a processor or feeder. Thus, for processors and feed manufacturers to have been net long was legitimate hedging, but there were 269 farmers who were net long six million bushels. Was all of this purchased to cover a feed requirement until cash corn could be bought? A banker was long 10 thousand bushels, two lawyers were long 30 thousand, a teacher was long 5 thousand,

and three skilled workers were long 130 thousand. What sales or requirements could have been opposite the net long position of 95 thousand bushels held by 11 retired people? One suspects that some people said they were hedging because they didn't really know the difference and that others preferred the term because, to many people, hedging is good and speculation is bad.

Speculators were net long and hedgers were net short 101 million bushels. The general proposition is that hedgers shift ownership risks to speculators.

Corn Trade Speculates. People in the business of producing and marketing corn are among the more active speculators. Of the net long speculative position of 101 million bushels, 39 million, more than one third, was held by farmers. It appears that some farmers sell their cash corn and buy back futures—or perhaps decide that if holding the cash that they raise is a good idea the operation should be increased by buying futures. There were more than 900 accounts held by people actively engaged in the corn trade, people who are in the business of buying and selling cash corn. Some of the people in the business have confidence in their own skill.

The total number of people engaged in the corn trade is not known, but it is much greater than 900. Similarly, there are many times 4,032 farmers who produce corn in the U.S. Neither all nor a high percentage, of people in the trade speculate. At the same time, it should be recognized that the people who had positions on January 27, 1967 are not nearly all of the people who trade corn futures.

Commodity Trades. The professional commodity fraternity made up a small percentage of the total traders in corn futures (4.3) and held a modest share of the positions (21% of long and 19% of short). Corn futures trading appears to be a game played by the corn trade and amateurs. The striking thing about the positions of professionals is their balance of opinions. The brokerage houses and floor traders were almost evenly divided in their positions and thus, presumably, in their expectations about prices. Professional speculators were few in number, net long, but far from unanimous in their expectations.

Commodity counselors are professional analysts who form opinions about prices and advise clients. Their number exceeded the number of professional speculators but their positions were much smaller. Presumably, their positions were indicative of their advice. If so, their vote on whether the price would go up or down was essentially tied—long 3,040 and short 3,030.

Relative Skill. It is not relevant to the topic of risk shifting but, while looking at the positions of different occupational groups of speculators, it is possible to make some comparisons of skill. The price of corn went down subsequent to January 27, 1967. July futures closing prices were:

Table 4. Corn Futures: Occupational Distribution of Accounts, by Number and Class, Chicago Board of Trade, Jan. 27, 1967 (Positions in Thousands of Bushels)

	Speculators			Hedgers			Total		
	No. Accts	Long	Short	No. Accts	Long	Short	No. Accts	Long	Short
Corn Trade									
Mrchnt, Exptr, Wrhouse	450	9,480	3,785	973	71,975	191,340	1,423	81,455	195,125
Processors, Feed Mfgrs	62	935	460	97	37,960	22,140	159	38,895	22,600
Farmers & Farm Mgrs	4,032	53,500	14,480	269	6,870	850	4,301	60,370	15,330
Other	415	11,275	4,905	100	5,665	2,350	515	16,940	7,255
Total	4,959	75,190	23,630	1,439	122,470	216,680	6,398	197,660	240,310
Commodity Trades									
Brokerage Houses	261	20,845	19,255	10	685	465	271	21,530	19,720
Floor Traders	125	36,295	35,400	4	55	70	129	36,350	35,470
Pro. Speculators	80	16,545	11,370	0	0	0	80	16,545	11,370
Commodity Counselors	87	3,040	3,030	1	200	0	88	3,240	3,030
Total	553	76,725	69,055	15	940	535	568	77,665	69,590
Business									
Agr. Proc. (not corn)	15	1,835	1,750	7	1,510	10,380	22	3,345	12,130
Commodity Dealers	61	1,650	860	8	265	20	69	1,915	880
Bank Officials	156	4,740	3,105	1	10	0	157	4,750	3,105
Manufacturers	126	2,540	2,875	4	135	0	130	2,675	2,875
Retailers	569	8,750	4,025	2	30	0	571	8,780	4,025
Other	817	13,785	5,925	11	725	295	828	14,510	6,220
Total	1,744	33,300	18,540	33	2,675	10,695	1,777	35,975	29,235
Professions									
Medical	385	4,500	2,300	0	0	0	385	4,500	2,300
Lawyers	178	2,810	950	2	30	0	180	2,840	950
Teachers	195	2,035	945	1	5	0	196	2,040	945
Other	885	9,475	6,015	1	0	10	886	9,475	6,025
Total	1,744	18,820	10,210	4	35	10	1,647	18,855	10,220

Table 4 Continued	Speculators			Hedgers			Total		
	No. Accts	Long	Short	No. Accts	Long	Short	No. Accts	Long	Short
Other									
Sales	283	3,300	1,930	0	0	0	283	3,300	1,930
Insurance	315	6,415	2,425	3	45	10	318	6,460	2,435
Clerical	122	955	510	1	10	0	123	965	510
Skilled Workers	341	3,340	2,100	3	130	0	344	3,470	2,100
Service, labor	284	2,690	975	0	0	0	284	2,690	975
Total	1,345	16,700	7,940	7	185	10	1,352	16,885	7,950
Miscellaneous									
Housewives	339	6,665	3,320	0	0	0	339	6,665	3,320
Students	66	785	640	0	0	0	66	785	640
Retired	776	10,040	4,765	11	130	35	787	10,170	4,800
Other	284	2,610	1,580	0	0	0	284	2,610	1,580
Total	1,465	20,100	10,305	11	130	35	1,476	20,230	10,340
TOTAL	11,709	240,835	139,680	1,509	126,435	227,965	13,218	367,270	367,645

113

Jan.	31	144	Apr.	30	133⅜
Feb.	15	140½	May	15	134½
Feb.	28	145⅞	May	31	135½
Mar.	15	145½	June	15	131½
Mar.	31	145¼	June	30	130¼
Apr.	15	140			

The shorts were right and made money and the longs were wrong and lost money. Grading on the basis of positions held January 27 assumes that the composition of the market did not change abruptly, a reasonable assumption. As we shall see, the general structure of the open interest did not change significantly. The longs had already lost money because the price had been declining since the previous August. There is a marked tendency for speculators to stay with losing positions. It is doubtful that the positions of the various groups changed appreciably for at least several weeks.

The ratios of long to short by speculative groups were:

Corn trade	3.2:1
Commodity trades	1.1:1
Business	1.8:1
Professions	1.8:1
Other	2.1:1
Miscellaneous	2.0:1
Total	1.7:1

The corn trade was the worst, the commodity trades the closest to respectable, and there were no significant differences among the other groups. The most notably bad performance was that of farmers with a 3.7:1 ratio. The single group with a passing grade was manufacturers who were slightly net short. The grade of students at 1.2:1 was better than professional speculators at 1.5:1.

Geographical Distribution. Table 5 summarizes the geographical distribution of accounts. All states and 25 foreign countries were represented. There was a hedger short 200 thousand bushels in Liechtenstein and a speculator long 10 thousand bushels in South Vietnam. Of the 250 accounts in foreign countries, 143 were in Canada, the largest single state was Illinois with 3,316, of which 921 were in Chicago. Iowa was in second place with 2,327.

The geography of corn futures trading tends to resemble the geography of corn production just as speculation tends, proportion of the population taken into account, to be concentrated in occupations close to corn production.

Size of Positions. The average size of positions can be derived from Table 4. Table 6 shows the size distribution of the positions of selected groups of speculators. The bulk of speculative positions were small. Forty percent were

Table 5. Corn Futures: Distribution of Accounts by Geographic Areas, Chicago Board of Trade, January 27, 1967

	Number Accounts	
Area	*Speculators*	*Hedgers*
North Atlantic	797	57
East North Central	4,170	726
West North Central	3,855	530
South Atlantic	703	42
South Central	803	68
Western	1,185	18
Insular	14	0
Total U.S.	11,527	1,441
Foreign Countries	182	68
Total	11,709	1,509

just 5,000 bushels and 75 percent were 15,000 bushels or less. There were 936 positions of 50,000 bushels or more. Ten thousand bushels is not very much corn. The 14 cent decline in price from the end of January to the end of June was $1,400 profit or loss on 10 thousand. But 50 thousand is a fairly substantial position—$7,000 from a 14 cent move and a half million is a lot by the standards of most people—$70,000. While most speculators played for modest stakes there were a few swingers.

The size distributions fall into two general categories. The public accounts were about equally numerous in the two smallest categories and fell off rapidly from 20 thousand bushels up. The doctors gave up before one half million and the chemists and engineers quit short of 200 thousand. It is possible that at least three farmers were more concerned about the price of corn than they were their farming activities. At least two bankers did not fit the general public image of prudence bankers enjoy. One wonders about the 16 housewives who had positions of 100 thousand bushels and over, and hopes, in the interest of the preservation of family budgets, that they were short. Large scale traders are found in many different occupational groups. On the other hand, the size distribution of commodity trade group positions were nearly uniform by size of position—note particularly the professional speculations. When they turn professional they trade in large units—they can't afford to stay around for small sums.

Table 7 is an attempt to explore the category "Non Reporting Traders" that is reported by the CFTC on a monthly basis. The January 27, 1967 data was divided at the 200 thousand bushel reporting level.

Small scale speculators were net long 81 million bushels, large scale speculators were net long 20 million, small scale hedgers were net long about 14 million (rounding accounts for the one million discrepancy). Ownership risks associated with inventories of cash corn were shifted from large scale hedgers to the speculating public (70%), large scale speculators (17%) and to small scale hedgers (13%). A total of 354 million bushels of risks were shifted by hedgers—126 long and 228 short. The net shift of risks from hedgers to speculators was 101 million bushels.

The positions of the under and over the 200 thousand reporting level developed in Table 7 were compared with the regularly reported positions on January 31, 1967. They were: (million bushels)

	Long	*Short*
Non Reporting Traders		
Regular Report	184	83
Table 7	179	83
Reporting Speculators		
Regular Report	93	78
Table 7	94	74
Reporting Hedgers		
Regular Report	84	201
Table 7	94	210

The match is satisfactory, indicating that the detailed survey made on January 27 described the composition of the category "Non Reporting Traders" at that time.

The non reporting traders category was made up of a large number of small accounts which were predominantly speculative. Eighty two percent of the long positions and 78 percent of the short positions were held by speculators. This probably understates the predominance of speculation as earlier noted in raising questions about some of the smaller positions reported as hedges. The long to short ratio of the small speculators was 2.3:1 while that of the small hedgers was 1.8:1. Doubtless a large part of the small short hedges were offset by inventories of cash corn on farms, warehouses, and in factories. How much of the 32 million bushels reported as long hedges was offset by sales already made or requirements subsequently purchased is conjectural. Ten million of it was owned by farmers and the speculating public. Adjusting and guessing we can reasonably generalize that the composition of non reporting traders' positions were: (Percent)

	Long	*Short*
Speculative	88	12
Hedging	80	20

The anatomy of the corn futures market as shown by the detailed cross section of January 27, 1967 was similar to the anatomy of other markets at other times. Special studies of corn at other times, of wheat, soybeans, potatoes, and onions all revealed the same characteristics of a large number of small scale

Table 6. Corn Futures: Size Distribution of Speculative Accounts of Selected Occupations, Chicago Board of Trade, January 27, 1967

		Number of Accounts by Size of Long and Short Position (1,000 Bu.)						
Occupational Group	*Total*	*5*	*10–15*	*20–45*	*50–95*	*100–195*	*200–495*	*500+*
Grain Mrchnts, Exptrs, Wrhousemen	450	119	135	138	38	13	6	1
Brokerage Houses & Employees	261	56	61	59	27	29	19	10
Floor Traders	80	13	12	27	19	25	9	20
Professional Speculators	385	12	12	12	13	12	8	11
Farmer & Farm Managers	4,032	1,650	1,500	706	127	31	15	3
Medical Profession	385	170	126	64	18	6	1	0
Chemists & Engineers	400	227	120	42	9	2	0	0
Bank Officials	156	65	44	25	9	7	4	2
Retailers	569	220	201	102	31	9	4	2
Insurance & Real Estate	315	123	112	49	16	8	6	1
Housewives	339	147	118	40	18	10	4	2
TOTAL All Speculators	11,709	4,760	4,003	2,010	533	228	110	65

Table 7. Corn Futures: Distribution of Accounts by Classification and Size of Position, January 27, 1967

Size Group (000 bushels)	SPECULATORS					HEDGERS				
	Number Accounts	Gross Positions Long	Short	Average[1] Size	Net	Number Accounts	Gross Positions Long	Short	Average[1] Size	Net
5	4,759	18,320	7,720	5.0	10,600	246	1,070	240	5.0	830
10-15	4,003	35,735	12,610	11.2	23,125	379	3,490	1,080	11.4	2,410
20-45	2,001	42,230	16,935	27.3	25,295	387	8,190	3,310	28.6	4,880
50-95	532	24,650	13,010	64.5	11,640	202	8,875	4,470	65.0	4,405
100-195	228	25,955	15,195	144.1	10,760	135	10,660	8,730	136.1	1,930
Sub Total	11,523	146,890	65,470	16.5	81,420	1,349	32,285	17,830	35.7	14,455
200-495	109	25,725	18,515	333.1	7,210	90	15,095	13,505	315.0	1,590
500 & over	67	68,220	55,695	1,553.6	12,525	70	79,055	196,630	3,938.4	s117,575
Sub Total	176	93,945	74,210	797.1	19,735	160	94,150	210,135	1,900.2	s115,985
Total	11,709	240,835	139,680	28.2	101,155	1,509	126,435	227,965	233.4	s101,530

[1] Gross positions include spreads, average does not.

speculators, a few large scale speculators, and a few hedgers with the speculators predominantly long and the hedgers predominantly short. In all cases, the positions of non reporting traders were predominantly speculative, predominantly long and were very small—mainly one to three contracts—much below reporting levels. The classification "Non Reporting Traders" is mainly composed of the speculating public.

Hedging and the Open Interest

We now back away from this detailed focus to take a more general look at corn futures trading. But first, a few facts about corn production and marketing are necessary.

The production of corn in the U.S. was about 5.5 billion bushels per year in 1971–75. The U.S. is, by far, the largest producer in the world. Production is concentrated in the central part of the country and there is a tendency for this concentration to increase. Corn is primarily a livestock feed, both in the U.S. and export destinations of U.S. corn. For example, in 1973–74 the use was:

Feed	4,193 million bushels	
Food, industrial, seed	440 ”	”
Export	1,243 ”	”

Exports increased rapidly during the 1960's, from 200 million bushels at the beginning to nearly 600 million at the end. They doubled to 1.2 billion in 1972–73 and in 1976 were more than 1.6 billion.

The corn industry has become increasingly commercialized since World War II. Production units have increased in size and the relative importance of the inputs of entrepreneurial labor and land have decreased. The use of hired labor, fertilizer, herbicides, and machinery increased so that out of pocket cost increased. The harvesting method was changed, beginning about 1963, from ear corn to shelled corn that was artificially dried and mainly stored off of farms, resulting in an increased farm to market movement at harvest.

Formerly, most corn was fed on the farms where it was grown; it was estimated that 85 percent was consumed in the local area. As livestock enterprises became specialized and as exports and industrial use increased, the movement off farms increased so that by 1975 more than half of the crop was sold by farmers and was moved long distances—to terminals, export points, and to livestock feeding areas, particularly the southeastern states.

Farmers begin selling corn before the planting season in May. These are cash forward sales made for harvest delivery. Sales are made to local elevators who, in turn sell to grain merchants. The amount that is sold during the planting and growing season varies from year to year, depending on farmers' expectations about production and their reactions to existing prices. Some farmers sell at least enough corn to cover out of pocket costs. These cash purchases become long positions of the merchants and they hedge all or part of them by selling new crop futures contracts. Farmers sell more corn at harvest but hold substantial quantities on farms and in local commercial storage for sale throughout the year, finally finishing up the selling just ahead of the harvest of the next crop.

During the summer, importers in destination countries buy from U.S. exporters for fall and winter shipment. These transactions become short cash positions of U.S. exporters who hedge by buying new crop futures. The amount of this business varies from year to year and generally increased as U.S. exports increased.

Industrial processors and feed manufacturers generally have product commitments at more or less firm prices which makes them short cash corn. They thus, to some extent, cover requirements by purchases of futures contracts.

These are the underlying forces that establish the pattern of hedges that exist in futures markets. The hedges, short and long, are the means by which the commercial world of corn relates to corn futures trading.

The crop year for corn is October 1 to September 30 because corn is harvested beginning late in September. The production, stock, and use statistics are kept and published on this basis. The futures crop year is longer. Until recent years, trading in December futures was started in January, that of March futures in April, etc. However, in 1970, the trading period for most contracts was extended out to as much as seventeen months. On October 26, 1970, trading in December 1971 corn futures and March 1972 corn futures was initiated so that there were seven contracts traded at one time with the March 1972 contract given a life of seventeen months. Decisions of this nature usually depend upon the interest evidenced in the market. The number of contracts traded and the length of the trading period varies from commodity to commodity and from year to year.

Fourteen years of open interest. The open contracts and commitments of the three classes of traders are shown in Table 8. The table is divided into the ten years preceding the commodity upheavals of 1972, a swing year and the three years following the major changes. The first ten years, 1961–62 through 1970–71 are typical of the long history of corn futures trading and illustrate the risk shifting process. The last three years picture the changes that have recently taken place and that raise some interesting questions about the future. First are some comments about the first ten years.

Note first, that our year of detailed look, 1966–67, was the largest open interest—studies tend to be made when there is especially great interest in markets. Second, the average size of open interest varied from year-to-year and there was a general pattern of growth through the decade. This was related to the increased commercialization of corn production and marketing; the size

Table 8. Corn Futures: Long, Short and Net Commitments of Traders, Annual Average of Month-end Data, Crop Years 1961–74 (Million Bushels)

Year	Net Open Contracts	Reporting Hedgers			Reporting Speculators			Nonreporting Traders		
		Long	Short	Net	Long	Short	Net	Long	Short	Net
1961–62	147.1	25.6	89.6	−64.0	25.3	7.6	+17.7	96.2	49.9	+46.3
1962–63	98.7	31.2	65.1	−33.9	20.4	4.3	+16.1	47.1	29.3	+17.8
1963–64	104.5	41.6	65.1	−23.5	19.4	6.3	+13.1	43.5	33.1	+10.4
1964–65	140.4	70.5	96.1	−25.6	21.6	6.8	+14.8	48.3	37.5	+10.8
1965–66	177.9	61.8	123.4	−61.6	28.9	12.3	+16.6	87.2	42.2	+45.0
1966–67	239.8	65.2	152.9	−87.7	29.8	12.6	+17.2	144.8	74.3	+70.5
1967–68	193.8	84.1	114.5	−30.4	18.1	18.2	− .1	91.6	61.1	+30.5
1968–69	196.5	75.8	120.6	−44.8	23.6	11.3	+12.3	97.1	64.6	+32.5
1969–70	180.3	72.4	116.7	−44.3	21.8	10.2	+11.6	86.1	53.4	+32.7
1970–71	259.5	97.2	169.1	−71.9	33.3	9.9	+23.4	129.0	80.5	+48.5
Mean										
1961–70	173.9	62.5	111.3	−48.8	24.2	10.0	+14.2	87.1	52.6	+34.5
1971–72	219.2	108.3	149.5	−41.2	16.2	12.2	+ 4.0	94.7	57.5	+37.2
1972–73	357.1	227.0	260.1	−33.1	28.9	10.2	+18.8	101.2	86.8	+14.4
1973–74	334.9	215.3	232.1	−16.8	28.0	10.3	+17.7	91.6	92.5	− .9
1974–75	358.2	259.6	222.3	+37.3	22.5	15.3	+ 7.2	76.1	120.6	−44.5
Mean										
1972–74	350.1	234.0	238.2	− 4.2	26.5	11.9	+14.6	89.6	100.0	−10.4

of the crop gradually increased and an increasing proportion was sold into commercial channels.

Non-reporting traders were net long in all years and there was a tendency for them to be long more in relation to short as the open interest was larger. For the period, the ratio of long to short was 1.7 to 1.0 and they held an average of 50 percent of the long open interest. Reporting speculators were net long in all years but one and their ratio of long to short was greater than that of non-reporting traders: 2.4 to 1.0. The reporting speculators held an average of 28 percent of the long side of the market and 6 percent of the short side.

The reporting hedgers were net short and there was a greater stability in their long positions than there was in their short positions. The ratio of hedgers short-to-long was 1.8 to 1.0 and they held an average of 64 percent of short open interest.

Figure 2 compares the annual average short hedges to the net open contracts. The ratio of short hedges to open interest averaged .64 to 1.0. The relationship was close, strongly indicating cause and effect. As farmers sold corn to merchants in excess of immediate requirements and merchants hedged by selling futures, speculators entered the market on the long side; they came in as there were short hedges and did not come in when there were no short hedges. The size of the market, as measured by open interest, was determined by the amount of short hedges placed.

Figure 3 shows the seasonal pattern of the open interest of the three classi-

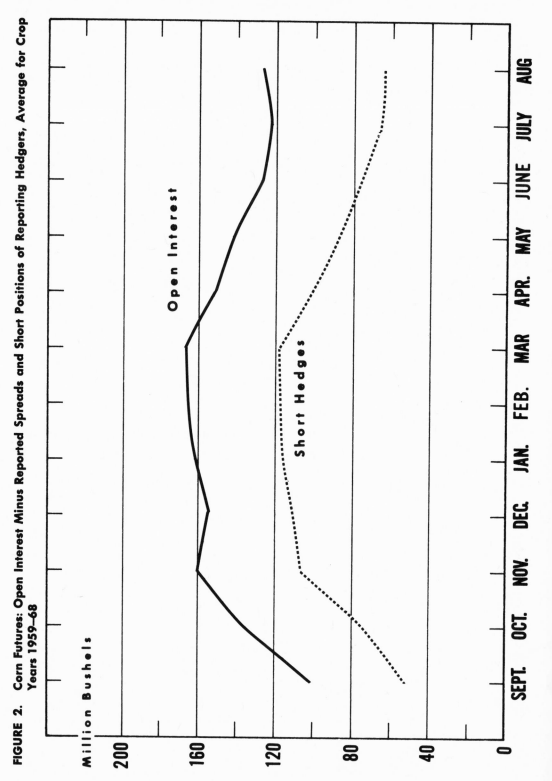

FIGURE 2. Corn Futures: Open Interest Minus Reported Spreads and Short Positions of Reporting Hedgers, Average for Crop Years 1959–68

Million Bushels

Open Interest

Short Hedges

SEPT. OCT. NOV. DEC. JAN. FEB. MAR APR. MAY JUNE JULY AUG

200 160 120 80 40 0

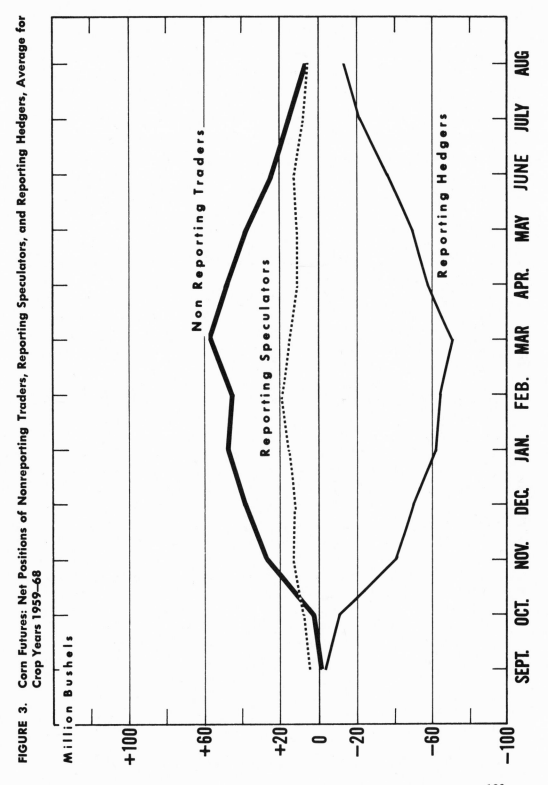

FIGURE 3. Corn Futures: Net Positions of Nonreporting Traders, Reporting Speculators, and Reporting Hedgers, Average for Crop Years 1959—68

123

fications of traders. This is the basic risk transference pattern of annually produced crops. Hedgers were net short and speculators were net long. The seasonal pattern of net short positions of hedgers followed the seasonal pattern of off-farm inventories and accommodated the hedgers. There was a marked difference in the seasonal pattern of net positions of non-reporting traders and reporting speculators. Reporting speculators assumed a substantial proportion of the risks shifted, but did not vary the level of their net long positions greatly within seasons. The non-reporting traders—predominantly speculators—varied their net long positions to accommodate the variability in the net short positions of hedgers. Farmers sold, merchants hedged, and the speculating public stood opposite.

This succession of events from farmer to speculator can be carried one step farther by comparing short hedges to off-farm stocks of grain.[3] The numbers are difficult to work with because so much off-farm stock was owned by the government for many years, but the relationship is generally fairly close. The relationship was established, not only between years, but within years as well.

The large scale speculators tend to play a balancing role in the market, more often net long, but sometimes net short, particularly at the beginning and end of the crop season. It has long been thought that the speculating public has a strong bias toward the long side of the market while the large speculators are more flexible between long and short. When the buying tendencies of the speculating public were greater than the selling tendencies of farmers, the large speculators were net short and vice versa.

The functional relationship between farmer sales and the size of the open interest is clear but we can still raise a question about the line of causation. Do speculators buy because farmers sell or do farmers sell because speculators buy? At all times there was sufficient liquidity in the corn futures trade to absorb all of the hedges that merchants placed without discernible price concession. Merchants base the prices they bid to farmers on the futures prices at which they can sell. Thus, farmers look favorably on the prices bid by speculators and sell or look unfavorably and hold. As they like the market price they sell, hedges are placed, and the open interest grows. The answer to the question seems to be that the speed of sales by farmers determines the size of the open interest but that futures prices affect the speed of farmer sales.

In the first year of big open interest, 1966–67, the crop got off to an excellent start and prices were high relative to preceding years and high relative to the government price support rate. Farmers were willing sellers early in the season —May and June—so that new crop hedges increased rapidly. But disappearance of the preceding crop was also large and the weather deteriorated during the summer so that a crop smaller than requirements was threatened. Speculators

[3] See Schonberg, J. S. *The Grain Trade,* Exposition Press, N.Y. Chapter XII: and *Marketing Grain,* North Central Regional Publication No. 176, Purdue University, Chapter III.

were willing buyers, bid the price up, and farmers continued to sell. There was a contest of judgments between farmers and speculators. The peak price was reached in mid-August at about $1.57 for July 1967 futures. It remained strong at $1.50 at the end of November when the open interest reached its high for the year. As we have seen, prices gradually declined to $1.30 by the end of June. Some farmers sold too soon and regretted it while others held too long and regretted it but speculators generally accumulated at high prices and liquidated at declining prices, suffering net losses for the season. The farmers won the contest. It is worthwhile noting that large speculators participated in the losses taken, having a wide long to short ratio (Table 8). At the end of November they were long 56.1 million bushels and short 8.0 million. They did get net short by the end of April while the speculating public remained long through July. The pros did not do so poorly as the public which may help to explain why they are professionals.

In the second year of big open interest, 1970–71, the crop got off to a good start, July weather was excellent and there were adequate carryover stocks in sight. The first of August, a unique blight struck the corn crop throughout the midwest and by the end of the first week of August it was clear that severe damage had been done. (The 1970 crop was 4.1 billion bushels compared to 4.7 billion in 1969). The price of July 1971 corn rose from $1.35 to $1.65 in eleven trading days. It remained in the $1.60 to $1.65 range until late January, 1971 before declining to $1.45 in July, 1971 as it gradually developed that the 1971 crop would be fully adequate. Short hedges increased from 71.9 million bushels at the end of July to a peak of 268.6 million at the end of November. This compared to 130.1 at the end of November the year before. Non-reporting traders long positions increased from 79.8 million at the end of July to 195.5 at the end of September which compared to 53.7 the year before. Short hedges were up 138.5 million and the long positions of the speculating public were up 141.8 million. Farmers sold the rapidly rising price and speculators bought the prospective shortages.

It should be noted that the two years were similar: prospective shortages, rising prices, farmer sales, and eventually, declining prices. Beware of the long tail of a short crop.

We should now look at the changes following the upheaval that followed 1972. Basic to it were a doubling of the exports and a large increase in both the level and volatility of prices. For the decade prior to 1972, the price of corn at Chicago was fairly stable around $1.25 per bushel. During the three crop years 1972–74 it averaged $2.55 and had a monthly average range of $1.24 to $3.70. Prior to 1972, government farm programs played a dominant role in the price of corn so that price variation and the need to shift risks were much less than in the subsequent period.

The net open contracts in the second period were twice the average of the first period; the size of the market doubled. Short hedges increased a like amount, 2.1 times. There was increasing need to shift risks so that there were more hedges and a proportionate increase in open interest; the relationship and lines of causation remained intact.

Between the two periods, the average positions of reporting speculators changed very little. Their risk exposure was substantially greater because of increased price volatility and their capital requirements were much greater because of increased risk exposure and margin requirements. They were a much smaller proportion of the total market: 9.8 percent in the first period and 5.5 percent in the second.

Non-reporting traders had the same size average positions in the second period as the first. They essentially doubled their short position so that they went from long by a wide margin to short by ten percent. Their share of the total market decreased from 40.2 percent to 27.1 percent. The risk bearing function performed by the speculating public was more than taken over by the importers in destination countries. They accommodated and adjusted to the changed circumstances by shifting to a net short position. It may well be that the long side bias of the speculating public is more imagined than real or that they lost their bias as time passed.

The most significant change between the two periods was the decreasing importance of speculation and the increasing matching of producers long side risks with the long hedges of exporters.

We can sum up and generalize from all of this. Markets relate back to and are built upon risk shifting. Their size is a function of supplies in hedgeable position: they develop when there are risks to be shifted and fail to develop when there are not. Speculators come in when they are needed to assume risks and do not enter when they are not needed. There is a margin of speculative liquidity over and above the hedges that is necessary to get speculative participation but this margin is a moderate proportion of the open interest. This is the standard doctrine, chapter and verse. Gray[4] puts it thus: "The importance of hedging is best expressed in the categorical statement that futures trading depends upon hedging. Evidence of this dependence abounds in the statistics of commodity markets, and the habitué of the markets comes against such a constant stream of first-hand evidence that he takes the relationship for granted. Study the open interest in any commodity futures contract and you obtain insight into the economics of the commodity, so strong and general is the relationship. Find two commodities for which the open interest pattern differs markedly and consistently and you will find that their production and distribution differs in such a way as to account for the contrasting open-interest patterns."

[4] Baaken, Gray, Paul, Hieronymus, *Futures Trading Seminar,* Vol. I, Mimir, Madison, Wis., 1960.

Some Reservations. This was all to the good, and life was simple, but then came pork bellies. As we have seen, the fastest gaining of the futures markets during the 1960's was pork bellies, traded on the Chicago Mercantile Exchange. Trading was started in 1961 and languished for three years until taking off in 1964. It has since been a star performer. It breaks the rules that we have so carefully derived. Volume of trading and open interest far exceed risk shifting requirements. The average stocks of frozen pork bellies and open interest (both expressed as contracts of 36,000 pounds), fiscal years, were:

Year	Stocks	Open Contracts
1961–62	1,414	68
1962–63	1,818	61
1963–64	2,382	81
1964–65	2,111	5,246
1965–66	961	9,250
1966–67	1,454	10,071
1967–68	1,964	12,861
1968–69	1,552	14,794
1969–70	1,270	15,617
1970–71	1,921	14,407
1971–72	2,587	18,475
1972–73	1,245	14,454

The market started slowly, grew like crazy, and then grew into one of the most popular of speculative mediums.

Pork belly trading came under the jurisdiction of the Commodity Exchange Authority in 1968 and, thus, information of reporting traders became available.

Stocks of frozen pork bellies, reported short hedges, and net open interest, annual averages were:

Year	Stocks	Short Hedges	Net Open Interest	Percent Speculative
1969–70	1,270	721	12,305	95.3
1970–71	1,922	924	11,434	92.3
1971–72	2,587	1,209	13,358	93.9
1972–73	1,245	1,080	12,112	93.9

In the first three years, approximately one-half of the stocks of pork bellies were hedged. These were years of relatively low belly prices. In the fourth year an average of 87 percent of stocks were hedged. These percentages of stocks hedged are unusually high compared to other markets (as we shall subsequently see, 10 percent is a more normal amount). Thus the pork belly market was a hedging medium. But the ratio of net open interest to short hedges was completely outside of the data of other futures markets. A huge speculative open interest was built on the hedges so that the market was about 95 percent speculative. Not only did speculators move in to absorb hedges, but many more came in as well.

A special survey[5] of the positions of all traders was made on January 31, 1969. The market was highly speculative:

		Positions	
Classification	*Number Traders*	*Long*	*Short*
Speculative	5,722	18,256	16,773
Hedging	113	682	2,173
Total	5,835	18,938	18,946

The occupational distribution was comparable to that shown in the special survey of corn futures trading. There were 357 speculators whose occupations were closely related to the meat industry and 5,365 members of the general public—594 farmers, 306 physicians, 125 lawyers, 381 chemists and engineers, 289 salesmen, 164 craftsmen, 210 housewives, 54 students, and 391 retired people. There were 61 hedgers closely related to the meat industry and 52 hedgers from the general public. Thirty of the general public hedgers were farmers who were long 166 contracts and short 167. It is doubtful that any farmers had either long or short positions in cash pork bellies opposite the alleged hedging positions. If we are quite loose with our definition of hedging we can presume that the farmer short hedges were opposite to actual hogs the farmers were raising, but how to rationalize the long farmer hedges defies imagination. The market was probably even more speculative than the data shows. The geographical distribution of traders was comparable to that of corn—world-wide but with a tendency toward concentration in the midwest.

The positions of small-scale speculators were predominantly long and those of large-scale speculators predominantly short:

	Commitments	
Size in Contracts	*Long Only*	*Short Only*
1–4	3,772	2,047
1–24	2,884	2,189
25–49	483	581
50–99	348	1,005
100–149	467	660
150–up	421	410
Total	8,375	6,892

While the structure of the pork belly futures market was predominantly speculator against speculator there was also an element of small-scale speculator versus large-scale speculator present. The price of July pork belly futures rose from 33.25 cents per pound on January 31, 1969 to 40.80 cents on May 29.

[5] *Trading in Frozen Pork Bellies*, CEA, USDA, October, 1969.

Thus, if the large and small traders maintained their relative long and short positions, the small traders got the better of the contest.

The pork belly market is the only U.S. futures market for which data are available in which speculation so greatly predominates. The Azuki bean market in Japan appears to have the same general characteristics. In looking at the rapid growth of silver futures trading the U.S. one must wonder about the role of hedging.

It would seem that we should modify our standard doctrine. It appears that the size of markets is generally limited to the risks that need to be carried, but such is not always the case. Speculation can far exceed hedging. The limitation of market risks to the general size of need to carry risks is a peculiar and imponderable phenomenon. Speculators couldn't care less about the economic need to absorb hedges. They are in the game of trading to make money, buying when they think that the price will rise, and selling when they think it will decline. Whether they make money from the short positions of hedgers or from other speculators is a matter of complete indifference. It is thus with some relief that we find an exception to the rule.

The second part of our doctrine says that when there are risks that need to be shifted, markets develop and the necessary speculators come forth to absorb them. This is how markets originated and developed and is a characteristic of active futures markets. But it may be that there are risk problems for which markets have not developed or have not prospered when organized. We should keep open the possibility that the world of futures trading is far too small to accomplish the necessary job of risk assumption.

A couple of examples are suggestive. We earlier noted that there is a ham futures market, started in 1964, in which trading has languished. Every economic case that can be made for trading pork bellies can be made for trading hams. On the basis of stocks and price variability it should do quite as well. Perhaps belly trading will decline or ham trading will increase.

Sorghum grain is a major crop in the U.S. and production increased rapidly during the period 1950 to 1975. Production in 1975 was 13% as great as that of corn. It moves extensively in export and in commercial feed channels. Prices are as variable as those of corn. A futures market was started in Chicago in the 1950's but was unsuccessful. There was no trading after 1964 (Table 2, Chapter 2). However, trading was resumed in 1971 at the Chicago Board of Trade and in 1971 started at the Chicago Mercantile Exchange. (Neither market was active in 1975.) Grain sorghums futures have been traded at Kansas City for many years without success.

CHAPTER 7

Equity Financing

In the preceding chapter the processes by which risks of losses resulting from changes in price are shifted from one group of people to another were described. It is clear that the need to shift risks was the original impetus for the development of the markets and that, for more than a century, hedging of price risks has been the dominant force in determining the size of the markets and the fluctuations in the level of trading. However, this description does not explain why the activity takes place; why some businessmen involved in commodity production, marketing, and use have a compulsion to hedge risks while others do not. To observe the practice is useful and adequate for understanding the past and present. It is necessary to inquire into the motivations of hedgers and the institutional arrangements lying behind the hedging activity if we are to fully understand the why of that which has taken place and to make progress in charting the course that lies ahead.

Financial Instrument

A futures contract is a financial instrument and futures trading is a financial institution engaged in gathering and using equity capital. It is not a financial institution in the sense of a bank in which money is received from one group of people and loaned to another. Rather, it is a means by which loans made by banks or operating money otherwise secured by businesses is guaranteed against loss. When bank loans, or capital from any other source, can be protected from part or all of potential losses they are more readily forthcoming than when they cannot. Operating businesses acquire debts that they add to their own net worth to build a total operating capital structure. By this process, they can control capital without owning it and the people from whom they obtain funds can own capital without administering its use. The financial system is the means by which the ownership of real capital is separated from its control. Futures markets are a part of the system. In this context, a futures contract is the exchange of a monetary obligation, or debt, for a commodity obligation, or debt. The long speculator exchanges his own monetary obligation to pay for the commodity for the obligation of the hedger to deliver the physical commodity. The short speculator exchanges a monetary obligation to buy and deliver for the commodity obligation of the hedger to accept and use the commodity. Thus, the hedgers remove themselves from financial debts by substituting commodity debts for them. The financial obligations are assumed by the speculators.

This process of debt exchange through the financial system enables resources to be used more productively and it is from this that the social benefits of the financial system flow. The consolidation of resources through the exchange of debt enables increased productivity associated with large scale enterprises. The ownership of scarce resources is widely diffused and, if it were not possible to consolidate their control, production would be quite as diffused as ownership. This would result in small-scale production, limited technological advance, and less total productivity. Control of capital needs to be consolidated into the hands of the people who can use it most efficiently and people who can operate businesses most efficiently need access to capital beyond their own equity.

In the last chapter we tended to look on speculators as the people who accommodated the hedgers in a null fashion, appearing when and only as needed. As we turn to borrowing money from banks to finance stored inventories, we tend to merely note that warehousemen who have their inventories hedged can borrow more money than those who don't. This does not do justice to the speculator. By committing his wealth to commodity futures he influences the warehousing activity and its cost, and, thus, becomes an important financier.

Financing Process

The process by which equity capital is raised through futures trading can best be seen by some examples. First, the importance of hedging in financing stored inventories of grain has long been recognized. Terminal elevator operators, cotton merchants, grain processors, and, to a lesser extent, country grain warehousemen are often able to borrow in excess of 90 percent of the value of stored commodities at prime rates of interest, providing the inventories are offset by short positions in futures markets. Warehouse receipts serve as collateral for the loans so that the general balance sheet and liquidity of the company are not affected by the inventory ownership except for the small difference between the value of the cash commodity and the amount of the loan. In some cases in which the capital position of the company is so fully extended before borrowing to buy inventory that the commodity loan would restrict financing of noninventory activities, separate warehouse companies are established or a system of field warehousing is used. In such cases the commodity inventory does not enter the balance sheet.

The inventory loans are sometimes worked up to quite high levels. Banks frequently loan the margin deposit on the futures transactions as well as a high proportion of the current value of the inventory. Or, they loan the full value of the inventory on the basis that the margin deposit is quite enough protection. As we shall see when we consider hedging operations, the value of stored commodities tends to increase in relation to the futures price as the storage season progresses. For example, corn in country locations may sell 40 cents under the July futures price at harvest and typically sell for 5 cents under the July on July 1. There is thus a highly probable 35 cent storage profit in a hedging operation. Armed with this information, the country elevator operator may go to his banker and ask for the full purchase price of the corn, the margin requirements, and a part of the storage earnings and thus finance part of his operating costs in addition to the inventory. Bankers are not inclined to go so far, but the operator may get away with the full purchase price and margin plus a promise of the storage earnings as they accrue.

As time passes the price of the commodity, hence, the market value of the warehouse receipts, changes. If the price goes down, the bank, reasonably, wants part of its money. It is readily available out of the increased value of the short futures position. The warehouseman asks his commission futures merchant for the money the bank wants. If the price goes up, the short futures position shows a loss and the commission house calls for margin. The value of the warehouse receipts has increased and the additional margin is forthcoming from the banker.

The point of this is that ordinary bank financing is readily available for purchase and storage of hedged inventories. This is not the case for unhedged inventories. The transaction is put on the balance sheet and a normal liquidity margin is required. The proportion of the loan may be sixty percent or so—certainly, a great deal less than for hedged inventories. The equity capital that the operator must furnish is very much less for hedged than for unhedged inventory. The uncertainty of the warehouseman's return is reduced by hedging but the total uncertainty of the venture is not. The fact remains that the market value of the commodity may decline so that the return to storage may be less than zero or it may increase so that the return is much more than the cost of storage. Commodity price variations are great relative to the cost of storage. Losses are taken out of someone's equity and gains are paid into someone's equity. As we have seen, on the other end of the hedges stand the speculators. The flow of funds from commission house to warehouseman to bank or from bank to warehouseman to commission house as prices decline or increase, flows further to the clearing house and from then on to the speculators, decreasing or increasing their equity. The speculator is thus a financier, furnishing the equity capital required to absorb changes in price level.

This process of financing is roundabout and specialized. It would be theoretically possible for the warehousemen to go directly to individuals for the money, selling them warehouse receipts and charging them storage. The individuals would, in turn, go to banks and borrow, on the basis of their net worth, the money to buy receipts. It would be a clumsy system with banks making many small loans to speculators instead of a few large loans to hedgers (note the relative size of positions of hedgers and speculators shown in Chapter 6). More importantly, it would have little attraction to speculators because they would be furnishing the total of the funds rather than the equity necessary to finance price variations. Further, it is difficult to visualize such a scheme sufficiently sophisticated to afford liquidity comparable to that of futures trading. More likely, the warehousemen would reorganize the financial structure of their businesses in a way that would make the assumption of equity financing possible.

As developed in Chapter 4, futures markets originated out of a need by country merchants for equity capital just as egg warehousemen turned to their friends for the equity capital to carry inventories. It is worth noting they did not necessarily lack the net worth to obtain funds from the banking system; in the case of eggs, net worth was more often adequate than not. They simply preferred not to endanger their capital structure to the extent they judged the price risks of a full inventory would endanger it. The system evolved over a long period of time as the most attractive among the alternative ways of gaining access to equity capital.

A second example relates to cattle feeding. The production of market beef is a two stage process. The animals are raised from breeding herds on the grazing lands of the west and south and moved into specialized feeding yards or on to grain producing farms for further growth and fattening. The traditional pattern was from the forage producing lands of the plains and mountain states to the corn production lands of the central states, particularly Iowa and Illinois, and then on to the central markets for slaughter and shipment to eastern consumption markets. The farmers buy feeder cattle, feed them grain and other concentrates, and sell them for slaughter. Their profits and losses depend on their skills in feeding cattle and on the price of fat cattle in relation to the cost of feeder cattle and the cost of feed. The feeding process takes time (up to 12 months and an average of about 6) and the price of fat cattle fluctuates over wide ranges. Thus, cattle feeders are exposed to substantial amounts of risk unless they develop some kind of a risk shifting program.

In this traditional feeding process, the farmers are part cattle feeder and part cattle speculator. Some follow the same pattern, year in and year out, buying the same size and quality of feeders at the same season each year and feeding them to the same weight and quality for sale. For these people, variations in the feeding margin average out over a number of production cycles so that, in the long run, they get the industry average returns (plus or minus their own technological skills in relation to those of the industry). But the long run may be several years so that a large reserve of equity capital is necessary for survival. These people are speculative nulls. Most cattle feeders, however, vary their operations on the basis of existing and expected prices and price relationships, becoming active participants in the speculative game. They buy different sizes, kinds, and qualities of cattle and sell at different weights and qualities in different production cycles. At times, they leave their lots empty and sell part of the feed supplies that they have produced on their farms, and at other times, they increase the size of their operations and buy additional feed. The extent to which programs are varied differs greatly within the cattle feeding fraternity. Some of the members are more speculator than feeder.

In the main, the equity base of the traditional, midwest cattle feeders is large enough that they can readily absorb the risks associated with the business and can command the necessary capital to finance the operations.

Starting in the latter 1950's the industry changed rather dramatically. Beef production nearly doubled from the early 1950's to 1975. Part of the increase was the result of increasing cattle numbers, but a substantial part of it was the result of putting more cattle through the feeding process so that slaughter weights were increased. Many of the small feeding operations went out of business. Large scale, commercial feedlots were developed. By 1968, the proportion of cattle fed in the traditional, small operation had decreased to about one-half and the other half was fed in commercial feedlots (1,000 or more head per year). Nineteen of these fed more than 32,000 head per year. The heaviest concentration was in yards of 8 to 32 thousand.

The increase in scale resulted in a new set of risk and financing problems. The equities of the firms would not support risks associated with price variability nor did the firms want to take as large risks as they could. The practice of custom feeding developed, in which the cattle are owned by someone other than the feedlot and the feedlot is paid per pound of gain or feed cost plus overhead. The risking-financing activities are carried by someone other than the feedlot. The cattle owners are speculators. By the late 1960's, approximately one-half of the cattle on feed in commercial feedlots were custom fed.

The cattle custom fed are owned by ranchers, cattle feeders, meat packers, livestock marketing agencies, and investors. Many of the cattle feeders and investors use the operation in part as an investment and in part as an income tax shelter. They obtain leverage by borrowing from banks. The price of cattle followed a generally upward path from $25 per hundred weight in 1960 to an average of $36 in 1972 and to a peak of $60 in the summer of 1973. The investors pyramided successfully. The price of cattle collapsed in 1973. The inventory value of all cattle and calves in the U.S. decreased from $40 billion on January 1, 1973 to $20 billion on January 1, 1974. Heavy losses were taken and many loans could not be repaid to banks. The tax shelters work well in the context of tax avoidance, but poorly in the context of preserving income.

It was in this context that futures trading in live cattle was started in 1964. It grew rapidly to an average open interest of 18,265 contracts of 40,000 pounds each (38 fat cattle) in fiscal 1968–69. The average open contracts and reported short hedges were:

Fiscal Year	Open Interest	Short Hedges
1968–69	18,265	6,982
1969–70	21,564	4,839
1970–71	13,638	3,709
1971–72	18,752	4,233
1972–73	28,217	8,494
1973–74	32,830	7,827
1974–75	26,434	11,320

The impact of the price decline of 1973–74 is readily apparent in the increase in short hedges. The feedlot operators shifted from individual investors to the futures market as sources of equity capital. The bankers were a strong force in the shift. When their loans to feedlot operators are secured by futures contracts, they avoid the credit risks that were troublesome and in some cases, ruinous, in 1973–74. The equity capital is furnished by the speculators in futures markets.

Pyramiding of Capital

The command of resources can be greatly increased by hedging inventory risks or by pricing finished product before operating costs are committed. A loan rate of 90 percent on hedged inventory enables a firm with $1,000 of equity capital to contract and use, in a storage and merchandising activity, $10,000 worth of a commodity. A loan rate of 60 percent is two thirds as much, however, it enables the control of only $2,500 of inventory. Thus, the increase in the borrowing rate from 60 to 90 percent enables the control of four times as much capital. This is illustrated here at a 60 to 90 increase so that the numbers remain finite. As we have seen, a 60 to 100 increase is feasible in which case the equity capital requirement for price protection is zero and the multiplier is infinite. Constraints on the growth of the business are from sources other than equity capital for inventory control.

The impact of equity financing through fixing sales prices of products ahead of production is equally impressive. Suppose that a corn producer is operating 1,000 acres and is contemplating expanding to 2,500 acres by leasing additional land. His lease cost is $100 and his operating cost other than return on fixed investment in machinery and equipment is $100 per acre, his anticipated yield is

100 bushels, and the net price that can be obtained is $2.50 per bushel. He thus has a prospective operating margin of 50 cents or a total of $125,000 compared to a current $50,000. He will use up virtually all of his balance sheet liquidity in the purchase of additional equipment. He has to furnish a bank guarantee for payment of the lease. How much of his own equity must he hold for operational costs? It depends on the percentage loan. Price vulnerable, the bank may loan 60 percent, requiring $100,000 of operator equity but not price vulnerable the bank may go 90 percent, requiring only $25,000. This latter amount is not really a price vulnerability equity but rather a guarantee of the organization and management skills of the operator in the production process—his technical ability. If his past performance record is excellent, the bank may loan the whole of the operational cost and the lease guarantee.

The ability to obtain the operating capital is not the only consideration in fixing sales prices. It protects the operator from his own mistakes. The market may not offer a price as high as $2.50, making the expansion less attractive or possibly unprofitable. The operator may optimistically—as is the nature of farmers—expect the price to eventually turn out to be $2.50, commit his own equity, and fail. If the futures market won't furnish the equity and he can't otherwise obtain it, he the operator, is protected.

More importantly, the process protects the equity capital of the operator. He may not elect to make the expansion if it must be done at the hazard of his equity. He may be willing to hazard his net worth on his ability as a corn producer but not as a corn speculator, especially if he recognizes that he is tied to the long side of a speculation with no flexibility. He would be long 250,000 bushels of corn, throughout the production period and thus a speculator on the price of corn. The old 100,000 bushel level may be more attractive. If this is the case, the expansion may not be made. Equity capital from futures markets may affect the business structure and efficiency of corn production. This is but one example. Others can be drawn from all commodities actively traded.

Attraction of the Speculator

There is something ridiculous about explaining to a chemist or a private detective that he, fine and noble entrepreneur, is furnishing the equity capital to feed cattle or produce plywood. Told, he is apt to reply, "Who, me? I'm just trying to make a fast buck in a market where I can get high leverage on money that I am willing to lose (heaven forbid)." Shades of Adam Smith's invisible hand.

This process of equity capital flow from speculative markets is an example of commercial specialization among financial institutions. The process of gathering up money is separated from hazarding equity. One is the business of the banking system while the other is that of speculators.

The division and specialization is the thing that attracts speculators. Had they to furnish the whole of the operating capital to produce corn or buy feeder cattle there would be little attraction. They are only interested in furnishing the equity and taking the risks. A high proportion of commodity inventories for which futures markets exist are hedged. But only a small part of the production of corn, cattle, plywood, orange juice, etc. are forward priced in futures markets; the equity capital is otherwise forthcoming. How good the futures system is compared to others is a question that can only be answered after more of market operation has been considered. As we proceed, we will note that the cost of equity capital is very near zero and more likely negative than positive. A zero or negative interest rate on high risk capital compared to a bank interest rate on nonrisk capital is an interesting anomaly. Such is the behavior of speculators.

CHAPTER 8

Speculative Pricing

The Speculation Controversy

The history of futures trading in the 19th century was quite as much, if not more, about rampant and enthusiastic speculation as it was about risk shifting. The risk shifters sought out the speculators at the outset but as soon as the speculators learned of the game they rushed in and took over. The growth of futures trading from 1960 to 1975 was, necessarily, an increase in speculation. Our review of the open interest in corn indicated that, while the pattern of hedging dominated the market and appeared to determine the amount of speculation, there was a large amount of speculator against speculator. One must look at the structure of the open interest in pork belly futures and conclude the market was mostly about speculation.

The literature of futures trading is, in large measure, dominated by discussions of the desirability of speculation and its effects, some favorable and some unfavorable. Few can resist evaluation. The long public controversy has hinged around this point. Emery[1] discussed the difference between speculation and gambling at length before stating the case for speculation. Baer and Saxon[2] used most of their chapter on speculation for evaluation and defense. The key attacks on onion futures trading that finally resulted in prohibition were related to "excessive speculation." Most defenses of speculation in futures markets have been directed toward the need for speculators to carry risks. It is with a sigh of relief that authors find the close relationship between short hedges and long speculative positions and thus, establish that speculation does not greatly exceed the minimum necessary to absorb risks of prudent businessmen.

[1] Op. cit. Chap. IV.
[2] Op. cit. Chap. III.

Some of the attacks are more fun. Emery[3] quotes an English writer, "The option, future, and settlement systems which have been introduced into various forms of produce and food products, with the result that gradual misery and ruin have entailed all classes." And a broker in the U.S., "The New York Stock Exchange, which is the soul, the motive power of Wall Street, is an evil in the land, a danger to private wealth, a disturbing force in general business, and a foe to public morals. . . . The Chicago Board of Trade is a den of speculators whose operations are even more permissive." There was this exchange in Senate Hearings:[4] Senator Norris. "You would call that gambling?" Mr. Vesecky. "You might call it gambling or speculation." Senator Norris. "I am not one who objects to speculation in a modified way. I think that it is probably legitimate. I think, as a matter of fact, that when a man buys wheat for future delivery in a sense he is a speculator because he doesn't know what the price is going to be when the time comes, but if he buys without reference to the handling of the commodity itself, just goes in and buys and sells without reference to anything, is he a hedger then or a gambler?" Mr. Vesecky. "He is not a hedger at all. He is either politely called a speculator or otherwise might be called a gambler, which ever one you want to call him." Senator Norris. "If that were prohibited by law, or prevented in any way, your idea is that it will have a beneficial effect upon the market generally?" Mr. Vesecky. "I think if excessive speculation, excessive long lines or short lines—either one—and excessive sales and purchases on any one day are limited or prohibited, that it will have a beneficial effect on the market. It was proven several times during this last big flurry in July, 1933 that it was the creation of these long lines at one time that made the bad break. At other times, the big short lines made the bad break."

Much of the historical controversy about commodity speculation, particularly in futures, has related to a confusion of speculation and gambling. Gambling is almost universally condemned as wasteful and as working great evil on the gambler himself. Commodity speculation has been said, many, many times, to be the "biggest gamble of them all." It is said that speculation is merely gambling, without reference to actual trade, except that it consists of betting on the course of prices. This was obviously the case with bucket shops. Speculation and gambling are alike in several ways. Both depend upon uncertainties. Both involve the risk of loss for the sake of possible gain. The occurrence of certain events results in losses to one player and gains to another while other events have the opposite result. Both may involve the careful calculation of probabilities and development of forecasts or both may be based on pure chance.

The essential distinctions made in defense of speculation generally fall along

---

[3] Op. cit. p. 97.

[4] _____ Committee on Agriculture and Forestry, U.S. Senate, Seventy Fourth Congress on H.R. 6772, April 1936.

two lines: 1. Gambling involves the creation of risks that would not otherwise exist while speculation involves the assumption of necessary and unavoidable risks of commerce, and 2. In every futures transaction, the speculator incurs the duties and acquires the rights of a holder of property and thus is an integral part of commerce. Whether the impact of his activities is "good" or "bad" is neither here nor there—they are inevitable and necessary. Both of these distinctions are fairly easy to dispute. Gambling is an integral part of the commerce of the economy, certainly that of the state of Nevada. A ticket in the Irish Sweepstakes is a property right. Much of the argument is moralistic which is not relevant to economics. Good or bad, gambling is an economic activity just as speculation is an economic activity.

A good example of this attitude is found in some comments of The Joint Committee of the Economic Report (December, 1947). Mr. Mehl, who was the administrator of The Commodity Exchange Authority, said, "I believe that if we are to maintain the present system of marketing, with the incident of hedging which enables processors and dealers to transfer the price risk from their shoulders to speculators who are willing to assume these risks, we will have to tolerate some degree of speculative trading in order to take up the slack between the merchant and processor who wants to buy for hedging purposes, and the one who wants to sell for hedging purposes." In immediate response, Representative Rich said, "I am not interested in trying in any way to stop legitimate business; I want that to proceed. But I thought if there was anything that you could suggest to our Committee whereby we might, from your experience, stop speculation, pure and simple, and let legitimate trade go on, I wish you would make that recommendation."

This fairly dominant point of view reflects the recognition of the importance and usefulness of futures trading in the transference of risk and the raising of equity capital but also reflects a widespread conviction that the price effects of speculation are disruptive of trade and commerce. More importantly, it reflects a widespread lack of recognition of the role of speculation in price formation and, for that matter, a lack of recognition of the role of prices in the economic processes. Our purpose here is to describe the speculative pricing function and the role of speculators in price formation.

Prices have several essential functions to perform in a competitive economic system. The lists compiled vary among authors but generally include, (1) The allocation of productive resources, (2) Determination of the amount and kind of product, (3) Direction of inventory accumulation and liquidation, (4) Distribution of products among people and places, and (5) Distribution of the rewards for production among productive resources. Individual prices combine into a set of price relationships that determine production and distribution. There is one and only one set of prices and price relationships that will result in a balanced production and use; that will equate supplies and demands. This is the equilibrium price or set of prices. In a dynamic economy, equilibrium is never achieved—something is always out of balance. The underlying conditions affecting supplies and requirements are in a constant state of flux, resulting in constantly changing prices and price relationships.

There is a major element of futurity in prices. Investments made today affect production tomorrow and throughout the life of the investment. Inventories are accumulated or liquidated today in anticipation of tomorrow's requirements. Consumers spend all or more than their incomes or forego consumption until a later time, depending upon their expectations about the future. The implementation of expectations results in the establishment of prices that apply not only to the present but to the future as well. Today's prices are a function of expectations about the future as well as today's spot market situation. Forward prices are established on the basis of expectations about the situation and prices that will exist in the future.

The future is unknown and uncertain. *To speculate is to contemplate the future, reach conclusions about the shape of things to come, and to act on the basis of these expectations; in short, to buy now in anticipation of higher prices or to sell now in anticipation of lower prices.*

In connection with futures trading we are concerned with speculation in stored commodities and with speculation in production of commodities of which there are not significant inventories.

Stored Commodities

Throughout its long history, futures trading has been primarily associated with commodities having major seasonal patterns of production and inventory accumulation and liquidation. Prices of seasonally produced commodities are speculative. The supply that is harvested during a short period of time must be made to last until the next crop is available. At the same time, the supply must be used down to a small carryover going into the following year. This job of rationing the supply is a function of price. There is one and only one average price that will make the supply just clear the market. If the price is held at higher levels, some of the users will be priced out of the market and there will be more than a necessary carryover. If the price is held at lower than the equilibrium level, additional users will be drawn into the market and the supply will not last until the next harvest year.

Rationing and Supply. When allowed to work, market prices effectively accomplish the necessary job of rationing. No matter how short the crop, we never run out. Enough users get priced out of the market to leave something when the new corp is harvested. No matter how large the crop, new users are brought into the market by bargain prices; and even though there is a substantial carryover, the expanded use makes an inventory appear desirable, building a supply for the next year.

From this explanation it is apparent that at all times there are two kinds of demands. One is demand for current use and the other is demand for inventory to be used at some time in the future. If it appears that the supply is short at the current price, the demand for inventory increases. The bidding up of prices slows down the rate of use. If it appears that the supply is so large that it will not be used before the next harvest at the current price, the demand for inventory decreases and reduced prices speed up the rate of use.

At the same time, there are two kinds of supply: one is corporeal or physical inventory and the other incorporeal or speculative short sales. As prices reach levels which the inventory holders believe are high enough to make the existing supply last until new crop harvest, they sell. This situation prevails whether it be for unhedged cash commodity or for hedges held by speculative longs. Thus, the inventory holders become inventory suppliers. Speculators who judge that current prices are higher than necessary to make the existing inventory last until the new crop make contracts for deferred delivery of actual grain. They reason that the prevailing high prices will discourage utilization and result in an undesirable carryover. They are induced to acquire and furnish commodity they do not have. They increase the available incorporeal supply of the commodity which may later result in deferred delivery. As time passes and the contracts become current, they must either buy the contracts back or acquire physical commodity for delivery. Either action increases the current market supply and reduces the deferred supply.

Maintaining Reserves. Some commodities such as potatoes and onions cannot be effectively carried from one crop year to the next. As the harvest approaches, the demand for inventory of old crop decreases until it is zero at the beginning of new crop harvest. The speculative game of the inventory holders is to let the inventories run out with precision but not one day too soon. This leads to some fascinating pricing problems of which onions are one outstanding example. The demand for onions is highly inelastic so that, in the case of a short supply, the price may be very high. Yet when new crop onions become available, the old crop onions become, literally, garbage and valueless. The timing of new crop harvest is not precisely determinable as it may be delayed by cold, wet weather. The game is to have onions until the last day but then be out. This accounts for the wild fluctuations in onion prices at the tag end of the season.

Pricing problems occur at the end of crop years for storable crops as well. The 1964 crop of soybeans was small and had to be severely rationed with high prices. The 1965 crop prospects were favorable so that supplies appeared adequate at lower prices. Thus, the inventory holders tried to make their inventories run out the day that harvest started. It was a good plan, but just as harvest got under way, the rains came and the price of old crop rose sharply. As soon as harvest could be resumed, the prices came together sharply. Old and new crop prices by weeks were:

	Old Crop	*New Crop*
August 20	$2.58	$2.37
August 27	2.62	2.40
Sept. 3	2.75	2.41
Sept. 10	2.55	2.39
Sept. 14	2.80	2.41
Sept. 24	2.58	2.41
Oct. 1	2.38	2.38

There were comparable gyrations in the September futures prices which was blamed on speculation. The responsibility was properly placed. The market was speculating about when the crop would mature and the rains stop and just what price would be required to make the rapidly dwindling supplies last.

For the more storable commodities such as grain, the inventory liquidation is more complex. Speculators must establish a desirable carryover. On one hand, as old crop supplies are relatively large and prospective new crop supplies are relatively small, the demand for the old crop increases and a carryover is generated. On the other hand, as we move from a short crop year to a large crop year, inventory demand is reduced and supplies are allowed to decline toward zero.

Thus, a part of the speculative game is the establishment of an appropriate size reserve held in anticipation of later demand increases, supply decreases and unforeseeable contingencies. The market must weigh the cost of carrying stocks against the prospective value at a future time. It must also measure the utility of a reserve supply to meet unforeseen events such as droughts, wars, increased foreign demand, and like exigencies. The market carries forward the amounts it judges appropriate, the cost of carrying taken into account; that is, the amounts that speculators think profitable.

Balance of Judgment. At any given time price is the result of an interplay of two sets of demand and supply forces. It strives to strike a balance between these forces. Thus, in the short run, the resulting price depends on the decision of inventory holders and suppliers. The question that the inventory holders and suppliers ask is simple: "Shall I hold or sell?" The answers depend upon whether they think the price is going up or down. The inventory holders and suppliers must forecast prices. They must look ahead and appraise the effect on price of changes in supply and in requirements for various uses. This is a complicated and difficult job as is well known to all who have tried to un-scramble the price outlook. The equilibrium price is uncertain. After the season has been completed, all of the prices for the year can be averaged and the equilibrium price established but in the meantime, all of the holders and suppliers of inventory are attempting to forecast what the equilibrium price will finally turn out to have been.

At any given time the price at which inventories are either held out of use or supplied for use is the result of striking a balance of judgments of the holders and suppliers of inventory. On the one side the people who think the price is going down will sell; if the consensus is that the price is going down, selling quickly puts it down, and vice versa. All things that are expected to affect the price in the future are quickly discounted. The current price then reflects the composite judgment of the traders in forecasting the equilibrium price. The composite judgment of all of the market participants is that the equilibrium has been found and that prices will not change. But none of the individuals who make up the composite think that the equilibrium has been reached, else they would not have a position.

Obviously, the composite is always wrong. Prices do change, almost never remaining constant, even from one day to the next. This is because some things are not yet foreseeable, because the market does not foresee all things that are foreseeable, and because the market does not weigh properly all of the things it does foresee. If the market were omniscient, able to foresee all things and weigh them properly, the price would never change except seasonally to reflect carrying costs. *Changes in price level, thus, are the result of speculative error.*

The owners of inventory are speculators. They have taken a position at the risk of loss and in the hope of profit. He who holds an inventory is speculating. He is pitting his judgment about the direction of price change against that of the market by deciding to hold rather than sell. If he is right, he makes money; if wrong, he loses.

In the case of agricultural commodities, the most important speculators are farmers. At any given time they hold more of the inventory than other group and not many of them hedge as is clear from the anatomy of the corn market. Probably the second most important inventory controlling group are speculators in futures markets. A high proportion of the inventories not owned by farmers are hedged in futures just as a high proportion of the cash commodities sold for future delivery but not bought are hedged by long positions in futures. The speculators are long the amount the hedgers are short and short the amount the hedges are long. Hedgers, being long cash and short futures or vice versa do nothing more than act as custodians. As far as prices are concerned, they are nulls—eunuchs, fit only to guard the harem. They act, in their storage operations, in response to basis behavior, but fundamentally their actions are determined by the speculators whose actions influence the basis that influence hedgers. Until users outbid the speculators for the stored commodity, hedgers must hold grain in store. The hedgers buy back their short futures contracts so they can sell the cash commodities to users.

Commodities in Production

Until the mid-1960's almost the whole of futures trading related to hedging and speculation in stored commodities and the speculative pricing function to regulation of the rate of use of inventories. As we have seen, it was generally accepted that only those commodities with a high degree of storability were eligible for trading in futures markets. But this changed with the advent of trading in live cattle, live hogs, fresh eggs and broilers. While the older function of hedging and pricing stored inventories of commodities with seasonal production patterns remains, a new function of forward pricing commodities not yet produced has been added. Farmers sell enough corn to cover out of pocket costs ahead of planting, cattle feeders sell fat cattle for deferred delivery before feeder cattle are purchased, and broiler producers sell finished products before the baby chicks are hatched.

Farmers who sell ahead of production are producing for the speculative market. The corn farmer may sell in January for delivery to his local elevator at harvest and the elevator hedge by selling futures so that the contract is quite indirect but the basic arrangement is from producer to speculator. The market the cattle feeder is producing for when he sells futures is the speculative market. The feeder is a contract farmer, manufacturing finished beef out of feeder cattle and feed. A speculator is on the other end of the contract and thus directing his activities.

The speculative job of the people who put the producers under contract is to forecast the price that will just clear the market at the end of the production period. These speculators must take into account the supplies that *will* be available, quantities of competing products that *will* be available, consumer incomes, response of consumers to prices, etc. and arrive at a price forecast. They must judge how much there will be and the price at that time in the future.

The pricing of as yet unproduced products has an added dimension. In the case of pricing inventories to balance use and requirements within the year, the quantity is fixed but in the case of pricing production forward, the supply at maturity of the contract becomes a variable, dependent on producer response to the forward price. Futures prices become supply determining as well as supply rationing. Speculators control hedged inventories of stored commodities; they control production of the unproduced commodities that are contracted forward in futures markets.

Consequences of Speculative Pricing

Speculators in futures markets affect prices; they accumulate and liquidate inventory which puts prices above the levels that would otherwise prevail when they are accumulating and puts prices below levels that would otherwise prevail when they are liquidating. There is only one rate of inventory accumulation and liquidation that will hold the price constant at its equilibrium throughout the crop year. As too much inventory is held off of the market early in the season the price is held above the equilibrium and must later decline, as too little is held off the market early, the price is too low and must later increase, and these excesses—mistakes in rates and prices—can, and do numerous times during the season, flip from one excess to the other.

Speculators affect interim prices to the extent they control inventory. Some measure of control can be obtained by comparing open interest in futures contracts and total supplies. On January 1, 1975 the stocks of certain grains and the open interest in futures markets (Mil. bu.) were:

	On Farms	*Off Farms*	*Open Interest*
Wheat	440	659	239
Corn	2,533	1,080	412
Soybeans	491	505	305
Oats	388	123	15

A little of the farm stock was doubtless hedged and a substantial proportion of the off farm stock was owned by farmers in country warehouses. The size of the latter is not known. The general conclusion is that a substantial proportion but not all of the nonfarmer stock is hedged and in the control of the speculators but the bulk of inventories are controlled by farmers.

A large share of the January 1 stock on farms does not enter commercial channels but is fed on farms and so is not priced. A sufficiently high price of corn or a very low price of livestock would attract some of it to market but extremes that, as a practical matter, never exist would be required. Accordingly, the price making influence of speculators in futures markets is greater than their share of the total inventory.

Speculators do influence intraseasonal price patterns. So what? As they forecast prices accurately, prices are stable and as they forecast inaccurately, prices are variable. Price stability is desirable in the marketing processes. Thus, the quality of job that speculators do in discounting events and prices to come into current prices is of consequence but not great. Within a season, the total supply is not affected. Price variability may decrease the use of commodities but not greatly. The price to primary producers is higher than would exist in the absence of speculators in futures. The merchants who buy farmers' products at harvest hedge rather than assume the inventory ownership. Because they are neither able nor willing to carry the inventories themselves at the existing prices, it follows that they would bid less if they could not hedge, enough less to make the risks worth assuming. In so far as this increases the average price paid to producers by reducing marketing margins, it increases the long run supply, reduces user costs and increases total product.

Speculators in the nonstorable commodities influence production in proportion to the amount of production they control. In 1975 this was not great. On January 1 there were 19.9 thousand open contracts, representing 756 thousand cattle. There were 9.6 million cattle on feed. The open interest in live hog, broiler, egg, and orange juice futures was smaller in relation to production in process. But these were new and rapidly growing markets. Their importance was much greater than in 1969 and infinitely greater than in 1964.

The importance of speculators in the nonstorable commodities is greater than their proportionate control of production because the production controlled is marginal. It is the amount that is brought on stream or taken off stream depending on the prices offered by speculators. Marginal increments are particularly important in price determination.

The consequences of the accuracy with which speculators forecast prices of nonstorable commodities are much greater than for storable commodities because production is affected. With the growth of these markets, speculators were being given and were assuming responsibility for directing production—were becoming the planners.

The livestock industries have long been notable for bad planning. There have been well established hog and cattle production and price cycles. The broiler industry has always been feast or famine, boom or bust. Aggregate hog and cattle production decisions have been directed by many individual small farmer decisions. Cyclical theories have related to decisions about the future that are based on the current market situation. When prices are high and hog production profitable, farmers hold back breeding stock which reduces the market supply and further increases market prices. In due course, production catches up so that prices decline, farmers liquidate, causing further declines in price, the liquidation phase is overdone so that eventually the process starts over. The cycle is based on lack of foresight and the formation of expectations on the basis of things that are rather than on things to come. The cattle cycle is comparable but longer. Small farmers are responsible; perhaps speculators can improve on the formation of expectations.

Most broilers are produced by large, vertically integrated companies. Their track record is not very good. They, too, appear to respond to the current market situation.

Production of commodities must be planned. If prices are to be stabilized and an equilibrium of supplies and requirements established, speculators must anticipate events to come and estimate their impact on prices. This is true whether the speculation be done by individual farmers, by corporate planners, or by the speculating public. Beginning in the 1960's an increasing responsibility for production planning was turned over to futures market speculators.

CHAPTER 9

Cash and Futures Price Relationships

There is one more building block before moving on to the operations of people who trade in futures markets: The relationship of the prices of cash commodities and the various futures contracts. An understanding of these relationships and factors affecting them is essential to an understanding of how operational firms hedge and of hedging profitability. It is the key to the effective use of futures markets by primary producers in fixing sales prices ahead of production and the use of futures by processors and exporters in covering requirements. Speculators need to understand cash and futures price relationships if they are to accurately forecast prices and make money. Behind these statements is the fact that futures contracts are for real; futures contracts mature and turn into cash commodities; they represent cash inventory in store or not in store but committed for delivery or they represent commodities in the process of production that will inevitably move to market. Futures contracts are temporary substitutes for cash commodities. The real world of supplies of and requirements for cash commodities determines price.

The study of price relationships is more meaningful if it is placed in the context of hedging and the reasons hedgers hedge. The knowledge of price relationships can then be used in considering how to hedge.

Hedging

The first step in considering hedging is to unlearn a standard concept. The standard doctrine says that hedgers are prudent businessmen who shift risks of ownership to speculators so that they avoid the danger of ruinous losses and have access to equity capital. This has long been the basis for the defense of futures trading against legislative inroads. Unfortunately, the story has been so

148

often told that it has found its way into the textbooks and the literature evaluating the effectiveness of futures markets as hedging media.

It is less than kind to quote and then contradict an author, but Baer and Saxon[1] so aptly put the proposition that it is impossible to resist: "The whole purpose of hedging is to remove credit and price risks or to minimize them. Hedging is not used to make a profit, either speculative or otherwise, but to insure one already existing or to limit a loss already threatened. It is this purpose which has caused the hedge to be termed price and credit insurance. Businessmen can, through established insurance companies, insure against such major casualties as fire, employers' liability, explosion, and other contingencies which, though remote, contain the possibility of great loss to anyone who suffers the casualty. The organized insurance companies do not, however, offer insurance against price and credit risks inherent in commodity contracts and commodity positions. Yet the risks inherent in such contracts or market positions are much less remote and sometimes more devastating than those defined as strictly insurable casualties.

"The hedge, therefore, is used to insure the producer, dealer, or manufacturer against loss due to price changes or credit risks in commodities. Its purpose is to insure his profit or minimize his loss, one of which is always an integral part of the business transaction in which it is employed. Its object is not to return a speculative profit, for the reason that any profit derived in the futures merely equalizes or offsets a loss which has been increased on a transaction or market position in the physical market or vice versa. The physical market transaction and the exchange transaction are complementary. The hedger, however, by insuring against speculative risks, must forego the chance of speculative profits."

From this it follows that a perfect hedge is one that neither gains nor loses. A perfect hedge, it is said, requires that profits or losses on cash commodities be precisely offset by profits or losses on the futures positions. For this to happen, the price spread between the cash commodity and the futures contracts in which it is hedged must remain constant during the life of the hedge. The extent to which this price spread varies is said to measure the degree of imperfection of the hedge. Studies have been made[2] comparing variations in cash prices and cash-futures price spreads to determine the percentage effectiveness of hedging markets. For reasons that we will eventually evolve, futures markets did not show up well.

The first of the standard propositions that we should lay to rest is the one that says that hedging is like insurance—it is not. Insurance is based on the law of large numbers that make actuarial computation of average losses in any given

---

[1] Op. cit. pp. 203–204.
[2] Howell, L. D. *Analysis of Hedging and Other Transactions in Grain Futures,* USDA, Tech. Bul. No. 971, 1948.

time period, say one year, possible. The average loss plus operating costs and returns to the insurer are spread over the insured population as premiums. It is a scheme for socializing losses in which one insured pays a share of the losses of the other insured and they, each, a share of his. The risks are not assumed by the insuring company but rather pass out of existence.[3] When risks are transferred by hedging they continue to exist in quite as large measure as before. They are assumed by the principal(s) on the other end of the futures contract(s). They are spread more widely (note the number of speculators compared to the number of hedgers) and are less onerous (else the speculators would not play). Presumably, the consequences of risk to the economic systems are reduced but the total of the risks remain.

It is important that hedgers understand that hedging is not insurance. Hedging is an intricate activity, requiring substantial knowledge and operational skill.

Hedging was defined in an earlier chapter as the assumption of a position in futures equal and opposite to an already existing or immediately anticipated cash position. This is a definition descriptive of the process. We now add a second definition: to hedge is to insulate one's business activities from price level speculation while retaining the opportunity to speculate in basis variation. This definition takes hedging out of the academic context of risk shifting and puts it in the business context of trying to make a profit.

As we have seen, holders of inventories hedge to avoid the risks of ruinous loses or because they lack equity capital. In broad context, then we can say that the purpose of hedging is to shift the risks of price level changes. But this does not explain why business firms hedge. They could avoid risks (or reduce them to negligible levels) by simultaneously buying and selling the cash commodity. The country elevator could buy only as it has firm bids, it could leave its space empty except as it is rented to others, the exporter could sell only as he is able to buy cash commodities, the wheat miller could buy wheat only as he makes and sells flour, the soybean processor could sell soybean oil and meal only as they are ready to ship, etc. But they do not. Instead, they substitute futures transactions for the selling or buying of cash transactions that would complete the original exchange. They avoid the completing transactions and the risks of price level changes by substituting futures contracts in their place. They shift the risks of price level change while retaining the opportunity to profit from changes in price relationships if the original decision to purchase or sell was correct. Hedgers hedge to retain a profit making opportunity, that is, they do not hedge to avoid risk but, rather, to make a profit.

Price relationships are variable and uncertain. Accordingly, positions taken in

---

[3] This is completely true only if the number of insured is large enough, the time period long enough, and the actuarial computation accurate. But it is the business of the insurance company to see that they are.

price relationships—one short and the other long—are speculative. Profits and losses are realized depending upon the change in relationship; profits, if the change is in line with expectations, and losses if it is not. The game that hedgers play is one of anticipating changes in price relationships, implementing their expectations with equal or opposite positions in cash and futures, and profiting as they are correct and losing as they are wrong.

Hedging and Speculation. The relationship of hedging and speculation needs to be brought into focus. It is sometimes said that hedging is the opposite of speculation. This is not so. They are different kinds of the same thing. The thing that is usually identified as speculation—that is, long or short positions in futures contracts—is speculation in changes in price level. The thing that we identify as hedging—that is, long cash and short futures or vice versa—is speculation in price relationships. We may be able to make this difference clearer by considering the case of a farmer with a bin full of wheat. He is long cash wheat. He is speculating in the level of wheat prices and in the relationship of the price of his specific lot of wheat to the general level of wheat prices. If he hedges, he ceases to speculate in the level of wheat prices while continuing to speculate in the relationship of his wheat to the general level. Thus, hedging and speculation are not opposite; in fact they are conceptually similar. They are just different kinds of speculation.

The process of hedging divides the process of speculation into two parts: price level and price relationship. We have noted that futures become a sale for the hedgers who are long and a purchase for the hedgers who are short. Because hedging is extensively practiced by people who market commodities for which there are futures markets, futures become the central focus and pricing point of the system. Futures prices represent the general level of the price, and the multitude of cash prices that exist at any given time are established in relation to the futures.

What, then, is a perfect hedge? If we accept the notion that hedgers hedge to make profits, it follows that a bad hedge is one that loses money and a good hedge is one that makes money. Extending this, a perfect hedge is one that makes all of the money.

Basis in Storage Markets

Before looking at price relationships we must divide the world of futures trading into two major parts—storage and nonstorage markets. Until recently futures trading was limited to commodities suitable for relatively long term storage. A body of knowledge about price relationships was built up. This, unfortunately does not apply to futures markets for nonstorable commodities.

The essence of hedging is speculation in basis. The analysis of basis is a field of its own, quite separate from the field of price analysis. It is a study of cash and futures price relationships.

Basis. The basis is the price of a cash commodity at the delivery point in relation to the nearby or dominant future. If in February we say that the corn basis is 2 over, we mean that No. 2 yellow corn is selling for 2 cents more than March futures contracts.

Statements of basis can be modified by location and by time. For example, we can say that the east-central Illinois basis is 7 under, or the New Orleans basis is 14 over, in these instances designating a location different from the delivery point but again referring to the nearby future. It is sometimes useful to refer to the cash price in relation to the more distant future. For example, in October we may be concerned with the price of soybeans at interior elevators in relation to the May future. In this case we would say that the track basis is 15 under May. For users of futures markets, the important basis is that one that applies to the operational problem at hand.

One Price. The various individual prices of a commodity are functionally interrelated. On November 13, 1975 some prices of No. 2 yellow corn were:

Track, Illinois Points	$2.42	December futures	$2.64¼
To Arrive Chicago	2.52	March futures	2.72
Minneapolis	2.49	May futures	2.76¼
Baltimore	2.65	July futures	2.77¾
Gulf Ports	2.75	September futures	2.70

These several prices are an integrated part of the price level of corn. They should be thought of as one price; the parts of which vary only with time and place of delivery. The system of price differences is intricate but simple in concept. There is one central price of corn; the multitudinous individual prices over time, space, quality, and state of processing fall into place about the central price. The principle of one price within one market, in which the market is construed as the area of economic intercourse, applies to commodities traded in futures markets more than in any other area of the economic system.

Cash and Futures Prices in the Delivery Month. The price of the cash commodity and its futures price must be equal in the delivery month. If the futures price were above the cash price, the cash commodity would be bought, the futures sold, and delivery made. If the cash price were above the futures price, users would buy futures and stand for delivery as the cheapest source of supply. Thus, arbitrage in cash and futures markets forces the two prices to be equal.

All of this is fine in theory, but even the most casual student is aware that cash prices of storable commodities, particularly grains, are nearly always higher than the futures during delivery months. These differences arise out of technical considerations of delivery, are limited in their possible size, and do not violate the principle. There are several reasons for the cash premium:

1. The precise time of delivery is not known. Delivery is made at the option of the seller, and the buyer does not know whether he will get delivery on the first day, the last day, or somewhere in between. It is not possible to run plants or meet shipping schedules on such an uncertain basis. Thus, the cash commodity is worth a bit more than the futures. The premium may be substantial in periods of short cash supply where the commodity is needed immediately. Cash and futures are not perfect substitutes until the last day of the month, typically several days after futures trading has been stopped (seven business days in the case of grain). While premiums may be large early in the delivery month, they decrease as the month progresses.

2. The precise quality is not known. Several different grades can be delivered on most futures at discounts from or at premiums to the contract grade. Users have specific quality requirements and therefore prefer buying in cash markets to taking delivery.

3. Sometimes load-out and switching charges must be paid. For example, grain bought "To Arrive" by rail can be switched to any point in the Chicago area without additional freight charge but if delivery is taken, load-out and switching charges are incurred. This is the principal reason for the premiums on cash grain.

4. The value of freight billing accompanying some commodities (grain in particular) on delivery is different for different lots. Minimum-value billing is usually furnished with delivery.

There are occasions when the cash is at a discount under the futures during the delivery month. These arise when the cash commodity does not meet delivery requirements with regard to its location. For example, grain must be in store in a certified warehouse in Chicago for delivery except during the last three days of the month when delivery in rail cars is permitted. If there is no available warehouse space, the cash price may be below the contract price by the cost of holding grain until space is available. This sometimes occurs during the first month of the crop year—December for corn, July for wheat, etc. Another example, the price of cash pork bellies may be below the futures price during accumulation months by the cost of putting bellies in storage. The point of this is that spot commodities differ from the in-store commodities that are priced by futures. In-store commodities can be bought and these prices do, indeed, equal the futures prices at the conclusion of trading.

There are two points to be kept in mind about cash and futures prices in the delivery month:

First, because of delivery provisions, futures contracts are commercially real and prices must reflect values at which the commodity can be moved into consumption. Although only a very small percent of contracts are actually delivered, the opportunity to make or take delivery is always present and enough deliveries are made and taken to keep futures contract values in line with cash values. Note, that in a sense, the moment of truth comes in the delivery month. Prices of futures contracts can be out of touch with reality until first notice day but during the delivery month the assets are put on the auction block and must go for what they will fetch for use.

Second, in the delivery month the differences between cash and futures prices are based on commercial factors that are consistent from year to year and that can be expected to prevail at future times. That is, if No. 2 yellow corn trades at four cents over the July in July, 1975 it will probably trade four cents over the July in 1976, etc.

Cash and Futures Prices Over Time. The relationship of cash and futures prices is based on the theory of the carrying charge. This theory rests on three facts: (1) Storable commodities are produced at one time of year and used at fairly even rates throughout the year so that inventories must be carried from harvest forward, (2) There are costs in storing and maintaining the quality of commodities, and (3) There is virtually no cost in holding futures contracts. From these three facts it follows that cash prices should increase in relation to futures prices as the storage season progresses.

One of the clearest examples of this seasonality and the behavior of price relationships is that of corn. We will illustrate with it.

If one buys a July corn futures contract in October with the intention of taking delivery and processing, distilling, or exporting the corn, the only cost is incurred in the small margin deposit required to guarantee the contract. On the other hand, if one buys cash corn in October for sale or use the following July, one must provide space that has an investment, depreciation, and maintenance cost, operate the space, and have the full value of the grain invested. Because there is no cost in holding futures contracts, there is no reason to expect futures prices to increase regularly from harvest to the following summer. Because there are costs in holding cash corn, there should be, on balance, an increase in price during the season equal to the cost of storage.

The delivery months for corn are December, March, May, July, and September. Basis theory suggests that at harvest the price of cash corn should be below the December futures price by the cost of carrying corn from harvest to December, that December should be less than March by the cost of storage from December to March, etc. We should not expect September to fit the pattern because it is a transition month, coming before the new crop is readily available but being affected by early harvest in some parts of the country. Such a general pattern was noted in the prices of November 13, 1975 above. At the end of the crop year, the cash price should fall to reflect, again, the new crop situation with its cost of storage. Schematically, the pattern appears thus:

FIGURE 4.

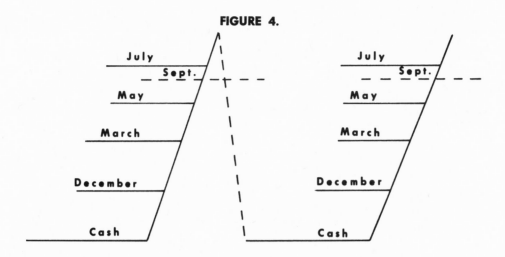

This pattern assumes no change in the price level of corn, the only change being in the relationship of cash and futures prices. The level of price does change, and it changes almost continually, so that at any given time the nature of change in cash grain prices is twofold: price level change and basis change.

The reason for the differences among prices of the several futures contracts for each grain is the carrying charge. The carrying charge consists of three parts: storage, interest, and insurance. In 1970 the warehouse tariff for grain delivered on the Chicago Board of Trade was 6/100 cents per bushel per day. Grain in storage must be owned. Money can be borrowed on hedged grain at 1/2 point over the prime rate. Insurance rates could not exceed $1.00 per $100 valuation per year, and in modern elevators they were less. The carrying charge for December to March is equal to the elapsed time from the first delivery day in December (Dec. 1) to the first delivery day in March (March 1), or 90 days. At 6/100 cent the total storage charge for 90 days was 5.4 cents; at $1.00, the maximum insurance cost was 1/4 cent for the period; interest at 7 percent with corn at $1.15 per bushel amounted to 2 cents. The total carrying charge was thus 7.65 cents for the three month period or 2.55¢ per month.[4]

The full carrying charge as illustrated is the maximum discount that the

[4] The calculations shown here use the rates applicable to 1970 so that they are consistent with Figure 5. Inflation during the 1970–75 period results in nonrepresentative averages, hence the use of the decade of the 1960's.

nearby future can be under the next delivery month. Should the difference be wider, speculators could take delivery, hedge in the next delivery month, pay the charges, and make a profit. And so this does not happen. But if the basis and the spreads are determined by the carrying charge, we should expect a long run tendency for the relationships to approximate the charges.

So much for theory. What really happens? Figure 5 is a basis chart of corn prices for the 10 crop years 1959–68. Basis charts can be constructed in several different ways and each experienced basis operator tends to develop his own eccentricities. Three general forms are described here. The purpose of a basis chart is to visually describe the changes in price relationships that have taken place in the past and that are currently taking place. This is an aid to forecasting the changes in relationships that determine the degree of success of hedging operations.

The essence of making a basis chart is to set one price equal to zero and plot the other prices under consideration around it; they differ only in which price is set equal to zero. One type is to make the cash price central to the hedging problem equal to zero. If the storage-merchandising operation is located at the terminal where the futures market is, the terminal cash price is used. If it is located in the interior the local price is used, etc. This procedure has the advantage of focusing attention on the price of the cash commodity that is central to the hedging operation. A second advantage is that the cash price is continuous through time whereas futures come into existence, mature, and expire so that if a futures price is set equal to zero the zero line has to be changed from time to time—no one zero line is good for the whole of a crop year, from preplanting until harvest of the succeeding crop year.

A second form of basis chart is to set the last maturing contract of a crop year equal to zero and plot all other prices in relation to it. This has the advantage of portraying the cash price as gaining in relation to the future—of the futures remaining constant because of their lack of carrying cost while the cash gains because of its carrying cost, a la the theory of the carrying charge. The disadvantages are that such a chart will not span a whole crop year of 18 to 20 months and the focus is on the distant future while the focus of trading is on the nearby.

The third form is to set the nearby future equal to zero and switch to the next future as the nearby expires, etc. This has the advantages of portraying the cash as gaining in relation to the future and of concentrating attention on the nearby cash-futures relationship as the market does in actual practice. Further, it will span an entire crop year.

Figure 5 is the third type. The December future was set equal to zero and the two cash prices—To Arrive Chicago and On Track, Central Illinois Points— and the other futures prices plotted over and under. The cash prices prior to harvest were for harvest shipment—by December 15—rather than spot ship-

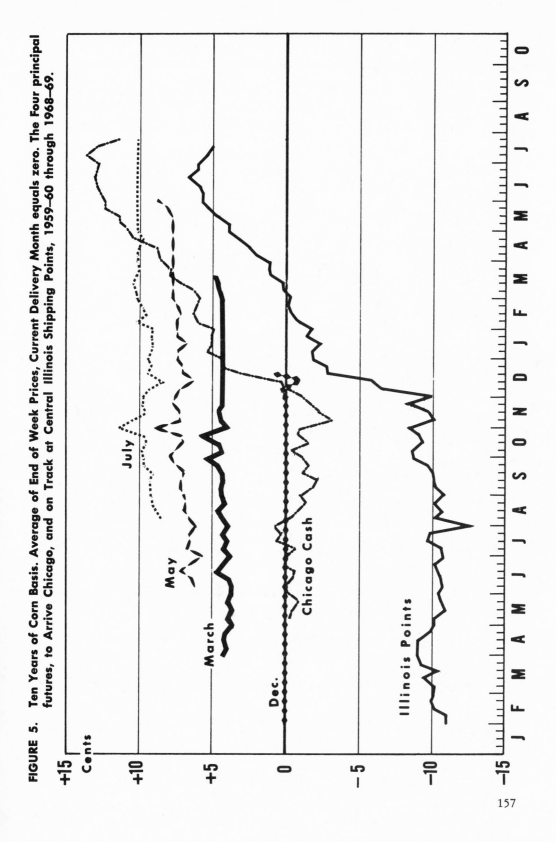

FIGURE 5. Ten Years of Corn Basis. Average of End of Week Prices, Current Delivery Month equals zero. The Four principal futures, to Arrive Chicago, and on Track at Central Illinois Shipping Points, 1959–60 through 1968–69.

157

ment and were thus forward contracts. The change to the next delivery month was made on the first delivery day of the expiring month. The next month was located in relation to the expiring month on the basis of the difference that existed on the changeover date. The ten year average difference between December and March on the last Friday in November was 4.3 cents; this amount determined the location of the March zero line.

The figure is broadly and generally consistent with the theoretical pattern. The cash prices gained in relation to the futures, nearby futures were below the later deliveries, and the futures prices maintained generally stable relationships. But there were two major deviations from the theory that require its modification. First, the cash price did not gain in relation to the futures at a regular rate At four week intervals the To Arrive price relative to the July futures was:

October 13	11.0 under	March 31	1.7 under
November 10	11.8 under	April 28	.5 over
December 10	8.0 under	May 26	2.2 over
January 6	3.7 under	June 23	2.8 over
February 3	3.9 under	July 14	2.9 over
March 3	4.2 under		

From harvest to early January the cash gained 7.3 cents in relation to the July future, a rate of .261 cents per day, more than the full carrying charge rate of .085 cents. From early January to the expiration of trading in the July future the gain was 6.6 cents or .035 cents per day, an amount on the general order of one half of a full carry. This pattern was consistent throughout the ten year period so that the average was representative.

Second, the differences among the futures were much less than a full carrying charge. The average differences among the futures during their common periods and full carrying charges were:

	Average Difference	*Full Carry*
December–March	3.2	7.7
March–May	2.7	5.2
May–July	2.3	5.2

An example is useful in describing the processes by which differences are established. During the delivery month the basis and the spreads are established by the actions of terminal elevators in making deliveries and placing hedges. On October 29, 1964, the price of to-arrive corn was $1.15. December futures were $1.18½, and March futures were $1.22¾. A terminal elevator has to decide whether to buy cash corn and hedge in December futures or to merchandise such purchases as it makes and whether to place hedges in the nearby December or in March or even farther forward.

The cash corn decision is made on the basis of anticipated earnings. The potential earnings for putting corn in storage were 3½ cents for the month of November, more than a full carrying charge because at that time the market was glutted by the corn harvest. Corn was crying for a home and bidding a stiff price to get it. Two weeks earlier the decision would have been very different because to-arrive corn was 2½ cents over the December.

The decision whether to place hedges in the December or March futures was more difficult. The spread was 4¼ cents, substantially less than a full carrying charge. Elevators would like to have a full carrying charge but will take less to avoid the risk of losing control of inventory. When hedged grain is delivered, it may be taken and held by the receiver; in that case the elevator no longer holds title but acts as a public warehouse.

Elevators are reluctant to lose control for several reasons: (1) The grain may be ordered shipped, leaving empty space that earns nothing; half a loaf is better than none. (2) If grain is delivered, the elevator must keep a sufficient amount of the delivered quality on hand to back the warehouse receipts, reducing the quantity that it can use for blending with off-grade grain. (3) Merchandising opportunities are lost; terminal elevators are primarily merchandisers, and grain that is out on delivery cannot be merchandised. (4) If elevators lose control, grain may remain in position when the elevator could make more money by moving it out to make room for the next crop.

Typically, elevators do not place grain on delivery if they do not expect to recapture it. If the spread between futures is narrow, they may place grain on delivery, expecting that the delivered grain will be redelivered by speculators. This action will depress the nearby future in relation to the more distant ones so that the nearby can be bought and the distant sold at a more favorable spread. The elevator management must formulate a judgment of the most favorable spread at which it can move its hedges forward and, at a smaller spread, deliver grain. In making this judgment, it looks at existing supplies, supplies to come, demands for use and shipment, and the amount of available space. It is a complex judgment, and first delivery day is nearly always a time of intense interest.

The opposite ends of these futures trades by warehousemen are taken by speculators; they buy the hedges. They pay premiums for the deferred deliveries. If they are to make money the cash price must increase by more than the amount of the premium. They pay, indirectly, the storage that the warehouseman receives indirectly. As the spreads are wide, they are paying more storage than when the spreads are narrow. Thus, they, on occasion, take delivery to try and narrow the spreads and move their long positions forward at less cost. There is a contest between hedgers who try to widen carrying charges and speculators who try to narrow them. Any speculator can take delivery and carry the cash commodity forward by paying the full carrying charge but few do. The warehousemen are large scale operators who have skill and money. Only the professional speculators are equipped to oppose them; the effective competition in the storage market is provided by the large scale speculators.

In the final analysis, the nearby basis and spreads boil down to the supply of and demand for space. When stocks at the terminal are large and grain is flowing to market rapidly, the cash price is weak in relation to the nearby future and spreads are wide. But when stocks are small, the commodity is flowing to market slowly, and demand for shipment is vigorous, the price of storage decreases.

The basis and spreads, then, are the going market price of storage, based on the principle of the cost of storing the cash commodity, but modified by the specific supply-demand situation. Commodities move into storage when the price of storage is favorable and move out of storage when the price is unfavorable. In the short run, the critical price-of-storage decisions are made by the terminal operators. But these decisions are conditioned by the flow of the commodity out of country locations. The rate of flow is affected by the supply of and demand for storage in nonterminal locations. If the price of storage at outside points is favorable, the commodity does not move, and vice versa. Thus, terminals and country locations compete in the storage market, and the price of storage reflects the total storage supply-demand structure.

Selected Variants. The ten year average experience for corn is a good norm from which to depart. It is typical of price relationship behavior for stored commodities. But there are major individual year variations that are significant in actual hedging operations and that are useful in understanding the factors affecting basis. Figures 6 and 7 show two individual years of soybean basis. Here the charts were drawn with July, the most distant old crop future not affected by new crop conditions, equal to zero.

The crop year 1965–66 was selected because of its typicalness. The futures were arranged in a carrying charge structure and traversed fairly parallel courses. Both cash prices moved essentially parallel courses. Both cash prices moved essentially parallel to the futures prior to harvest (there is no cost of storing a growing crop), gained rapidly immediately after harvest, and gained gradually during the balance of the growing season; our modified theory is vindicated.

The crop year 1966–67 was selected because of its atypicalness. The relationships broke every rule of reasonable behavior that we have developed to this point. The season started well with cash and futures prices arrayed in a carrying charge structure, but starting in October the cash gained in relation to the futures and the nearby futures gained in relation to the more distant ones so that the market was turned upside down. Note particularly that the November expired 6.5¢ over the July, that in mid-January the price of January was 7.8¢ over the July, and that the cash price in January was nearly 10¢ over the July. Following March, the market righted itself so that during May, June, and July the pattern was similar to the preceding year. Actual prices on four selected dates were:

Date	*Ill. Points*	*Cash Chi.*	*Nov.*	*Jan.*	*Mar.*	*May*	*July*
Sept. 30	2.92	2.97⅝	2.98½	3.03½	3.09	3.12⅝	3.14
Nov. 18	2.93⅝	2.99⅝	3.05⅝	2.98	2.97⅛	2.99	2.99⅝
Jan. 13	2.91⅝	2.97⅜		2.95½	2.91⅜	2.89¾	2.87¾
Mar. 10	2.84	2.90⅜			2.88	2.88½	2.88⅜

What happened? An understanding requires that we look at the specifics of the crop year. The price of soybeans had been high during the preceding crop year. There was an unusual increase in product demand which, coupled with a moderate sized crop, appeared likely to pull the carryover down to minimum pipeline supplies. Weather was bad through mid-August, threatening a small 1966 crop. Prices of the new crop rose rapidly during the summer. As was noted in an earlier chapter, this threat ended with the crop estimate of September 9. From that time on the general course of prices was downward; from $3.44 the July futures declined to $2.75 at the expiration of trading in July, 1967.

Encouraged by the high prices of the preceding summer, the major price increase from harvest of 1965 to summer 1966, and the threatened shortage, farmers held an unusually large proportion of the crop. Exporters had made sales of cash soybeans for harvest shipment and covered by buying November futures. Processors had sold cash oil and meal and covered in futures. On September 30, Reporting Hedgers were long 85 million bushels and short 31 million bushels. At no time during the entire crop year did the hedgers get net short. The hedgers stood for delivery and the price to the country was bid up to draw enough supply to satisfy the immediate requirements. At the core of the matter, the farmers were long cash and the speculators short futures which, as contracts matured, turned into cash positions. But the speculators knew that the crop was back in the country and would eventually move to market. They judged that the equilibrium price would turn out to have been less than the harvest price plus the cost of storage and refused to bid up the distant delivery months. As time passed, it became increasingly apparent that there would be a major increase in carryover and the planting intentions released in March indicated an increase in the size of the 1967 crop. Farmers gradually gave up and sold, letting the speculators out of their short positions. From the basis chart it is apparent that the farmers held the whip hand with the expiring of the

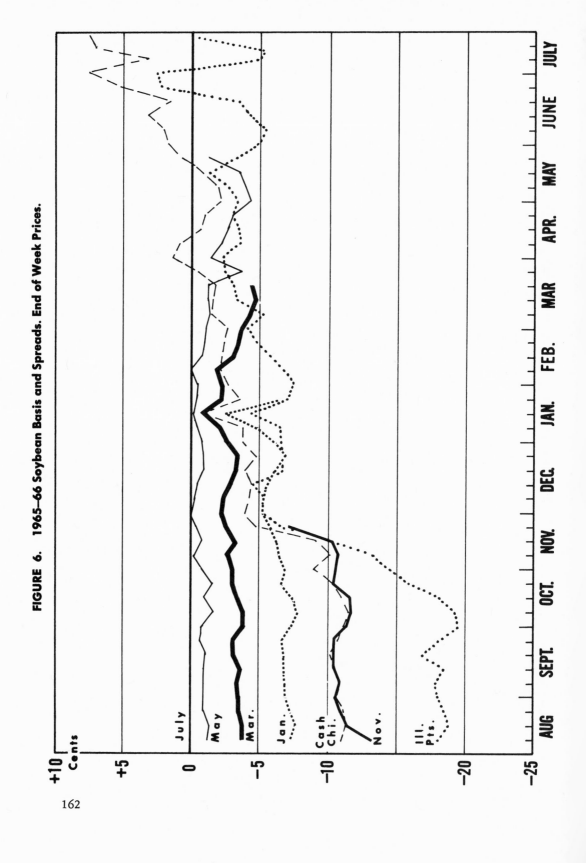

FIGURE 6. 1965–66 Soybean Basis and Spreads. End of Week Prices.

162

FIGURE 7. 1966-67 Soybean Basis and Spreads. End of Week Prices.

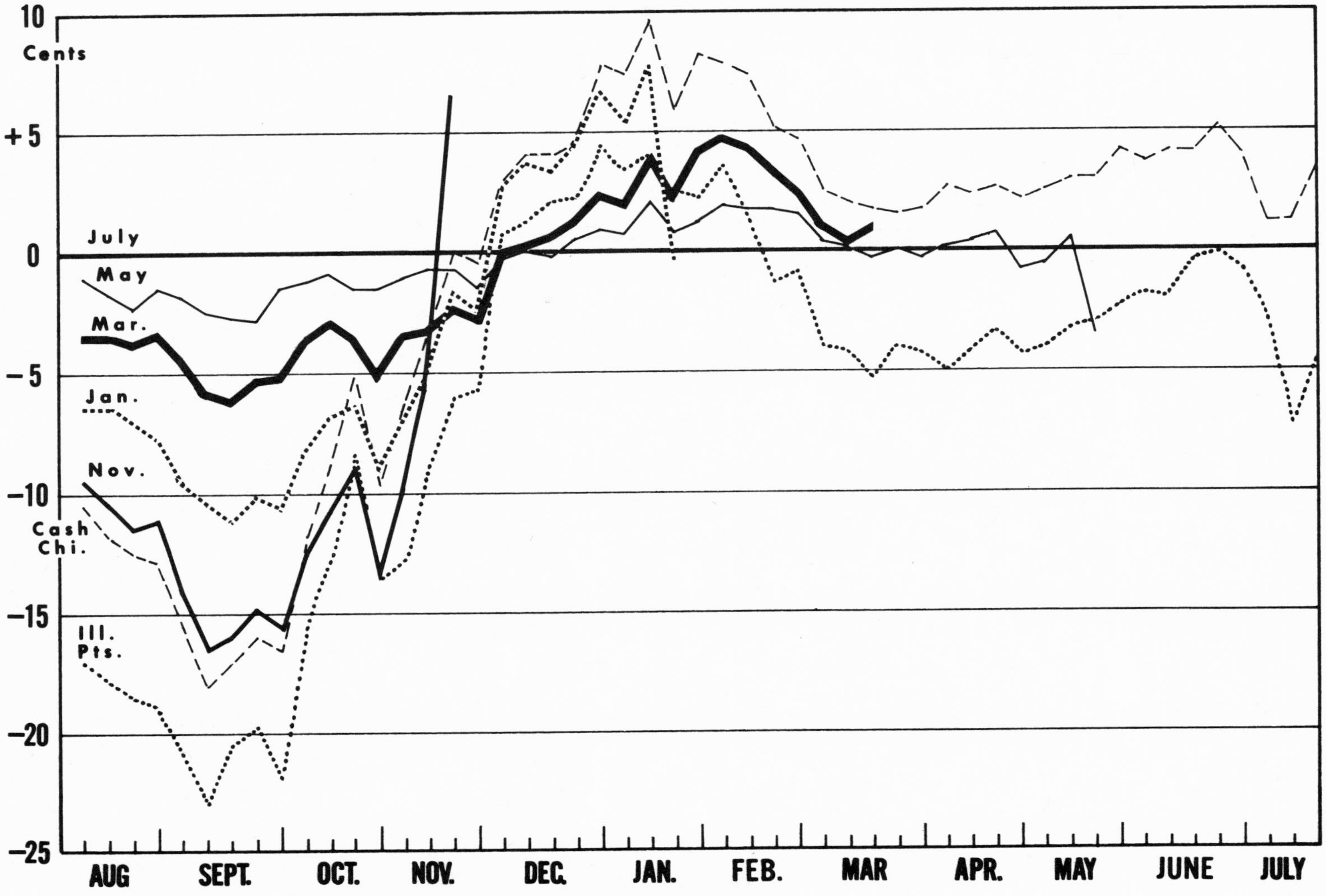

November contract and through most of the trading in January futures but they lost their power with the trading in March. Note that the March contract declined from nearly five cents over the July at the first of February to expire barely even with July.

Inverse carrying charges, such as these, are a negative price of storage; the market is not only failing to offer payment for storage, but is charging for the privilege of owning cash inventory. On January 13, "To Arrive" soybeans Chicago were 9.7¢ over the July futures. The market was saying: "You may buy cash, store until July, and deliver at a guaranteed loss of 9.7¢." In the face of this unprofitable proposition he who wanted to own soybeans because he thought the price was going up should have preferred the ownership of futures to cash. As it turned out, any ownership was a bad idea but the ownership of futures, rather than cash, lost less as well as avoiding the cost of storage. Had prices gone up, owning futures would have been a great deal more profitable than holding cash.

It appears that the cause of this carrying charge inversion was the failure of farmers to respond rationally to the cash-futures price relationship. Had they sold cash as soon as the price of storage, as shown in price relationships, went below cost and replaced the cash with futures the inversion would not have occurred.

The matter of inverse carrying charges is not this simple. It gets involved with normal backwardation, risk premiums, market bias, and the effects of speculation on prices. It has been much discussed in the literature of futures trading. At a later point, we will consider the question further but for operational purposes we can consider that the relationships of cash to futures and among futures are the going market price of storage.

Carrying Charges in Nonseasonal Markets. The seasonality of production is an essential part of the carrying charge structure. At the beginning of each new season the cash price goes back to its beginning of the year before and the first new crop future begins at the level of the same maturity the year before as shown in Fig. 4. If it is anticipated that supplies will be greater or requirements smaller in the second year, the right hand side of the diagram slides down so that the whole of the new crop structure is lower and vice versa. So long as the price level of the commodity remains stable over several seasons, as commodity prices tend to do except for monetary inflation, there is a seasonal rise and abrupt fall in cash prices and futures prices move generally sidewise.

However, some commodities, as, for example, silver are stored in substantial quantities, but inventories do not have a regular seasonal pattern. Silver is primarily a by-product of the production of other metals. Production is on the general order of 250 million ounces and use on the order of 430 million ounces per year. The size of silver stocks is unknown, but various estimates run up to

5 billion ounces. An unknown amount can be melted from ornaments and coins that have been fabricated over the centuries. The point is that some day silver stocks will be exhausted and prices will have to go high enough to increase production and/or reduce use. In the meantime stocks will be carried.

The existence of inventories forces a carrying charge because of the cost of storage and interest. Metal dealers and warehousemen carry their inventories hedged in silver futures. As the carrying charges are less than full, they deliver and move hedges forward only as full carrying charges are offered—there is no danger of losing the inventory because of the large stock. Speculators pay the current spot price plus storage and interest to the more distant delivery. The effect is to force a continually rising price of spot silver relative to silver futures. If the carrying charge is greater than the normal secular increase in silver prices resulting from inflation, the total price structure must periodically collapse or silver futures must have a chronic downward bias.

Assume that the rate of inflation is six percent per year, that the real rate of interest is a positive three percent so that the nominal rate is nine percent, and, for purposes of simplification, that there is no warehouse charge. If the spot silver goes up at the inflation rate, futures will have to decline. Diagrammatically it is:

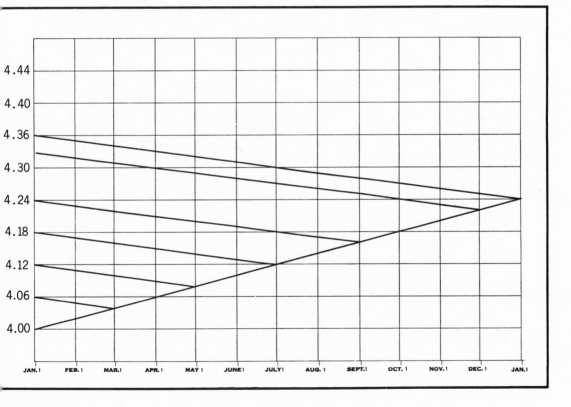

In theory, such a chronic erosion of carrying charges should exist. But the nature of price uncertainty and speculative behavior is such that it does not. Were spot prices to remain on such a stable course such a bias would develop and the market would die. A consistent downward bias is too discouraging to long speculators to persist. Instead, the market moves upward in speculative surges and periodically collapses.

Temporal Price Relationships in Nonstorage Markets

The essential characteristic of price relationships in storage markets is the functional interrelationship that is forced by the need to store until a later time and to ration the supply over a protracted period such as one year. This functional relationship is a key consideration in the use of futures markets. The essential characteristic of price relationships in futures markets for nonstorable commodities is that there is no functional relationship. The price of each delivery period is a true forecast of the equilibrium price that will prevail at that future time. It is not possible to carry product forward to a time in the future, increasing present price and reducing the price in the future. The product that is ready for market at a given time must move through marketing channels and into consumption at that time and no other. It must carry the price that it will fetch in consumer markets; there is no waiting for tomorrow for a smaller supply or greater demand. Production cannot be accelerated and moved into consumption in response to current high prices; an unlaid egg can be neither fried nor poached—only done without.

This overstates the case because nothing is perfectly storable nor completely perishable. Some commodities approach perfect storability as in the case of silver or platinum and others can be stored for quite long periods. Under price support programs, the government has held such items as corn, wheat, cotton, and cottonseed oil for several years without major deterioration—they made futures contract grade when taken out. Even the most perishable items can be held for a limited time. Cattle can be fed to heavier weights and still make contract grade or sold at lighter weights to increase current market supplies but the variability is limited.

Some futures contracts are written to guarantee some minimum degree of perishability. For fresh eggs, only one reinspection is permitted; past one day following reinspection, a given lot is no longer deliverable on a fresh egg contract. While pork bellies are in the storable category, there is a limit on the age of bellies that can be delivered. Bellies placed in storage prior to December 1 cannot be delivered on contracts maturing in the following calendar year. This planned perishability is especially interesting in view of the long held notion that futures trading is feasible only for fully storable commodities. A key rationalization—not the reason—in banning futures trading in onions was their relatively high degree of perishability. The success of cattle, hog, and fresh egg futures trading is conclusive proof of the error of the earlier thinking.

The first of the strictly nonstorable commodities traded was live cattle. At the outset traders were confused about the price relationships that should exist. Bound by tradition, they looked for a crop year and a carrying charge structure. Who would hedge in a noncarry market? It became quickly apparent that to buy the more distant months because a proper futures market should have a carrying charge was a nearly certain way to lose money. Being artists at survival, the traders quickly modified this notion and started looking at potential changes in market supplies and consumer demand that might result in change in the current market price by the time of contract maturity.

Table 9 shows three years of cash and futures prices of cattle.[1] The 1973–75 period was one of unusually great variability. There was general inflation with rising consumer incomes; hence, increasing demand for meat. During 1973, the supply of beef per capita decreased for the first time in many years, putting upward pressure on prices. In the spring, consumer resistance moderated the increase. Price ceilings on meat were imposed in the early summer. This had two strengthening effects: (1) consumers lost their price sensitivity in the face of threatened shortage and bought everything available, putting much of it in storage in home freezers and (2) anticipating an end to ceilings, cattle feeders held cattle off of the market and fed them to heavier weights. Prices rose. The two forces reduced consumption and increased supplies. The bubble broke in August and there followed a long period of liquidation into summer, 1974. Feed production conditions were very poor in 1974 threatening feed supplies and cattle prices rose. The very poor crop materialized and a liquidation of cattle herds followed, with range cattle going directly to slaughter instead of to feed. The increased supplies weighed on the market into early 1975 before the real decrease in production took effect and prices again rose. Consumer resistance again put prices down during the second half of 1975. In 1975, feed crops were of record size and the number of cattle on feed was increasing rapidly, foreshadowing eventually larger beef supplies as 1975 ended. Such were the commercial forces behind the gyrations in cash cattle prices. Examination of the data reveals three things: (1) all prices rise and fall together, (2) variation in cash prices and nearby deliveries is greater than in more distant deliveries, and (3) there is substantial independence of the more distant deliveries and the cash and among the various deliveries.

Summarization of the table in which the eight up and down legs of cash

---

[1] Cash cattle and futures prices during the delivery month are not exactly comparable. The cash is the average for the entire month, while futures is the average before trading was suspended in the delivery month, about ¾ as long. In strictly comparable periods cash, Omaha, averaged $0.67 below futures.

Table 9. Cash Cattle and Cattle Futures Prices, Chicago Mercantile Exchange, Monthly Averages of Daily Closing Prices, Dollars per CWT.

Month	Choice Steers Omaha	Feb. 1973	Apr. 1973	June 1973	Aug. 1973	Oct. 1973	Dec. 1973	Feb. 1974	Apr. 1974	June 1974	Aug. 1974	Oct. 1974
1973												
Jan.	40.31	42.84	42.71	42.70	41.98	41.42	41.28					
Feb.	43.07	44.47	43.84	44.09	43.43	42.62	42.50	42.34				
Mar.	45.28		45.92	45.74	44.91	43.80	43.32	43.37	43.28			
Apr.	44.76		44.38	43.25	43.11	42.65	42.81	43.06	42.99			
May	45.71			45.91	45.52	45.15	45.25	45.35	45.03			
June	46.65			47.63	47.24	47.14	47.21	47.35	47.02	46.83		
July	48.11				50.93	51.75	52.41	52.59	51.87	51.68	50.94	
Aug.	53.39				56.72	55.64	56.50	57.07	56.67	56.72	55.92	
Sept.	44.79					43.48	45.40	48.11	48.31	48.42	47.91	47.42
Oct.	40.65					41.71	44.91	48.30	48.94	49.16	48.59	47.89
Nov.	37.47						40.56	45.28	46.27	46.38	45.71	45.02
Dec.	38.87						38.64	46.06	48.00	48.13	47.60	46.86

1974		Feb. 1974	Apr. 1974	June 1974	Aug. 1974	Oct. 1974	Dec. 1974	Feb. 1975	Apr. 1975	June 1975	Aug. 1975	Oct. 1975
Jan.	47.22	50.95	53.80	54.30	52.93	51.81	51.60					
Feb.	46.22	46.57	48.61	51.50	52.26	52.07	52.14					
Mar.	42.42		43.17	46.23	48.32	48.83	49.36					
Apr.	40.86		42.20	45.65	47.64	49.91	47.02	46.96				
May	40.04			41.04	41.59	39.69	39.26	39.13	37.06			
June	37.50			36.47	37.21	37.49	37.42	37.12	36.73			
July	43.60				46.02	46.30	45.73	45.51	45.41	45.65		
Aug.	46.52				48.46	46.70	45.19	44.81	45.38	46.10	46.33	
Sept.	41.24					39.41	38.11	41.21	41.77	43.02	43.30	
Oct.	39.72					41.09	42.96	44.06	44.03	45.29	45.02	
Nov.	37.77						38.53	40.57	41.28	42.46	42.24	
Dec.	37.13						38.12	41.14	41.90	42.60	42.68	42.43

1975		Feb. 1975	Apr. 1975	June 1975	Aug. 1975	Oct. 1975	Dec. 1975	Feb. 1976	Apr. 1976	June 1976	Aug. 1976	Oct. 1976
Jan.	36.17	37.10	38.00	38.70	38.82	38.69	38.83					
Feb.	34.68	35.08	36.72	37.54	37.22	36.81	36.93					
Mar.	36.14		37.96	38.59	37.65	36.77	36.90	37.02				
Apr.	42.68		42.50	43.29	41.08	39.27	38.92	38.74				
May	48.35			48.47	43.86	40.33	39.39	38.81				
June	52.21			53.42	48.63	43.51	41.74	40.67	40.17			
July	50.41				46.77	41.91	40.84	40.37	40.05	40.61		
Aug.	47.84				47.27	42.07	42.04	42.77	42.98	43.65		
Sept.	49.64					47.79	47.21	45.29	44.45	44.92	44.77	
Oct.	48.27					47.79	44.59	41.69	40.81	41.72	41.53	
Nov.	45.49						45.83	43.48	41.90	42.79	42.16	42.05
Dec.	45.62						47.03	43.70	41.71	42.81	42.69	42.16

cattle prices are compared to the maturities about six months forward is as shown on following page.

Note that the cash prices had a net increase of $5.18 during 35 months, but traded up and down to a total of $93.58, leaving intramonth changes out of account. Futures contracts about six months forward had a net increase for the period of $.62 but traded up and down to a total of $71.06. Futures moved about three-fourths as much as cash. Only in late 1975 did cash and futures

Cash		Futures		
Jan.–Aug. 1973	+13.08	Dec. 1973	+15.22	
Aug.–Nov. 1973	−15.92	Feb. 1974	−11.79	but stayed 7.81 above cash
		Apr. 1974	−10.40	" " 8.80 " "
		June 1974	−10.21	" " 8.91 " "
Nov. 1973–Jan. 1974	+ 9.75	June 1974	+ 7.92	and remained above cash
		Oct. 1974	+ 6.79	" " " "
Jan.–June 1974	− 9.72	Dec. 1974	−14.18	and returned to cash
June–Aug. 1974	+ 9.02	Dec. 1974	+ 7.77	but below cash
		Apr. 1975	+ 8.65	" " "
Aug. 1974–Feb. 1975	−11.84	Apr. 1975	− 8.66	and was above cash
		Aug. 1975	− 9.11	" " " "
Feb.–June 1975	+17.53	Aug. 1975	+11.41	and was 3.58 below cash
		Dec. 1975	+ 4.81	" " 10.47 " "
June–Nov. 1975	− 6.72	Feb. 1976	+ 2.81	but was below cash
		Apr. 1976	+ 1.73	" " " "

move in opposite directions. The dominant influence on cattle futures prices is the cash cattle price.

In nearly all cases, the movement in futures prices was less than in the cash. The only exception was the runup in 1973. The futures market appeared to participate in the expectation that prices would rise with the ending of price ceilings.

But futures prices do not just move up and down with cash prices, with the amount of movement dampening the farther forward the contract reaches. Note in August, 1973, the ascending price structure through February with a decline subsequent to February. The market may have been saying: "Strength will persist until enough time passes to produce a larger supply and then the price will decline." Note that the forward contracts increased much less than cash during the first half of 1975 in contrast to 1973. The market seemed to be saying the rise was a fluke and wouldn't persist. Note that there was a tendency for June futures to be above April and August, suggesting a concept of a normal seasonal price variation.

What do these things tell us about how traders think in buying and selling contracts? First, the dominance of the cash price suggests that the basic forecast of the market seems to be that the price is as it should be and will not change. Second, there is a substantial skepticism about the validity of recent change. While saying that the present price will generally continue it also appears to say that the recent change is an aberration, will not last, and that prices will return to their earlier level. There is apparently an element of surprise when prices change. Third, markets do look ahead, anticipate supplies to come to market at a later time, and adjust prices in line with expectations.

While it is true that there can be no relationship of prices induced by storage stocks in the case of nonstorable commodities it should be recognized that there is a functional relationship that results from production planning. Presumably, producers form expectations about supplies and requirements that will exist at future times and adjust their own production up or down. If this is the case, resources are committed to production in a way that is expected to result in stable prices. The effect of production planning on price relationships among several delivery periods is toward an equalization of prices which is precisely the phenomenon that we have observed.

Price Relationships over Space

The use of futures markets by people engaged in the cash commodity trades is not restricted to firms located at futures delivery points. While futures contracts for some commodities provide for delivery at a multiplicity of points, most do not. In most cases delivery is restricted to a single delivery point, generally, at the point of the futures market. But only a small fraction of the commodities to which the futures transactions relate move to or through the delivery point. Thus, the relationship of prices at the delivery points to prices elsewhere is important. Such questions occur as: How can corn purchased at New Orleans at a price higher than Chicago be hedged in Chicago futures? Or can soybeans located in Yokahama, Japan be satisfactorily hedged in Chicago futures? Answers are that they can be so long as prices at the nondelivery positions have a functional relationship with those at the delivery point. It is only necessary that the futures prices be representative of the general level of prices and that prices at the many locations be functionally interrelated.

Prices of a commodity at its multitude of locations are functionally interrelated by transportation costs. For each commodity some areas are surplus and others are deficit. Therefore, commodities must move from area to area. There is a single set of price relationships that will cause the commodity to flow in a pattern that will just equalize supplies and requirements at all locations. Similarly, there is just one flow pattern that will minimize total transportation costs for the required movement. A commodity is bought where it is cheapest and sold where it is dearest, the cost of transportation taken into account. When the price is low in a supply area, the commodity is bought and the price is bid up to the point where purchases in that particular area cost just as much as in some other supply area. When requirements at a particular point are larger than receipts, prices are bid up enough to pull the commodity away from some other destination until an equilibrium flow and price pattern is achieved.

A delivery point on futures contracts must take its place in relation to other points. If the price at the delivery point is too high in relation to that at other destinations, a disproportionate supply will be attracted that will weigh heavily on the delivery point price, putting it back to its equilibrium relationship. If the delivery point price is too low, supplies will be inadequate for local use and shipping demand and the price will be bid up to an equilibrium level. That is, the delivery point price is no different from the price at any other point. It must be at its equilibrium level in the total spatial price pattern.

The actual purchase and sale decisions are made by merchants. They seek out the lowest purchasing points and highest selling points. They make purchases and sales without regard to whether the commodity can actually move between the two points. They base both purchases and sales on the expectations that distorted relationships will be restored to normal and that a profitable outlet will be found for the purchase and a profitable source of supply will be found for the sale. In this connection, futures markets become another source of supply for sales and another outlet for purchases.

Merchants are active and competitive. They do not let distortions become very large before they take corrective actions. The price surface for a commodity may be likened to the waves on the surface of a lake. It is never quite at rest, each individual spot moving up and down, traveling over a large aggregate distance but getting nowhere. The waves on the commodity price surface are kept small by the actions of merchants.

The thing that lends fascination to all of this is that it is never certain just what the equilibrium set of price relationships is. Price relationships over space do change and, at times, such changes may be large. One reason for this variation is changes in supply and use by areas. Specific regions have different surpluses of supplies for use in different years, and others have different excesses of demands over local supplies in different years. Some regions shift from surplus to deficit from year to year, and some regions have a surplus at some seasons and a deficit at others. Changing supply and use patterns require changing price differences to generate an optimum commodity flow.

A second reason for the differences in price relationships is that transportation rates and modes change. Such changes are frequent and have a major impact on price relationships. As transportation rates change, price relationships must also change if supplies and uses are to remain in balance over space.

A third reason for the variation is imperfection in the process of establishing the equilibrium set of differences. It is not possible to know just what set of relationships will optimize commodity flow. As a result, errors are made and price relationships become distorted. Such errors are the stuff out of which merchants record losses.

Artificial Distortions

This discussion of price relationships over time and space had assumed effective competition and the absence of distortion related to the operation of futures markets. Yet we saw in Chapter 4 that markets have not always been without suggestion of distortion resulting from futures trading; in fact, the history of futures trading in the latter part of the 19th century had the appearance of being more disruptive than not. Nor were such suggestions left in the last century. Modern futures trading is continually subjected to criticism on the basis that it results in distortion of prices between times and between prices at delivery points and outside points. We will delay discussion of the question of manipulation to a later point and content ourselves for now with some warnings for users of markets.

One possible distortion relates to an inadequate supply at the delivery point. The open interest at the beginning of a delivery month invariably exceeds the deliverable supply. Effective liquidation is dependent upon the willingness of longs to sell out. If supplies are small, longs may persist, forcing prices above spatial equilibrium levels. Such distortion will, in due course, attract additional supplies, forcing restoration of price equilibrium. But due course may be longer than the time allotted for settling contracts or the shorts may elect to sustain losses rather than go through with the process of obtaining supplies and moving them into position. As we have seen, speculators are numerous and generally have quite small positions. They are not very strong opponents of the large scale operators who might stand pat.

This kind of a distortion works to the disadvantage of the outside hedger. It results in a loss in the value of his cash position relative to his futures position. It is also disadvantageous to the small scale speculator who ventures to be short. The defense against this kind of unhappy occurrence is quite simple: Stay out of the delivery month. As we have noted, the delivery game is one played between the terminal merchants and large scale speculators.

The other side of this coin of delivery point shortage is artificial delivery point abundance. It is sometimes suggested that large scale merchants put more supplies in delivery positions than would be profitable except for purposes of advantage in futures operations. They may simply put large supplies in delivery position to aid in forcing wider carrying charges. This can not be profitable on those inventories alone but most such merchants and warehousemen also operate large amounts of space in outside locations; a terminal merchant in Kansas City may own a line of country elevators that he has full of hedged grain. Losses might be sustained on the terminal operation to protect the profitability of outside points.

A second and more sinister part of this game is to move large amounts into position, sell futures contracts against it, and sell additional contracts. Delivery is expected to depress the price so that any small losses taken on the hedged supplies are more than offset by speculative profits from the short sales. This is one of the games that was alleged to have been played with onions and the allegation was a factor in banning futures trading in onions.

Any of this type of distortion that exists is helpful to the outside short hedger. It strengthens his cash price relative to the futures and increases his profits. It is harmful to the outside long hedger; it reduces the value of his futures position without reducing his procurement cost. The long speculator is also hurt. Again, the defense is simple: Stay off of the long side of the delivery month contracts when delivery point supplies are large.

Part III

USE OF FUTURES MARKETS

Having looked at what futures markets are and what they are about, we are in a position to look at the way that markets are used by firms and individuals to increase the profitability of their production, marketing, and processing activities and to make money from futures trading. Futures markets are tools; they are not means of making money for the principals in trades. They are tools for implementing speculative judgments and enabling specialization in some aspects of the commodity trades while avoiding participation in others. It is important that prospective users from the commodity trades—agricultural producers, warehousemen, merchants, processors—understand that futures markets are not a new-found road to riches that can automatically assure business profitability. A poorly run cattle feeding operation is just that, with or without the use of futures markets, and is therefore unprofitable. An uneconomic country elevator operation will remain just that even though the management is highly skilled in futures market operations. Futures markets are a device by which a skilled speculator can greatly increase the exercise, hence the profitability, of his skills. But they are also a means by which an unskilled speculator can exericse his mistakes with great facility and lose his money rapidly. Futures markets are a means of implementation, not an enterprise in themselves.

The use of futures markets in connection with a commodity business or as a commodity speculator is a game of skill. The rudimentary futures operation, such as hedging a stored inventory, are simple and require little skill. But almost never is the game so simple. Price relationships are complex and uncertain and there are many factors that affect them. Similarly, multitudinous factors go into the makeup of prices so that an understanding of them requires detailed knowledge and skill in interpretation. Each of the commodity trades and each commodity price is surrounded by its own practices, facts, and behavior. While these tend to be generally similar in their broad outlines, they are specifically quite different. Thus, it is impossible for any one person to possess the knowledge and skills necessary to cover the whole field. Further, there is too much information to condense into one volume, let alone one section of one volume. What is attempted here is a general description, strengthened (hopefully) by a few examples.

CHAPTER 10

Warehousemen and Merchants

The area of futures trading about which there is the most literature and about which there is the most complete understanding is the use of futures in warehousing and merchandising storable commodities, grains in particular. This is the use of futures to shift price level risks while retaining the opportunity to speculate in basis. It is our point of departure in the use of futures markets.

Hedging in Detail

To hedge is to assume a position in futures equal and opposite to an already existing cash position. While in broad context the essence of hedging is risk shifting, the hedger should realize that he does not actually shift risk; he offsets the risk of price level change. He does not cease to speculate; he takes on an additional speculation. Because the additional speculation is opposite in short futures when he is long cash and long futures when he is short cash—profits and losses, because of changes in *price levels,* cancel and leave only profits and losses that result from changes in *price relationships.* The hedger should be under no illusion that he has no market position; he has two where previously he had only one.

The two positions, cash and futures, should be taken as near the same time as possible. But futures contracts are traded only a limited number of hours—9:30 A.M. to 1:15 P.M. (central time) for grains—and most cash commodities are bought and sold before and after these times. Should the hedger sell futures equal to the amount of cash grain that he expects to purchase after the close, or should he wait until he knows how much he has bought and then sell an equal amount at the opening the following day? There is some room for judgment about overnight price change. During periods of heavy movement, experienced

175

hedgers tend to sell futures in anticipation of purchases, and during periods of light movement, tend to sell futures contracts after making purchases.

Futures contracts are traded in fairly large units—5,000 bushels of the grains—while purchases are of all sizes. Thus, the hedger necessarily carries a small open position—it should not, however, exceed 2,500 bushels of grain. Whether he should be net long or short is a matter of speculative judgment about price change. But the positions should be as nearly the same size as possible.

Two rules (1) take offsetting positions simultaneously, and (2) keep offsetting positions as nearly the same size as possible, must be observed in a hedging program. To fail to observe both rules is to speculate in price level. Warehouse operators frequently talk about anticipatory hedging—selling futures well ahead of buying cash commodity—or about waiting for a postharvest recovery before placing hedges. Neither is part of a hedging program. To dress them up in hedging terminology does not change their nature. They are both examples of price level speculation.

Warehousemen—country elevators in particular—frequently go long cash grain, watch the price go up, and pride themselves on their speculative skill. The fact may be that the futures actually went down and the price appreciation was less than the basis gain, with the result that the speculation actually lost money. Many warehousemen do not speculate, but many do. But price level speculation is not a part of the warehouse business. It should be kept separate and should not be done in the cash commodity. People in the warehouse business who have an irresistible urge to speculate in price level should open a separate account—perhaps in their wives' names or their own rather than in the companies' names—and test their skill without the aid of the built-in upward bias of cost of storage of cash commodity prices.

The Mechanics. The country grain elevator is the simplest hedging case and a set of instructions for them is used as an example here. The principles are applicable to all warehouse operations.

Hedges should be set up on a "T" account system, with one side of the account for cash and the other for futures. Only rarely do country elevators make, and never do they take, delivery. Accordingly, the two accounts should be kept separate, cash transactions with subsequent cash transactions and futures transactions with subsequent futures transactions.

But the accounting of the cash and futures transactions must be made in a single hedging account. Many elevators have a composite account for cash grain and a separate futures account. The cash grain account, showing a gross profit or loss from sales of the various grains handled, contains elements of handling margins, storage returns on owned grain, speculative profits and losses, and sometimes storage on customer owned grain. The futures account is generally kept separate, showing a profit or loss without regard to the offsetting profits and losses in cash grain resulting from price level changes.

Frequently when firms keep cash and futures accounts separately, they note losses in the futures account and think and act negatively with regard to futures trading even though their hedging operations are successful. An integrated cash and futures accounting system is essential to a good hedging program.

The cash price entered in the hedging account should be the price the cash grain would have brought had it been sold instead of hedged, rather than the price paid to producers. That is, the amount of the handling margin should not be entered in the hedging account. If corn is bought at $2.75 on a six cent margin and hedged, it should be shown in the hedging account as bought at $2.81.

Illustration 1 shows a cash inventory hedged in futures. There was a gain of 10 cents per bushel on the cash and a loss of 5 cents on futures before commissions. (Commission is roughly ¾ cents per bushel for nonmembers.)

Illustration 1

Date	Cash Account		Futures Account	
Oct. 10	Bought 10,000 bushels	$2.65	Sold 10,000 bushels Dec.	$2.85
Nov. 15	Sold 10,000 bushels	2.75	Bought 10,000 bushels Dec.	2.90
		+ .10		− .05
	Gain	.05		

Illustration 2 shows a short cash position hedged in futures. This hypothetical hedge was placed ahead of harvest and shows a cash gain of 12 cents and a futures loss of 7 cents.

Illustration 2

Date	Cash Account		Futures Account	
Aug. 15	Sold 30,000 bushels	$5.17	Bought 30,000 bushels Nov.	$5.39
Sept. 30	Bought 30,000 bushels	5.05	Sold 30,000 bushels Nov.	5.32
		+ .12		− .07
	Gain	.05		

Illustration 3 shows how a hedge is moved forward as the delivery month in which the hedge was originally placed approaches.

Illustration 3

Date	Cash Account		Futures Account	
Oct. 15	Bought 50,000 bushels	$2.50	Sold 50,000 bushels Dec.	$2.80
Nov. 25			Bought 50,000 bushels Dec.	2.90 −.10
Nov. 25			Sold 50,000 bushels May	3.10
Apr. 15	Sold 50,000 bushels	2.90	Bought 50,000 bushels May	3.20 −.10
		+ .40		−.20
	Gain	.20		

Note that the sources of the net gains were from changes in the relationship of cash and futures prices. In Illustration 1, the cash gained 5 cents in relation to the futures while the grain was in store. The cash grain could have been held unhedged at a larger gain but only at the hazard of an adverse price change. The hedge may have been placed because the operator elected to separate the storage business from price level speculation as a matter of specialization, because he thought the price might go down, or because he couldn't finance the inventory except on a hedged basis. By the same token, he could have sold the cash grain and realized an ordinary merchandising margin. But in doing so he would have foregone the earning of revenue from otherwise unused space.

In Illustration 2, the gain was from a widening of the basis. Note that the cash sale was made at 22 cents under the November and bought at 27 cents under. The operator anticipated, for whatever reason, that the cash price would decline relative to the futures. It did. He made money from implementing his correct speculative expectation. The motivation was obviously not risk shifting, else he would not have sold cash soybeans six weeks before he bought them. However, speculation in price level was separated from speculation in price difference. He would have been better off to speculate in both level and difference but price level was not his game.

In Illustration 3, cash gained in relation to the futures during the October 15–April 15 storage period. The price level increased 20 cents and the cash gained 20 cents in relation to the futures. Again, the hedger would have been better off had he speculated in both price level and price difference. He may have hedged because he thought the price level would decline, he didn't have an opinion about price level, he wanted to avoid the risk of price level decrease, or because he could not borrow the money to own the corn unless he hedged.

Hedges should not be thought of as being placed and removed at specific prices but rather in terms of basis. In Illustration 1 the cash was bought at 20 cents under and sold at 15 cents under for a gain of 5 cents. In Illustration 2 the cash was sold at 22 cents under and bought at 27 cents under for a gain of 5 cents. In Illustration 3 the cash was bought at 30 cents under the December future, the hedge was moved forward at a May premium of 20 cents, and the cash was sold at 30 cents under for a gain of 20 cents.

There are two reasons for thinking in terms of basis rather than price: (1) The arithmetic is much simpler, and (2) the hedger is concerned about basis rather than price. When he hedges, he decides not to speculate in price. When he thinks in terms of basis, he is helped to remember that price is of no concern to him. If he thinks in terms of price, he is likely to regard all three illustrated hedges as losing money. True, more money would have been made by speculating in cash than by hedging. However, the hedges, per se, were successful.

Country Elevator Hedges

The primary interest of country elevators in hedging is to earn returns from otherwise empty space. However, hedges can be profitably used in other ways. Five kinds of uses are discussed here.

Storage Hedge. This type is the fundamental use of hedging by warehouse-men. It is the means by which warehouse space is sold. The underlying concept is that warehousemen have space, equipment, labor, etc., available and they wish to sell the storage service for as much as possible. They necessarily watch the going market price of storage for the various grains and decide when to commit space and which grain to store. They must choose from that which is available, but most elevators have less than enough space to store the amount of grain they buy.

By way of example, suppose that an elevator has 300,000 bushels of storage space and buys 200,000 bushels of soybeans and 400,000 bushels of corn during the fall harvest period. Further, suppose that 100,000 bushels of space is taken by farmer customers. This leaves 200,000 to sell on the storage market. The elevator will thus sell and ship two of every three bushels purchased and hold one for hedged storage. In other words, it has a one-third selectivity of hedging bases. The hedger can reject two-thirds of the basis opportunities offered and keep one-third. His objective is to choose the most profitable one-third. The chronic question is: "Should I take this basis or wait for a better one?" It is an interesting game and, watching it, it is again apparent that hedging is not the opposite of speculation, but rather a different kind of the same thing.

As the hedger reaches the other end of the line, a similar question arises: "Should I sell cash and buy in my hedges now, or will the cash gain further on the futures by enough to cover costs?" The answer to this question is not clear-cut either. In some years it is profitable to unwind hedges on the same basis that one would find profitable to continue in other years. Selecting the right time to unwind hedges is generally easier than selecting the basis on which space is committed.

A third question in the storage hedge is the delivery month to hedge in. Should hedges be placed in the nearby month with the expectation that they can be moved forward at more favorable spreads between futures than currently exist, or should hedges be placed in a distant delivery month near the end of the storage period? The answer depends upon what the hedger expects to happen to the price of storage in the various periods from Dec. to March, March to May, etc.

Coverage of a Cash Sale Ahead of Harvest. On occasion, elevators can profitably sell grain ahead of purchase from farmers and cover the resultant short position by buying futures. If the hedger observes that cash grain for delivery at harvest is selling unusually close to the nearby futures contract and if he expects a heavy harvest movement, he can sell to interior merchants for harvest delivery and buy an equal amount of futures. In doing so, he becomes short the basis. If the basis widens as in Illustration 2 (page 177), he will profit as he buys cash grain from farmers and sells his hedges. If the basis narrows, he will lose. Note that such transactions in soybeans would have lost money from August to October in both 1965 and 1966. (See figures 6 and 7.)

This kind of basis operation is fundamentally speculative. All of the merchants in the market are playing the same game. When they think that the basis will narrow, they buy cash and sell futures, going long the basis. When they think the basis will widen, they sell cash and buy futures. Thus, before harvest, the basis is representative of the aggregate market expectation of the harvest basis. Country elevators are in a relatively good position to judge crop size and farmer thinking about whether to hold or sell. These are two important factors in establishing the harvest basis. Preharvest purchases are often dominated by exporters who must get their purchases lined up well ahead of harvest because of purchases by firms in recipient countries. So long as such purchases exceed preharvest sales by farmers, there is upward pressure on the basis. But the elevator hedger must accurately anticipate farmer willingness to sell at harvest.

When this kind of hedge is successful, some hedgers are tempted to use the advantageous cash sale to raise bids to farmers in the interest of increasing volume. Such procedure is not wise. This kind of hedge is about as likely to lose money as to make money, and farmers are not likely to be willing to participate in losses. Such strong bidding is really margin cutting and should be regarded in that light.

Coverage of a Cash Sale During the Marketing Season. Occasionally elevators have an opportunity to make an especially favorable cash sale for deferred shipment; as elevators are bid for cash on a basis higher than the basis they expect to prevail at the time of shipment. There are a variety of reasons why such bids are made in connection with export sales, processed product sales, and freight rates. But the elevator should keep two things in mind: (1) The normal basis change works against being short the basis during the marketing season, and (2) some merchant has had the same opportunity to make the short basis sale and passed it up.

More usual are premium bids for deferred shipment, such as corn for January shipment during harvest. For example, on Oct. 29, 1964, corn for immediate shipment was bid at $1.07, track Illinois points, corn for January shipment was bid at $1.15, and the March futures closed at $1.22¾. The spot price was 15¾ cents under the March. On January 4 the spot price was $1.21, and March closed at $1.26⅛. The spot was 5⅛ under the March. The premium offered was 8 cents, and the basis narrowed by 10⅝ cents. A short sale of cash for January shipment, covered by a purchase of March futures, would have caused the elevator hedger to lose 2⅝ cents per bushel plus commission. It is a fair bet that the interior merchants making the premium bids were going long cash and short futures.

This is not an isolated example. Rather, it was chosen for its typicalness. It demonstrates the speculative nature of basis formulation. It is a game played among basis traders in which there are rewards and penalties for being right and wrong in basis expectations.

Hedging Off Purchases on a Weak Basis. Occasionally the basis at some locations is unusually weak. Such locations are usually tied to one or a limited number of markets because of freight rate considerations. If the destination effectively goes out of the market by bidding low, the elevator has trouble in meeting competition in its bids to producers. If the elevator has reasonable confidence that its usual destination will come back into the market with a competitive bid, it can hedge off its own purchases made at competitive levels and wait for a favorable basis before selling.

Futures markets react quickly to unusual news, such as war or drought. Cash markets often do not follow immediately. Purchases made from farmers at such times can be more profitably hedged than sold in cash markets. These things happen infrequently, but the astute hedger takes advantage of them when they do occur.

Hedging to Defer Pricing to Farmers. Farmers often want to deliver grain at harvest and defer pricing until later. If the elevator has a sufficient amount of space and makes an appropriate storage charge, no hedging problem arises. But frequently the elevator has insufficient space and is faced with the question of selling cash grain and buying futures. The simple solution is to buy the grain and let each farmer buy his own futures. But because individual farmers have small amounts of grain to store, limited understanding of futures markets, and because elevators are pressed by competition, they seek other solutions. Under warehouse laws, grain not physically present cannot be "stored" and a "storage charge" made. It must be purchased on a contract specifying a price relationship. Two different kinds of contracts are written:

a. The elevator agrees to pay the farmer the same amount under a given futures contract as the market price on the day the contract is written. If the bid to farmers is 24 cents under the May futures on the day the purchase contract is made, the elevator agrees to pay the farmer 24 cents under the May on whatever day he elects prior to May 1. The contract can be written in relation to any futures contract. The elevator can then sell the cash grain and replace it with a futures contract. Because the elevator buys and sells on the same basis, it can neither gain nor lose from basis change.

b. The elevator agrees to pay the farmer the going market price on whatever day he elects, minus a specified amount that varies among elevators and depends on when the farmer elects to sell. These are typically called delayed price contracts. Some of them are written at a monthly "storage" equal to the storage rate charged by elevators. Others have a charge for "deposit" plus a monthly storage. A third type is a flat charge for the season regardless of when the grain is priced. A charge for delayed pricing is a procedure farmers understand and tend to prefer. Elevators sell the cash and price it in a comparable delayed price arrangement or, more often, replace it with futures. When the elevator replaces the cash with futures it protects itself from price level changes but retains a basis risk. If the basis narrows more than the charges made, the elevator loses money and if the basis narrows less, it makes money. The elevator typically receives payment for the cash grain but does not pay farmers until it is priced. Thus, it can obtain interest income to partly offset the narrowing of the basis.

If a contract is to be realistic in the discounts in lieu of storage charges it must be written so that the discounts minus an estimate of interest earnings parallel the basis pattern. At $2.75 corn and seven percent interest, monthly interest earnings are 1.6 cents. In the mid 1970's the month-to-month change in corn basis in the midwest was about:

October to November	0	March to April	+ 3
November to December	+14	April to May	+ 2
December to January	+ 2	May to June	+ 1
January to February	+ 3	June to July	− 4
February to March	+ 3		

The total is 24 cents. If an elevator had a schedule of charges exactly equal to these amounts minus an allowance for interest it would break even on average. In years of greater basis gain it would lose, and in years of smaller gain it would profit. But in years of a wide harvest basis there is usually a greater demand for delayed pricing and vice-versa, so that the elevator tends to lose more when it loses than it gains in profitable years. It is particularly important that the charge system offset the large basis gain immediately following the end of harvest because many farmers sell in January. A monthly charge of 2.5 cents would cover the basis gain adjusted for interest earnings for the corn held to June. But corn held only to January would return only eight cents versus a basis gain of sixteen cents.

Hedging Program. This enumeration of kinds of hedges can be expanded by subdividing the several types so that the process is made as complicated as we have patience to think it through. The specialized warehouse operator has both time and patience. His operations can be made just as complex as his skills and willingness to work at basis analysis permit. But work at it he must because the essence of hedging is basis analysis and forecasting. The several kinds of hedging activities are not separate enterprises carried out in succession but rather are a part of an integrated whole that makes up a hedging program. Nearly all warehouse firms handle several different commodities—the country elevators as many as four kinds of grain. Each is continually buying, selling, receiving, shipping, and storing. All of the individual operations must be fitted together to form an integrated whole; each is done in relation to the existing operations going on in the others. The whole of the program must be related to the total activities and objectives of the firm. A hedging program is a supplement to the primary business activities of the firm.

The purpose of a hedging program is to enable the firm to supplement its income and to most efficiently use the facilities that it must have and operate in connection with its cash commodity operations. The nature of the country elevator operation changed rapidly during the 1960–75 period and was far from complete at the end. As grain farms became larger and harvesting methods changed the volume of receipts at harvest and the demands for storage increased rapidly. To effectively serve their customers, and thus stay in business in a highly competitive industry, elevators had to expand their capacity to receive, condition, and store grain, corn in particular. They had to make storage facilities available to farmers in as large amounts as farmers wanted. Sufficient plant to accommodate the harvest peaks resulted in excess capacity during most of the year. The basic purpose of a hedging program in this context was to increase income from otherwise unused capacity while avoiding the risks of price change inherent in cash grain ownership. They cannot maximize the use of available space without owning cash grain inventories and can neither finance cash grain inventories nor absorb losses from price decreases without hedging. The situation in Illinois corn producing areas in the 1960's was remarkably similar to that of a century before.

A second purpose of elevator hedging is to maximize selling prices. Hedging is a supplemental outlet for cash grain that is useful in merchandising activities. It enables the elevator to avoid temporarily depressed local prices without reducing bids to farmers or assuming price risks. It enables full play of the elevators merchandising skills.

If some elevators implement hedging programs that enable them to increase earnings it is essential that the others also do if they are to survive. It is an intensely competitive industry.

Operational Tools. The essence of a successful hedging program is forecasting basis. What are the tool for analysis? They can be divided into two main groups: (1) records of past behavior, and (2) records of factors affecting basis.

As we have noted, basis charts for a grain at a location are broadly and generally similar from year to year but individual years are specifically different and the differences are sometimes substantial. It is knowledge of the specific differences that is responsible for success or failure in merchandising and hedging programs.

To operate successfully, each hedger must develop his own series of data. There is no shortcut to success. A good job of hedging requires a lot of work, along with careful and continuous attention. Only by keeping his own data will the hedger be familiar (day by day) with the basis situation, with the factors affecting basis, and with comparable basis situations at other times. Only in this way will he have the hedging information pertinent to his location.

Each operator is concerned with basis at his location. From this point of view, the whole world of prices revolves around his location. The data pertinent to a single location is not available except as the individual himself develops it. The first category of records should include:

1. *Price and basis tables.* Tables of cash prices—generally, the selling prices at the location of the hedging operation and at the delivery point of the futures market and the closing prices of all futures contracts—should be kept. The prices themselves can be entered on one half of a page. On the other half, so that both are visible at the same time, the relationship-basis of the local cash price to each of the futures prices—should be entered. The spot cash prices are related to the old crop futures, and the deferred shipment prices are related to new crop futures.

2. *Spread tables.* A tabulation of the spreads as they exist each day is useful in forming judgments about which delivery month will be most profitable for hedging and about what spreads should be placed ahead of the cash grain purchases that will eventually be hedged.

3. *Basis charts.* The tabulated data are used to make charts for easy inspection of basis patterns and trends. Some people read tables of data easily; others best understand charts. Keeping both is useful.

4. *Long and short records.* Each firm must have an integrated record of cash and futures transactions. The cash commodity is priced into the hedging account at the spot selling price. The offsetting futures price is entered, and the ingoing basis computed. When hedges are removed, the gains and losses can be easily computed.

The second category of records is more general. It is also more difficult to deal with in specific terms. A lot of data on the production, use, and flow of commodities are available—much on a weekly basis.

The data kept should include: (1) production by states, (2) receipts, disappearance, and shipments at the pertinent terminals, (3) terminal stocks, (4) primary receipts, shipments, and stocks, (5) exports by points, (6) farm stocks, (7) total stocks, and (8) open interest in futures markets and its breakdown between speculators and hedgers.

Equipped with the tools, what does one do? Analytical techniques for basis behavior have not been developed in a specific or quantitative sense. In analyzing a current basis situation certain questions should be asked: (1) How is this basis going to change in the future? (2) What happened from this time onward last year? (3) What has been the average behavior over the past several years? (4) What is specifically different about the current year that will cause a deviation from past patterns? (5) Is this a basis situation that will prove profitable? (6) Is this situation more or less profitable than one that may exist next week or next month?

Most of the answers are matters of judgment. Good judgment is acquired from experience and diligent examination of all of the factors. When the hedger learns to explain that which has happened before, he is in a position to anticipate that which will happen next.

What Do Elevators Really Do? The thing described above is a complete hedging program of a kind recommended for warehouse and merchandising operation. It rests on the twin assumptions of a high degree of sophistication and a policy of not speculating in price changes, and the constant maintenance of a fully hedged position. It is not representative of the real world of warehouse operations, grain and otherwise. There is no systematically assembled knowledge of what country elevators really do but some impressions are worth listing.

Some elevators, probably a small percentage, do run hedging programs by the book and with a high degree of sophistication. The number is greater than it was 10 or 20 years ago before the increase in size and amount of nongovernmental storage associated with changes in grain production took place. Some of these are small, independent companies while others are a part of line companies.

Something of the change taking place is shown by an exchange that took place before the House of Representatives Agricultural Committee when it was considering a futures trading bill in 1966. Mr. Hagen of California. "Do you speculate on the market yourself?" Mr. Brouilette (a country elevator owner-operator from Indiana) "I think that I would be a little bit remiss to say that sometime in one's life he has not made a trade. However, our banker will not let me speculate so I, at the present time, do not speculate." Mr. Brouilette had previously described the rapid increase in the storage of corn bought at harvest that had taken place and his use of corn futures associated with it. What he meant was that prior to the change in his operation he did speculate in grain prices, both cash and futures, but that he had been forced to stop out of financing considerations. There was a note of wistfulness in Mr. Brouilette's expression.

At the other end of the scale are elevators whose managers know nothing of hedging or futures market operations. There are provisions in the by-laws of some firms, farmer cooperatives in particular, prohibiting any activities in futures markets. These stem from a history of speculation in futures that led to company bankruptcy. This is not to say that companies that do not trade futures contracts do not speculate. Nearly all elevators take cash grain positions and some of these positions are quite large. A high proportion are on the long side—buying cash grain and waiting for the price to go up which it typically does from harvest onward. Instances have been found in which elevators have been long as much as a quarter of a year's receipts of cash soybeans while having by-laws prohibiting futures trading because it is speculative.

Selective hedging is common. Elevators acquire cash grain inventories and hedge when they think the price is apt to decline or hedge part of the inventory so that risks are kept at "sleepable" levels. The percentage of the inventory that is carried hedged is varied as the managers' expectations and certainty-uncertainty change. Anticipatory hedging is the short side of the selective hedging game. Here, managers place hedges against inventories that they expect to buy at lower prices. Their thought is that grain will come to market, put pressure on prices as it does, and that they will be in an excellent basis position by placing hedges in advance. If the harvest movement does not put pressure on prices they can cover their mistakes as an abnormally small basis gain.

Another variant is to hedge and fail to offset the futures position when the cash grain is sold. This tends to happen when the futures position is a losing one and the manager either thinks or hopes that the price will decline so that he will, at worst, break even on the futures side.

A thing called a "Texas hedge" should be mentioned as an extreme case. Here the elevator accumulates an inventory of cash grain and, expecting the price to go up, holds on to it. This seems like such a good idea that he regrets that he hasn't a larger stock and does the next best thing, buys an equal amount of futures. This, of course, has no resemblance to a hedge but is sometimes done.

These impressions lead to some generalizations. First, the favorable image the term hedging has, in contrast to speculation, leads to all sorts of things being called hedging. Second, country elevators speculate in prices of both cash and futures. It appears that some amount of speculation is difficult for most elevator managers to resist. Commission futures merchants tend to regard their country elevator accounts as generally speculative in establishing margin requirements. Third, there is need for a better understanding of the use of futures markets by interior warehousemen. There is a lot of genuine misunderstanding and an even greater lack of appreciation of the opportunities to improve operations presented by futures trading.

Interior Merchants

Interior grain merchants are those firms located in the main surplus grain regions. This is specially true for areas not directly tributary to terminal markets. They are most numerous and of greatest importance in the surplus grain producing areas of Illinois. The fundamental reason for the development of interior merchandising is the great diversity of flow of grain. As the direction of flow became more diverse in the western part of the North Central Region, additional interior merchandising points developed.

These people are merchants in the purest sense. They do not receive, store, ship, or, for that matter, even see the commodities they handle. Their physical equipment—operating plant so to speak—consists of a telephone, desk, set of books, and, sometimes, a price quotation ticker. Their primary asset is their merchandising skill; they live by their wits.

The interior merchant buys, takes title to, and sells grain. On the buying side, he provides a market outlet for the grain purchased by country elevators. On the selling side, the merchant provides supplies for processors, terminals, and exporters. A key consideration in the success of the interior merchant is that he must stay continuously in the market. He serves as a clearing house of information with news of the markets to the country and news of the country to the markets.

In large measure the merchant makes the market, standing as he does in the middle, so that he can see both the supply and demand sides. His actions and information have important effects on the actions of speculators in futures markets and so they influence the price level. More importantly, the operators affect price relationships over time and space. More than any other group, the interior merchants establish the structure of the grain price surface by buying grain when and where it is cheap and selling it when and where it is dear.

Merchandisers are arbitragers. They do the job of satiating the demand for consumption and the demand for inventory. This entails movement of the commodity from locations of supplies to points of use. Reconciling these divergencies in demand is a complex and intricate operation. Grain is produced in thousands of locations and is consumed all over the world. The relationships of prices at different locations guides the flow from points of production to the points of use. The specific decisions about where and when to send any given lot of grain are made by merchants on the basis of existing and prospective price relationships. They buy and sell in an attempt to make a profit. These merchants deal in large quantities and their gross margins are quite small in relation to the variation in the level of grain prices. They must either buy and sell simultaneously or hedge to avoid the price level risks that they are neither able nor willing to assume.

It is possible for merchants to limit all transactions to cash grain, and in large measure they do, but they also hedge. They hedge because they judge that merchandising profits can be increased by hedging; that the relationship of prices will change in their favor during the time that they are hedged.

For example, a merchant may find producers and country elevators offering large quantities of a commodity. He judges it an appropriate time to accumulate stocks from which he can supply processors, terminals, and exporters. He probably cannot sell as rapidly at advantageous prices as he purchases so he hedges. As he gradually works off the inventory he buys the offsetting futures contracts. Note again that futures contracts stood, for a time, in the place of cash transactions.

On the other side, merchants may sell ahead and buy futures as price level protection. For example, an exporter may buy a large quantity, as much as one million bushels, to cover part of a sale. This is more than the interior merchant can expect to buy in cash markets immediately. He covers by buying futures and liquidates as the cash commodity is gradually accumulated.

A merchant may conclude well before the season begins—e.g., in January for corn—that the new crop cash price (October–November delivery) is high in relation to new crop futures (December). He sells cash for harvest delivery and buys new crop futures to hedge. In this case he is arbitraging between current inventory demand (typically importers in other countries) and the next year's production. He is short the basis in an attempt to profit from an expected subsequent decrease in cash prices in relation to futures.

Another game these people play is to use the time lags in the marketing process as storage space. Suppose that a farmer goes to his local elevator and sells 10,000 bushels of corn that he has stored on his farm. The elevator, in turn, sells to a merchant and the merchant hedges. The farmer arranges for transportation and delivers the corn ten days later. The elevator orders rail cars in and loads them. This takes another ten days. With the cars sealed, the elevator draws a sight draft on the merchant and the merchant has some money tied up but still holds title to the corn. He orders the corn shipped as far as possible, say the east coast. In the leisurely process of the railroads, he will be notified several weeks later that the corn is approaching destination. He sells the cash corn to an eastern export house and removes his hedge. In the usual course of events the basis will have narrowed during the 30 day or so time lag and the merchant will have earned a carrying charge without the cost of space operation; he will have used a phantom elevator. Spread over enough bushels, this can be quite lucrative. But, again, life is not so simple. As he buys from the elevator with these happy thoughts, the elevator may tell him the corn is loaded and ask for billing instructions, having played the game himself. Or the exporter may know the corn is enroute, realize it has no feasible alternate destination and offer a low price, resulting in a loss to the merchant. But there is enough in this kind of operation that merchants tend to operate out of long cash—short futures positions after the peak of harvest is past.

The operating margins of interior merchants—the difference between the prices that they are offered and that they bid—are quite small—too small to be profitable. If they were wide enough to be profitable the users would find it profitable to buy directly from the country or the country would find it profitable to sell directly to users. Interior merchants have commented that they sometimes lose money or break even on three quarters of their trades but make enough on changes in price differences on the balance to stay in business. Casual observation of their living standards suggests that they manage to stay in business at favorable levels of return. But they live by their wits.

In these several illustrations individual transactions have been isolated. In practice, the matter is more complex. Merchants buy and sell continually, attempting to buy cheap and sell dear. Because favorable purchases and sales only occasionally occur at the same time, futures transactions are made against sales until purchases can be made and against purchases until sales can be made. Actually, of course, only the net positions are hedged.

As described here, the merchants are closely hedged so that they are not subject to risks of price level change. But they do most of their cash business before the opening and after the close and so cannot avoid market positions. Do they prehedge or wait to hedge? The answer depends upon how they feel about prices at a given time. When they are totally uncertain they try to do half one and half the other or to offset cash purchases with cash sales and vice versa. But they are not always totally uncertain and so lean one way or the other. Sometimes they are fairly certain and lean heavily one way or the other. Under some circumstances they take substantial market positions, speculating in price level. There are times when they are firmly convinced that farmers will not sell below a certain price and are willing to go long futures when the basis between this floor price and the futures is narrow. On the other hand, they sometimes sense that the country will sell large quantities should the price rise to a certain level. At prices above this level, normal basis taken into account, they are willing sellers of futures. These actions sometimes put brackets around futures prices for protracted periods of time. But they sometimes make mistakes and are forced to liquidate hurriedly, resulting in fairly sharp changes in prices.

The positions that merchants take are much smaller relative to their volume of operations than those of country elevators. Their gross margins are very small and their operating capital is small relative to the volume handled. Thus, their risk absorption capacity is small. They are not in a position to finance major decreases in price and so take small losses quickly and content themselves with small profits. They are price making forces over small ranges of price but not major ranges. The market positions that they take are sometimes in cash grain and sometimes in futures.

Ingredient Merchants

The kinds of trading activities and function performed described above are similar to, and thus examples of, activities of merchants trading in other kinds of commodities. One other kind is feed ingredient merchants. The list of ingredients used in the manufacture of compounded livestock feeds is quite long, including five kinds of oilseed meals, fishmeal, animal by-product protein, wheat millfeeds, corn gluten feed and meal, brewers dried grains, bone meal, alfalfa meal, and various grains. Excepting the grains, alfalfa meal, fishmeal and soybean meal they are by-products of various agricultural product processing industries. The most important ingredients in terms of values and cost are corn and soybean meal. There are a lot of processors of various kinds and many mixed feed manufacturers. The ingredient merchants buy from processors and sell to feed manufacturers. They are locators of supplies and markets and, for most ingredients, operate on generally understood and acccepted margins. The grain trade with feed manufacturers is handled by the grain merchants.

Soybean processors have soybean meal sales departments. They sell to feed manufacturers when they are the best outlets at the time that the processors want to make sales and to the ingredient merchants when they are the best outlet. The converse is true of the feed manufacturers' ingredient buyers. Thus, the ingredient merchants stand in between two sets of specialists, carving out an income. One function they perform is the convenience one of locating and servicing markets, of matching supplies to requirements, furnishing market information, and routine shipments to minimize transportation cost. A second function is the bridging of time gaps between sellers and buyers. The sellers time their offers out of one set of considerations such as soybean purchases and margins in the case of soybean meal and the buyers out of another set of considerations such as price and mixed feed sales. The merchants bridge the time gaps, sometimes accumulating inventories and sometimes committing inventory they do not own. They, too, are true merchants in that they have no physical facilities beyond a telephone, desk, and set of books.

There is a large volume, active futures market for soybean meal at the Chicago Board of Trade, started in 1951. For some years prior to that time there was a moderately active futures market in soybean meal and cottonseed meal at Memphis. For many years there was a wheat millfeeds market in Kansas City but trade died out. A millfeeds market was attempted in St. Louis but it failed to get off of the ground. There is a fishmeal market in New York but the volume of trade is quite small.

Feed ingredient merchants make extensive use of the soybean meal futures market. They hedge their purchases and their sales in futures. They spread between delivery months as a further means of smoothing out the time gaps between purchases and sales by manufacturers and users. They make and take delivery when they judge that forthcoming changes in basis will make these operations profitable. The essence of their operations in futures is basis speculation. They make purchases of cash forward meal and hedge when they judge that current selling pressures have forced prices below the levels relative to futures that will prevail at a later time and they make cash forward sales when they judge the opposite to be true. This kind of use of futures makes it possible for the merchants to maintain an ownership inventory out of which they can sell or a backlog of sales for which they can later make purchases.

Much of the activity of feed ingredient merchants is in the arrangement of the details of trades. Processors store little meal; most is loaded directly into railcars from the production stream and must be shipped immediately. Soybeans are processed in transit so that the destinations of meal and incoming locations of soybeans are interrelated. Meal has different values depending upon the destination that it can go to and yet recover a part of the inbound freight on soybeans. The upshot is that processing plants allocate shipments in a pattern that is related to the pattern of origin of soybean receipts. They must work out shipments schedules by specific time and kind of freight billing in advance of loading. They like to establish the specific prices as well. For example, in the latter part of March a processor offers a large quantity of "fully unrestricted" meal for scattered April shipment, at $140.00 per ton. His plant, his price, or his billing may not fit the bids of the feed mixers then in the market. A merchant buys it, and he then sells it, gradually, some here and some there, fitting it in to the production requirements of several users, both large and small. He tends to the details of shipment, exchange of money, quality adjustments, etc.

How do futures fit into this? The processor may have sold meal futures against an inventory of soybeans well in advance of March as part of a process of establishing a processing margin. When he makes the specific cash sale he has the meal part of the margin tied down tight and buys his futures back. The merchant, who is now long cash meal may hedge by selling May (or some other delivery) futures. He may sell the cash meal (or part of it) on a basis. A feed mixer may like the origin and the timing but not the price. He may agree to pay the May futures price on whatever day he elects prior to the arrival of the meal at plant. When he says "now" the absolute price is fixed and the merchant buys in his short position. It may be that the feed mixer already holds a long position in futures. In this case the merchant and mixer may exchange futures "ex-pit." In "ex-pit" transactions the brokers agree to report identical prices to the clearing house without actually executing the trades. Under the rules this is permitted only when there is an accompanying cash transaction. It may also be that the mixer, instead of saying "now" and letting the merchant buy futures, prefers to buy May futures and exchange. If, in fact, the merchant has sold July instead of May he is in the position of spreading back into May to make the exchange.

Obviously, the possible complications of these people trading futures against cash positions are nearly endless. We have tried to keep the example simple. In addition, this is an isolated transaction that is but one part of the total cash-futures positions of all three. The use of futures by merchants is complex and requires a high degree of specialized knowledge and skill.

"Pricing" by users, not only in soybean meal but other commodities as well, sometimes results in quite volatile futures prices. The merchant who is short futures is short to speculators and the user is buying from speculators. In situations of short supply of the spot commodity, the speculators may be quite difficult to bargain with and the user, especially if he has over-waited hoping for a lower price, in a nearly defenseless position. He can either pay up or go without. In these situations there is a marked tendency for the users to find a way to give up a car here and car there or delay shipment for a week or two. High and rising prices in a delivery month tend to uncover spot supplies not thought to exist. Such is the role of price and such is the role of the speculator in price establishment.

From this brief description of the activities of ingredient merchants it should be especially noted that theirs is an arbitrage activity between cash and futures prices and among delivery months and that the risks of price changes are carried within the futures market. Prior to the development of a futures market in soybean meal merchants and jobbers bought cash forward contracts and carried price risks (see Chapter 4). But nearly all of them eventually made price level mistakes large enough to put them out of business; their mortality rate was high. This is not to suggest that the survivors do not take market positions, both cash and futures—they do. Their market positions are small relative to their total volume of operations but they may be absolutely of substantial size. There are occasions, particularly near the expiration of trading in a delivery month, when an individual merchant may hold most of the open contracts on one side of the market. This is a situation they try to avoid because they almost invariably wish to even up and in doing so they find that they are making the market and fouling their own nest. The locals catch them in a nonliquid position and punish them. Both liquidity and security of identity of positions are important to merchants.

The size of positions that merchants take vary in relation to the certainty of their opinions about the direction that prices will take. They, the survivors, are not notably speculative but they are in an excellent position to see both the supply and demand sides of the market and recognize good speculative opportunities. Their price making role is fairly great within narrow price ranges and they are highly skilled in taking advantage of small price variations. They do not participate importantly in major changes in price level.

Cash Grain Merchants

The classical illustration of hedging in operation as a risk shifting system is the use made by consignment merchants. To describe it is somewhat pointless as it is almost a thing of the past. Until about the time of World War II most grain moved from country locations to terminal markets for storage, processing, and transshipment. Most grain was tributary, in terms of transportation, to a terminal such as Kansas City, Omaha, Duluth, Minneapolis, Milwaukee, St. Louis, or Chicago. The trading at the terminals was conducted by cash grain commission merchants. Country elevators bought from farmers, placed orders with the commission company at the terminal to sell futures as a hedge, and consigned the grain to the terminal in the care of the commission company. When the grain arrived, it was inspected, usually by the exchange, and a sample brought to the trading floor. There, the buyers for elevators and processors traveled among the cash tables on which the samples offered by the commission companies were displayed and negotiated on basis—so much under for this carlot and so much over for that one. When agreement was reached they looked at the futures quotation board so that the absolute price was fixed. The merchant, also a commission futures merchant, then went into the pit and bought back the country elevator hedge. Or, the buyer and commission merchant discussed the futures positions and sometimes exchanged futures in ex-pit transactions. These people offered a complete line of service to the country elevator—market information, cash commission business, futures commission business, and, in many cases, financing. The commission companies handled sales for a fee, usually a percentage of the value, the amount of which was set by the exchange. This process is illustrative of a classical system of cash and futures relationships and the arbitrage between the two and of a stylized system of risk shifting.

Several things happened to change the system. The flow of grain diversified so that a small percentage was tributary to terminal markets. This was partly a matter of decentralization of processing and partly a matter of increasing of U.S. exports so that grain flowed directly to Gulf and East Coast ports; the development of inland waterways was particularly important. Second, as communications improved and country merchants became better informed, they were reluctant to lose control or risk dead-ending a shipment in a terminal. Third, the system of interior merchandising described above developed and intercepted the grain. In view of the country's obvious preference for pricing at country location the terminal merchants shifted to buying "to arrive" so that this method replaced consignment selling as the dominant procurement means. Fourth, terminal elevators vertically integrated forward into exporting and backward into ownership and control of country facilities. Fifth, services were overpriced. The exchanges had set the consignment sales commission rate and when the shift was made to "to arrive" purchasing, they regulated this rate as well. But the country merchants would do it cheaper and by-passed the terminal merchants to sell directly to the terminal elevators. The "to arrive" rules were eventually dropped but not before the damage was done. This is not to suggest that the rates were high enough to be outstandingly profitable to the merchants; they were not. Rather it is to suggest that the interior merchants make their money out of skillful trading in price relationships and that a competitive pricing system is more ruthless in establishing handling margins than is a trade association.

The principal reason for introducing this discussion of cash grain merchants it to call attention to the dynamics of the use of futures markets and to broaden the concepts of the use of futures markets from the classical textbook descriptions.

Terminal Elevators

In discussing independent terminal elevators we are again looking at the activities of a dying breed. Their numbers and importance have decreased because of changes in the flow of commodities such that terminal markets are by-passed and they are losing ground to large, vertically integrated merchandising-warehousing firms that operate on an international scale. Operational costs of terminal elevators are higher than their country counterparts so that facilities are not replaced as they wear out, burn down, or become obsolete. Consideration of their activities is useful because it isolates and simplifies some futures trading activities.

Terminal elevators are the classic hedgers. They are located at the delivery points so that it is the stock in their warehouses that is interchangeable with futures contracts during the delivery months. They are both merchants and public warehousemen so that part of the inventory in their houses is their own and part is out on warehouse receipts owned by merchants, processors, exporters and speculators. As we have seen, they make the key decisions of delivery or nondelivery that affect basis and interdelivery month price spreads for stored commodities. They are merchants who buy and accumulate reserves during periods of inventory buildup and who sell and supply markets during periods of inventory liquidation so that their decisions are important in determining the amount of inventory accumulation. Their decisions are based upon existing and anticipated price relationships.

These differences are the market price of storage. This price is paid indirectly by the speculators because they are long the contracts that the elevator operators hold as short hedges. Thus, it is the speculators who make the inventory decisions. Inventory is accumulated when speculators are willing to pay enough more for distant contracts than nearby to encourage accumulation and hedging, and inventory is liquidated when speculators will pay little more or even less for the more distant contracts. It follows that an objective of terminal elevator operators is to maximize carrying charges while an objective of speculators is to minimize carrying charges. They are natural opponents in the make and take delivery contest. The thinking of terminal elevator operators is described by Ted Rice, Vice President, Continental Grain Co.[1] "Typically, we make delivery on a futures contract when we are unable to merchandise the cash article at as good as a delivery basis. To be frank and realistic, we seldom make the delivery if we believe the grain will be ordered out. Usually the recipient of the delivery does one of two things: (1) he pays for the warehouse receipt, leaves the grain in our house and starts paying us carrying charges, or (2) he retenders, i.e., he sells out his long futures and passes the delivery to someone else. If the grain remains in our house we are: (1) relieved of interest and insurance costs and (2) are paid 1/20 cent storage per bushel per day. If the grain is retendered day after day it tends to weaken the nearby contract relative to the distant. As carrying charges are widened, we will tend to buy the nearby and sell the deferred contract. We recapture our grain and have been able to rehedge it in the next deferred contract at a better basis than was possible prior to delivery." Such is the

---

[1] Leslie, Conrad, *Guide for Successful Speculating,* Dartnell Press, Chicago, 1970.

game plan but note the sentence. "To be frank and realistic, . . ." The defense the speculator has is to take delivery and order grain out.

Terminal elevators tend to be pure hedgers in the sense that they maintain balanced long and short positions. Terminal elevators hedge because they must if they are to operate at a volume consistent with their available space. Elevators are large and are the more profitable as they are kept the fuller. A decline of five cents per bushel on the 10 million bushels of grain that may be in an elevator is $500,000. The financial structure of terminal elevator companies will not bear this kind of risk and if it could, the elevators would elect to employ the capital in expansion of their ordinary merchandising business.

But, terminal elevators cannot make money storing commodities on a hedged basis. Their costs are higher than the carrying charges usually offered by the price relationship structure. They are not as high as a full carrying charge as calculated by tariff, interest, and insurance so that they make money on grain they have out on delivery. They are indeed pleased to have grain out on delivery when they are fairly certain that it will not be ordered out. This is why we say that the defense of the speculator is to take delivery *and order grain out*. To take delivery and hold can only cost him money. The essence of the business of terminal elevators is merchandising on a basis. Their success is determined by their skills in merchandising and by the volume that they are able to put through each bushel of capacity.

They attempt to buy grain to move into their space at net cost of less than the futures in which they hedge and to sell for local consumption or out shipment at a net price higher than the futures. They make money on some trades and lose on others with their success dependent upon making mostly profitable trades and on making a large number of trades. Their losses on space operation must be more than offset by merchandising profits. The more profitable merchandising trades they can make, the wider the overhead cost of space operation can be spread. Thus, success is dependent upon throughput. An elevator with an annual throughput of eight times its capacity is invariably more profitable than one with a throughput of three or four, etc. Operators have said: "Tell me the throughput of an elevator and I will tell you its profit." This is an overstatement because there are a lot of ways to move grain through unprofitably but the generality is true.

We should not leave the subject of terminal elevators with the notion of pure hedging as is developed above. There are variants. They have a selection of delivery months in which they can hedge. As the purest of hedgers they must hedge in the delivery month in which they expect to merchandise the grain out, typically nearby. But if the spread between that month and a more distant one appears, to them, as if it will narrow they reach further out, expecting to pull hedges in closer as the spread narrows. The fact is that they spread back and forth fairly continually.

Spreading opportunities sometimes become sufficiently enticing that hedges are placed outside of the crop year pertinent to the grain being hedged. For example, September soybean futures tend to be a new crop month, that is, harvest is usually early enough to make Chicago delivery by September 30. This tends to finally force September down to only a moderate premium over the November. There are occasions when September is high in relation to November during late spring. If the elevator operator is firmly convinced that the spread is out of line he is tempted to place his hedges in September even though he expects to merchandise his cash soybeans out in June or July. Or if the purely new crop delivery November futures is under the July by substantially less than a usual carrying charge from November to the subsequent July and new crop prospects are favorable, the operator may place hedges against old crop soybeans in the November. In this case, he expects the normal backwardation from old crop to new crop to develop. He will not do this willy nilly but will look carefully at terminal receipts, deliverable stocks, and prospective outshipments in formulating his judgment. The point here is that terminal elevator operators do form speculative judgments about prospective changes in price relationships and wander from purely hedged positions.

On occasion they wander to other markets in placing hedges. Elevators in Minneapolis or Kansas City may place wheat hedges in Chicago futures rather than at the delivery point of the cash wheat that they are hedging. Elevators in Chicago sometimes hedge in other markets. The Chicago hedges placed in the other markets are there because the operators expect a favorable change in price relationship—there is no other reason to go outside. Placing hedges in Chicago from Minneapolis and Kansas City is also the result of expecting a favorable price change although in former times it was often the result of insufficient liquidity in the home markets. Prior to the middle of the 1970's the volume of trading, particularly speculative trading, was often so small that hedges could be placed only at severe price discounts. The large exports of hard red wheat that developed made Kansas City the world's commercial trading center for wheat. This expansion also made Kansas City arbitrage center for the three markets. The slow transition underscores the importance of liquidity from a hedger's point of view.

Finally, while they are not large relative to the total volume handled and are not frequently taken, terminal elevators do take open market positions in both cash and futures. In the first place, they do most of their cash business outside of the trading hours of the exchanges and are thus necessarily prehedged or hold open cash positions—long or short—overnight. They must estimate how much business will be done and take appropriate actions in futures. They may make a careful estimate and act on it but they have a tendency to add a bit "to be on the safe side." The "safe side" toward which they lean is invariably in line with their price expectations.

The out-and-out price level speculative positions that terminal elevators take tend to occur either at the peak of the harvest movement or near the end of the crop season. When prices are low at harvest, and the movement appears nearly over, elevators sometimes delay hedging purchases in anticipation of a post harvest recovery. Near the end of the crop year—say May in wheat or September in corn or soybeans—cash prices tend to become quite erratic relative to futures. Occasionally an open position appears less risky than a hedged position. More often, the elevators are in a good position to know how much of the remaining terminal stock has been sold for outshipment prior to the expiration of the last old crop futures and act on the basis of this knowledge. When they have a good basis for thinking that essentially all of the stock is scheduled to move they sometimes hold cash inventories unhedged. They do this to make a profit but they are quick to point out that it also renders a service to the speculators who are imprudently short by making some supplies available to them. They also render a service to the market by holding some supplies in position so that wildly gyrating prices that discredit markets are avoided.

Exporters

Exporters buy grain, direct its movement to ports, load it aboard ships, and supervise its delivery to destination. Most grain, other than Public Law 480 shipments, is sold CIF (cost, insurance, freight) destination ports. P.L. 480 shipments are made FOB (free on board), port of shipment. Exporters buy from terminal merchants and elevators, interior merchants, and country elevators.

In some seasons of the year they accumulate supplies at a faster rate than they sell them and in others they sell faster than they accumulate. Thus, they sometimes have net long cash positions. These net positions are hedged in futures. Sales are always accompanied by hedge lifting in futures markets. The timing of hedge lifting against a large sale is an interesting tactical exercise. Large export sales are generally known in the market and the futures activities of exporters are closely watched by other traders. Their problem is to get the hedges out of the market without affecting the price. They often remove hedges gradually, preferring the risk exposure of net short positions to the cost of rapid hedge buying. They also go to different delivery months and to the other two markets which leaves them with both intra and inter market spreads. They go where liquidity is greatest.

One device that exporters use is the ex-pit exchange of futures. If the exporter is short futures and must buy in hedges when he sells, it may be that the purchasing importer is long futures. If so, they arrange an exchange and cancel the futures they hold without going into the pit.

Exporters also remove hedges in anticipation of sales so that when sales are actually made, they are nearly, if not completely, through with pit activities.

The announcement of export sales often has an effect upon prices in the futures market. Several export firms may be making offers, vying for a particular lot of business; all of them may remove part of their hedged positions in anticipation of getting the business. These maneuvers may tend to influence market prices in an opposite direction from that which would normally be expected as a result of export sales. When a sale is actually made one of the firms has some more hedges to buy, but the others need to rehedge. Thus, hedge sales following a major export sale may increase, putting prices down. Similarly, speculators know of pending export business and they buy in anticipation of hedge removals. This is sometimes overdone and prices recede.

Exporters play an important role in equalizing the price of grain spatially, particularly on a world wide scale. This role is well described in a paper by Rice of the Continental Grain Company, in which he said, in part:[2]

"Somebody asked me how we determine the 'basis', i.e., the premium or discount of grain relative to a futures contract at a given point. I should like to give you a rather simple illustration. I will use corn for my example because it avoids the complication of grades and class differences inherent in wheat. For purposes of simplicity of calculation some of the values in the example are slightly different from actual. Remember that ocean freight rates including the differential between Gulf and St. Lawrence change constantly.

"Today, there is a 'world price of corn.' I shall not try to demonstrate whether the U.S. makes world prices or the world price determines the U.S. price. It's like trying to prove which came first, the chicken or the egg. Suffice it to say the prices are interdependent.

"Let me emphasize that these are only approximately correct since I have rounded transportation costs. Also, let me emphasize that barge and ocean freight rates fluctuate. (For example, ocean freights have just about doubled since early summer.) Further, the prices I have calculated are for prices to an elevator usually on a barge or rail car, not to a farmer. Elevator margins vary— usually widest at harvest and narrower as elevators try to clear their space. All I have tried to show is that there are logical ranges of values relative to Chicago at a number of points. (Buying basis vs. selling basis.)

"Let's say Chicago December corn futures are $1.23. Let's assume during harvest we can buy corn delivered at our Minneapolis river elevator at 9 under or $1.14. Let's also assume we chartered a barge to New Orleans for 13¢ per bushel. If New Orleans is selling at 9 over Chicago or $1.32 our net selling price Minneapolis parity would be $1.19. Our margin would be 5 cents per bushel.

"But what if we are buying corn faster than we can sell it? We sell futures at $1.23 and buy cash at $1.14. We are long the basis or premiums at 9 under. We have eliminated our risk only if both fluctuate in equal magnitude and direction.

[2] Rice, S. T., "Remarks at Oklahoma State University," January 8, 1965.

The skill of the grain merchant lies in being on the right side of the basis changes more often than on the wrong side."

As a general proposition, exporters find themselevs more comfortable merchandising out of a long cash-short futures position than the other way about. Export sales are made in large quantities, oftentimes for prompt shipment. Accumulation of grain must be made in relatively small units and at the gradual rate that primary producers elect to sell. To cover a large sale quickly in cash markets is difficult. Thus, exporters attempt to build up inventories in interior locations so that they do not force a tightening of basis with hurried purchases when sales are made. Futures markets offer much greater liquidity than do cash markets.

Following harvest, exporters are usually able to maintain cash positions from which they can merchandise. However, during several months preceding harvest, sales of cash for new crop shipment positions tend to exceed sales by primary producers for new crop shipment. The exporters cover the short cash positions by buying futures so that the long open interest of reporting hedgers builds up sharply. The size of this pre-harvest buildup of open interest is proportional to export sales so that some indication of the size of exports, particularly corn and soybeans, during and immediately following harvest is available during the summer months.[3]

Integrated Merchants

As a final note in this discussion of warehousemen and merchants, we should point out that this compartmentalized description of the series of processes is only partially accurate. There are independent merchants and warehousemen at all stages but there are also large integrated merchant, warehousing, and export firms that cover all of the kinds of activities. They own country, subterminal, terminal, and export elevators. They operate interior acquisition points and terminal merchandising offices. They have sales offices and sales agents in foreign countries. They are members and clearing members of commodity exchanges. They have their own brokers on the exchange floors. They are licensed commission futures merchants, handling accounts for independent merchants, processors, and, to a limited extent, speculators.

Some of these large firms are compartmentalized into separate profit centers. These usually handle futures positions on a profit center basis so that one company may have both long hedges and short hedges in the same market. At the same time, they have both long and short customers positions. While floor traders and brokers watch the actions of brokers who handle trades for such firms, little can be told from their activities about their market positions.

Other integrated firms funnel all cash positions into a central futures office

[3] Note the changing structure of the corn open interest shown in Chapter 6.

where the decisions about the placement of hedges and spreads are made and from which trading instructions are issued. Long and short cash positions are offset and only the net positions are hedged.

Stocks in delivery positions and the effect of these on basis is of greater significance to the large integrated firms than their effect on the profitability of space operations at the delivery markets. Basis and spreads at the delivery points affect hedging profitability at outside locations. It is therefore desirable, from the point of view of holders of outside space, that stocks be maintained at delivery markets. We have noted that operating costs tend to be higher at terminal markets than in country locations. We should also note that there is a tendency for terminal space to gravitate into the hands of the large firms who control large amounts of outside space. It is sometimes said that they are the only ones who can afford to operate in terminals. The implication is that terminal space is used to increase the profitability of outside space and basis operations generally. This is an involved question about which no precise judgment can be made. It is a consideration that exchanges take into account in establishing contract terms.

CHAPTER 11

Primary Producers

Because the bulk of futures trading is in agricultural commodities and the information about the use of futures markets is generally limited to such commodities, the discussion here of the use of futures markets by primary producers is limited, mainly, to grains and livestock. The same general principles apply to other commodities traded whether they be other agricultural commodities, forestry products, or metals. Futures markets are available for some primary commodities but the list is far from inclusive. For example, in 1975 the viable futures for grains and oilseeds were limited to wheat, corn, oats and soybeans which left out barley, grain sorghums, cottonseed, flaxseed, rye, sunflower seed, and peanuts. Of fruits and vegetables, only orange juice and potatoes were actively traded. Of the long list of secondary products used in livestock feeding only soybean and fish meals were actively trading. It is worth noting, however, that both the number of commodities and volume of trading increased from 1960 to 1975.

Since the beginning of time, farmers have complained that they are forced to pay the prices set by sellers for the things they buy but must accept what the market offers at the end of the production cycle for the things they sell; that the prices of the things they buy are set at profitable levels by the sellers but they are at the mercy of the market for the prices of their products. And, further, that the prices of the things they sell fluctuate greatly—generally downward— during the production process. Without commenting on the accuracy of this bit of agrarian folklore we observe that it is no longer true. Through the mechanics of an expanding futures trading system, farmers have an opportunity to contract production forward at essentially fixed prices. They can accept or reject, or adjust production. They can, during the production process, capitalize on profitable prices offered whether the product is ready for market or not.

The structure of agricultural production units changed rapidly during the period 1950 to 1975 and appears likely to change at an even faster rate in the future. Production is becoming more specialized, concentrated, and commercialized. Out-of-pocket costs are becoming a higher proportion of total costs. Producers are using increasing proportions of borrowed capital. Farms, those engaged in poultry and livestock production in particular, are becoming factories that buy a high proportion of their inputs. Grain farms are increasing in size and a decreasing proportion of the land is owned by the operator. Farmers are operating on increasingly thin cash flow margins so that changes in selling prices have major effects on cash positions and net returns. A moderate change in price can easily double or halve the net profit. Expansion has stretched operator equities quite thin and operators expand just as far as their equity capital allows. Because of these changes, primary producers have lost much of their financial capacity to absorb price variability and so much search out ways to produce at firmly contracted prices.

This quest for surcease from the hazards of market price variability is not undertaken with unbridled enthusiasm, for farmers have a strong propensity to speculate. Whether this is a matter of the optimistic temperament that is required of one engaged in a vocation so inherently hazardous because of the vagaries of nature or it results from a normal component of avarice is unknown. Yet, it must be recognized when contemplating farmer use of futures markets: if there is a way to shift a futures program toward risk assumption rather than risk aversion, at least some of the subjects will find a way to do so. The anatomy of the corn market examined in Chapter 6 showed farmers as the largest single classification of speculators. And this is typical of all cross section studies of markets.

Futures markets are management tools to be used in the operation of a production business. They are not ways of making money. Their effective use has the potential for increasing and stabilizing income and, through this, enabling more rapid growth of the farm business. They provide latitude in the timing of sales (and purchases) so that prices can either be fixed at profitable levels or production foregone. But they also provide latitude for the full implementation of speculative judgments. The profit-loss outcome of the use of futures markets depends on the skill of the manager. A hammer and a saw are useful tools for building outhouses but it is the carpenter who does the building and the quality of the outhouse is more dependent on his skills than on the quality of the hammer and saw.

Purposes of Futures Trading

Futures trading can be used by primary producers for two purposes: to implement speculative decisions and to produce known profitable prices. These two purposes are conceptionally quite different but in actual practice tend to blend together into one kind of use. The emphasis on speculative decisions is great in some instances of use while it may be totally absent in other circumstances.

The implementation of speculative decisions tends to be the central consideration in grain operations. Because of land use, the production of grains has a high fixed cost. Accordingly, its production is not importantly affected by the prospective selling price. Prices affect, to a minor extent, the amount of fertilizers, herbicides, and insecticides used, and differences in price relationships among grains result in shifts in land use but the fact remains that the grain producer is confronted with a decision of when to sell rather than a question of whether or how much to produce. In addition, the production of grain is inherently variable because of the vagaries of weather. A farmer can fix a sales price per unit but there is no way that he can fix the gross returns from production.

It rains on the just and the unjust alike—but only if they are in close geographic proximity. Farmers in a limited area may be adversely affected by weather even though the total of the crop is not significantly reduced. In this case, forward contracting before planting may be the best of bad courses. But if damage is so general as to affect the size of the crop, hence its price, returns may be more variable at a fixed forward price than at a variable price.

There is no way to avoid uncertainty in the sale of grain. One can reduce uncertainty of gross returns by taking production probabilities into account but their total elimination is impossible. Thus, decisions about when to sell grain are inherently speculative. A purpose of futures in pricing grain is to give full range, for better or for worse, to the implementation of speculative decisions.

Production to known profitable prices tends to be the central consideration in livestock operations, particularly cattle feeding. There are production considerations, such as disease, that affect the quantity produced but these are not great. Variable costs are a much greater proportion of total costs than for grain. There is an opportunity cost of leaving a cattle feeding facility idle but it is in no way comparable to leaving land idle. Hog, broiler, and egg production is an ongoing process that cannot be totally started and stopped as forward prices fluctuate. But the quantities produced can be adjusted readily. A production cycle foregone is a lesser loss than a production cycle that will not cover variable cost.

There is a more general consideration than individual profit maximization involved in producing to fixed selling prices. If the industry continues to produce at maximum capacity on blind faith that prices will finally turn out to be profitable, the inevitable result is elimination of the producers who can stand losses the least so that an equilibrium is finally restored. But if most of the industry declines to produce except as profitable forward prices can be fixed, adjustments of production can be orderly with only the noncompetitive producers being forced out and without the industry as a whole falling into a loss position.

In discussing the use of futures in connection with the farm business two words need be said about hedging: "It isn't." Farmers don't hedge nor can they. Their problem is to establish selling prices. They can contract forward at firm prices or they can delay pricing past the completion of production. But they cannot avoid the decision about when to sell. The word hedging has a favorable connotation, hedging is a practice of prudent business people, and bankers look favorably on loans to hedgers. It is well and good for farmers to tell their friends and bankers that they are hedging so long as they do not confuse themselves. The difference between futures activities of farmers and hedging is that in hedging risks of price level change are avoided but farmers cannot avoid the speculative decisions of when to sell. They use futures better as they clearly understand this difference.

Transactions in futures must be related to the farm business in the amounts traded and the objectives of the trades. This involves two things: an effective accounting system and the avoidance of any more speculation than is inherent in the farm business. The specific objectives of futures transactions are to establish net selling (or buying) prices. Producers should never make or take delivery on futures contracts. They should sell cash commodities at their regular outlets—country elevators, livestock yards, etc. Futures transactions are offset by opposite transactions and gains and losses realized. The net price received is the cash price plus or minus the gains and losses from the futures transactions. The producer's accounting system must be organized so that the net price is clearly established. Part of the futures transactions result in profits and part in losses—on the general order of half and half. The success-failure of the use of futures tends to be judged on the basis of profits or losses from futures transactions alone, which is inappropriate. Farmers tend to blame futures for their speculative errors. The use of futures should be judged by how closely the net price objectives are achieved. This can only happen if net prices are clearly established in the accounting system.

Additional speculation is not one of the purposes of farmer use of futures. Those farmers who have an irresistible urge to speculate in prices past the speculation inherent in their operations must separate such transactions—probably by opening a second account. Speculation in commodity futures is an honorable practice but it is not a part of a farm business.

Arriving at this prohibition of assumption of additional risks via futures trading results in the loss of some potential traders, particularly cattle feeders because some of them are in the business for the purpose of speculating in prices. Some cattle feeders vary the weight, class, and numbers of cattle that they feed at different times. They buy those cattle that they expect to appreciate in price during the feeding process and leave their yards empty when they expect all cattle prices to decline. Some of the most successful midwest cattle feeders in years past have been more cattle speculator than cattle feeder and their success has depended more on their ability to judge quality and prices than their skills in feeding. For this hearty breed, futures offer the ultimate. They can have the use of an unlimited number of cattle for a small margin investment, hire no labor, buy no feed, own no land, pay no vet bills, wade in no mud, have no frozen water lines, etc. while plying their trade of speculation. But it is not a part of a farm business.

Development of a Marketing Plan

Each farm business should have a marketing plan into which the use of futures is fitted. The marketing plan should be tailored to the specific business it is designed to serve. The plan should take into account:

a. Income objective of the farm. In some operations regularity of income is important while in others it is of little importance. The range is generally greater for land owners as some are heavily dependent, say widows, on rental returns while to others land return is of little importance to total income.

b. Growth objectives of the business. As we have seen, futures markets are a means of raising equity capital to finance price variability. Thus, effective use of futures can free up equity capital to finance expansion.

c. The financial and equity position of the business. A heavily mortgaged farm is in a quite different risk bearing position than an unmortgaged farm, etc. A conservative approach to forward pricing is warranted whenever a possible price decline could put the firm out of business.

d. Skills and temperament of the farmer. Different farmers have different abilities in price forecasting. The more skilled should have more flexible marketing plans. Some people thrive on uncertainty while others abhor it. The marketing plan must be atuned to the psychological characteristics of the operator.

Marketing plans must be flexible enough to be stuck to. As we shall see, there are reasons for changing futures positions as the production and marketing season progresses. At the same time a plan is of little value if it is not adhered to. There is a delicate balance of allowing change without flitting about continually. The key consideration is to not panic. Futures positions tend to be disturbing, particularly the first few times that they are taken. Farmers are fully conditioned to—and accept—changes in cash prices with aplomb. But they watch gains and losses in futures closely and get excited even though they have reduced their total risk; even though the changes in futures are offset by changes in cash. They get margin calls which are disturbing. They watch profits in futures positions accrue and find them hard to resist taking. If they are short futures against a growing crop and get ahead on the futures side, they want to take profits, wait until the market rallies, and sell again. While it is a waste of capital use, there is merit in overmargining the futures account. A change in price of five cents looms much bigger when the original equity is eight cents than when it is eighteen. There is a tendency to compound mistakes when plans are changed. A classic case is putting more weight on cattle or hogs when the price declines. Farmers often hold cattle and hogs for some weeks after optimum weights are reached, when market prices are declining, hoping for recovery. The additional weight compounds the price weakness.

Importance of Basis

Farmers must know basis if they are to use futures markets successfully. They must know what a given futures price means in terms of the price of the cash commodity at their usual, generally local, markets. If the price of December corn futures is $2.75 in January an Iowa farmer must know that this means, should he sell it, a net price of about $2.35 at his local elevator at harvest. Or, it could mean a net price of about $2.65 should he sell December futures, buy back and sell July, and carry the corn in storage until July 1 of the following year. Or a Nebraska cattle feeder must know how much under (or over) the appropriate futures price the class, quality, and weight of cattle he contemplates feeding will sell for at his local market at the end of the feeding period.

Farmers plan operations and work out budgets and cash flows on the basis of the selling prices of commodities. They formulate speculative judgments about prices at their local markets. These are the prices with which they are most familiar, that they watch continually, remember from last year and the year before, and are most capable of forming judgments about. Their marketing decisions must be made in terms of local prices and their line of reasoning must be from local prices to futures prices.

The concern of farmers with basis relates both to time and place. As was shown in Chapter 9, price relationships vary between cash and futures over time. The relationship between the cash price and the price of the nearby futures is not the same at all seasons of the year, the difference tending to be wider at harvest than during the following spring and summer. More significantly, the cash-futures difference at a given time of the year varies from year to year. $2.75 December corn does not always mean a $2.35 farm price at harvest. This may be the central tendency for a particular location but there is substantial variation from year to year. The cash-futures spread is more variable at harvest than it is toward the end of the storage season. For example, farmers need to know, for corn, what the local price has been in years past at harvest relative to the December futures, in February relative to the March futures, in April relative to the May futures, and in June relative to the July futures. This knowledge need include, not only the central tendency, but the ranges as well.

In addition to knowing the local price relative to the nearby futures farmers need to know, for storable commodities, the spread relationships among futures. They are not limited to selling the delivery month in which they expect to sell the cash commodity and offset the futures contract but are free to sell the highest month. They must be able to judge which is the highest, for example: Is July the highest at 15 over the December? To answer the question correctly requires a knowledge of spreads. Further, the delivery month in which the farmer plans to sell the cash commodity may not be traded when he plans to sell cash. For example, he may elect to contract to grow, harvest, condition, and store corn for June, 1976 delivery in January, 1975. But July, 1976 futures are not traded until August, 1975. He must sell December, buy it back and sell July at some time between August and December. He needs to be able to recognize a favorable difference when he sees it.

As we have seen, the price of a cash commodity at the delivery point must equal the futures price in the delivery month. For those commodities away from the delivery point the relationship to the futures is variable. Those located tributary to the delivery point have a close relationship that can be dependably anticipated but, as the distance increases and the movement is not to or through the delivery point, the relationship becomes more variable. There is a consistency about the price surface that is reasonably dependable so that the markets are usable. But knowledge about variation is essential to effective market use.

The governors of the markets attempt to establish delivery points and terms so that they are usable from all locations of production, storage and processing. The absence of a local discount from the futures large enough to cover transportation costs frightens some producers away from use of futures. This is particularly true in locations where the local price is typically higher than the cash price at the delivery point. This lack of deliverability becomes less troublesome as primary producers realize that they sell cash products in cash markets and offset futures with futures, never making or taking delivery.

Specific Uses

Primary producers can use futures markets in a large number of ways with almost limitless variants of these. For simplicity, six have been chosen for illustration here.

To Fix the Price of a Growing Crop. By selling futures before planting or during the growing season, farmers can assure themselves, within fairly narrow limits, of the net price they will receive at harvest. Let us follow through an experience for corn: On May 3, 1965 the price of December futures was $1.21¼. A farmer noted that the average cash price of cash corn at his local elevator had averaged 12½ under December on October 15 during recent years.

Subtracting this amount from the current December price he arrived at a target price of $1.08¾ The market as a whole was saying that it expected the price of December to remain at $1.21¼ through its expiration, which, as we know, was the least likely of all things. The market was also saying that, come what would, it would assure the farmer approximately $1.08¾ per bushel at harvest. Again looking at the history of October 15 price relationships for the preceding five years the farmer discovered that the range had been 14⅞¢ under to 9¾¢ under and concluded that approximately $1.08¾ meant some place between $1.06⅜ and $1.11½. For whatever reason, he found this an acceptable price range at which to contract and so he sold 50,000 bushels of December futures, an amount equal to his anticipated production. On October 15, he completed harvesting, delivered, and sold 50,000 bushels of cash corn at his local elevator for $1.02½. At the same time he bought December futures, offsetting the original contracts and closing out his futures position. The December futures price on October 15 was $1.14⅞. He sold at $1.21¼ and bought at $1.14⅞, thus making 6⅜ cents or $3,187.50 minus commission. Adding this 6⅜ to the cash price of $1.02½ yielded $1.08⅞, only ⅛ cent away from the target and a quite good market performance. The farmer was pleased. The market not only produced the promised market price but it was a higher price than he would otherwise have gotten. He had found a new tool and a new game to play.

Let's play again in 1966. On May 3, the December futures price was $1.19⅜ which, subtracting the 12½ cent basis, established a target price of $1.06⅞. Judging this acceptable, the farmer sold 50,000 December. It was a long and troubled season but we will skip to the end. On October 14, with harvest finished and the crop delivered, he sold cash for $1.28 and bought December for $1.34¾. He lost 15⅜ cents or $7,687.50 plus commission. Subtracting this 15⅜ cents from $1.28 yielded $1.12⅝ which was 5¾ cents better than the target. The market performed admirably but this did little to salve the man's pain. He not only lost money on the futures but, because of the weather impact on yield, had rather less than the projected amount of corn to sell.

1966 was a year in which the crop was threatened by drought but recovered with excellent August and September rains. The price of December futures increased gradually from $1.20 in early May to $1.25 by June 15. The threat of drought then became generally apparent and the price rose rapidly to a high of $1.52 in the third week of August. The rains came and the price receded to $1.34¾ on October 15.

In our illustration we have put the farmer in a forward contracting position and held him there. But let's turn him loose and let him swing his inherent speculative inclination. He originally sold because the target price was above the net government loan rate and he doubted that the market price at harvest would be. By June he knew it was hot and dry for he was in the field from sunup to sundown. He regretted his sale because he thought that the crop was apt to be damaged and the harvest price would be above the target so he bought his December futures for $1.26⅞, losing 7½ cents or $3,750.00 plus commission. Now he could watch the drought develop, knowing that the price of corn would go up more than enough to offset the loss of yield. When the rains came in August, he was among the first to know and among those most capable of appraising their impact on yield. The $1.50 December price looked like $1.37½ at his elevator so he sold. He finally sold for $1.28 and bought the December futures back for $1.34¾. Net, he got $1.28 minus the 7½ cent loss on the first sale plus the 15¼ cent profit on the second for $1.35¾ minus two commissions. The market served him well and he speculated well. True, we all have 20/20 hindsight and can speculate brilliantly in retrospect. But note that the farmer only changed his mind and plan once and speculated only on the basis of things he knew and understood well.

To further illustrate the play of speculative judgment, we skip 1967 and go to 1968. December corn futures traded in the $1.27 to $1.29 range during February, a target price of $1.14½ to $1.16½, well above the then current cash price and above the government loan of $1.08 (which was a net harvest rate of $.95, storage taken into account). Our farmer friend sold December. The season progressed beautifully with optimum temperatures and rainfall. Both acreage and yield estimates were large. The price declined to $1.20 in April, $1.15 in June, and $1.05 by the end of July. At this level, the December futures established a target price of $.92½ which was below the net loan. Our now very smug farmer reflected that he was happy to have recognized a good price when he saw it and was relieved that he was not in the position of considering a target price so low; if he were, he would by no means accept it but would rather own the corn. Realizing that he did not own his growing corn but had it sold to some speculators he bought in his December futures. December futures continued down to $1.01 by the end of August. Our now not so smug farmer, backed by the U.S. Treasury, stood his ground and, when he completed harvest at the end of October, sold for $1.01. He made 23 cents on his December futures which, added to $1.01 was $1.24, rather better than the target price. Buying in the December at less than the net loan did not require great speculative skill. The point is that at some prices long speculation becomes quite attractive, especially to those people who are backed by the government.

The record of corn prices is replete with examples in which circumstances changed during the season in ways that justified changes of mind, and the kinds of changes were such that farmers had early opportunity to recognize them and their impact. In June, 1970, December futures traded in a $1.28 to $1.35 range, an amount much above the net loan rate. Crop conditions were excellent and a sale of at least part of the crop was a prudent practice that many farmers followed. At the end of July a blight struck that severely damaged the crop. Prices rose rapidly, making a peak of $1.57 in mid-September. A prudent sale became imprudent. But farmers had until the fifth of August, about ten days after the blight struck, to recognize the problem and buy back their short commitments without loss. In March, 1974, December corn sold at over $3.00, a highly profitable and risk-laden amount. To price part of the crop was a prudent decision. Land preparation proceeded rapidly and conditions were excellent until early May when the rains came. Rains were followed by drought and drought by a record early frost so that the crop was severely damaged. December corn traded between $2.31 and $2.48 in May and did not start its major upward movement until early June. Farmers had quite a long time to recognize the problem developing under their noses. The top of the market was reached on October 3, 1974. The strength from the 1974 drought carried over to the next crop so that December, 1975 corn sold for $3.50 in October, 1974 and nearly $3.00 in January, 1975. The reduced rate of use, the large prospective 1975 crop, and highly profitable prices were good reasons for pricing at least part of the 1975 crop. December futures declined to less than $2.40 in June. News of crop failure and drought in Iowa and Nebraska entered the market and prices rose, sound reasons for buying back at least part of the priced grain.

These several examples of position reversal raise a question of the frequency with which operating farmers should reverse positions. Position change from having sold a crop to a return to being long a growing crop should be a part of their repertoire, first because the timing of crop sales before the size of the crop is known is inherently speculative and second, because some crop producers have the financial capacity to speculate and the capabilities of occasionally speculating successfully. The reversals shown in the examples were less speculative procedures than holding the positions through to completion. However, frequent reversal, trading in and out, taking profits as they develop with the intention of reinstating the position on subsequent rallies, or taking small losses while attempting to find the top of the market is a speculative game that is not a part of a farm business. Either procedure has the strong possibility, if not probability, of leaving the farmer standing on the dock after the boat has sailed. They are out of his speculative element; he is playing someone else's game. Further, such in and out trading is apt to lead him to take futures positions larger than justified by his projected crop size and positions in the same direction as his cash position. It would have been quite easy for our farmer to decide in June, 1966 or May, 1974 that he not only should buy back his growing crop but should buy more futures to make up for the prospective production loss.

The guideline to the frequency of mind changes is that the farmer should act the role of a farmer selling his cash crop. He should sell futures when he deems the target price to be satisfactory because of its level, he thinks that it is apt to decline, or he is totally uncertain about the direction of price changes. He should maintain his short futures position until he comes to genuinely regret it, not because it is costing him money or shows a profit that he would like to latch on to, but because he has a sound basis as a farmer for thinking the price will go up enough to justify the resumption of a long cash position.

How much of a growing crop to sell is a comparable question. The answer that some farmers make is: "I think that I will play safe on part of the crop by selling futures and gamble on the rest." The size of the parts tends to relate to the farmers' cash flow requirements. They may wisely sell enough to cover out of pocket costs for seed, fertilizer, fuel, etc. and leave their net returns variable to the extent of price variation. The questions of frequency of mind change and the amount to sell are related to the amount of risk the farmer wishes to assume. This, in turn, depends upon his risk absorption capacity, temperamental inclination, and speculative skill. There are no pat answers.

To Fix the Price of a Commodity in Storage. The objective of this game is to earn storage income in those years in which a long position is not attractive. It is a matter of taking advantage of the usual seasonal basis gain. A high proportion of storage costs are fixed. The ownership of farm storage facilities can only be profitable if they are used every year, but space isn't profitable if the price of the stored commodity declines. The ground rule is that space will always be filled at harvest and kept full so long as the target price is higher than the current spot price by more than the out of pocket cost of space use.

The procedures are the same as pricing a growing crop forward. A target price is established by reviewing the history of local cash prices relative to the nearby futures price at the end of the storage period. The decision whether to accept the target price or remain long the stored commodity is made, and the appropriate quantity of the more distant futures is sold or not sold.

Again the decision about whether to accept the forward price is a speculative one. The opportunity to price forward is always present and depends upon: (1) whether the person holding the grain thinks that the level of price, as measured by the distant futures, is going to go up and (2) the extent to which the farmer can afford, and wishes, to assume risks of a price decline. In the case of a stored crop, the decision to contract forward or not is purely one of whether to speculate in contrast to the decision of whether to contract a growing crop. The size of the farmer's crop and the total crop is known. Income uncertainty, after a crop has been produced, is at an end when the farmer wishes to end it.

In contemplating the question of a forward sale, a farmer must look at the price of the distant future, calculate what it means in terms of the price at his local elevator during the month of maturity of the futures contract, and then decide whether or not he wants to be long at that price. For example, on October 27, 1966 the price of cash corn bid to a farmer at his local elevator was $1.28 and the July futures price was $1.57. Looking back at the preceding five years the farmer found that the cash price bid to him on July 1 averaged 6½ cents under the July futures and the range was 5¼ to 7¼. Thus, his target price was $1.50½. The proper question he should have asked himself was: "Do I want to be long corn now priced at $1.50½ for delivery next July 1?"—not "Do I want to be long corn at $1.28?"

The difference between the current price and the target price, 22½ cents, is the prospective payment for storage. It will exist whether futures are sold fixing the price, or not. (Actually the basis turned out to be a quite narrow 35⁄8¢ so that the storage payment was 253⁄8¢.) On July 1, 1967 the farm price was $1.26½ and the July futures was $1.30⅛. Holding corn without considering futures a farmer might well consider that he lost only 1½¢, a not too bad result. But this is not so. He would actually have made 253⁄8¢ storing and thus lost 267⁄8¢ speculating. It is important to ask the right question.

The two uses, fixing the price of a growing crop and fixing the price of a stored crop can be worked together into one continuous program covering some 18 months. The whole operation of production and storage can be priced before it is begun. The procedure is to sell the first new crop future, buy it back and sell the more distant some time during the period that they are both traded— August through December for corn. This switching of futures requires a decision of when, which is based on the history of the spreads and conditioned by the supply-demand situation for the storage in the year in question.

An examination of 56 transactions in futures related to pricing growing and stored crops of corn, soybeans, wheat and oats, showed 32 profits, 23 losses, and one break-even meaning that the price went down 32 times, up 23, and did not change once.[1] The average size of the profits was 77⁄8 cents, and the average size of the losses was 9¼ cents. On average it was more profitable to be short than long, but this was not a meaningful average. It was too near even to be ascribed to anything other than chance. Profits and losses from futures transactions tend to average out to zero. The use of futures in a routine way does not, in the long run, add to or subtract from the realized price of a commodity. Thus, futures serve two purposes: 1. They are tools for pricing forward when a farmer's best speculative judgment tells him it is time to fix the price; tools for implementing speculative decisions, and, 2. They assist in regularizing income from season to season, releasing equity capital that would otherwise have to be held in reserve against possible losses.

To Delay Pricing a Sold Crop. Farmers sometimes want to delay pricing commodities past the time that they can be held on farms. They can do so by selling cash and replacing it with an equal amount of futures. This is speculation. They are long. If the price goes up they make money and if it goes down, they lose money. Speculation in futures is neither more nor less a part of the farm business than maintaining a long position in a cash commodity so long as it replaces a cash commodity speculation that formerly existed.

Farmers often ask if they can sell cash grain at harvest and replace it with

[1] Hieronymus, T. A., *Farmer Use of Futures Markets,* Ill. Agr. Exp. Sta. Bulletin 696, 1963.

futures to take advantage of the seasonal rise in price without incurring storage costs. This cannot be done. The more or less regular seasonal increase in cash grain prices is the result of increases in cash prices relative to futures; there is no seasonal pattern to futures prices. Accordingly, he who sells cash and replaces it with futures is, in effect, paying someone else to store.

How does a farmer know at what price he is going long? The answer is a matter of anticipating basis. A normal basis on first delivery day is established by looking at the historical record—say 9½ under the July on July 1 for corn. Suppose that at harvest the cash farm price is $2.40, and July futures $2.81. Should the farmer sell cash and buy futures? The cash price must rise to $2.72 before he makes anything. He is, indirectly, paying 32 cents per bushel storage. The appropriate question is not whether he should go long at $2.40 corn but should he go long $2.72 corn.

In the long run the routine replacement of cash with futures is a break-even proposition. To successfully use futures in this way requires a better than average job of speculation. A rather large payment for storage must be made.

There are occasions when it pays to replace cash with futures if one wants to remain long, but these rarely occur until well past the critical harvest period. As we have seen, the cash price almost invariably gains rapidly in relation to the futures immediately following harvest and then gains quite slowly for the balance of the season. If cash grain storage can be rented at a regular monthly rate that will total a reasonable storage for the year farmers are often well advised to rent space for a couple of months, then sell cash and buy futures. At any time that the cost of storage, including interest and taxes, is greater than the prospective basis gain, the cash commodity should be sold. Then, if the farmer wants to be long the crop he has produced, futures should be bought.

The most striking example of the advisability of replacing cash with futures is the instance of the inverse carrying charge as illustrated in Chapter 9, Figure 6. On November 15, 1966, the cash price of soybeans bid to Illinois farmers was $2.87 and the May futures was $2.98. A normal May 1 basis was 5 cents under leaving a scant 6 cents for storage. Interest cost alone was 8½ cents. Any farmer wanting to be long soybeans should have sold cash and bought futures. The situation in January was even more remarkable with the farm price two cents under the May futures. There was an almost guaranteed gross loss for storage. On May 1, 1967 the farm price was $2.73 and the May futures $2.81, a wider than normal basis. Being long soybeans was not a good idea that year. A long position in cash soybeans from November 15 to May 1 would have lost 14 cents plus the cost of storage while a long position in May futures would have lost only 17 cents total. A long position in cash soybeans from January 9 to May 1 lost 15½ cents but a long position in May futures lost only 9⅞ cents.

To Fix Cattle Feeding Margins. Cattle feeding is a high risk agricultural enterprise. Individual operations have distinct production cycles of substantial duration—from a few months to more than one year. The prices of finished cattle are variable and difficult to forecast accurately. When a feeder commits a production cycle by buying feeder cattle, it is an irreversible process, the outturn of which is dependent on the selling price of the finished cattle at the end of the cycle. In large feedlot operations where the inflow and outflow of feeder and finished cattle is essentially constant, short-term variations are averaged out so that returns are less variable. But cattle prices move in relatively long swings so that the end result of price variations are the same for the small feeder who follows one cycle with another and the larger feeder who runs numerous cycles simultaneously. Cattle feeding is a high leverage operation because a comparatively high proportion of the end product value is purchased as feeder cattle— the amount varying with the weight of the cattle fed. Price variations apply to the total of the product, original weight plus weight added.

Since the beginning of live cattle futures trading in 1964 it has been possible to eliminate price uncertainty from cattle feeding. The procedure is simple: sell finished cattle futures when feeder cattle are bought. For example, on January 2 a feeder buys 600 pound feeder steers at $40.00 per hundred weight, or $240 per steer. He expects to sell 1,000 pound choice steers in June. He will put on 400 pounds of gain at a cost of $51 per hundredweight, making the steer cost $444 and the break-even selling price $44.40. The price of June steers is $49.00. His local price for choice steers in June is $1.00 under the Chicago futures. Commission and interest on margin is $.20. The net selling price is $47.80. The prospective profit is $3.40 per hundred or $34.00 per steer. He sells June futures and buys them back when he sells the finished cattle about June 1. If the price of cattle is up he makes more on the cash cattle and loses an offsetting amount on the futures and vice versa.

Presumably the feeder knows the price at which he can sell June futures before he buys the feeders. It is a locked up feeding operation that is undertaken for a known profit. It is attractive when it shows a return above cost and is unattractive when it shows a return below cost. In the latter case, the feeder refuses to buy the feeders and waits until the combination of the futures price, feeder cattle price, and cost of putting on gain shows a profit.

So it goes by the book, but there are variants. Most discussions go a step farther and demonstrate how a feeder can lock in a profit resulting from a price increase with futures after the feeding cycle is in process. When the feeder sees too good of a thing to let get away, he sells futures before his cattle are ready for market, accepting speculative profits. The other side of this coin is to limit losses in a declining market. The feeder buys feeder steers at a price that will return a profit if the price of fat cattle holds. But during the cycle, fat cattle prices decline so that the feeder's break-even price is approched. He sells futures and thus avoids a loss. The thing that these two examples illustrate is that futures can be used as a tool to implement speculative decisions as well as a system for entering a feeding cycle at a profit.

Futures markets are useful guides to the kind of feeding operation that should be undertaken. There are numerous cattle feeding programs, ranging from feeding steer calves from 400 pounds to prime steers at 1,400 pounds, to heifer calves, to 600 to 700 pound steers to 1,000 or 1,100 pounds, choice or prime. The various programs include a range of qualities. The cattle feeder can look at the cost of various classes and weight of feeder stock, the cost of putting the appropriate amount of gain on each, and the futures prices for delivery at the different times the various classes and weights will be ready for market. He lets the judgment of the market tell him what to do. He then lets the market guarantee its judgment by selling futures.

What does the cattle feeder need to know? With regard to the use of futures he need only know the relationship of the price of the weight and quality of cattle he will produce to the futures price during the month that his feeding cycle will end. The appropriate price is the one at his usual selling point. If he is going to sell high good steers weighing 1,000 pounds at Kansas City in April, he should know the usual relationship between the price of such animals and the April futures price during April. This relationship can be learned from study of historical relationships.

There is no problem of selecting the appropriate delivery month as there is in the grains. Because the cattle futures delivery months are not functionally tied together by storage, the feeder should sell the month closest to the time his cattle will be ready for market.

To Contract for Hog Feeding Services. The production of hogs is a more ongoing type of business than cattle feeding. Thus, there is less opportunity to drop out of production when prices offered by futures markets are below cost. But production can be varied so that the quantities produced for a particular time can be reduced as the price offered for that time is low and vice versa. The gestation period for a pig is 112 days and hogs reach slaughter weights at about six months. The lead time on production, hence the planning horizon, is about ten months.

For the ongoing hog operation, geared to a particular level of operation, the selling decisions are basically speculative. The hogs must be sold some time or other; and futures markets provide an opportunity to separate the time of sale from the time of delivery at the market. Hogs can be priced forward as far as futures are traded or pricing can be delayed until hogs are delivered.

Two different strategies can be used in making sales decisions. First, the producer can make judgments about what will happen to the price of hogs for the time that he will have hogs ready for delivery. If he will have hogs at market weight in October he looks at the October futures price and decides whether it will go higher before October or not. If his judgment is higher, he waits; if it is not higher, he sells. In this strategy he must look at the whole set of factors affecting hog prices.

Second, the producer can follow a strategy of selling forward when a profit is offered and refuse to sell when the price offered is unprofitable. The underlying assumption is that at some time during the period that the applicable future is traded, a profitable price will be offered. But the assumption is not valid. The weakness of this strategy is that the producer must accept losses when profitable prices for a particular delivery are never offered while foregoing the more than breakeven prices that are offered as frequently as less than breakeven prices persist. This strategy can be modified so that only those prices at a certain percentage above breakeven are accepted. If he can get, say, a ten percent pad two thirds of the time, he can afford his losses when they occur. But the strategy is only effective if coupled with production adjustments.

The best strategy is probably a combination of the two. There is no way that a producer can avoid forecasting changes in hog prices nor is there a way to avoid making decisions about when to sell. One consideration entering a speculative judgment is that prices much above breakeven will not last. This is conducive to the adoption of the second strategy. The combined strategy suggests that prices moderately above breakeven should be accepted except as there is strongly persuasive evidence that indicates further increase.

Some of the total hog production is specialized into the two parts, feeder pig raising and hog feeding. The use of futures in connection with hog feeding is closely comparable to cattle feeding. The feeder is subject to the risks of hogs selling for less than anticipated and less than a profitable price relative to the amount he has paid for feeder pigs. He has the opportunity to bid for feeder pigs on the basis of hog futures prices and to refuse to buy and feed when hog futures are not high enough to let him lock up a profit. If he buys feeder pigs he can either sell futures or speculate in finished hog prices. His options are open. What he should do depends upon his risk bearing capability, his inclination toward speculation, and what he thinks will happen to the price of hogs.

The feeder pig producer is in a quite different position. His is an ongoing business that can be turned off for a time only at considerable cost. He cannot, practically, liquidate a breeding herd and replace it a month, or a few months, or a year later. An unpregnant sow eats nearly as much as a pregnant one. He must make speculative decisions about when to sell pigs. He has little latitude; there is no feeder pig futures market and the existing informal forward contracting market does not extend far into the future.

Can he use live hog futures? The feeder pig price is demand determined and appears to depend, primarily, on the profitability of *current* hog-feed price ratios. The buyers of feeder pigs do not seem to look very far forward. Fluctuations in feeder pig prices are somewhat less than are justified by current hog-feed price ratios, indicating some doubt that the current high or low profitability will persist the whole of a feeding period. Fluctuations in feeder pig prices are greater than fluctuations in slaughter hog prices because of the leverage of the greater weight of slaughter hogs. Suppose that pigs are purchased at 40 pounds, sold at 220 pounds, and the cost of gain is $30 per hundred weight:

	$35	$37	$33
Value of 220 pound hog	$77.00	81.40	$72.60
Cost of 180 pound gain	54.00	54.00	54.00
Value of feeder pigs	23.00	27.40	18.60
Percent change in hog price	0.00	+ 5.71	− 5.71
Percent change in pig value	0.00	+19.13	−19.13

Because of the covariance of hog and pig prices, hog futures can be used to forward price pigs. How many futures to sell is a difficult question. Hog for hog is too much because of the weight difference but pound for pound is too little because of the leverage. If the above illustration accurately reflected the feeder pig price variation, hog for hog would be just the right amount. What the feeder pig producer needs to do is work out the feeder pig price variation to hog price variation for his local market for various hog-feed ratios. This ratio should then be multiplied by the pounds of feeder pigs to be produced to obtain the quantity of hog futures to sell.

To Fix Feed Costs Without Taking Immediate Delivery. As a livestock feeder starts a program, he commits himself to the use of feed. The feed that he does not have on hand he must subsequently buy. He is short a requirement of feed. If, at the outset of a feeding program, he buys a sufficient amount of feed to last the entire season, he nails down one more cost item and thus reduces his total uncertainty. The feeding season is usually regarded as from fall to fall, so that we are talking about buying feed in the fall of the year. The discussion relates almost entirely to corn and soybean meal as the two most important feeds and feeds with major futures markets.

Producers who do not have a sufficient amount of storage space or who do not want to tie up money in inventories can fix costs by buying futures. As space is available and feed required, they buy cash feed and sell futures. Profits made on the futures transactions are subtracted from the price paid for the cash feed to get the net cost. Similarly, losses taken on futures transactions are added to the price of the cash feed to get the net cost.

If cash and futures prices moved up and down precisely together, the price of the feed item could be fixed at the price existing when the futures transaction was initiated. To illustrate let us suppose that a hog producer observes that the price of cash corn at his local elevator is $2.40. He likes this price and wishes to fix it for the supplemental feed corn that he will eventually buy. He buys futures at, say, $2.75, or 35 cents over the cash. Some months later when he needs the cash corn he pays $2.60. If the cash and futures have moved up the same amount, he will sell futures for $2.95, realizing a 20 cent profit. He subtracts this from the $2.60 that he paid for cash corn, for a net cost (ignoring futures commission charges) of $2.40.

However, cash and futures prices do not move up and down together, the cash typically gaining in relation to the futures. Increases in the futures will not offset increases in the cash price. This increase in cash in relation to futures is equal to the going market price for storage. In effect, the feeder pays someone to store the corn that he has bought until he needs it. And because someone is storing the corn for him, he should reasonably expect to pay.

There are benefits from pricing feed ahead even though in the long run it only breaks even. It is a means by which the approximate cost of feed can be established. The knowledge of cost is useful in planning feeding operations. Pricing feed ahead reduces the total risk involved in feeding operations.

The purchase of futures does not assume that the cost of feed will be the current price; it will be higher than the current price by the amount of basis gain. The problem, then, is to understand what the current futures price means in terms of the ultimate net cost. The feeder should subtract the basis that he expects to exist at the time he wishes to buy and take delivery from the current futures price. If he wishes to buy and take delivery of cash corn on April 2 and expects a basis of 23 under the July at that time, and the current price of July futures is $2.60, he should reckon his net cost at $2.37. This becomes his target price.

Relative Merit of Cash Forward and Futures Contracts

For grains and to some extent cattle and hogs, farmers can make cash forward contracts. Bids for harvest delivery of grains are usually made as early as January and there are bids for January, March, etc. from harvest onward. Thus, the farmer has a choice: he can contract ahead at a firm price with his local elevator for cash grain, or he can sell futures. Forward contracting has three advantages: The exact price is known, the quantity is divisible by less than units of 5,000 bushels, and it is not necessary to maintain a margin deposit as in the case of futures.

Using futures to sell ahead has two advantages: First, the average price is higher. As farmers sell ahead of planting or during the growing season, someone is selling futures. Perhaps the elevator is selling futures against its purchases from farmers, or it may be that the elevator makes a cash forward contract with an interior merchant or processor who, in turn, sells futures. Whoever is doing it is bidding enough less for the cash grain to cover the cost, including the risk due to variable results, and leave a profit.

The second advantage is that use of futures provides greater flexibility—greater ease for the farmer to change his mind. Suppose that at planting time a farmer notes that December corn futures indicates a net price for harvest delivery that he likes and so sells. During July the weather gets hot and dry and it begins to look as if the crop will be small. The price starts up. What looked like a good sale early now looks like an error. Our friend can reverse his sale just as quickly as he can call his registered representative and buy in his short futures position. All it will cost him to again be long his growing crop is the amount that the price has gone up while he was becoming alert to the developing situation.

In May 1966, corn planting time, many Illinois corn producers sold cash corn for harvest delivery for $1.10. At the time it looked like a good sale; the indicated acreage was large and the price was above the loan. But, as we noted, the weather degenerated in June and the price rose. The farmers regretted the sale but were stuck with their contracts.

Some Common Pitfalls

There are several ways that farmers can go wrong in their futures trading operations. In all futures transactions there is uncertainy because of variability in basis. A trade that fails to materialize as expected because of unusual basis behavior should not be scored an error.

The first type of error is improper calculation of basis—the failure to add the right normal basis to, or subtract it from, the right delivery month.

The second is the selection of the wrong delivery month. It is difficult to go wrong in markets for storable commodities because of the functional relation ship of the several futures prices. The only way to err is to go out of the pertinent crop year. But for nonstorable commodities the delivery month closest to the time the commodity will be ready for market must be sold. It is tempting for cattle feeders and hog producers to sell the highest priced futures.

The third is to fail to relate the futures transactions to the farm business in the size and direction of position. The futures position must be as nearly as possible the same size as the cash position. Margin requirements for trades in futures are small. Farmers are tempted to take larger futures positions than the cash positions that are being offset without realizing the large losses and gains that can result from small price changes. The temptation is particularly great to replace cash sales with larger quantities of futures. The reasoning is that if it is desirable to replace 10,000 bushels of cash soybeans with 10,000 bushels of futures, then it is even better to replace them with 50,000. To do so is to leave the farm busines and become a speculator.

Positions in futures must be opposite the cash positions. If the farmer is trying to establish a price for deferred delivery of a growing or stored crop, he is long cash and therefore must be short futures. If he buys futures, he is increasing his risk and trading in futures in a way that is not related to the farm business. If he has need for additional feed supplies, he is short cash and should therefore be long futures.

Fourth is the failure to close out both the cash and futures positions simultaneously. Many people are reluctant to take losses on futures. Suppose a farmer is long the crop that he has in store and is short futures against it and the level of prices goes up. He has made money on the cash and lost on the futures. The net of the changes may be meeting his target price exactly, but when he sells the cash he is tempted to stay short the futures in the hope that the price will go back down so that he can retain his cash profits without having to offset part of them with futures losses. He is reluctant to admit that he made a mistake when he priced his cash grain forward instead of staying long. He must learn to live with his decisions in the same way that he does if he sells the cash grain too soon. When he prices a growing or stored crop forward by selling futures, he is working with basis and is no longer concerned with changes in the level of price.

The fifth error is to trade in and out. We have described some situations in which farmers can wisely reverse positions taken in futures as they change their minds about the future course of prices. There is always the temptation to overdo this reversal, grabbing quick profits when the opportunity is offered, expecting to resell on a rally or repurchase on a dip. If a farmer trades in and out he is becoming a short term speculator which is something that most farmers are not qualified to do. They typically lose money doing this, and fail to accomplish their original goals as well.

CHAPTER 12

Users of Raw Materials

We now move to the other side of the commodity market—that of buying for use. This is the province of the purchasing department. Commodities are raw materials used in the production of manufactured products destined for consumer markets. There are numerous commodities and comparably numerous kinds of industries that buy, convert and manufacture, and sell them. Some commodities are converted into finished consumer goods in one process while others are converted into products for further conversion and manufacture. Some processes are fairly simple and the end products of some raw materials closely resemble the original commodity while other processes are complex and the end products are only remotely related to the original material. Sirloin steak is identifiable with a live steer and the conversion processes are fairly simple but a bottle of soda pop does not resemble raw sugar nor is a cake mix closely related to the soybean that was the original source of one of the ingredients in the package.

There are futures markets for some commodities but not others. The use of futures markets is an integral and major part of the management of some conversion and manufacturing industries while it plays no part in others. Within industries, the different firms make different uses of futures markets, ranging from total involvement to none at all. Each industry and each firm has its own peculiar set of procurement and inventory problems. These relate to the nature of the raw materials, the end products, the price and pricing structure, and the firm structure within industries.

The great differences among materials, processes, products, industries, firms, and pricing arrangements and customs make generalizations about the use of commodity futures difficult. At the same time, the large numbers make even a cursory description of each impossible. Nor does any one person know a great deal about the futures trading, inventory, and pricing activity of the gamut of processing and manufacturing firms. Very few systematic studies have been made in the area. Current positions and procurement and inventory policies are closely guarded company secrets.

Procurement and inventory management are areas of intense competition among firms and skill in these areas is of major importance in levels of company earnings. Company officials have been known to make such remarks as: "Anyone can operate a plant. We make it or lose it by buying, selling, and converting better than the competition" and "A plant is a thing we must put up with as an operating base for exercising our procurement, trading, and merchandising skills." These are overstatements but they do illustrate the importance attached to the area. It shows up in the company salary structure. The inventory management and price activity of one soybean processor is located in a small office deep in the bowels of a huge processing plant. It is under the control of one man who controls a few hundred square feet of office space and a handful of people. The plant is multi-storied, covers several acres, is loaded with intricate machinery, and has many employees scurrying about. It is controlled by a plant manager. The man who controls inventory and price usually has a higher salary than the plant manager.

Each raw material using industry has its own peculiar kinds of procurement and inventory management problems. Each firm within each of the industries is different from each other in such things as organization, size, financial strength, and marketing skills so that each has its own procurement or inventory management problems. Thus, market operations, futures market operations in particular, are highly individualized. Our objective here is to illustrate some of the kinds of problems encountered by operating firms and some of the procedures employed to cope with them. The literature in the area tends toward overgeneralization and stylized presentation. Most of it has been written by tradespeople who were, in writing, trying to put the best possible face on futures trading for the benefit of legislators, educators, and the public. This is not to suggest that they are less than candid but rather the circumstances of presentation usually make candid exposition impossible. The observations here have been gleaned from a miscellanea of literature presented to legislative bodies, symposia, seminars, and forums and from conversations with operating people about specific, immediate problems.[1]

Flour Millers

One of the classic and most frequently used examples of a commodity buying hedge is the flour miller. A flour miller is a converter of wheat into flour and

---

[1] It is worth noting that hospitality rooms at conventions are more conducive to candid comment than public forums, the proceedings of which are published.

feed by-products. The processes are fairly simple and flour is an undifferentiated product. There is one raw material and major product, the characteristics of which can be objectively measured. The process is a commodity to commodity conversion.

Wheat is not just wheat and flour is not just flour. There are several grades and classes of wheat and flour is made to the exacting specifications of individual buyers. The different flours require different classes of wheat and the principal flours are made from blends of several wheats. Soft wheat is required for the production of flour for cookie manufacturers and cake bakers. Low protein winter wheat is needed for production of family flour. High protein flour is made from northern spring wheat. Bakery flour is made from blends of ordinary protein winter wheat and high protein wheats. Clear flour for the export trade requires ordinary protein winter wheat. Semolina for the macaroni trade comes from durum wheat. There is a range of characteristics within these general classes of flour. The individual buyers have their own specific preferences for their own requirements. Advancing technology of milling has reduced the close identity of class of wheat to class of flour that once existed but has far from eliminated it.

Production of the different classes of wheat varies geographically. High protein spring wheats are produced in Minnesota and the Dakotas. The relatively high protein hard winter wheats are produced in the Great Plains states. Soft wheats and the not so hard winter wheats come from states east of the Mississippi River, particularly Illinois, Ohio and Indiana. Thus, Minneapolis is the market center for hard spring wheat and the delivery terms of Minneapolis futures contract require delivery of this high quality class of wheat. Kansas City is the market center for the high protein winter wheats and the delivery terms require moderately higher protein hard winter wheat. Chicago and St. Louis are market centers for soft wheat and the relatively low protein hard winter wheats. Chicago delivery terms permit delivery of nearly all classes of wheat. The geographic distribution, class considerations in flour production, and freight rate structure impose restrictions on the buying of cash wheat. The appropriate kinds of wheat for the specific kinds of flour to be made must be bought where and when they are available. Selection and purchase is a continuous process that cannot be coincident with the sale of flour.

Flour millers are price competitive. Flour users buy where they can buy at the lowest price and otherwise have little preference among millers. The per capita consumption of flour in the United States has declined, for many years, at almost exactly the same rate as population has increased, so that wheat used for human consumption has remained essentially constant. The lack of market growth, changing technology, and changing freight rate structure have resulted in more flour production capacity than there is demand for flour. There are numerous firms and plants. The industry is intensively competitive.

The price of wheat is independent of the price of flour. Wheat production in the U.S. has ranged from two to four times wheat use for flour for many years. Wheat is fed to livestock and exported. Prior to 1972, a high proportion of exports moved under government subsidy. Farmers were offered incentives to restrict wheat production and the government made nonrecourse loans to farmers. Large government inventories continually existed. This integrated, governmental wheat program dominated the price structure for wheat. Beginning with near failure of the Russian wheat crop in 1972 the control of wheat prices shifted from the U.S. government to world markets. World demand for wheat increased and there was another crop failure in Russia in 1975. Volatility of wheat prices was greatly increased. Flour milling is the highest value use of wheat but the price is established by forces outside of the U.S. flour-baking industry. Wheat is a small part of the cost—approximately 10 percent—of bread. Thus, price does not affect the quantity taken by the milling industry.

Flour is priced on the basis of the cost of wheat plus competitive milling margin minus the value of milling byproducts. The price of flour varies directly with and is closely related to the cost of wheat. The byproducts are millfeed— bran, shorts, and middlings—which are used in the manufacture of livestock feeds. The price of millfeeds is variable and must be taken into account in pricing flour.

The purchase of flour by bakers is seasonal and erratic. The buyers book substantial quantities at one time for deferred shipment. Some contracts extend as much as six months forward. The volume of forward booking varies greatly from year to year as well as within seasons. The period of heavy booking is in June and July. This forward booking is more typical of the bread bakery trade than it is of the specialty flour trade, but this is the bulk of the business. The bakers appear to base their purchases on three things: 1. Their price expectations about wheat. 2. A price of flour that will return baking profits at prices of bread that fit into merchandising programs, and 3. The price patterns and the proper timing of purchases the preceding season. They try to nail down their costs at levels that permit moderate and stable prices of bread. When flour prices permit the bakers preconceived bread prices they book heavily and vice versa.

Obviously, the bakery trade is highly speculative in its flour purchasing activity. This speculation is partly defensive and partly offensive. They book to defend a merchandisable price of bread on the one hand but book to fix a cost of flour lower than they judge their competitors can. In a sense, they are "damned if they do and damned if they don't." Note that this baker speculation in flour prices is not directly related to futures trading.

These several things make up the framework within which the flour miller must operate an inventory program. They can offset risks of price variations in the price of their wheat inventories by selling futures contracts. Their operations in this are the same as the merchant and warehouseman. Prior to harvest they tend to be long new crop cash and short futures. From the beginning of the flour booking period through most of the rest of the season, they are short cash flour and can offset risks by purchase of futures. The futures contract stands in the place of cash wheat until the appropriate class and quality can be accumulated.

Millers encounter problems in hedging flour sales in wheat futures. First, they must correctly anticipate the price of futures at which they can cover the flour sale. Sales that are made overnight must be anticipatorily hedged or the sale is vulnerable to the change in the wheat price from close to opening. The more serious price problem is the impact that millers' purchases may have on the price. The small, regular orders are not a problem but some of the bookings are large enough to require hundreds of thousands of bushels of wheat. Such amounts, purchased rapidly (within a session) may put the price up a cent, or two, or more. Bookings tend to come in epidemics. When one baker books, the rumors fly, and they all book. Such losses as may result from lack of perfect futures market liquidity must be correctly anticipated in pricing flour, for the milling margins are thin.

When wheat prices are active and speculators are trading in volume, liquidity is not a severe problem. Activity attracts the scalpers and pit traders who furnish short term liquidity. But when markets are quiet, the pit traders can't make any money and are elsewhere doing other things. Much of the time liquidity at the market where the hedges were originally placed is not sufficient to permit removal without price penalty. In such cases the flour miller must either wait with the accompanying risk exposure of a net short position or go to other delivery months or to other markets. What they do depends on their appraisal of subsequent changes in spreads within and between markets.

Second, millers must correctly anticipate the basis at which cash wheat will be purchased to replace the futures that serve as a hedge. The cash is accumulated over time and the basis changes. Flour millers must have and use skill in selecting the delivery month in which hedges are placed. Hedges must also be placed in the appropriate market. Ideally, the lower protein wheat hedges should go to Chicago, the ordinary protein wheat hedges to Kansas City, and the high protein spring wheat hedges to Minneapolis, but lack of liquidity may prevent this. The large hedges are placed in Chicago and sometimes gradually moved to the other markets as spreads can be executed at favorable differences. But "favorable" differences may never materialize; that is the hedger may have incorrectly anticipated the spreads that would prevail in the future. Hedgers must be competent intermarket spread speculators.

Third, there is no effective way to hedge requirements of high protein hard spring wheat. Delivery terms at Minneapolis require No. 2 Northern Spring

Wheat—13.50 protein or higher and No. 1 is deliverable at a 2 cent premium. But protein premiums are variable. They vary both within and between crop seasons. For example, during the first half of 1967 which related to the 1966 crop, 17 percent protein cash wheat at Minneapolis traded at the same price as 13 percent protein but during the second half of the year 17 percent sold at a premium of as much as 28 cents over 13 percent. A requirement hedge placed in Minneapolis March, 1967 wheat was quite effective but one placed in Minneapolis December, 1967 was not at all effective. Prior to 1972 the Minneapolis wheat price was tied closely to the government loan rate so there was limited variation in the base or deliverable price. Most of the variation was in the premiums and these were not hedgeable. Millers must speculate in protein premiums or forward contract cash wheat of specified protein content, letting someone else speculate in premiums.

Fourth, flour millers are subject to uncertainty because of variation in the price of millfeeds. About 28 percent of the weight of a wheat kernel is millfeed. Typically, this is 12 to 15 percent of the value. When millers cover flour bookings in wheat futures they are long millfeeds. In pricing flour, they must calculate a millfeed value that becomes a credit against the cost of wheat. To the extent that they overestimate the ultimate selling price of millfeed they suffer reduced milling margins and vice versa. Their preference is to contract millfeeds forward but this can be done only to a limited extent. Most of the millfeeds are consumed by cattlefeed manufacturers. Because these people book cattlefeeds forward in the fall of the year, they are interested in booking millfeeds. The feed manufacturers typically come in during September for millfeeds to be delivered from October through March. Their preference is October through January but the flour millers have a bigger problem and can put enough pressure on to get the longer period. This is at some price concession. Even so, 65 to 70 percent of wheat millfeeds are sold for spot shipment so that flour millers are chronically net long millfeeds to the extent of their flour bookings covered in both cash and futures wheat. If their forecasts are too high they lose part of their milling margins so they tend to be conservative, but if they are overly conservative they are not competitive in their flour price. Flour salesmen tend to be optimistic regarding millfeeds prices and in constant conflict with the analysis and conversion people within the company.

There is a way out; they can sell corn or oats futures. Millfeeds, corn, and oats prices tend to vary generally together, but the relationship is not close. Millers may hedge millfeeds in corn or oats futures when they judge the risks of variations in price relationships are less than those of a decline in millfeeds prices. They tend to do this only when they judge millfeed prices are inordinantly high, and corn or oats prices are high relative to millfeeds prices.

The preceding discussion assumes risk minimization activities by millers. The open interest of long hedgers in wheat futures contracts appear to be substantially less than the forward bookings of flour. Part is offset by cash wheat but an apparent discrepancy remains, suggesting that not all millers are fully hedged. Because of the size of their positions and because they borrow large amounts of operating money, the large millers maintain a fairly close balance between wheat inventories, cash and futures, and flour sales. They tend to accumulate net long futures positions in wheat ahead of the flour buying season. They judge the moods and expectations of their buyers and anticipate sales with wheat purchases. They do not always cover bookings promptly but may string the process out over several weeks when bookings of the industry as a whole are large and the millers judge that the coverage of bookings is the major price supporting factor.

Smaller companies appear to hedge a smaller proportion of their wheat requirements than do the large companies. Part of this difference stems from less exacting requirements on the part of their bankers, part from ignorance of the use of futures, and part from being out of position—out of the mainstream of the flow of wheat and flour. They can often buy wheat near their plants at prices that are dependent on flour prices; that is, their acquisitions are less competitive.

The integrated companies that mill wheat and manufacture branded products such as cake mixes, cookies, crackers, party snacks, etc. are less regular hedgers than the specialized millers. They can set prices on the basis of wheat costs more effectively than can millers of bakery flour. Their hedging activities are influenced more by their price expectations than are those of the straight millers.

Soybean Processors

The soybean processing industry is unique among the agricultural industries in that there are active futures markets on both the raw material and product sides. The industry is confronted by organized speculation in buying raw materials and in selling products. This participation in pricing of both sides of the process results in broad participation in the pricing of the process. In other industries, as flour milling, the competition in the processing margin is with other converters so that margins are set by the industry, but the whole speculative fraternity gets involved in soybean processing margins. In the final analysis, processing margins are determined by interprocessor competition but, in the meantime, speculative markets result in great latitude of opportunities for processor pricing of the conversion process. Their operations are sometimes quite intricate and much of the difference among earnings of processors is determined by differences in skill in maneuvering within the pricing complex. The games they play is a subject worthy of a book and can be only hinted at here.

The soybean has only one significant use—processing into two very different products, crude soybean oil which is used for further refining and manufactured into food ingredients, and soybean meal which is nearly all used for livestock feed. The soybeans that are exported from the United States are processed abroad so that processor competition is international. Soybeans are nearly homogeneous, having only minor differences in oil content. Both oil and meal are produced to standard grades so that they are fungible raw materials. There are two kinds of meal, one 44 percent protein and the other 49 percent. In making 49 percent meal the fibrous hulls are removed from the soybeans before processing. Soybean meal is valuable for its protein content so that 49 percent meal sells proportionately higher than 44 percent. Many plants are equipped to make both kinds of meal. The bulk of the meal produced (approximately 60%) is 44 percent, although most of the meal produced in eastern trunk line territory is 49 percent.

Most soybean processing plants are located in the soybean production areas. Soybeans move from farm to country elevator to processor. Some are stored on farms, some at country elevators and most processors have extensive storage facilities. Stocks at plants typically reach a peak in November and are usually reduced to negligible levels in mid September. For the industry as a whole, peak stocks are sometimes as high as 30 percent of a year's use. The firms located in the interior sometimes own as much as 50 percent of a year's requirement immediately following the harvest. Relatively few country elevators own soybean inventories, limiting storage to farmer owned beans. Thus, processors must buy soybeans as farmers wish to sell. Soybean prices are volatile; processors have major inventory and risk management problems.

Soybean products are shipped as they are produced. Processors provide facilities for the storage of some oil but their stocks never amount to a significant percentage of a year's production. Meal stocks at processing plants rarely exceed 2.5 percent of a year's production. Oil is sold to refiners and meal to feed manufacturers and feed ingredient merchants. Some sales of oil and meal are made for quick shipment but most are sold for deferred delivery. Most of the forward contracts are made for shipment in less than 90 days. Users also maintain limited storage facilities and the forward contracting is mainly a scheduling convenience for both processors and users. In addition to plant scheduling convenience, freight billing for meal plays an important part in processing operations. Outbound shipments of meal must be matched to inbound shipments of soybeans.

As noted in an earlier chapter, there was, in former times, very extensive and extended forward contracting of both oil and meal. Some of this remains, particularly for meal. Some meal for October-March shipment is contracted during the summer and the fall harvest period. The essential point is that the forward contracting option is open to soybean processors.

The soybean processing industry has grown rapidly as the market for soybean products has expanded: from a crush of 251 million bushels in 1950–51 to 402 million in 1960–61 and 738 million in 1969–70. In spite of this rapid growth, it has always been an industry of over-capacity. In only one year, 1969–70, was the supply of soybeans and the demand for products larger than the crush capacity. Prior to 1950 the main method of oil extraction was by machines called expellers. From the latter 1940's to the early 1950's the industry changed to chemical solvent extraction which essentially doubled the capacity for the time that the expellers remained in use. In the early days there were numerous small mills and a few large ones. There are economies of scale so that the industry gradually shifted to large mills with an accompanying overcapacity. In the early days soybean production was concentrated in four cornbelt states, Ohio, Indiana, Illinois, and Iowa. The rapid expansion of the industry was in the midsouth and southeast and plants were built in those areas. There are freight and tariff advantages to shipping soybeans rather than products, contributing to plant building in Europe and Japan.

Many soybean processing plants were built as vertical extensions of firms using soybean oil and meal. Starting in the 1950's, the oil users sold most of their facilities (or let them go out of use) so that little soybean oil to shortening, salad oil, etc. remains although some soybean processors have added oil refineries. Most soybean processors are part of companies that use soybean meal in feed manufacture. But meal is sold to feed manufacturers other than the parent companies and meal is bought from plants other than those owned by parent companies. Ownership is integrated but operations are not.

A few large firms have a large share of the soybean processing business but there are numerous firms. There is no price and margin domination or leadership in the industry. The market operations of some firms are watched closely by other firms and by speculators but market positions are carefully masked.

Market prices of soybeans, oil, and meal are fully competitive and reported. Thus, it is possible to compute existing processing margins. Processors operate in a fishbowl; all of their buying and selling prices are known and only the amounts traded at the various prices are private information. A bushel of soybeans produces about 47.5 pounds of 44 percent soybean meal and 10.6 pounds of crude soybean oil. The reference price of soybeans is track, Illinois points, that of meal is bulk, Decatur, Illinois, fully unrestricted rail billing, and that of oil is crude, Decatur, in tank cars. Thus, if the price of oil is 18.5 cents per pound its value is $1.961, if the price of meal is $160.00 per ton its value is $3.80 and the combined value is $5.761. If the price of soybeans is $5.53, the processing margin is 23.1 cents. Soybean and soybean product prices vary geographically and are different for different times of delivery so that this stylized margin does not measure actual returns to processors. But the price structure is interrelated over time and space so that the stylized margin is indicative of the general level and changes in actual margins.

Prior to 1972 operating costs, including overhead, depreciation, and nominal return on capital appeared to be on the general order of 18 cents per bushel. However, it also appeared that a stylized margin of 12 cents kept the vigor of processor complaints at moderate levels. A 12 cent margin tended to generate a maximum crush but at lower margins they cut back. Processing margins are highly variable between years and within years. Average crush margin for six years was:

1962–63	9.36	1964–65	6.12	1966–67	12.85
1963–64	−1.07	1965–66	22.65	1967–68	10.90

In 1963–64 there was a shortage of soybeans that resulted in a reduction in crush from 475 million bushels to 440 million. In 1965–66 soybean supplies were large so that farmers did not hold strongly. Product demand was excellent and prices rose substantially. Soybean prices also increased, but processors were able to get the best margins in many years. By months, the average processing margin for the six years was:

Oct.	19.8	Feb.	8.0	June	5.6
Nov.	15.7	Mar.	4.7	July	7.0
Dec.	9.7	Apr.	3.6	Aug.	12.7
Jan.	10.6	May	1.9	Sept.	23.6

The moral of this story would seem to be: Operate the plant August through January and quit. But closing down does not stop the overhead nor can a labor force be dismissed and reassembled so readily. A better solution would seem to be to buy soybeans at harvest and contract products forward, extending the favorable processing margins forward through the February-July poverty period. But it is not that simple.

There is one more parameter of the processing margin. There is a stock of soybeans that is carried hedged in soybean futures. This stock, with its accompanying cost of storage, forces a carrying charge structure in the futures market. Typically, there are only small inventories of oil and meal. Accordingly, there is no way to force a carrying charge structure. Cash soybean prices gain relative to the futures but cash product prices do not. The result of this is that spot margins may be profitable in the fall of the year while the margins shown by the forward futures—say May soybeans compared to May oil and May meal—may reflect a negative processing margin. For example, on May 25, 1970 processing margins as shown by various futures prices were:

Cash	soybeans	versus	Cash	products	19.38¢
July 1970	soybeans	versus	July 1970	products	22.13¢
Sept. 1970	soybeans	versus	Oct. 1970	products	11.04¢
Nov. 1970	soybeans	versus	Dec. 1970	products	7.68¢
Jan. 1971	soybeans	versus	Jan. 1971	products	1.40¢
Mar. 1971	soybeans	versus	Mar. 1971	products	−1.50¢
May 1971	soybeans	versus	May 1971	products	−3.75¢

Processing margins for immediate shipment were unusually favorable. The farther they were extended into the future the less favorable they became.[2]

Such is the world in which processors must operate. They attempt to buy soybeans and sell products at differences that result in profitable processing margins. While processing margins are unprofitable a high proportion of the time, in every season there is a time when they are profitable and there is a combination of positions and trades that permits a profit for the year. The options are numerous and complex.

An option that is always open to processors is to speculate in price levels of soybeans and products. They do this to varying extents; some not at all and some susbtantially. In the main, they must maintain fairly evenly balanced positions to avoid the ruinous losses that would inevitably occur and put them out of the game, and to obtain operating capital. As a general rule, the larger the firm the more closely balanced are the market positions. Price level speculation is regarded as a subtle form of cheating. It is outside of the game of trying to carve a margin out of price relationships. It may work but it doesn't require a processing plant and thus is not within the processing game. Some of the "legitimate" options are:

1. Buy cash soybeans as they are available, hedge them in soybean futures. Sell cash products as they are produced and remove the soybean hedges as products are sold. The result of this is to accept spot margins as they exist.

2. Buy cash soybeans and sell product futures, placing the product hedges in the months in which the soybeans will be crushed. Product hedges are removed as cash products are sold. By selling product futures rather than soybean futures, the processor is accepting the margins offered in futures.

3. Buy cash soybeans and sell products forward in cash markets. This can be varied by selling futures for one product and making cash forward contracts for the other.

4. Buy cash soybeans and sell product futures, placing product hedges in months other than those in which the beans will be crushed. For example, for soybeans bought in November the oil fraction might be sold in January futures and the meal in May futures if the oil market is inverted and the meal market has a carrying charge. This may result in capacity being oversold for oil and undersold for meal and so requires further action at a later time, moving some of the oil hedges forward and some of the meal hedges back to closer deliveries.

5. Buy cash soybeans and hedge in soybean futures while at the same time selling oil or meal or both cash forward and hedging these positions in oil and meal futures. This, in effect, postpones the acceptance of processing margins.

---

[2] In earlier times—about 1950 to 1960—this normal inversion of processing margins shown in futures was a source of profit to informed speculators. The negative margins usually turned positive as the delivery month approached, as they had to, to get soybeans processed. Early in the season speculators sold distant soybean futures and bought product futures. The game was called "reverse crush." Processors played it too. In time it became so widely practiced that its reliability and predictability was lost.

6. Buy soybean futures before cash soybeans are available and sell products either in cash forward or futures markets. This process is called putting on "board"[3] crush. The effect of this is to accept the current crush margins rather than waiting until cash soybeans are available. In the simplest form, soybean and product futures are matched, January soybeans to January products, etc. and the volume in each of the delivery months matched to the expected crush rate. However, positions need not always be matched by delivery month and capacity can be oversold.

7. Processors can and do reverse crush; selling soybean futures and buying product futures. It may be that they have put on board crush at profitable levels and reverse the position when margins turn unprofitable, taking profits. Or they may start with a reverse crush, particularly in forward positions, thinking that margins can only improve. There is no theoretical limit to the number of times that crush can be put on and removed within a season but there are practical limits. Processors do not like to reverse crush because they find that they are their own worst enemies when they merchandise cash products. They are selling cash at the same time they are liquidating futures positions.

The core of the processing activity is purchase of soybean futures and the sale of products futures, matched by delivery month and related to plant capacity. The relationship of futures to futures is the basic crushing margin. All of the other trading activities are basis and spread trades in relation to it. The combination of soybean and product futures gives processors very wide latitude in the selection of the time that they accept existing crushing margins. They can put on a year's crush months before the crop is raised or they can, by buying soybean futures and selling product futures after the cash soybeans are crushed and the products sold, delay the acceptance of crush margins until the end of the year. The key decisions that crushers make relate to the timing of putting on crush.

The intricacies of processor positions and trade stem from changes in price differences: cash soybeans to soybean futures, soybean futures to other soybean futures, cash meal to meal futures, meal futures to other meal futures, cash oil to oil futures, and oil futures to other oil futures. The purchase of cash soybeans as they are available and hedging them in soybean futures until oil and meal is made and sold has not been profitable during nearly all of the history of the industry. Processors make or lose money on the basis of their skills in timing the commitment of plants to crushing and in basis and spread trading. Price relationships are uncertain and variable. Trading decisions are speculative. Soybean and product futures are indispensable tools for the implementation of speculative decisions.

Processors tend to go about this business conservatively. They put on crush at gradual rates and reverse crush infrequently. They rarely over-commit crush

[3] Short for Board of Trade.

capacity. Their open position speculation is limited. They buy soybeans as they become available and keep products merchandised well ahead of production. They prefer to keep as many of their market positions as possible in cash rather than futures.

In all of this, processors are continuously matching wits with merchants, product buyers, and with the market. It appears that they are skillful because apparent processing margins have been below cost and the earnings records of processors respectable.

Feed Manufacturers

The mixed feed industry presents an interesting set of variants from standard doctrine of trade use of futures markets. The use of futures markets by feed manufacturers is but one part of a total inventory management program. The ways in which they use futures markets is a further demonstration of the futility of trying to set hedging and speculation apart as opposites or even trying to distinguish between the two. Futures operations of this group of firms might best be called speculative hedging.

Much of the feed consumed by livestock is compounded from ingredients into mixed feeds. Mixed feed is consumed by all classes of livestock—hogs, beef cattle, dairy cattle, egg laying flocks, broilers, turkeys, household pets, sheep and goats, and even fish. There are two broad kinds of feed, complete feeds which is the only ration the animal is fed, and supplemental feeds which are further mixed with other ingredients such as grain at the feeding site. There are hundreds of varieties of feeds made from different combinations of ingredients.

There are several thousand firms engaged in feed manufacturing—a few very large firms, a large number of medium sized firms, and many small firms. Some are national in scope with foreign branches while others are limited to one small town operation. There are all degrees of sophistication of management, including, for our purposes, ingredient procurement and inventory management. Individual feed manufacturing vary in many respects; size, location, kinds of feed manufactured, capital structure, capacity to withstand losses, and inclination to speculate. These differences affect inventory and hedging programs in such a way that it is not possible to apply one program to all firms. Inventory and hedging programs must be individually tailored.

There are probably 115 different ingredients used in feed manufacturing. The most important of these, in terms of tonnage, are the grains—corn, grain sorghums, oats, barley, and wheat. Second are the protein supplements—oilseed meals (soybean, cottonseed, linseed, peanut, copra), animal byproducts, fish meal, and alfalfa meal. Third are grain byproducts—wheat millfeeds, corn gluten feed and meal, distillers and brewers dried grains, soybean millfeeds, etc. These three groups make up the bulk of the tonnage and most of the cost. The rest of the list is composed of minerals, urea, synthetic amino acids, antibiotics, etc. There is even artificial coloring and flavoring in pet foods. The primary preoccupation with ingredient cost is with corn and soybean meal. A nutritionally balanced feed can be made from different combinations of ingredients; the real concern is with carbohydrate, protein, fat, fiber, etc. balance. Thus, some ingredients can be substituted for others. Substitution is a matter of relative price. A high proportion of the industry is sufficiently computerized to work out least cost combinations on a current basis and formulae are changed as price relationships of ingredients change.

As a general rule, mixed feeds are priced on the basis of replacement cost of ingredients and price lists are kept current on a weekly basis. As with all general policies, there are variations and shadings. A few firms price on average cost and a few on actual cost. Nearly all firms fail to fully follow the extremes of ingredient price changes or lag behind them. For example, when soybean meal prices suddenly shoot up 10 or 20 percent and feed manufacturers have sufficient inventory to avoid, or nearly avoid, spot purchases, feed prices do not immediately follow the change. If the change lasts, feed prices are adjusted to the new cost structure. Some of the peaks and valleys are leveled, but not much.

The single major exception to replacement cost pricing is beef cattle feed booking. In the fall of the year cattle feed is sold for shipment scattered over several months, price guaranteed against decline; if the market price is higher on the date of shipment, the contract price prevails but if it is lower, the customer pays the market price. This is a "heads I break even and tails you win" game. It is a good sales gimmick, but is hard on the nervous systems of ingredient buyers. The way this ridiculous policy came into being is lost in antiquity. The industry as a whole deplores it but nearly everyone does it to meet the competition. There is no way to cope other than to speculate in ingredient price levels. There is a marked tendency for ingredient buyers to be long and so vulnerable to price declines rather than short and vulnerable to price increases.[4]

Feed manufacturers must carry minimum inventories of cash ingredients and be long some ingredients in transit to assure uninterrupted plant operations. Problems of plant operation, sales variability, quality, availability of materials, and rail billing require a basic long cash position. But for the major ingredients, this position is not large and is partly offset by the lag in the changing of

---

[4] This probably relates to an almost universal tendency to be more willing to absorb losses resulting from price declines rather than losses from price increases. To be caught short in a rising market seems to be more difficult to explain to management than to lose money on an inventory that declines in price. Soybean processors who are long cash soybeans in a declining market quietly grind up their mistakes. Country elevators point with pride to price appreciation on long cash positions even though it may be smaller than the basis gain. It seems to take more courage to be short than long.

finished feed price lists. So long as these in process inventories are held constant at minimum levels, gains and losses from price changes are not large and tend to average out over relatively short periods. Such risks are not of major importance.

Feed manufacturers, as a group, do not hold inventory risks to a minimum consistent with adequate supplies of satisfactory quality. They accumulate much larger than minimum inventories when price increases are expected, and reduce inventories of forward contracted ingredients to minimum levels when price declines are expected. The amount of ingredient speculation varies among firms, both in absolute size of inventories and in relation to the length of time that inventories are expected to last. Whether the maximum inventory positions taken are expected to last three weeks or 12 months they are varied on the basis of price expectations. Because mixed feed is priced on replacement cost, manufacturers must take inventory profits and losses. The basic point of departure in considering feed manufacturers' use of futures markets is that their objective is not to minimize risk but rather to control risk. Their problem is how to manage inventories so that inventory profits can be maximized and losses held to a minimum. The first phase of the problem is how to avoid being forced into unwanted speculative positions, and the second is how to stack the cards in favor of gaining as compared to losing. Futures markets are one tool in a total inventory management program. Four uses of futures markets are distinguished here; three of which are called hedging.

Procurement. Futures markets can be and are used to accumulate inventory ahead of the time that cash ingredients are purchased or contracted. The primary use is in connection with soybean meal and corn to cover beef cattle feed booking. But this use is not great. Ingredients are usually available on cash forward contracts in sufficient volume to cover feed manufactures' speculative inclinations. They prefer cash forward contracts out of scheduling and freight rate considerations. They buy futures when they judge the cash buying basis to be less favorable than is probable at a later time.

Direct Hedging. Direct hedging is the maintenance of an even market position by taking opposite positions in futures in the same commodity. This is the traditional hedging method employed by warehousemen and pertains to grain. It is not the total answer to feed manufacturers' needs, however, because so few feed ingredients can be covered in this way.

Direct hedging is used, principally, by feed manufacturers to earn carrying charges. This is particularly true in areas where grains are produced, but not in sufficient volume to serve all of the needs of the area. For example, corn is usually worth substantially more in the eastern states than at Chicago, but at certain times—harvest in particular—the price in the east may be no more than or even lower than the price at Chicago. At such times, corn can be hedged in Chicago futures with the nearly certain expectation of a remarkable basis gain.

Cross Hedging. Cross hedging is the hedging of cash positions in futures markets for different commodities, that is, short sales of corn futures against cash positions in grain by-products, oats futures against millfeeds, corn futures against grain sorghums, etc. It involves generally balanced positions and logically considers each inventory separately in the hedging program.

Cross hedging serves several purposes. First, it is used to cover commodities for which there are no futures markets. There are futures markets for only a few feed ingredients but ingredient prices are interrelated so that a short futures position in corn or soybean meal may offer protection when none other is available.

Second, it is used to cover commodities for which the existing futures markets are not liquid enough to hedge in without serious price concession, in and out. Some feed manufacturers who do not feel they can hedge effectively in certain futures markets prefer cross hedging.

Third, cross hedging is used when the direct hedging basis is judged to be unsatisfactory. For example, farmer holding may keep the price of oats high in Iowa while a large crop in Illinois and Indiana may depress futures resulting in poor prospects for basis gain on an Iowa held inventory. In such a case, new crop corn tends to be a better hedge.

There is considerable difference of opinion about the advisability of cross hedging. Some firms do quite a lot of successful cross hedging, while others prefer to carry inventories unhedged. A thorough knowledge of price relationships is essential to effective cross hedging. There are problems in addition to the one of price relationships. One is the quantity to sell against an inventory. Whether to sell pound for pound, value for value, or in some combination of the two requires a careful study of historical price behavior. Another problem is locational price differences. Relative values at different points are more erratic in feed ingredients than in grains and this erratic behavior must be recognized in placing cross hedges. Cross hedging does, however, have the offsetting advantage of offering basis profits to those hedgers who understand it. It has the major advantage of offering the opportunity of getting short something, against cash or contracted inventories, in generally declining markets—any old port in a storm.

Selective Hedging. Selective hedging might be better called selective speculation; it is a fundamentally speculative program. It is, however, less speculative than carrying open inventory positions. Selective hedging is the careful selection of inventory positions and hedging plans in order to take maximum advantage of market changes with a minimum of price risk. It involves both direct and cross hedging, as well as generally unbalanced market positions taken on the basis of expected price and price relationship changes. A selective hedging program is a blending of the entire inventory management program with all of its separate prices into one coordinated balance of market positions. This seems to be the single hedging program that fits both the problems and the desires of feed manufacturers.

A selective hedging program should be designed to achieve several different goals. First, it must limit the total risk of the firm to the amount of loss that it is willing to take. If this involves hedging part or all of the minimum pipeline inventories, then it must provide these hedges.

Second, the program must assure liquidity of operations. Every purchasing agent must be able to make independent decisions. But the outlook for supplies, prices, and requirements changes rapidly, and he must be nimble enough in his thinking and trading to adjust to the changes. The inventory program must also be liquid enough to make it possible to adjust to changes. Taking a position and holding it for a long period without the possibility of adjustment is dangerous.

Suppose that a feed mixer buys soybean meal in October for delivery from January through March at $65 per ton. He believes that it is priced below the average for the year and that meal will cost more than $65 in January, February, and March. By December the price goes up to $75, which the mixer considers too high. He thinks the chances are the price will decline to $68. Suppose, further, that he is exactly right in his appraisal. If he carries the original position through to its conclusion without deviation, he will make a net of $3 per ton. Actually, he will have made ten dollars and lost seven. The inventory value of the meal in December is $75, not $65, no matter how archaic his accountant may be. With a flexible inventory program, he would have gotten off a sale against the meal contract and cashed the ten dollars.

A good military commander always plans his retreat before he launches an offensive. All feed manufacturers who take inventory positions get into situations that go against them. This cannot be helped. The thing to do then is to stop the losses before they get too large. One of the most important uses of futures markets it to provide liquidity; cash positions are relatively inflexible. They are tied to considerations of adequate supply, proper quality, and transportation costs. There is a tendency to get married to cash positions.

One serious inventory problem is the changing volume of feed sales. A decline in mixed feed price is usually accompanied, in the short run, by a decrease in the volume of sales, and an increase in prices by an increase in sales. Accordingly, an inventory of a given size lasts longer on a declining market than on a rising one. This is another reason liquidity is important. In a declining market, something in addition to feed sales is needed to get inventories down fast enough.

Third, a selective hedging program is designed to make profits from long positions. This is the *selective* part rather than the *hedging* part of selective hedging. The program calls for deliberate speculations after the potential gains and losses have been appraised and the gains outweigh the losses at the level at which the firm is willing to speculate.

Fourth, the program should fix profits from speculations when the balance of potential gains and losses is unfavorable. This is the hedging part.

Corn Wet Millers

To this point we have looked at the inventory management problems of industries whose end products are identifiable with the raw material and are priced relative to raw material prices with either the product prices dependent on raw material cost or raw material prices dependent on product values. Inventory management problems of corn wet millers are different because the end products and end product prices are less closely identifiable with the raw material and raw material prices.

By a process of soaking and centrifuging corn wet millers float the sperm away from the kernel and separate the starch portion from the gluten portion. The objective is to obtain the starch; the other two parts are by-products. A high quality edible oil is extracted from the corn germ and sold into the general edible oils market. The gluten, relatively high in protein, is made into gluten feed and meal and sold to mixed feed manufacturers.

Some of the starch is further processed into sugars. A high proportion of the corn sugars—corn syrup—are used as sweeteners in the manufacture of candy. In this market corn sugar competes with other sugar sources—cane and beet— but the price relationships are not close. Corn sugar moves into a specialized market and sells at a premium. There are specialized, highly concentrated products made from corn sugar—dextrose, sucrose, and variants of these—used in the pharmaceutical industry. Corn sugar prices, in this assortment of markets, are variable and only remotely related to the price of corn.

The principal products of the industry are starches. Chemically, starch is a highly flexible product that can be put together in many combinations. The starch industry continually changes its product list. At any given time, there are more than 80 different kinds of starches. Research and development is an important activity of the companies; some new starches are added each year and others are dropped. The bulk of the starches go into the paper and textile industries but there are multitudinous other uses ranging from pharmaceuticals, to cosmetics, to home laundry, and to absorbents for babies' behinds.

There are only a few firms in the corn wet milling industry—a dozen or so—and two firms account for more than sixty percent of the business. The firms have no monopolistic buying power in the corn market because wet milling consumes only five to six percent of the U.S. corn crop. Corn gluten feed and meal prices are closely related to the prices of competing feeds, hence cannot be controlled by the milling industry. Corn oil has specialized food uses, particularly in the polyunsaturated margarine market, and sells at a premium over the principal fats and oils as soybean and cottonseed oils and lard. Its price moves up and down generally with the fats and oils market, but the size of the premium is variable. Wet millers can have but little control over the corn oil premium because it is a by-product and its supply is uncontrollable.

There appears to be industry leadership in starch prices. Leadership is neither clearly defined nor specific. This is partly the case because the industry must be meticulously circumspect in observing antitrust regulations. It is also partly the case because the industry leaders are independent and competitive, continually contesting for a larger share of the market. Nor are the smaller firms content with the table scrapings that might be alloted them in a monopoly industry. More importantly, the weakness of leadership is the result of product quality competition. Product innovation and merchandising programs are important determiners of market share and individual company returns relative to the average price of starch.

The net effect of all of this is a set of prices of the various starches that is directly variable with the price of corn when the two sets of prices are compared over fairly long time spans. But the price of starch is sticky relative to the price of corn. Company price lists are understood to be good for fairly long time periods and the full amount of fluctuations in corn prices never get into starch prices. Starch is not sold on firm forward contracts but the effect is the same. In periods of rising prices, the informal forward commitment appears to extend about three months. But in declining markets, the price of starch is more responsive so that protection extends only about thirty days.

This, then, is the context in which the inventory managers of wet millers must operate. They attempt to acquire raw materials at an average cost lower than the average of spot corn prices and at an average less than their competition, and attempt to sell the byproducts, gluten feed and meal and corn oil at higher than the average of market prices. If they are not long, they are short. They are short by the amount of the understood starch price protection and they are shorter in rising markets than falling markets. When they are long corn against informal starch commitments, they are net long gluten feed and meal which is generally sold for prompt shipment and they are long corn oil which is also generally sold in spot markets. At any given time there is an inventory of corn that represents a minimum price risk or zero market position. The precise size of this position is variable and difficult to calculate; it is by no means clear that all, or most, wet millers make such a calculation.

Wet millers own varying amounts of storage space for corn. Generally, those with storage space can accumulate cash inventories and these inventories often amount to more than the informal starch commitments. Those without storage space can do a moderate amount of inventory accumulation in cash forward markets. Inventory accumulation to fill storage space is a separate game from inventory accumulation for processing. It is geared to corn availability and corn basis. The internal accounting system usually treats elevator operation separately from corn processing. Use of corn futures in connection with the elevator is the same as that in the operation of interior and terminal elevators. The usual futures position is short.

The use of futures in inventory procurement is simple. They establish a long position equal to the estimated size of the starch commitment and vary its size as their estimates of the starch price commitments vary. They then vary the size of this position on the basis of the extent to which they are willing to assume price risks and their expectations about the price of corn. Position parameters are set by company risk policy. They vary from company to company; some are quite narrow with little room for exercise of speculative judgment while others range up to several months requirements.

Two things should be especially noted. First, they grind up their mistakes. When they accumulate unprotected inventory that subsequently goes down in price, the result is reduced processing margins resulting from high cost of raw materials. This is a useful euphemism in making explanations to management and stockholders. Second, inventory procurement in excess of sales can be and usually is called hedging. Such is more apt to be the case in declining markets when losses are realized than in rising markets when profits are made. There is, however, an element of "damned if you do and damned if you don't." If the rest of the industry is long in a rising market and a company is not, its profits for the year will suffer. Some indeterminable element of speculation is forced on individual companies by inventory practices of the rest of the industry. But companies are well advised to recognize this speculation for what it is and make deliberate speculative decisions, keeping the estimated industry position in mind.

Corn against starch positions generally result in net long positions in gluten feed and meal and corn oil. Only a limited variability in the timing of sales of gluten feed and meal is permitted by normal cash trading practices. Positions can be protected by sales of corn and soybean meal futures. Gluten feed and meal is higher in protein than corn and lower than soybean meal. Its price follows the corn price to some extent, meal to some extent, and moves independently to some extent. The variability of relationship among the three is oftentimes greater than the variability of gluten feed and meal prices. Thus, the hedging operations undertaken are themselves considerably speculative. But the variations are the result of real market forces and are subject to analysis. There are rewards to be earned by careful analysis of price differences among gluten feed and meal, corn, and soybean meal.

Corn oil can be sold on cash forward contracts but not always to the extent that corn has been purchased against starch production requirements. The alternative is to hedge in soybean oil futures when the company elects to avoid a speculative long position in corn oil. It is not a very accurate hedge because the premium of corn oil over soybean oil is substantially variable. But rarely do the prices of the two oils move in opposite directions. Nearly always some protection is afforded. The use of soybean oil futures offers an alternative to the willy-nilly acceptance of corn oil prices as oil is produced. Whether soybean oil futures or cash forward corn oil should be sold depends upon expectations about changes in differences.

Again it should be noted that in considering sales of futures against byproduct inventories, the proper terminology is uncertain. Whether these are hedging activities or selective speculations is a moot question. They are part of inventory management.

Candy Manufacturers

For our last illustration, we turn to the opposite end of the commodity line—the manufacturer of finished consumer goods. Candy is a somewhat extreme illustration of the kind of inventory problems faced by manufacturers of consumer products. Consumer products are branded and not fungible and so cease to be commodities. These products typically have sticky prices. Such products as meats and vegetables have less inelastic demand schedules than branded meat products and branded, frozen vegetables. Consumers are used to and responsive to changing prices of meats and vegetables and to the branded meat and vegetable products but prices of the latter are less variable than the former. At the other end of the scale are such products as crackers, party snacks, potato chips, soda pop, candy, and chewing gum. Within limits, price is not a major factor in consumption. The price of a given brand must be competitive.

Some products sell at traditional prices and merchandising programs are tied to price. There are 15 cent candy bars and 25 cent candy bars and no prices in between. Soda pop sells for 20¢ or 25¢ in vending machines. Weather is the most important factor in soda pop sales. A change in the price of sugar is not reflected in the price or sales of brand x soft drink. The lower the price and the more highly advertised a product is, the less directly related is its price to the cost of ingredients used in its manufacture.

Candy is low in price, branded, and widely advertised. The consumer price is sticky. The only practical way to vary the price of a candy bar is to vary its size. This requires repackaging and takes considerable time. Candy manufacturers sell into a fixed price market.

The principal ingredients in candy manufacture are sugar and chocolate. Sugar prices are closely related to raw sugar prices and chocolate prices to cocoa beans. Both of these trade in world markets and their prices are highly variable. Candy manufacturers buy in variable price markets.

In planning their operations candy manufacturers must make assumptions about the finished product market. For example, one may conclude that he must make a candy bar that will sell in vending machines for 20 cents or the public won't buy it. He has his work cut out. He works backward, estimating his necessary expenditures for selling, overhead, packaging, and manufacturing cost. He now knows what he can pay for ingredients and still make money. If ingredient prices are below this level all is well. But if they are above he must form a judgment about their course in the future. If he expects them to forever remain too high, he must go back and adjust his operation—probably adjusting the size of the candy bar. But if he expects eventual price reductions he can wait to purchase, providing his inventory position is large enough to permit waiting.

The manufacturer must form opinions about market prices—know the cost parameters within which he can operate and know what his actions will be if certain things happen or do not happen. No matter what he does he is taking a speculative position—a short one by not purchasing his requirements for the selling season and buying hand-to-mouth or a long one if he covers his total requirements.

Two different approaches can be taken to this speculative problem. He can treat the acceptable, backed-off, ingredient costs as a reference point and his average cost objectives. As prices are below, he accumulates, and the farther they go below the more he accumulates. As prices are above he uses up inventory and the farther they go above, the farther he lets his inventory run down. It is possible to let inventories go below zero by selling cocoa and sugar futures. As he is forced to buy the cash commodities for use, he sells futures and waits to buy them in until the price goes below the reference point.

The second approach is to speculate without the bias of the profit reference point. In this case the purchasing agent's objective is to buy at the lowest average cost that his skill as a speculator permits. He builds inventory as he expects the price to increase and liquidates inventory as he expects the price to decline. The only thing that separates him from a pure speculator is the limitation imposed on him by the ingredient requirements of the firm. He must speculate, at a minimum, in an amount equal to plant requirements. His speculation, as a purchasing agent, is limited to positions no larger than plant requirements. As he goes past this point he changes identity from purchasing agent to speculator. This isn't a tight limitation. All he has to do to rationalize an even larger position is to project an indefinite life of the company and extend farther into the future.

The first approach has the implicit assumption that the prices of ingredients must finally depend upon the price at which candy can be merchandised and will finally return to this equilibrium level. This assumption is of questionable validity, particularly within any reasonable time span. Sugar and cocoa are used in products other than candy. Their consumption is world-wide so that the demand for the products of one company is not closely related to total demand. Supply conditions are highly variable and change over long periods of time. Periods of over-supply or under-supply can and do last for years. It would thus appear that the second approach has greater merit.

What do these people really do? Some, and probably only a few, beg the question and buy hand-to-mouth. The underlying assumption here is that there is a long run rational relationship between finished product and ingredient prices and that they cannot do a better (and perhaps worse) job of speculating than the market as a whole.

In practice, most purchasing agents appear to combine the two approaches. There is a great temptation to extend a profitable price forward and to extend it a long way forward when it is very profitable. But this is conditioned by price expectations that are formed independent of the need to acquire inventory. Some buyers are more oriented in one of the two directions than others. There is no way to judge which is the more successful but logic suggests that buyers whose price forecasting is not encumbered by nagging thoughts of the need to cover requirements get the better of the contest.

The extent of forward cover varies greatly by companies. Some limit maximum inventory to a season's requirement and keep a minimum of three months ahead. Others go much less than a full season at a maximum and let inventories run below three months. There are those hardy souls who will reach three years out or come in to as little inventory as three weeks. Company policies tend to be established in terms of time cover—a minimum below which inventories are not allowed to fall and a maximum beyond which they may not extend. There is a strong bias toward the long side of the market—net short positions rarely exist.

Positions in cocoa and sugar are taken in both cash and futures. Most cash trading is done relative to futures. Logistical problems of quality, plant supply of multiple plant firms, storage, and transportation are solved by basis operations when the best logistical solutions do not precisely coincide with the desired ownership position. But to discuss these would be redundant of early basis trading discussions. The basic inventory positions are taken in futures, either directly by the purchasing company or by the merchant who sells cash forward.

Some Generalizations

The three chapters, 10, 11, and 12, comprise a fairly long list of illustrations of kinds of uses made of futures markets by firms in the commodity trades.[5] In the context of the total of kinds of activities in the commodity trades it is a short list. The list is incomplete in that it treats only with physical commodities and leaves out of account the growing list of strictly financial instruments for which there are futures markets. Some generalization is worth attempting.

First, the description is a continuum of complexity from the simplest equal and opposite, intracommodity, risk aversion hedge to sophisticated management of price relationships, risk exposure, and capital. The world of use of futures in connection with commercial operations is tremendously complex. It defies

[5] For a more completely and more specifically described treatment of commercial use of futures markets see Arthur, Henry B., *Commodity Futures as a Business Management Tool.* Graduate School of Business Administration, Harvard University, 1971.

classification and simplification, for the world of commodities and commodity prices and price relationships is complex and continually changing. There is room within it for playing the most intricate of games. The games are fascinating to the people who play them and the skill with which they are played is of major importance to the success of firms that deal in commodities.

Second, all of the activities treat with price risk exposure and involve objectives relating to the management of risk exposure to levels consistent with growth and earnings objectives of companies. In the main, the activities are toward the reduction of risk exposure from levels that would prevail if the firms were operated in the same way without using futures markets. In a broader sense, the activities involve the management of capital to secure maximum use of capital in firm growth. The use of futures in risk reduction frees capital that would otherwise be needed to absorb variations in equity for use in expansion and development in other lines and gives firms access to low cost capital markets. These things are all illustrative of the notions advanced in chapter 7. Futures contracts are financial instruments.

We have now progressed to the identification of still another definition of hedging: *To hedge is to use futures contracts in managing risk exposure associated with commodity ownership and commitment and with variable price relationships among commodities and related commodity products to levels consistent with profit maximization and/or profit regularization and with capital preservation and expansion.*

Third, futures markets contribute to the efficiency of the production, processing, and marketing processes of commodities. They enable the more effective use of capital and free up other activities from the constraints that would otherwise be imposed by risk exposure. Over time the number of industries and firms within industries that have found the use of futures desirable in the interest of growth and increased efficiency and necessary to meet competition has increased. The growth of futures markets since 1960 is highly suggestive of a need for firms to increasingly use futures markets in times ahead. Futures markets are institutions that promote the extension of competition in the economic process.

Fourth, there are some central considerations that firms contemplating the use of futures should recognize. The use of futures is unique to industries and to firms within industries. Every individual use must be adapted to the problem context within which it is placed. There are very few standardized applications.

Satisfactory results in futures markets operations can be obtained only by persons with experience and knowledge in markets. The use of futures is complex so that not only is knowledge needed, but also judgment, and judgment comes not only of knowledge but from experience. The use of futures is subject to scientific scrutiny and application but there are major elements of artistry because the world of commodity prices is infinitely intricate and continually changing.

There must be a corporate philosophy and policy established. The objectives of the use of futures must be clearly understood and the constraints that are placed on people charged with operations articulated.

Finally, the commercial need for risk management and capital preservation and expansion increases as firm size and industry complexity increases. The need for futures operations increases with scale and sophistication.

CHAPTER 13

Speculators

Problem Setting

The orientation of this chapter is toward the customers of commission houses—the speculating public. The objective is to develop a framework that describes the problem, and establishes some guidelines that individuals can use in commodity speculation. It is not a blueprint, for commodity speculation is a lonely and highly individual business. There are many kinds of plans and programs that are used successfully and rather more that are used unsuccessfully. Each trader must develop his own and succeed or fail with its use. Every speculator is in the business of competing with the market for profits that, in the aggregate, do not exist. He is challenging the wisdom of the market, and the market is made up of the kinds of traders discussed in the preceding chapters and of other speculators. The challenges are not issued by groups but rather by individuals and every other trader is the enemy. When one speculates in commodities he is attempting to take someone else's money away from him. Thus, if there were a blueprint and it became known—as it would—everyone would make money. But this is not possible, so we shall not quest for the Holy Grail.

What motivates speculators? There are many specific motivations and combinations of motivations but these can be generalized into only a few. First, successful speculation can be used to increase a relatively unimportant amount of money into an important amount. Most people do not have important amounts of money. Most of us are born poor, die poor, and live our lives on our earnings. Most people would rather have an important amount of money than not. Some important amounts of money are accumulated out of earnings by such people as excel in sports, entertainment, the professions, business entrepreneurship, and the like, but only a few reach the top. Other important amounts are accumulated out of speculation. Speculation takes many forms but generally involves selling property at higher prices than those at which it is purchased. Gold, uranium and oil are sold at higher prices than mining rights are purchased; the trick is to locate and purchase the right rights. Large fortunes have been accumulated from real estate speculation. Precious jewels, art objects, and rare coins are popular speculative media. Securities are probably the most popular media in the United States.

Second, speculation is a means of supplementing income and gaining a return on capital. Here, the motivation is not to accumulate capital but to make some money to spend or save. Some speculators trade to get money for vacation trips, buy new automobiles, etc. They see what they think is an opportunity for a fast buck and grab it. There are professional speculators, particularly in commodities and securities, who do not intend to use markets for capital growth but as an income producing system and who plan to accumulate wealth by saving. This is a different game than using the market in quest of capital growth.

Third, some speculators are attracted by the stimulation of the game. People trade in the same way that others are baseball or football fans. Sports fans appear to get a vicarious thrill out of associating themselves with a team and its fate. The exuberance of winning and the dejection of losing are real. The thrills from speculation would seem to be greater because profits and losses are real; the trader is a participant. But for some, the money made and lost is not of consequence; money is only the way the game is scored. This is not to suggest that making money is not more fun than losing but rather that the game is the central motivation. One trader explained his motivation by saying, "I am not good enough to play golf for money and I like to compete at something." A chronic loser, on being asked why he continued to trade, explained that he could afford it and enjoyed speculation in the same way that his friends enjoyed an occasional trip to Las Vegas even though they knew they didn't really have much of a chance of winning. There is an urge to compete in a high proportion of people and speculation is a vehicle for competition.

Fourth, some people receive masochistic pleasure from losing. Unfortunately for the rest of the traders, these are neither numerous nor wealthy.

Commodity Futures as a Speculative Medium

Commodity futures markets have much appeal as a medium for speculation. First, the mechanics are simple and clean cut. Most security houses are also commission futures merchants. They maintain offices in most population centers and they all accept collect telephone calls. No one is farther away from the execution of an order to buy or sell than the nearest telephone. The opening and maintenance of an account is simple. Nearly all commission houses maintain research staffs, and account executives are liberally supplied with trading suggestions. Information about commodities and factors affecting prices is readily and abundantly available. Price quotations are instantaneous and widespread. The markets are usually liquid; entry and exit can be made without delay. Trading in commodities is for price gains and losses only. The commodity trader is not concerned with the dividends, options, splits, proxies, conversions, etc. that clutter up trading in securities. It is easy to keep score in commodity trading; one buys and sells and wins or loses.

Second, minimum capital requirements for entry into commodity trading are small. Just how much capital a speculator should have available before he tries the games is debatable but the minimum that he *must* have before he is allowed to play is quite small. Contract units and margin requirements are small enough that only a few hundred dollars is required to finance an initial transaction. It may be imprudent to enter with so little but it is possible. Commodity trading is one of the very few roads to big money that is open to the shoestring investor.

Commissions on commodity futures transactions are small relative to the size of price changes, hence contract value changes, that regularly occur. The speculator need not be eaten up by the overhead. Thus, his positions have greater flexibility than in other speculative media. One cannot readily trade in and out of most mutual funds because of load charges. He has to give away too much of his prospective profit to make the initial transaction.

Third, commodity trading has appeal because of the realism of the prices. Contracts mature and go out of existence by the end of the delivery month and are exchangeable for the cash commodity on first delivery day. It is possible for a speculative fiction about real market value to be maintained until first delivery day but then the real forces of quantities available, and requirements for them, take over. And contracts mature frequently—once a month for some commodities and as few as five times per year for others. The securities analogy to this would be to liquidate XYZ corporation five or more times per year and auction off the plant, equipment, patents, goodwill, etc. Securities prices are based, not only on current earnings, but on anticipated earning and not only on anticipated earnings but on expectations about prices at some far distant time in the future. A security has a presumed perpetual life expectancy while a commodity contract has a short life span. Thus, speculative fictions in securities can be long perpetuated but speculative excesses in commodities, up or down, are soon pricked by the test of the first delivery day auction block. Trading securities is often a matter of trading the psychology of the market while trading commodities is a matter of trading the cash commodity value in consumption.

The comparatively short life span of a commodity futures contract both adds to and detracts from futures markets as speculative media. It forces the speculator to accept profits that he has earned and to face his mistakes and take his losses. This forces a measure of discipline into his speculation that is not present in speculative media that have great longevity. Often securities that are bought in anticipation of a price increase are turned into long term investments when prices decline. One definition of an investment is a speculation gone sour. The discipline of futures contract maturity is often disagreeable, but it is also useful.

Fourth, commodities are a relatively low risk speculative media. This notion is in contradiction of standard doctrine and widely accepted concepts—commodity futures trading is said to be the fastest track of them all. Commodity trading can be made a fast track but it is not inherently fast and need not be.

The degree of riskiness is a function of price forecastability and price variability. It is impossible to reach a definitive conclusion about the relative forecastability of commodity and, say, security prices. Two considerations tend to suggest that commodity prices are more accurately forecastable. First, the short life of the contract and the exchangeability for cash commodities imparts a realism that, at least, gives a solid point of departure for forecasting price changes. It would seem to be easier to know where you are going if you know where you are. Second, information about factors affecting commodity prices is very complete and is made available to everyone at the same time. Information about factors affecting securities prices is much less complete and readily available. There appears to be more "inside" information with the result that a price move may be over before the thing causing it is generally known.

Security prices are more variable than commodity prices. A test of this hypothesis was made using 1968 as a reference period—a year of relative stability in security prices prior to the 1969–70 debacle in the stock market. A sample of 50 common stocks was selected at random from the listing of the New York Stock Exchange. The commodity sample was those commodities regularly traded in substantial volume on the major exchanges. These were wheat, corn, soybeans, soybean oil, soybean meal, cattle, pork bellies, potatoes, orange juice, cocoa, and cotton. The high-low range within the year for each of the commodities and securities was ascertained, the mid-point of the range computed, the range was divided by the median, and multiplied by 100 to obtain a coefficient of relative dispersion. This is a comparable and unit-free measure.

The average relative dispersion of the securities prices was 46.22 and the range was from 14.63 to 92.39. The average relative dispersion of the commodities prices was 28.03 and the range was from 8.28 to 58.03. The differences of means and ranges were statistically significant at the one percent level. The average relative dispersion of securities prices was 1.65 times as great as that of commodities.

The exercise was repeated using 1975 security and commodity prices. The year 1968 was chosen for its normalcy, but it may be that the turmoil in both security and commodity prices of 1975 is more representative of the future than is the relative stability of the 1960's. The average relative dispersion of securities prices was 55.42 and the range was from 15.75 to 112.22. The average relative dispersion of the commodities prices was 48.10 and the range was from 22.26 to 91.78. The variability in securities prices was little changed between 1968 and 1975, but that of commodities was 1.7 times as great and essentially as large as that of securities.   7.

The commodity trading game changed in 1972 from one of relatively low inherent risk to one of moderately large inherent risk, but still remained at a risk level lower than securities.

Fifth and finally, the great appeal of commodity trading is leverage. This is the way that the track is made fast. Margin requirements tend to be five to ten percent of the value of the contract. Thus, a five to ten percent move in the price is either double or nothing of the investment required. To use all of this great leverage is imprudent and conducive to failure, but the opportunity is present. Because of the great leverage, the doubling of one's capital in one year is not out of a reasonable realm of possibility. Now, $1000 doubled in each of ten successive years expands to something over one million dollars. For a speculator to double his money in each of ten successive years is not a reasonable expectation and is complicated by taxes, but it is clear that a successful speculator can turn an unimportant amount of money into an important amount.

The leverage of small margin enables speculators to take large positions on a small capital base. This feature of the markets has given commodity speculation its reputation for high risk. The high risk reputation stems from high leverage rather than price volatility. The degree of risk can be limited to the level that the speculator desires by using less than the total leverage. With the corn margin requirement at a typical 20 cents and the price at $2.50 it is possible to control an inventory of 50,000 bushels worth $125,000 with an investment of $10,000. If a speculator were to limit his commitment as if margins were comparable to securities, he would control less than two contracts or 8,000 bushels worth $20,000. A dime a bushel is a small variation in the price of corn. At maximum leverage this is 50 percent on investment (gain or loss) but at a margin comparable to securities, it is 8 percent. Without high leverage, commodity speculation would have less appeal and would not have its high risk reputation.

The Game Speculators Are In

The first step that one should take in learning to play a new game is to examine the rules—the nature of the game. All that has gone before in describing the markets and their use by producers, merchants, warehousemen, converters, and users is part of what speculators should know. There are some features of the game that are worth underscoring.

First, the Clearing House breaks even; it pays out the amount that it takes in. Futures trading is a zero sum game minus the cost of doing business—commissions. In the aggregate, the participants break even gross and lose net by the amount paid in commissions, brokerage, and clearing fees. Thus, when a speculator enters the market he is attempting to take money away from someone else who, in general, is most reluctant to lose.

In direct line, the pure hedgers are neutral with regard to whether they gain or lose from futures trading. But these hedgers represent cash principals, producers on the one side who have sold at a rate faster than consumption, and users on the other side who have bought at a rate faster than consumption. In a sense, producers who have sold ahead of a price increase are losers and speculators gain from their losses. And users who have bought ahead of a price decrease are losers to speculators. As we have seen, hedgers are more often short than long and speculators more often long than short. Thus, as prices increase speculators gain from producers and vice versa. But, as we have also noted, there is a major element of speculators offsetting other speculators with the result that speculators pass money back and forth through the clearing house, paying commissions en route.

Second, price variations in the major, highly developed futures markets, are random, at least on a day-to-day basis. Successive price changes are independent; that recent price changes have been up does not increase the likelihood that the next price change will be up, etc. The question or randomness (or nonrandomness) of price variation has long been the subject of investigation, both by traders and developers of trading plans, and by academicians. There remains much active controversy about the question and probably more people, particularly those actively trading in futures markets, disagree than agree with the statement that price variations are random. Space does not permit a full discussion, nor is the controversy really worth all of the attention that has been given it when looked at from a pragmatic trading viewpoint, but some central points should be made.

The theory of normal backwardation is based on the notion that speculators must anticipate an increase in price before they will buy; to merely break even is not enough. Because speculators accumulate predominately long positions at and following harvest and liquidate later in the season, it follows that there is an upward bias in the seasonal pattern of futures prices. But, such patterns are not consistent nor are they easily discernible in the highly developed markets.[1] This is as we should expect. A risk premium should approach the level of ordinary interest. The moves in commodity prices relative to margin requirements are so very much greater that the possible return for bearing risk, year in and year out, is completely obscured by the question of what will happen this year. To cash in on a risk premium a speculator would have to absorb and

[1] *Marketing Grains,* North Central Regional Research Publication No. 176, Chapter III by Hieronymus, T. A.

Gray, Roger W. "The Characteristic Bias in Some Thin Futures Market," *Food Research Institute Studies,* Vol. I, No. 3, November 1960, Stanford University.

average out all of the intrayear variations. This would require an inordinate amount of capital and is not the kind of action that speculators are looking for. The bias of speculators is in the direction of making a lot of money fast.

More complex than the question of seasonal variation is that of interior serial correlation, or trend movements, of prices. The belief that trends do exist and that successive price changes are not independent has given rise to technical systems of trading that are based on price charts and numerical computations, primarily moving averages. The basic assumption is that the past behavior of prices can be used to forecast the future. Books and an almost limitless number of articles have been written on the subject, more relating to securities than to commodities.[2] One can buy chart services and the results of numerical computations that are designed to identify trends and to indicate when to buy and sell. There are technicians who trade in markets on the basis of their charts and computations.

The question of randomness has been explored by academicians, particularly Working, Larson, Gray, Coatner, and Houthakker. The bulk of this work is summarized by Teweles, Harlow, and Stone.[3] They put the question in the context of the "random walk theory." The theory suggests that successive price changes are independent and that past prices are not a reliable indication of future prices. It is possible to generate simulated price patterns from a table of random numbers that cannot be distinguished from actual price patterns. Thus, real price patterns are like random price patterns. Numerous tests for nonrandomness have been made. Most of the tests made have been for positive serial correlation. There is some evidence of a positive relationship. One of the more interesting tests indicated some evidence of both positive and negative serial correlation in corn futures prices, suggesting that trading on the assumption that the next price change would be opposite the last, yielded as favorable results as trading on the assumption that the next price change would be in the same direction as the last. The authors conclude: "Statistical techniques are capable of detecting data that have come from a process which is significantly nonrandom. However, even if a process is random, the techniques cannot prove it. To date, no one has been able to show significant nonrandomness, and numerous tests have shown that the price data are consistent with these generated by a random process." The final comment is: "Technicians assume that there is dependence in series of successive price changes in commodity futures, and thus hold that the history of price change may be incorporated into meaningful predictions for the future. The random walk theory virtually refutes this basic concept of technical analysis. . . . Many empirical tests remain to be

[2] See especially articles by Jiler, Wheelan, and Donchian in *Guide to Commodity Price Forecasting.* Commodity Research Bureau, 1965.

[3] Teweles, Richard J., Harlow, Charles V., and Stone, Herbert L., *The Commodity Futures Trading Guide,* McGraw-Hill, Inc., 1969, Chapter 8; and Teweles, Harlow, and Stone, *The Commodity Futures Game,* McGraw-Hill, Inc., 1974, Chapter 4.

made. Although the present state of the art of statistical techniques is quite advanced, it is still inadequate to cope completely with the many complex features of a complicated process such as a commodity market. However, one of the greatest contributions to traders' welfare made by the advocates of the random walk hypothesis is the presentation of objective evidence which shows how difficult it is to make money in the market."

All of this is as we should expect in a competitive market. The search for a guaranteed technical system or systems for profitable speculation has been long and thorough. If such a system is discovered, and widely utilized, it would probably be exploited to its own destruction. No system can work if very many people use it, for futures trading is a zero sum game.

Third, the speculating public must compete with professional speculators and the group at markets that we have identified as facilitators—scalpers, pit traders, and floor traders. This latter group furnishes liquidity and presumably gets paid for it. Their objective is to sell at a bit over the market and buy a bit below, thus taking some of the money that speculators might otherwise make or not lose. True, they sell at prices lower and buy at prices higher than speculators would pay, or get in their absence, if speculators were to get orders filled as quickly as they do, but there is a cost of the liquidity service. Speculators should be aware of this. More importantly, the facilitators' game is the pit and the floor and they must be good at it to survive. Speculators are well advised to avoid competing with them.

There are a lot of people who would like to be professional golf players but no one will subsidize them nor are they good enough to win enough money to support themselves. So it is with many would-be professional speculators. It is difficult to imagine a professional speculator being subsidized, but some are good enough to speculate as their major use of time and source of income. Almost by definition, they are consistent winners—and they win from other players, presumably the nonprofessionals. Almost nothing is known about how these people operate in markets so that the road to riches for amateurs by emulating professionals is not feasible.

One detail of the operations of larger scale traders is regularly available for the regulated commodities. This is the CFTC reports of open positions held by classes of traders. The reports are published monthly, about 10 days following the end of the month. Some of the reporting speculators are professionals and others are not and some professionals do not take positions of reporting size. But once a month the public can have a look, for what it is worth, at what the larger scale traders thought at an earlier time. Examination of these reports over time is interesting in two regards: 1. Nearly always there are large scale speculators who are long and others who are short. At times, the longs and shorts are about equal and at others they are predominately long or short. Even among large scale traders there is great diversity of opinion. 2. Their positions are flexible. The size of the net long or short position varies greatly, both within and between seasons. They move from long to short and short to long fairly rapidly, yet it is not a flip-flop pattern. There is substantial continuity of position. They tend to be net long more of the time than they are net short but they don't show any strong bias toward either side of the market.

The significance of professional speculators to the speculating public is that they are there attempting to make money and they are presumably good at it. A speculator moving into commodity markets is playing in the major leagues.

Fourth, the speculating public must also compete with "hedgers." Those merchants, warehousemen, and converters who always maintain exactly balanced market positions are nulls in the market with regard to price. They take no net positions and so have no effect on prices. The same is true of users who always carry the same amount of forward cover. But as noted in the discussions of the use of futures markets by trade interests the "hedgers" do have market opinions and do take positions. Many of them are not particularly well qualified speculators but many are. There are large companies involved and they hire competent people to analyze prices and to trade.

Little is known about whether trade interests put money into or take money out of futures markets. Working[4] comments: "Recent studies of the behavior of futures prices have given reason to believe: (a) That the short-lived price dips and bulges occasioned by hedging orders are commonly larger than economists have ordinarily supposed, and of considerably longer duration, sometimes extending over as much as three or four days; and (b) that professional scalpers on futures markets, who aid in the absorption of hedging orders and profit from the service thus rendered, tend to lose money, on balance, to other speculators and to depend for their incomes on their services to hedgers.

"To the extent that hedging orders affect the price, hedgers tend to sell on price dips and to buy on price bulges, and therefore tend to lose money on their transactions in futures. The consequent losses, being incurred for the sake of obtaining prompt execution of orders, may be called the execution cost of hedging. If the dips and bulges occasioned by hedging orders are as large as has been indicated by the recent price studies, execution cost may be a major fraction of the total cost of hedging, and a major source of income to speculators in futures." Professor Working's evidence is persuasive but limited. It is consistent with market conversation about "hedging pressure" particularly at harvest time. There may well be an execution cost of hedging for the pure hedgers. But this by no means includes all of the trade interests nor should we suppose that many hedgers place orders in such a promiscuous fashion. Even more surprising is the notion that the facilitators turn and give up part of their earnings to speculators.

From the point of view of the speculating public the best posture to take is

---

[4] Working, Holbrook, "Tests of a Theory Concerning Floor Trading on Commodity Exchanges." *Food Research Institute Studies*, Supplement to Vol. VII, 1967, Stanford University.

that trade interests are speculators or represent cash interests who are speculating. A rather high level of expertise should be attributed to them. Until there is more conclusive evidence we should assume that, at best, hedgers don't take money out of the game. Certainly we should not assume that they put in substantial amounts that subsidize the play of the speculators.

Fifth; markets do not have a great capacity to forecast prices and, therefore, may not be all that difficult to beat. To this point the description of the game that the speculator is in is discouraging to the would-be speculators. It paints a picture of a tough, competitive world. There is a school of thought that says that markets are dumb and blind to the future, and all that is required is that the speculator be somewhat less dumb. As an example, note the variations in cattle futures prices shown in Chapter 9. There were eight legs of cash cattle price movement in three years for a total of $93.58 and futures prices approximately six months forward moved $71.06 in the same direction as the cash. One system of evaluation would say that traders in futures were 75.9 percent dumb and blind.[5] Cattle prices move in response to supplies of beef and consumer ability and willingness to spend money for meat. Because of the availability of information and biological considerations in beef production the forecasting of major changes in cattle prices would seem feasible. That the market does not do it well is encouraging to the would-be speculator.

The Results of Speculation

Little is known about how speculators make out; how many win and how many lose and the amounts. The attitude of market people toward the speculative public is generally cynical. Their skills are held in low esteem and popular guesses of the percentage that lose are extremely high. The most cynical of the commission house people say that even those customers who succeed for a time, eventually get greedy and give it all back.

On being asked to whom the speculating public's money goes, the commission house people are hard pressed for an answer. The most usual explanation is that a good share falls through the slot in the table. That is, into the paying of commissions, but this is only part of the story. It is said that the traders in the pits get some, the professionals a part, and it is generally thought that hedgers take out more than they put in.

On the other side of the coin, there are any number of experienced registered representatives who can cite cases of several customers who have traded for years and consistently made and taken out substantial amounts of money. National periodicals have reported legendary success stories of individuals who have parleyed thousands into millions.

However, it is evident from the consensus of informed opinion that the big

[5] See Leuthold, R. M., "Evaluating the Price Performance of the Live Beef Cattle Futures Contract," Illinois Agricultural Economics, Vol. 15, No. 1, January, 1975.

winners are relatively few in number and that the great majority of the speculators in the public sector are losers. The following limited studies would also
seem to bear out such a conclusion:

The Blair Stewart Study. A widely accepted notion about speculator success-
failure is found in a pamphlet entitled "Trading Techniques for the Commodity
Speculator," published by The Association of Commodity Exchange Firms, Inc.
It says "A U.S. Department of Agriculture survey of the record made by 8,782
speculators in the grain futures markets showed that 25% made a profit." The
reference is to a study made by Blair Stewart.[6] It is the analysis of the trading
records of 8,922 customers of a large Chicago commission firm (which went out
of business in the 1930's and turned its records over to the U.S.D.A.) over the
9 year period from January 1, 1924 to December 31, 1932.

There are two case studies presented, one the biggest loser and the other, the
biggest winner. The trading of the big loser, extended from November 17, 1924
to October 29, 1932. His trading resulted (after commissions) in losses of
$400,089 in wheat futures, profits of $1,694 in corn futures, and losses of
$13,996 and $821, respectively, in oats and rye. The bulk of his trading was in
wheat. He traded in moderate amounts (5,000 to 90,000 bushels) from 1924
through the spring of 1928 at which time he had a moderate cumulative profit.
He then traded in much larger amounts—up to 875,000 bushels and lost
heavily. He bought wheat at harvest and sold it in the spring for four successive
crop years, 1928 through 1931. He didn't last through the 1932 crop year. This
accounted for the bulk of his losses. He was persistently long wheat, on a
seasonal basis, during a protracted period of declining prices.

The successful trader made $255,000 trading corn, nearly $28,000 in wheat
and $12,000 in rye. Nearly all of his trading was concentrated in the first three
quarters of 1924. He started buying corn in early 1924 and accumulated a
maximum position of 925,000 bushels in March. He stayed basically long substantial amounts until October, 1924. He was long rye and wheat in the same
period but in smaller amounts. He apparently foresaw a rising corn price,
bought heavily, made a lot of money, and disappeared from the scene of that
particular commission house. The price of corn rose $.50 per bushel, from $.75
to $1.25.

Some significant summary points from the study are:

1. Trading was confined to the four major grains, wheat, corn, oats, and
   rye.
2. Traders were concentrated in Seattle, Los Angeles, Chicago, Omaha,
   Spokane, Long Beach, and San Francisco with a strong bias toward the
   northwestern wheat producing areas.

---

[6] Stewart, Blair, *An Analysis of Speculative Trading in Grain Futures,* U.S.D.A. Technical Bulletin No. 1001, October, 1949.

3. There was a broad occupational representation with the usual heavy farmer participation.

4. The period studied was one of predominately declining prices with wheat falling from $1.50 to $.50, corn from $1.35 to $.30 and oats from $.50 to $.20 from early 1925 to the end of 1932.

5. General results were:

Commodity	Profit Traders			Loss Traders		
	Number	*Total Net*	*Ave. Net*	*Number*	*Total Net*	*Ave. Net*
Wheat	2,045	1,508,407	738	5,496	9,411,620	1,712
Corn	1,525	1,183,993	776	2,403	2,222,602	925
Oats	589	124,038	211	997	772,132	774
Rye	497	293,042	590	816	825,838	1,012
All grains	2,184	2,064,800	945	6,598	11,958,200	1,812

6. Distribution of traders by size of Profits and Losses:

Amount (1,000 dollars)	Number of Traders	
	Profits	*Losses*
0– .09	856	1,080
.1– .9	979	3,428
1.0– 1.9	168	912
2.0– 4.9	118	721
5.0– 9.9	37	275
10.0–19.9	14	109
20.0–49.9	9	58
50.0–over	3	15

7. Speculators in the sample exhibited a preference for the long side of the market but this preference was not so great as had been generally thought. The trading cycles identified as long exceeded those identified as short by a ratio of 1.72:1

8. Speculators who confined themselves to the long side of the market had more loss cycles than profit cycles. Consistent shorts had more profitable than unprofitable cycles. This is as to be expected in a declining price structure.

9. There was a marked tendency for the size of losses to exceed the size of profits so that even the consistent shorts who had more profits than losses, had net losses. Unprofitable trading cycles in general covered more trading days than profitable cycles. There was a clear tendency for traders in the sample to take their profits and let their losses run. There was little evidence to indicate that the reaction of large scale speculators differed significantly from that of small scale speculators.

10. There was a tendency for long speculators to buy on days of price declines, and for shorts to sell on days of price rises. Trading against the current movement of prices was the dominant pattern on both sides of

the market, but was not nearly so definite for shorts as for longs. The tendency of longs to buy on price declines and for shorts to sell on price rises indicates that traders in the sample were predominately price level rather than price movement traders.

The study is a classic of its kind and much of the results are consistent with impressions that one gets in talking with commission house officials. However, it was made a long time ago from data even more ancient. It had a strong bias toward trading in wheat by residents of the northwestern wheat areas. The study shows that a group of commission house customers lost money and their losses greatly exceeded the money they paid in commissions so there was a net pay to the clearing house. It should be noted that there were some winners and these were substantial in number, if not in proportion. It does not tell us a great deal about the flow of funds among commission house customers and from commission house customers to the clearing house.

A Cursory Look.[7] For purposes of this chapter, the summary records of some customers of a major commission house for the calendar year 1969 were obtained. The sample consisted of all of the accounts identified as speculative (in contrast to trade) for three major offices of the company, all metropolitan, two in the midwest and one in the south. The information for each account consisted of the commissions paid, the profits (after commissions) realized, the losses (after commissions) realized, and the profits and losses carried from 1969 to 1970. It did not include unrealized profits and losses carried from 1968 to 1969. It was assumed that these were offsetting and the analysis was confined to positions closed in 1969. In the limited number of instances where the carry-out was of major significance, the carry-in was obtained and adjustments made.

No great claims can be made for this cursory look as being representative of the fate of public participants in commodity futures markets. It is but one house—a large house that puts a lot of resources into the care and feeding of its customers. It is but one year—the winners may have been losers and the losers winners in other years. Little is known about the longevity of the customers— some may have been around for a long time while 1969 was the only experience for others. Some may have had accounts in other houses—a not unusual practice. The trading was in the full gamut of commodities—silver, to pork bellies, to orange juice, to grains, etc. 1969 was a year of stability in the general level of commodity prices—some up, some down, some volatile and some stable. The best claim that can be made is that it is all we have. It is the record of how a group of traders made out in a year.

Aggregate results. The aggregate results of the review were:

---

[7] A more recent and more complete study obtained essentially the same results. See Ross, Ray, "Financial Consequences of Trading Commodity Futures Contracts," Illinois Agricultural Economics, Vol. 15, No. 2, July, 1975.

Number of accounts	462
Number of accounts with profits	164
Total profits (dollars)	462,413
Profit per account (dollars)	2,819
Number of accounts with losses	298
Total losses (dollars)	1,127,355
Losses per account (dollars)	3,783
Average result (loss) (dollars)	1,439
Net loss, all accounts (dollars)	664,942
Commissions paid (dollars)	406,344
Put to clearing house (dollars)	258,598

The ratio of winners to losers was 1:1.8; the ratio of total profits to losses was 1:2.4; the ratio of average size of profit to average loss was 1:1.3. Nearly twice as many people lost money as made money and the losers, on average, lost more each than the winners made. The average loss per account, all accounts considered ($1,439) was not great. A total of $1,589,768, involving 462 people, changed hands. This is an average of $3,441 per person. It was not, *on average,* a real large game.

It is readily apparent from a comparison of the net trading results and commissions paid that the gross trading results were not nearly as bad as the net results. The winners paid $191,422 in commissions and the losers paid $214,922. Adding commissions to the profits and subtracting them from the losses reveals gross trading profits to gross trading losses as 1:1.4.

Of the total of $1,127,355 put into the game by the losers, 41 percent went to the winners, 36 percent lodged with the commission house, and 23 percent went to the clearing house to be paid out in profits and commissions in some other part of the system.

Table 10 is a frequency distribution of the trading results. It is readily apparent that most traders neither win nor lose large sums—49% won or lost less than $1,000 and 84% less than $5,000. Second, a few people were big losers. The net loss of people, 22 of them, whose results were over $15,000 was $350,560. Their loss before commissions was $252,053. The total paid into the clearing house was $258,598. Third, except for the few big losers, the players tended to pass money back and forth among themselves, paying commissions as they played. There were 38 losers who would have had profits had it not been for commissions. Thus, among the traders whose results were under $15,000, 196 made money gross and 244 lost. Among the traders whose results were under $5,000, 175 were gross winners and 212 were gross losers.

In shortest summary, it appears that few big losers contributed heavily on a gross basis, it is a fairly even game among traders, and that commissions are expensive.

Table 10. Frequency Distribution of Trading Results, 462 Speculators, 1969

Class Interval Dollars	Number		Net (Dollars)		Ave. (Dollars)		Commissions ($)		Gross (Dollars)	
	Profit	Loss	Profit	Loss	Profit	Loss	Profit	Loss	Profit	Loss
0– 199	23	31	1,959	2,937	85	95	2,424	5,833	4,383	2,896
200– 999	63	110	33,361	58,270	530	530	27,196	39,382	60,557	18,888
1000– 4999	53	109	122,636	264,837	2,430	2,430	68,378	73,533	191,014	191,304
5000–14999	19	32	153,883	300,177	8,099	9,381	50,600	40,491	204,483	259,686
15000–over	6	16	150,574	501,134	25,096	31,321	42,824	55,683	193,398	445,451
TOTAL	164	298	462,413	1,127,355	2,819	3,783	191,422	214,922	653,398	912,433

In view of our objective of exploring ways to speculate successfully, it is worth noting that a few people did quite well. Twenty-five people made over $300,000 and half of this went to six who did handsomely indeed. This is as we should expect; in all fields of endeavor—sports, business, entertainment, and politics—it takes a lot of losers and also rans to support a few champions.

One Time Traders. A large number of accounts showed only profits or losses suggesting single trades or a series of trades in a single commodity, in which the trader came in, won or lost and left. No one who trades very much has only profits or losses. There were 170 of these accounts, 37 percent of the total. There were 44 winners and 126 losers. The winners made $37,237 and the losers lost $461,659. The net loss of $424,422 compares with $664,922 lost by the entire group. That is, 37 percent of the people traded only once, had a very poor win to loss ratio (1:12.4), and contributed 64 percent of the total losses. A few people lost a lot of money; the ten biggest losers contributed $242,267— 36 percent of the losses in the game.

A crude approximation of the number of contracts traded per account can be obtained by dividing the commissions paid by $25 (the average commission per contract in 1969). The winners traded 167 contracts and made an average of $223 per contract and the losers traded 689 contracts, losing an average of $670 per contract. It is true that the winners tend to take profits quickly and the losers let their losses run, sometimes to extremely large amounts.

In general, the one time traders traded in small units. The frequency distribution was:

Number Contracts	Number Accounts
1– 5	131
6–10	21
11–20	12
21–+	7

There were 47 single contract accounts, 38 two contract accounts, and 22 three contract accounts. More than 10 contracts is a substantial position that puts a significant amount of money at risk and more than 20 contracts is a big position. There were 19 positions of substantial size and 7 real swingers. All 7 of the big ones lost money, ranging from $2,500 to $30,000 and totaling $125,385. Of the 47 traders who traded only a single contract, 12 made a total of $2937 ($245 per contract) and 35 lost $52,488 (1500 per contract).

Regular Traders. The large number of one shot traders and their extraordinary capacity to lose suggested a further classification to identify the regular players. A session on the practice range or one trip around the links does not make a golfer or test his ability to play the game. Rather low criteria were established: a minimum of $250 paid in commission and minimum profits and losses of $500 each. That is, a trader who traded a minimum of 10 contracts and lost at least $500 and made at least $500 was considered to have played the game. There were 193—42 percent—accounts that met these criteria. The results were:

	Profit Accounts	*Loss Accounts*
Number	80	113
Profits	1,493,602	664,618
Losses	1,094,763	1,085,648
Total	2,588,365	1,750,266
Net	398,839	421,030
Commissions Paid	211,192	153,454
Gross	610,031	267,576
Number	112	81

Forty-one percent of this group of traders made money. The net profits were nearly as large as the net losses so that the total results of the group was a loss of $22,191. They paid $364,647 commissions so that the gross result was a gain of $342,455. That is, they almost made enough to pay commissions. Adjusting for commissions to obtain the gross trading results almost exactly reversed the won-loss numbers. One way of looking at it is that they took money away from the nonregular traders and paid it to the house for services.

The number of accounts that met the low criteria of trading activity was surprisingly small. A high proportion of commodity speculators traded but little and lost heavily. The regular players paid 90 percent of the commissions. The winners both made and lost a lot of money in achieving their net profits. The losers also made and lost a lot. Interestingly, their losses were almost equal those of the winners; their problem was that profits were much smaller. The profit accounts were more active than the loss accounts, suggesting that even seasoned traders tend to lock on to losses.

A frequency distribution of net trading results of the regular traders is:

	Range	*Number Accounts*	*Group Total*
Loss	15,000 and over	7	143,063
"	10,000–14,999	6	75,273
"	5,000– 9,999	7	51,598
"	3,000– 4,999	14	53,883
"	1,000– 2,999	39	75,753
"	0– 999	40	21,460
Profit	0– 999	26	13,948
"	1,000– 2,999	21	40,035
"	3,000– 4,999	11	45,142
"	5,000– 9,999	11	81,714
"	10,000–14,999	5	67,426
"	15,000 and over	6	150,574

It is a nearly normal distribution, highly peaked in the center. The center is skewed moderately to the loss side but it would lean moderately to the profit side had it been constructed from gross rather than net trading results. At the extremes, the distribution is skewed to the profit side with the big winners making more than the big losers lost, but the difference was not statistically significant.

One significant observation is that a high proportion of regular traders neither made nor lost substantial sums; 126 of the 193 were within the plus or minus $3,000 range. This apparent lack of result obscures a lot of activity. For example, one account made $29,000, lost $23,000, and paid $5,000 in commission. His gross trading results were a modest profit and his net a modest loss: But it was an active game. The closest to dead center was an account with profits of $2,208 and losses of $2,205 for a net $3. The gross profit was $580 but $577 went for commissions.

A second significant observation is that a few people made substantial sums and a few people lost substantial sums. The game was quite expensive for a few of the regular players just as it was quite lucrative for a few. The game is played and won by some people; it can be done. It should, however, be kept in mind that this was a one year sample.

Do regular, active, speculators make or lose money? The indications from the limited examination made are that the answer is neither. They pass money back and forth among themselves, gathering up enough money from the nonregular players to pay the cost of playing.

Recapitulation. The two selections of one time traders and regular traders omits a third group of traders who had both profits and losses but who failed to meet the regularity criteria. Their profile is derived and the final summary is:

	Regular	One Time	Other	Total
Number Accounts	193	170	99	462
Number Profits	80	44	40	164
Number Losses	113	126	59	298
Profits	398,839	37,237	26,337	462,413
Losses	421,030	461,659	244,666	1,127,355
Net	−22,191	−424,422	−218,329	−664,942
Commissions	364,646	21,403	20,295	406,344
Gross	+342,455	−403,019	−198,034	−258,598

The classification "other" obviously had the same characteristics as the onetime traders. They had a better won-loss ratio but their profits were small and their losses large. They were major contributors.

How To Speculate

There is no single plan for successful commodity speculation, rather there are many. It is clear from the foregoing discussion of the results of speculation that there are successful commodity speculators so that we know it is possible to win and there are losers so that there is money available for winning. Important money can be made by those people who can devise and execute successful plans and programs. This is not simple, for the game is intensely competitive; there is no easy road to riches. Trading is a highly individualized game. No two traders are alike in their capital positions, objectives, skills, time available, and temperament and all of these things go into making up a trading program.

Should you trade? For many people the most successful involvement with commodity markets is none at all. The question is one that each prospective, or active speculator must ask himself and carefully answer. The answer boils down to a dichotomy of questions: Can I win and is the winning worth the time and effort? or will I lose?

The markets and commission houses are quite circumspect in promoting public participation. They point out that there is money to be made but quickly say that commodity speculation is not for everyone and that one should not trade unless he meets certain requirements. Some commission houses impose a "know your customer" rule on registered representatives in their solicitation of new business and refuse accounts when they judge that the prospective customer should not trade. Some houses impose trading limits on the basis of net worth and earnings that are far smaller than the positions permitted by the available capital. Others reluctantly accept business on the basis that the man is going to find a way to lose money and it might as well be here as some place else.

It is said that the first requirement is that there be available cash funds which is genuine risk capital—that one should only speculate when his financial responsibilities have been met with regard to living expenses, an adequate retirement and insurance program, equity in a house, and educational program for his children. But strict adherence to this would rule out a lot of the people whose incentive to speculate is the greatest. If one already has all of these things, why bother? It is the getting of them that lends real incentive and incentive is important in success. This is not to suggest that one should hazard the rent money, but it leaves open the possibility that some people should postpone buying a house in the interest of one day, perhaps, owning a finer house. Each person must decide what he has he is willing to risk in the interest of getting more.

A second bit of advice is that the amount of genuine risk capital be large enough to withstand a series of initial losses that may occur before a profit is made and large enough to keep the risks taken on individual positions down to a modest proportion of the capital available. True, one must have some staying power in a program or a position but there is a counter argument. As we have seen, the big contributors to the game are the people who badly overstay positions. Their biggest error is in having too much money. One school of thought is that if you are good, the money will come to you and if you are not, you are going to lose what you put in, so keep it small.

Commodity trading is basically a game of skill in forecasting prices and managing capital in risk situations. The prospective trader must either possess or be capable of and willing to develop forecasting skills. It is not a game of chance and those people who play it as such inevitably lose if they persist. There are elements of chance that must be compromised by effective capital management but success or failure depends upon forecasting skill.

Not all people are temperamentally suited to commodity trading; in fact, more people seem unsuited than capable. But the temperamental requirements are not that great. The trader must be competitive. He must get a thrill from winning and react to defeat with an inclination to hit back. He must be more of a participant than spectator and prefer losing to not playing. There are chronic losers who persist in trading, not only out of hope or optimism that they will eventually become winners, but out of the enjoyment of competing. There are probably elements of all three in the chronic losers. It is worth noting that people, once hooked, do not give up easily.

Second, successful speculation requires a highly disciplined personality. The facts of a situation have to be faced immediately and without equivocation. A trader must have the discipline to recognize a mistake when he makes it and take his loss. There can be no alibis, no hoping for some improvement before getting out, and no waiting to see what happens. Most importantly, the trader must recognize that there are no "paper" profits and losses. An unrealized loss is just as real as a realized loss. The trader must be able to live with profits and losses without letting his judgment about the future course of prices be affected. A position must be appraised on the basis of the current price without regard to whether it has a profit or loss. Unrealized profits and losses are only important in capital allocation and management. The trader's attention must be focused on what happens to prices next without regard to whether he has a profit or loss in the position. The area of profit-loss discipline appears to be one of the aspects of trading that is most difficult to master. There is an adage that says "Keep your position down to a sleeping point," but one of the most common faults of traders is to sleep too well on losses; to be able to put losses too easily out of mind; to be "locked in the market." It is out of this that big losses are most often made. This fault is more common with novices than experienced traders; the experienced traders have coped else they would have gone broke and disappeared from the scene. Experienced traders tend to treat accrued profits too lightly. They tend to be more comfortable pursuing a questionable position with "someone else's" money. But it is not someone else's money. Some professionals scale down the size of positions that they take after a succession of profitable trades because they know they have a tendency to give it back.

Part of the personality discipline required is that of hard work. Markets are in a continuous state of flux and price changes are based on new information and appraisal of its effects as it becomes available. The trader must do the work required to collect information and continually review its probable effect on the course of prices. It is easy to ignore the eventual impact of new information when all is going well. Sometimes markets react immediately to new market forces but at other times, reactions are delayed. The trader may be long in a rising market and become complacent. New and obscure information may come in that will eventually turn the price down and be ignored by the market. The trader must not only be aware of the new information, but he must consider it carefully enough that it waves a danger signal.

A third personality trait that seems necessary is a combination of bravery and cowardice, of egotism and humility. When he takes a position the speculator is challenging the wisdom of the market. He is saying, "I know more than the market does about the price that will equate supplies and requirements; about what the equilibrium price will finally turn out to have been." This requires a strength of ego that borders on arrogance. Backing this challenge with money is not a game for the faint of heart. Yet every speculator is wrong part of the time. He must recognize and admit errors before they become serious. When a player loses an athletic contest, he is beaten and that is that, by how much is not of major importance. Once committed, his only course is to continue with courage to the end. But not so the speculator. When confronted with defeat, he must turn tail and run. The thing that should be done in response to an adverse price movement can be determined only after subsequent events evolve. With the benefit of hindsight, the reaction of the speculator who has liquidated a position at a loss may be: "I was wrong in the first place. I'm glad I got out when I did." or "I was right in the first place. I should have stood my ground. What a coward I am." Excessive courage and excessive cowardice are equally ruinous. Again, the key is disciplined analysis.

Vanity can lead to losses. The more people who know that one has been wrong, the more embarrassing it is. Seasoned speculators tend to avoid expressing strong opinions about prices and to avoid revealing their market positions lest their vanity get in the way of their trading. Embarrassment is limited if only the commission house knows of the losses. A speculator who was also a football enthusiast said, "I have a much better job than a coach. Only my broker knows of my mistakes, but he must make his in front of 60,000 people."

The place of greed in the temperamental makeup of the speculators is difficult to appraise. Acquisitiveness is an essential characteristic, necessary to get people in the game, give them incentive to work, and promote the aggressiveness needed to exploit market situations. But greed leads to ruin. The oldest saw in the trade is "The bulls make money, the bears make money, but the hogs get slaughtered." People enter markets in pursuit of a fast buck. They stay with winning positions past reasonable expectations in hope of making more and hold on to long positions on dips, waiting for a rally because they don't want to face the loss of part of the gain they once had. They take positions and pyramid positions past the prudent use of capital out of sheer avarice. Thus, the speculator should be acquisitive and aggressive, but not greedy. The problem is that the words mean much the same thing. To be greedy is to be acquisitive beyond reason. That is, if one plunges in heavily and makes it big, he is acquisitive but if he overstays and loses it all back, he is greedy. The reconciliation is that the speculator must have the temperamental discipline to make decisions based on considerations of capital management and price forecasts without regard to how much is made or lost on a particular trading operation.

Should you trade? The answer is yes for those people who possess or can develop the necessary skills and who are temperamentally structured so that they enjoy competition and can avoid ruinous mistakes. One can only find out by trying. He who decides to speculate in commodities must take the matter seriously. As we have seen, the people who do not trade regularly and consistently are the biggest contributors to the game. Objectives must be established, trading plans developed, and markets continuously and carefully studied. The speculator must develop a program that is adapted to his objectives, his skills, and his temperament. He must do the work that is involved in program execution.

Capital Management. The purpose of commodity speculation is to make money. It is not to make cents per bushel of soybeans, cents per pound of copper, or dollars per ton of meal. It is not to make x thousands of dollars. Five thousand dollars may be an unreasonably large return for speculator A to try to make but not for speculator B. The purpose is to make a given amount of capital grow into a larger amount; to obtain a return on investment. How well one does speculating is measured by how much money one makes in relation to how much money he has invested. The number of profits versus the number of losses and the size of individual profits and losses contribute to the end of capital increase or decrease but are, in themselves, unimportant. The measure of skill must be made over a protracted period of time. The investment of $750 in a contract of pork bellies that results in a quick profit of $3,000 is not a great speculative accomplishment. Likely, it is a matter of luck. It is what happens to $750 over time and the $3,000 next that counts. Trading must be done and results measured in relation to the capital on which it is based.

Returns to speculation accrue out of the risks that are taken and the potential returns are proportional to the risks of potential losses that are assumed. Returns are also proportional to the amount of time and effort that are put into trading. The full time, professional speculator should be expected to make more in relation to his capital than a physician whose speculative time is limited. The first step, then, is to establish trading objectives. There are all gradations in between, but three kinds of situations can be isolated for illustration. First, an individual may be interested in trading as an avocation; to give him something to get up for in the morning other than his mundane job or because he has gotten bored with being a sports fan and wants a game in which he can participate. Because his basic objective is to play he should be first concerned with holding his capital together or, at least, limiting losses to levels that keep his hobby cost within affordable limits. His original capital should be limited to the minimum necessary to margin some diversity of positions and absorb several losses without being forced out. His profit objectives should be limited to the minimum that will provide him with the kicks that he is seeking. These will grow rapidly enough, if not too rapidly, if he is successful.

Second, an individual may have some capital that he wishes to carry in commodities as a part of a diversified investment program. His objective is to obtain returns comparable to those from savings accounts, securities, small businesses and the like. His will be a limited risk program, probably at a higher risk, higher profit objective than the more generally understood investment media.

Third, it is possible, through commodity trading, to turn a small, unimportant amount of money into an important amount of money. This seems to contradict the generally accepted principle that it is more painful to lose a given amount of money, say $2,000, when one has a small net worth, say $5,000, than it is to lose the same amount of money when one has a larger net worth, say $50,000. From this it follows that losses are always more painful than profits are pleasurable and a progressive income tax structure augments the proposition. However, if one doesn't have much to begin with, he can't be hurt very much and to accept this modest risk of pain for the possible substantial pleasure of having a lot is an attractive exchange to many people. As we have noted, 1000×2^{10} = $1,024,000. To double one's money in a year is not an unreasonable profit objective. To do so for ten successive years is something else. One does it at the continued risk of being sent back to the starting line. It is part way up that the matter gets sticky. At some point, say $64,000 at the end of year six, the sum impresses the trader as being important. Does he set aside part, say $60,000 and go back to the end of year two or does he shoot the works? Or does he shift to more modest profit objectives with lower risk? There are numerous alternatives.

Each speculator must review his own situation and establish his own objectives for return on capital and these objectives must be continually reviewed as his capital position changes. Capital management decisions must be made on the basis of risk to profit appraisal. Is the potential gain worth the risk of loss assumed? These are pain-pleasure evaluations.

The first rule of capital management is to defend against excessive incursions of losses. If the trader loses his capital he doesn't get to play anymore unless he can find a new source and finding new sources is painful and eventually becomes impossible. Experienced traders count their money frequently and adjust their operations to what is happening to it. If the net worth of the account is declining they pull back and reappraise. No matter how good a position may look on the basis of market forces it is not worthwhile if it is seriously impairing capital. Impairment of capital is a sufficient reason, in and of itself, for abandoning a position.

The minimum amount of capital needed to start commodity speculation is an area of frequent injury. The minimum needed is just enough to comfortably survive a moderate series of losses while waiting for the first profit. At a very minimum, it would seem that one should be reconciled to losing one half of a margin requirement three times while still retaining the full amount of a margin plus one half of a margin to survive initial adversity on the fourth trade. Should the fourth loss occur, the neophyte trader should reconsider the whole thing. This adds up to three initial margins with the absolute amount varying by commodity. The appropriate amount may be larger. A strong case can be made for diversifying; trading over several commodities with some long and some short positions. The minimum needs to be multiplied by the number of commodities. The appropriate amount may also be larger out of time and attention considerations. Speculation is a game of skill and to be skillful requires work. The pay that the speculator gets for his work is proportional to the size of the position that he takes. It takes the same amount of skill to be right about a 10 cent move on 10,000 bushels of corn as to be right about a 10 cent move on 100,000 bushels. One pays $1,000 and the other $10,000. The amount invested needs to be large enough to make the pay worth the work. What is worthwhile varies among individuals. To a major extent, it is a function of the individual's net worth and his earnings from other sources. The amount of the investment need also be large enough that the outcome of the venture is important. If the amount is so small that its loss is of no consequence, the speculator is apt to take the matter too lightly to succeed.

Forecasting. Commodity prices fluctuate and it is out of these fluctuations that profits and losses are made. Commodity prices are real, responding to market forces of supplies and requirements so that an equilibrium price is established. Thus, the essence of successful commodity speculation is accurate price forecasting. The market, as a whole, forecasts prices and the current price is the composite forecast of all of the market participants, weighted by the size of their positions. To take a position in a market is to challenge the aggregrate judgment—to say that the market is in error. It is from the mistakes of other people that speculators make money and from their own mistakes that they lose money.

Discussion of methods of price forecasting is obviously the key, and beyond the scope of this volume. There are some general comments that are appropriate. First, the forces affecting the price of a commodity are numerous and subtle in their effects. Information about them is never absolutely complete or accurate. Many of the forces are nonrepetitive and change over time. As a result, the use of advanced statistical techniques and econometric models as a sole forecasting system are not sufficient. They are useful but they relate to the past and the forecaster is concerned with the future. Statistical forecasts are developed in probability terms and have a band of probability parameters around them. Advanced techniques can be used to accurately forecast, within a range. The problem is that composite wisdom of the market tends to hold the price within the range.

Second, the current price is the market's forecast of the price that will prevail at the moment of truth—first delivery day. To forecast a change is also to identify an error. It is not only necessary to make a positive forecast of price change but to identify the source of the market's error. Before challenging the wisdom of the market, it not only behooves one to know why he is right, but to form an opinion about why the market is making a mistake. This is a useful process in identifying the reasons that the speculator may be wrong. Not only does he probe for weakness but he establishes check points that will confirm or deny his forecasts as time passes and more information becomes available.

Third, there are numerous kinds of forecasts and numerous things about which forecasts are made. The scalper is concerned about whether the next order received by a broker will be to buy or sell and the pit trader with the flow of orders during the next hour or two as these are the things that affect the very short term price changes. There is a sequence of information that flows into the market. This consists of acreage estimates, yield estimates, stock reports, movement into and out of storage, cattle on feed, etc. Much of this is information furnished by the federal government on a schedule that is known in advance. The market forms its own aggregate opinion about what the next report will show. If it is right, there is no effect on price but if it is wrong, the price changes and the change may be large. A major change in the crop estimate from the one made a month before sometimes has almost no effect while unchanged crop estimates sometimes cause shape price changes. When stock reports differ from the expected, prices change. For example, in the first quarter of 1969 the price of corn remained stable at a price adjusted to a moderate increase in carryover which tied the price tightly to the government loan. The April 1 stocks in all positions report was scheduled for release after the market closed on April 24. The report was unexpectedly small, indicating a very large disappearance and an outflow from government stocks that would require a higher price. July corn closed at \$1.22½ on April 24 and \$1.26¼ on April 25. The market was wrong and adjusted quickly. The price of July futures continued to rise, reaching a peak of \$1.30¾ on May 21. It then settled down to trade in a \$1.26½ to \$1.29½ range until the contract expired at \$1.27 on July 22. Most of the price impact was instantaneous and to capitalize on it, the speculator had to have anticipated a big disappearance and bought ahead of the report.

The next check point for old crop corn was the July 1 stocks in all position report, to be issued July 24. It was larger than expected and the September contract declined from \$1.25¾ on the 24th to \$1.21½ on the 25th and traded quietly in a narrow range for several weeks. The market believed the April 1 stock report and concluded that the disappearance for the year would be large. To make money, the speculator had to disbelieve it, thinking that it did not square with all of the other information about animal numbers, prices, exports, etc.

On July 25, 1969 the price of the new crop December future declined $5\frac{1}{8}$ cents. The stock report affected the new crop price as well as the old. It said, "We are not using as much corn as was thought and, therefore, we will not need so much next year." That is, the minutia of a pair of stock reports went into making up the aggregate expectation about the equilibrium price for the subsequent crop year. The market was not only reacting to the short term impact of a new bit of information but fitting the new information into the long term price picture as well.

The market forecasts many things that have short term effects while en route to its long term goal of discovering the equilibrium price for the crop year. Sometimes it does this well and sometimes it makes mistakes. Thus, forecasting is a continuous process, made up of a succession of bits and pieces that finally form a whole.

Different speculators have different forecasting skills. At one end of the spectrum is the pit trader who senses the flow of orders into the pits and is skilled in estimating its impact. Close to him is the floor trader who specializes in getting new information and acting on it quickly. He anticipates what the weekly report of export loadings will show, or what effect today's weather report will have on what the general crop report of next week will show about the progress of planting, or the effect of the early morning cash prices of sunflower oil in Rotterdam will have on today's soybean oil futures prices at Chicago, etc. At the other end is the long term equilibrium analyst who works with consumer incomes, expenditures for food, export demand, producer supply reactions, changes in and impact of government programs, etc.

The import of this is that each speculator must identify and do his own thing. Perhaps more importantly, he must stay out of someone else's game. Scalpers and pit traders frequently say, "Do not tell me any facts about the factors affecting prices. Such knowledge will only serve to louse up my feel of what is going on in the pit. The market will tell its own story and my only problem is to read it fast." At the other end, the long term equilibrium forecaster's skills relate to basic price moves from one level to another. They must ignore the short term moves and trade outside of them. They are concerned with the long term effects of the flow of information, not the immediate impact. For example, the price of pork bellies moves up and down in response to weekly reports of bacon slicings, storage stocks, and in and out movement. There are traders who are skilled at anticipating these reports and their short term impacts and who trade for short term profits. But the reports are only significant to the price level in their cumulative effects. The short term variations are the result of market imperfection in appraising long term effects. The long term analyst must use the reports to modify or not modify his equilibrium projections. He must not be distracted by the false scents that the market frequently throws off in its zig-zag, groping course to its final goal. The long term analyst must stand ready to absorb the short term profits and losses that result from the flow of information. If he tries to trade these short term moves, he is playing someone else's game and will almost certainly lose. One of the most frequent questions that novice speculators ask is "I think that the price of ———— will finally go much higher but it has gone up sharply; shouldn't I take profits here, wait for a reaction, and reinstate my positions?" If he does this, he can be assured of three things: (1) he is responding to the general inclination to take small profits, (2) he will finally miss the major move if it develops, and (3) he will wind up paying most of his profits (if any) in commissions.

Fourth, markets respond to pressures that are not readily quantifiable and that are sometimes recognized by very few people. These pressures may be farmers selling at a faster than usual rate before or during harvest and reflect a larger than estimated production. Or the flow of hogs may be smaller than expected on the basis of production reports, reflecting an error in estimating production. They are more apt to come from the demand side as demand information is less readily available and more difficult to appraise than supply information. The price of cattle in the late spring of 1969 was a classic case. Prices were forecast on the basis of supplies—which turned out to be right—and the usual patterns of consumer buying. But consumers shifted their demand schedules to the right faster than their incomes increased. They spent more money chasing the limited supplies of beef than was to be expected on the basis of past performance. Real market forces assert themselves whether they are foreseen or not.

The market response to unseen pressures has given rise to a school of thought of omniscience of markets. It says that the wisdom of the market is greater than the sum of its parts; that, somehow, the market gets and weighs all of the information and seeks its own level. This is a persuasive argument, particularly to those people who have challenged the market's wisdom and lost. But the forces that move prices can always be understood and the nature of forecasting mistakes determined with the benefit of hindsight. The fact remains, however, that the things that seem to be market errors often turn out not errors at all but things that were overlooked. In such cases, realizing rather than anticipating markets exist.

The existence of realizing markets presents a problem to the speculator. His role is to challenge the wisdom of the market, yet he must recognize that the market may be right and he wrong. Accomplished speculators develop a sense of feel of danger that they cannot see that seems to come out of experience in dealing with adversity. And they seem to learn more from being wrong than right. Much of forecasting is a science based on hard information and its interpretation but some aspects of forecasting remain an art.

Fifth, the forecaster must possess a lot of information about a commodity, have it systematically collated, and be experienced in forecasting its price. There is a tremendous amount of information available about every commodity that is traded, often so much that it is difficult to see the forest for the trees. However, one weakness of speculative markets is that relatively few people systematize information sufficiently well to be interpreted. It is said that the market has an excellent memory for yesterday, a week ago, and a year ago but has little knowledge of other times. This is the case because reports tend to refer to yesterday, a week ago and a year ago.

A key consideration in forecasting is to ask the right question. Out of the mass of information, the forecaster must select the germane facts and he cannot do this without identifying his question correctly. Suppose that the price of soybeans is rising in July and a speculator is long. He knows that the price will be affected by the size of the crop and that an estimate of the prospective size will be released on August 10, based on August 1 conditions. The new information that he needs relates to planting and growing conditions to date relative to normal. Suppose further that he checks weather to date and judges conditions to be normal. The question that he must answer is what will be the August 1 yield estimate, not what is a normal yield. To answer it, the information that he needs is a series of August 1 yields and the accompanying description of crop conditions up to August 1. The yield of the preceding year or a series of final yields is not as good as these that include the effects of weather beyond August 1. The concern is with what the market will have to look at on August 10 rather than what the crop will turn out to be. The market tends to look at last year's yield or a series of final yields in estimating the August 1 estimate because these are readily available while the past August yields are not so readily available. Asking the right question and having the right information available can yield the careful speculator an edge.

There is no substitute for experience in trading a commodity. The speculator must live with a market to understand it. Experience can be simulated by collecting all of the pertinent information about past seasons and reviewing the price patterns that evolved. In addition, practice forecasting on previous price patterns is useful because forecasts can be checked and practice errors do not cost money. Much discipline is required to do this because nothing is directly at stake. Practice, however, lacks the elements of stress that are present in actual trades.

The need for work and experience raises a question about how many commodities the speculator should trade. The first requirement is that he be concerned with enough that there are opportunities for trades—that something be active. All commodities turn dull and inactive at times. But almost no commodity remains quiet for protracted periods so that only a few commodities are needed for ample trading opportunities to be presented. More importantly, the number needs to be small enough that the speculator can achieve a substantial knowledge about each. The number is a function of the time available and the effort the speculator is willing to make. There are related groups of commodities for which the same general body of knowledge is used in analysis. The feed grain complex is one. Soybean meal is a part of the feed complex. Thus, there is a close relationship of the analysis of the soybean complex and the feed grains. The prices of livestock and livestock products are interrelated. Most of the knowledge needed to trade eggs is gathered in the analysis of broiler prices. Silver and copper are related and knowledge of these readily expands to the other metals. But pork bellies and cocoa are not related and rarely is sufficient knowledge of both mastered by one person.

More speculators go wrong by trading in too many commodities than in too few. They tend to score a success or two in a commodity and become overconfident, thinking that they can trade in any commodity and go where the most action is. But a success or two in corn does not make one an expert in cocoa or silver. The merit of limiting one's trading to commodities of which one has intimate knowledge is well illustrated by the story told of Pete and Joe who were pit traders on a major exchange. They were walking off the floor after a trading session when Pete noticed that his friend was quite downcast and asked if he had been having difficulty. Joe replied that he was not having difficulty, he had the ultimate difficulty; he had lost his money and membership, had to leave the fraternity and go into the world to earn a living. "But what went wrong?" asked Pete. "I don't know," replied Joe, "everything I did went wrong." "Where have you been trading?" further inquired Pete. "In the wheat pit." "Oh! That is the trouble. You should have been in corn pit with me." "What? me trade corn? I don't know anything about corn." Just as a salesman must know his territory, a trader must know his commodity or small commodity group.

Sixth, markets tend to be better informed about and do a better job of interpreting supply factors than demand factors. They anticipate supply information and respond quickly to it but changes in demand are recognized and registered more slowly. Supply markets are anticipating markets while demand markets are realizing markets. This suggests that speculators are well advised to concentrate attention on potential demand changes and their impacts. The principle is to challenge the markets where they are weakest.

Finally, the prospective speculator need not be overwhelmed by the amount of knowledge and analysis required. There are usually one or two limited issues on which the price turns in a particular situation. Perceptivity is more important than intimate knowledge; perceptivity is developed out of intimate knowledge but not all people with intimate knowledge are perceptive. Much of forecasting is an art. He should be consoled by the knowledge that the market is made up of other mortals.

Technical versus Fundamental. Much of the literature on speculation relates to the contrasting approaches of "technical" and "fundamental." The technician works with charts, moving averages, volume of trading, open interest, new buying, new selling, and the like. Mechanical systems of trading based on market action are developed and implemented. Lengthy and elaborate tests of various systems are devised and made. Basic to the technical approach is the assumption of nonrandomness of price variations. The objective is to identify trends and to trade with them. The argument is that all forces are fed into markets and they tell their own story; that you, as a speculator, had better believe the market. Positions are initiated by stops that are triggered by price patterns and liquidated by stops when the trend has reversed. Stops are used to limit losses and the trader is warned that he should expect more losses than profits, but that losses will be small and profits large so that an overall profit will be realized.

The fundamentalist works with economic forces of supplies and requirements and their effects on price. His underlying assumption is that there are intrinsic commodity values that must be realized in the market place. The argument is that the market does willy-nilly things, responding to the psychology of traders, and making errors but in the final analysis it must go to a rational equilibrium price; that you as a speculator, must challenge the market and be more right about intrinsic value than it is. Positions are initiated when an error of sufficient size to make a trade attractive is recognized and liquidated when the market error has been corrected by a change in price or the speculator has decided, on the basis of new information or new interpretation, that he, rather than the market, is in error.

In so far as it is necessary to treat with the argument, the position taken here is on the side of the fundamentalist. All that has been said about the speculative function, randomness of price variation, commercial reality of futures prices on first delivery day, and the need to challenge the market with superior information and analysis dictates such a primary position.

There are many players in the commodity markets who utilize charts, computers and a variety of technical systems in their quest to beat the game. This approach has many adherents who rely exclusively on the performance of the market and the track record of their particular system. If it is true that price variations are random, a good technical system will gross break even and net lose commissions. However, Commodity Research Bureau, Inc., has thousands of subscribers to their chart services, many of whom have renewed their subscriptions continuously for over a dozen years. A survival rate of this order must certainly be considered mute testimony to a degree of effectiveness of this approach. Commodity Research Bureau also claims that their computer research can prove conclusively that a trend following method, paying all commissions, was successful on a theoretical basis for a ten-year period from 1961 to 1970. Such results would argue strongly against the "randon walk" school.

The "random walk" school rests on the efficient market theory which says that new information enters markets in a random fashion and competition causes the effects of new information regarding intrinsic values to be reflected instantly in commodity prices. If this is true then price patterns are truly random, and no system based on past market behavior can do other than gross break even and net lose by the cost of commission and any liquidity cost of entry and exit. However, if markets are less than totally efficient prices do gradually move toward the inevitable. The efficient market theory is not reasonable. Successful business enterprises invest heavily in price analysis and forecasting. Large numbers of people make a living as price analysts. Their performance is obviously much less than perfect but it is extremely unlikely that so many people would be so long engaged in a totally futile activity. Also, analysts can frequently look back when they have failed to foresee a major price move and identify the things that they should have foreseen and did not or that they should have interpreted differently. Our brief look at cattle price behavior tends to discredit the efficient market theory. It is interesting to note that the efficient market theory and the numerous tests made of it is more closely associated with the behavior of security than with commodity prices. As we have noted, security prices need face reality only in the very long run whereas commodity prices are confronted with the facts of life every first notice day.

What all of this says is that prices probably move at random when they are going nowhere and move in a trending fashion when events require a change in the level of prices. A good trend following scheme will make money when there is a trend and lose money when there is no trend. Prices are always in a state of flux. A price that is going nowhere continually reverses itself, giving off false trend signals. In such markets mechanical systems tend to buy the highs, sell the lows, and get stopped out with losses.

People do trade on the basis of charts, moving averages, and computerized trend following systems. The extent of this kind of trading increased sharply during the early 1970's when commodity prices became more variable and less forecastable and computer technology had become more fully developed. Some of the systems were sold to people who developed commodity funds so that substantial sums of money were traded on the basis of signals sent out by computers. Many commission houses developed their own computerized systems and the market actions of many customers were based on computer signals. The systems are not all alike but they all rest primarily on past price behavior. Out of a common input they tend to send out similar signals. To some extent trading systems are self fulfilling and price trends grow on what they feed on. The extent and impact of mechanical trading systems has not been investigated. Market observers generally think that the impact is substantial.

The controversy between some technicians and fundamentalists is unfortunate and the disdain of each for the other is regrettable. The systems are not contradictory and both are useful tools in the bag of careful speculators. The mutual exclusiveness—the either/or—of the two is more apparent than it is real. The strict chartist says, "I only read my charts. I do not know and do not want to know any fundamentals." However it is virtually impossible to find a chartist who does not know what the last crop report was, when the next crop report will be released, and who has not formed a judgment about what the market thinks the next report will show. Few, if any, chartists can refrain from reading commission house letters, news service reports, and weather maps. Some self-styled fundamentalists refuse to even look at charts, much less keep them and say that all chartists have holes in their shoes. However, fundamentalists invariably know the patterns that prices have made recently, the highs and lows for the season, the patterns of prices in other, comparable, seasons, and have a feel of the market action. They keep charts in their heads if not on paper. They watch the price action and develop a sense of whether it is strong, weak, or indecisive. The fundamentalists are usually aware of the price patterns that, should they develop, will trigger further action.

Even so, markets do move systematically from one price level to another. These moves are in response to real economic forces. The moving force may become apparent with one bit of new information and its effect be completely registered at once. Such were the corn stocks reports of April and July 1969. More often, information about the changes in economic forces that dictate a change in price level evolves gradually and is registered gradually. For example, the knowledge of a smaller crop that will lead to higher prices is developed over a period of several months. There are straws in the wind about farmer reactions and then an acreage intentions report. Weather and progress of planting reports follow and then an acreage planted report is made. During the season, weather and crop reports are punctuated by periodic estimates of production. There are final reports of acreage and yield. All of this grows from the faintest early suspicion that the crop may be smaller to full confirmation at the end. The price adjustment proceeds as the confirmation evolves.

As has been noted, markets respond to pressures that are not foreseen or are foreseen by very few people. Such realizing markets truly tell their own story, not out of past price behavior but based on the pressures that are registered by buying and selling in nearby cash markets. The detection and exploitation of these is the place that charts and trends are useful to the speculator, to help him avoid mistakes, and sometimes to make profits. Sometimes the speculator must aggressively challenge the market and sometimes he must run from it. He must not only ask what he knows that the market doesn't but what the market may know that he does not. Further, the fact that a market is making a mistake and should be challenged does not mean that the mistake won't get bigger.

Successful speculation is usually based on a combination of fundamental analysis and response to market action and the importance of each varies among speculators. Speculators who lean toward technical systems can trade closer to the full capacity of their capital became such systems limit losses to small amounts. Fundamental traders must be prepared to absorb more short term variability. The trading system used must be related to capital management.

Independence versus Commission House Advice. Successful speculation requires knowledge, forecasting skill, and experience even for speculation in one or a small group of commodities. One way to acquire knowledge, information on a current basis, and to observe analysts in action and learn from them is from commission houses. Speculators are customers of commission houses and the execution of orders and the keeping of accounts is but part of the service provided by the houses. They are also in the information and analysis business. Many hire staffs of trained and experienced analysts, each of whom specializes in one or a small group of commodities. They publish daily, weekly, and periodic situation reports that sometimes contain position recommendations from the staff work and these are furnished to the registered representatives who, in turn, communicate with the customers.

This procedure opens the possibility of trading on the basis of house recommendations. It is clear from the behavior of commission house customers that the houses are of major influence. The customers go where the house takes them. But when they get into a position they are pretty independent. It is difficult for the house to get them out of losing trades or keep them from taking profits prematurely. They lose faith quickly when they lose money and gain independent confidence quickly when they make money; when they lose it is the houses' fault and when they make it is their own brilliance.

One reservation that the speculator must have about following commission house advice is that if these people know so much why do they bother with commission business? A second is that if one samples the opinion of enough houses and enough people within a house, one finds substantial disagreement. There is a bias toward the bull side because speculators better understand about buying something that will go up than they understand selling something that will go down. The third reservation, then, is that there may be a commission house bias toward telling the customers what they want to hear. A fourth reservation is that to follow house advice is to be a follower instead of a challenger and to take away part of the fun of the play of the game, both of which are a part of successful speculation.

Most commission houses are quite circumspect in placing the responsibility for the trades made on the customer. They tell him, "Here are the facts and here is what we think, but its your money and what you do is your own responsibility." Different houses exercise different degrees of supervision of accounts but all try to keep customers from making ruinous mistakes.

As with most things, there is a compromise ground. The customer has access to information, analysis, and opinion that he can use in the degree that best fits his own circumstance. The novice is well advised to follow suggestions fairly closely and to assert increasing independence as he gains experience and knowledge. A rule of experienced and successful traders is to accept and digest house information, analysis, and advice and to exercise their own judgment while avoiding flying in the face of strong opinions held by the house.

A final observation about the use of the commission house advice is that, except in a few cases, it relates only to price changes. The whole area of capital and risk management is left to the customer.

Allocation of Capital and the Selection of Trades. Both bridge and poker are excellent card games, requiring knowledge, skill, and experience to play well. But to the speculatively oriented, poker is the better of the two. Bridge has a couple of disadvantages. First, the player must cope with a partner, often selected at random. Partners have to be understood, communicated with, and excused for the multiplicity of mistakes that they invariably commit. On the other hand, they can be blamed for failure but this doesn't help the cause of winning. Second, a bridge hand is dealt and has to be played. A poor hand has to be lived with through all thirteen miserable tricks. On the other hand, a poor poker hand can be thrown in behind the ante while the player goes to the refrigerator for another bottle of beer. A first rule of poker is to play only the good hands and to have the patience to wait for them. Poker has the advantage of variable investment. The high probability hands can be pursued with greater than usual vigor while the lower probability hands can be held with less investment.

So it is with commodity trading. The opportunities for profit are almost without limit and no ante is required. For some of the Chicago Board of Trade March 1976 futures contracts the season's ranges, value per contract, and margin requirements were:

Commodity	Range	Value/Contract	Minimum Margin
Wheat	$ 4.79½–$ 3.16½	$19,900.00	$2,500.00
Corn	3.58 – 2.39	14,925.00	2,000.00
Soybeans	8.60 – 4.39½	32,487.50	3,000.00
Soybean Oil	27.35 – 15.55	12,870.00	2,000.00
Soybean Meal	175.00 – 124.00	14,950.00	2,000.00

Not only did the ranges exist but prices wandered back and forth over the ranges. If one were to capitalize on all profit opportunities in one commodity and pyramid his capital by taking continually larger positions, the game would soon be over because he would have all of the money. The problem is not in the existence of opportunities but in the identification and selection of favorable opportunities. The opportunities are so numerous that the speculator can be quite selective and he need never capitalize on the whole of a move. Obviously, part of a move is sufficient to double his money. It is not necessary to go where the action is; there is action all over the place.

The first step is to establish profit objectives, keeping in mind that risks are proportionate to potential gain. The speculator who is concerned with earnings on capital invested rather than turning an unimportant amount of money into an important amount may select twenty percent per year while the speculator who chooses rapid capital growth may select 100 percent per year. To the puritanical, work ethic oriented, a more ambitious goal is unseemly. For purposes of discussion let us assume a modest growth objective of 50 percent per year.

A second step is to decide on the maximum capital commitment to be made at any one time. A commitment consistent with a 50 percent goal may be one-half. This leaves substantial capacity to absorb adversity and yet survive. It also contributes to the peace of mind that is essential to the maintenance of poise while winning and losing.

A third step is to establish the size of price move that the speculator is looking for. This should be determined by the attention and skill at his disposal. Those whose sources of information are complete and rapid should be expected to foresee smaller market moves and trade in and out much more than the trader who only understands the long term fundamentals. The long term, basic, analyst may be better able to foresee the larger moves. It is difficult to simultaneously see both the forest and the trees. Again, an assumption is necessary. Suppose that the speculator decides that his skills are such that he can foresee potential moves of a full margin requirement or more but the fine tuning of the market should be left to the more nimble.

A fourth step is to decide the level of risk the speculator is willing to assume to gain a profit. A one to one ratio does not yield the kind of edge that we are seeking. A ratio of a potential profit of two to a potential loss of one is a convenient one for discussion but one and one half to one or three to one makes quite as much sense. The ratio must be individually selected so that it is consistent with the trader's skill, objectives, and temperament.

Under our assumptions we are now in the position of a speculator saying: "My objective is to make 50 percent on my capital per year, I am willing to commit up to one half of my capital, I can foresee a move of a margin requirement in the commodities with which I am familiar, and I will take the risk of loss of half of a margin requirement to gain a full margin." He now has a basis for selecting trades. Suppose that corn and soybeans are his area of specialization. He looks at soybeans and decides that the price should go down twenty cents. He appraises the danger of an increase to a fifteen cent loss equal to the profit potential of twenty cents. The trade fails on two counts: the profit potential is less than the 70 cent margin and the risk of loss for the gain is greater than .5. He tosses the hand in and goes to the refrigerator. On his return, he may foresee a 45 cent increase in corn with an equal risk of a decline of only 20 cents. It is more than a margin move and better than two to one. All systems are "go" and he may commit half of his capital. But he may foresee a potential gain of 80 cents in soybeans against an equal risk of loss of 30 cents, a comparable return on capital and comparable profit to risk ratio. He may split his capital, one fourth to each.

Additional adjustments are readily apparent. As the profit potential in relation to margin requirement increases, or the profit to loss potential widens, a larger capital commitment may be desirable. The attractiveness of a trade is conditioned by the length of time that is expected to pass before the forecast materializes. The shorter the time span, the greater the contribution to the overall capital objective.

The allocation process is a never ending one. Forecasts must be continually reviewed and changed as new information becomes available. As prices move the profit-loss potential ratio changes. As gains are made and losses sustained, the capital position changes so that the size of position should be adjusted.

The allocation and selection system shown here is limited by several assumptions that each speculator must remove and replace with the real world of his own circumstance. Each plan must, however, include the essential elements of capital allocation and preservation, price forecasts consistent with the speculator's own skills, and appraisal of the profit-loss potential.

It should be especially noted that a liquidation phase is built into the plan. Getting out effectively requires greater discipline than developing and entering. All plans are made and implemented in the happy atmosphere of anticipation of success but many must be liquidated in failure and loss of money. Two thoughts, if kept firmly in mind make liquidation at a loss more palatable: (1) One's trades are known to only the trader and his registered representative and (2) There are endless opportunities offered by commodity markets—the game goes on every business day of the year. No battle need be or should be decisive in the outcome of the war. Never should a speculator take such a determined stand or assume such risks that he seriously impairs his capital. The market welcomes heroes because they are soon gone, leaving their money behind.

The plan calls for liquidation of the position when one or more of five conditions come to pass:

1. When time runs out. There may be a time line on the forecast that says if the price does not change by thus and so it will not change at all. Seasons end and contracts expire and, lacking anything else, this will end a trade.

2. When the original forecast is realized and review of the forecast reveals no basis for changing it. Sometimes things do work out according to plan.

3. When review and adjustment of the forecast reveals a profit-loss potential ratio that is below an acceptable level.

4. When commitment of the remaining capital is excessive. Losses on positions sometimes become large enough that a disproportionately large share of the reduced capital (including unrealized losses) is committed. The game plan calls for liquidation of part or all of the position regardless of the forecast.

5. When a more attractive trade appears. The problem is less often one of

finding something to do than of choosing among attractive alternatives. The experienced speculator tends toward diversification which is prudent but even though two or more positions are maintained, the size of each should be proportional to the attractiveness. A position in progress should be eliminated on a relative attractiveness basis just as quickly as a completed position.

Some Tactical Considerations. After the game plan is developed—and developed in such a way that it is automatically adjusted as the game proceeds—there remain some tactical considerations in its execution. In the main, these are defensive, designed to prevent violation of the game plan during the stress of play and to keep the speculator from committing financial suicide.

Timing in initiating trades is a first consideration. When he makes a trade, the speculator is saying that the market is in error. He must further ask himself, "If the market is dumb enough to do this, how much dumber is it going to get?" Timing is really a part of the forecast; as a general proposition, a trade should be initiated when the forecast and risk evaluation is favorable and liquidated when they are unfavorable. Timing is overemphasized in the literature on trading. There is too much waiting for dips to buy and rallys to sell or, the opposite, waiting for strength to buy or weakness to sell. To try to squeeze out the last bit of opportunity is to get too cute with the market; to be too disdainful of the intelligence of the market. The locals are in the business of fine-tuning the market and outside speculators who try to fine-tune will probably pay more and get less than those who execute at random.

The kinds of orders that are placed depend upon the trading characteristics of the market, primarily on its liquidity. The objective of the speculator is to get orders executed at the going market price without paying a premium or taking a discount. Thus, conceptionally, market orders are the best and should be used in highly liquid markets. In less liquid markets, limit orders are a useful tool for avoiding premiums and discounts but they have the disadvantage of the danger of being left behind. How independent the speculator should be in holding for a price depends upon how urgently he wants the order executed and this varies with the circumstance of the individual trade. The registered representative either has or can obtain from the broker in the pit an estimate of the price at which an order can be filled within a short period of time and this expertise should be used.

The kind of trading program outlined above does not admit the use of the various kinds of contingent orders described in Chapter 3 because they are just that, contingent on price action. To use contingent orders is to be led around by the market rather than exercising independent judgment in opposition to the market. The only place that these orders have is as a convenience device for the speculator who is not in close touch. If a speculator, for example, judges that a long position in wheat meets his criteria at $3.60 and the going market price is $3.70 he can advisedly leave a resting order when he is out of touch.

Stop loss orders have a special place in advice to speculators; they are almost universally recommended. Their use, however, contradicts the basic thesis here that decisions should be made independently of market action. There are times when losses must be limited in the interest of preserving capital, regardless of forecasts and profit-loss potential appraisal. The speculator must attach a loss limiting feature to every trade. Whether he places a stop loss order with his registered representative or maintains a mental stop depends on how closely he keeps in touch with the market and on how well disciplined he is. In so far as possible, the speculator should preserve his independence and thus not use stop loss orders. Ideally, he keeps a current tabulation of his account value—counts his money—and when his capital position does not warrant the existing positions, adjusts them downward. The adjustment may be made by liquidating losing positions or by liquidating winning positions depending on independent forecasts and appraisal of profit-loss potential. Some winning positions become less attractive as price changes are favorable and some losing positions become more attractive as price changes are unfavorable. An adverse price change does not automatically make a position more attractive; it may be a danger signal that calls for a careful look at the forecast. A professional speculator once said, "I bought oats during the great depression because they were cheap when they got down to five cents per bushel. But they went to two for a nickel."

Stop loss orders are so universally recommended because they help prevent the greatest error that speculators make: staying with losing positions. Speculators are notoriously undisciplined with regard to losses. Each must decide whether he needs the additional discipline of a stop loss order. The effectiveness of stop loss orders is limited because they can be so easily removed; they are of no value if they are not allowed to become operative.

In Chapter 3 we noted the process of shooting stops that is sometimes practiced by pit traders. Often the impression of the speculator who uses stop loss orders is that the market goes down (or up) to pick his stop and then recovers (or declines). Likely, this is more often apparent than real because competition among pit traders tends to police pit behavior and punish traders who push prices out of line. However, it does happen, and speculators who place stops must recognize that other speculators are doing the same thing so that exit from the market may be made on a less favorable basis than if the speculator acted on his own initiative. More importantly, the trader must place stops outside of the likely indecisive fluctuation range. The closer the stop, the more likely it is to get picked but the farther away from the market a stop is placed, the less effective it is in limiting losses or preserving profits. Placing a stop is a traumatic experience: the trader doesn't want to be stopped out of the game but his inborn avarice makes him want to put stops close.

Speculators who are stopped out and see a quick reversal of the market are quick to cry foul. Whether or not a foul has been committed is neither here nor there—the unhappy outturn is still the fault of the speculator. He must know the characteristics of the market he is trading in and adjust his tactics to them.

Some experienced speculators take experimental positions. A trade appraisal may call for a position of 10 contracts. The speculator may, however, start with one or two to see how they fit. They focus his attention more keenly on the market and sharpen his appraisal. Something is added by feel. He likes the position or he senses danger, which brings up the question of intuition. Having stressed systematic and disciplined analysis and execution and independence from the market, it is contradictory to give a place to intuitive judgment. But some of forecasting is an art and the human mind is a tremendously intricate memory bank and computer. Not all thoughts can be articulated nor the facts on which all conclusions are based identified. Some speculators should trust their intuitive judgment while others should not. Each should test and appraise the feel that makes him comfortable with some positions and afraid of others.

A further tactical question is that of pyramiding. In pyramiding, additional contracts are added as they can be financed from profits. In major moves, pyramiding has exciting possibilities that appeal to the avarice of speculators. The great profits made from a tiny base that are part of the lore of the market are made by getting in at the start of a big move and adding as fast as funds permit. But the probabilities are much less attractive, for a small adverse price change can wipe out the gain at any time and an adverse price change will inevitably occur if the position is held long enough. The literature stresses conservatism if pyramiding is attempted, that is, say an initial position of four contracts, a first addition of three, a second of two, and third of one. This, at least improves the odds but it does not correct the basic error. Additions to positions should be based on the criteria of capital allocation, forecasts, and profit-loss potential. The proper size position is not affected by the history of the original position. A new position is just that, whether in the same or a different commodity. The game is to pyramid money by the total program rather than to make a lot of money from a single trading cycle.

Our last tactical comment is a rule: Minimize commissions. Commissions on commodities are small when related to the total value of the commodity. They are large, however, when related to the minimum margin requirement. As is clear from the preceding section, they loom especially large when the net gains and losses of groups of speculators are considered. For many speculators, the cost of commissions is the difference between profit and loss.

Commissions have a major effect on the profit-loss potential ratio and nearly prohibit speculators who pay full commissions from trading for small price changes. Commission on corn futures is approximately $3/4$¢ per bushel. A gain of one cent is a net of $1/4$¢ while a loss of one cent is a net loss of $1\,3/4$¢. A three cent potential gain against a one-cent potential loss is a net ratio after commission, of approximately 1.3 to 1. A potential gain of 12 cents against a potential loss of four cents, the same gross ratio, is a net ratio of 2.4 to 1. Odds should be computed on a net basis.

However, the cost alone is not the most important reason for minimizing commissions. Keeping a sharp eye on commissions helps prevent overtrading. Speculators have great difficulty in resisting the lure of trading and tend to reduce the standards for selecting trades when they do not have a position. If they count up the money spent on commissions they quickly realize that trading can be quite expensive even though gross profits are equal to gross losses.

The discipline of minimizing commissions helps to keep the public speculator playing the game at which he has the greatest chance of success. His long suite is forecasting and capitalizing on major market moves. As he is attracted by the excitement of market action and short term price changes, he moves out of his element and greatly increases the probability of losing. Awareness of the high-cost of commissions tends to make the speculator more thorough and careful in evaluating and selecting positions which in itself, adds to the chances of success.

None of this is to suggest that the cost of commissions should stand in the way when a trade should be made. When a forecast has materialized and the trade is no longer attractive, profits should be taken and when disaster looms, the commission is but a small part of the loss.

Part IV

MARKET OPERATION

The purpose of this brief concluding section is to call attention to some things that might be done to improve the way that futures markets work and to pick up some loose ends, particularly having to do with controversial issues, that have been left dangling. To this point we have looked at what the markets are, how they operate, and how they have developed, looked at what they are about in terms of the economic functions undertaken and performed, and looked at how they are used by people in the commodity trades and by speculators. It is sorely tempting at this point to say that to understand is enough and end the discussion. But no member of the economics fraternity can resist an opportunity to evaluate and pontificate.

Futures markets are dynamic institutions: new exchanges are formed and old ones decline and disappear, commodities come and go, the total volume of trade doubled during the decade of the 1960's, and increased even more rapidly in the 1970's, the rules under which exchanges operate are continuously changed, and the laws regulating exchange operation and trading are continually revised. The changes in futures trading are influenced by the commodity context within which markets operate, by the governance of the exchanges and by the regulation of exchanges and trading. The future development of markets will be influenced by changes in the economic needs for their use and knowledge of their operation by people in the commodity trades, by actions of exchanges, and by regulation.

In the past, markets have had to swim upstream against an extensive ignorance of their usefulness in the commodity trades, against efforts to maintain less than fully competitive positions by industry, against a generally negative governmental attitude, and against exchange operations that have both failed to grasp the economic role of futures trading and pandered to the negative clamor surrounding them. What is needed now is not more controversy over the same old ground, but a positive look at the potential role to be played in a competitive economy and the weaknesses in the system that impair expansion to fill the role. There needs to be much less passing of aggregate judgment about good or bad and more acceptance of markets for what they are so that the bits and pieces can be examined for points where improvement is needed. The markets need to be accepted for what they are. They are old and venerable institutions that have stood the test of time. Economic usefulness is proved by persistence and by use. At the same time, there are weaknesses in operations that impair usefulness and changes that need to be made.

CHAPTER 14

Market Performance

How good are these markets? The question has to be answered in terms of how well they perform their economic functions in relation to how well the functions might be performed in the absence of the markets on the one hand and how well they perform in relation to how well they might perform if changes in their organization and operation were made. In the past, most of the evaluation has been made in the context of "there ought to be a law," either to abolish and prohibit all futures markets or specific markets as onions and potatoes or to further regulate markets to prevent speculative excesses and abuses. This context has resulted in a choosing up of sides in which the protagonists tend to be either for or against and find only good or evil. The weight of the arguments has tended to find futures markets "not guilty," at least not guilty to the point that they should be banished from the scene or completely circumscribed. Only in the one instance—onions in 1958—has a market been executed by law although numerous other attempts have been made. A large amount of legislation and regulation has been passed and exists. However, a major revision and extension of regulation was largely rejected by the Congress in 1966. The major revision passed in 1974 was very different than the original punitive bills proposed in 1973. There appeared to come out of the extensive hearings the most favorable (or least unfavorable) image the institutions have had. It would almost seem that the "either/or" controversy was laid to rest and a decision made to limit circumscribing legislation.[1] Perhaps never before have comprehensive legislative proposals been so thoroughly battered by so many people. If this did end broadside attacks and put discussion out of the halls of

---

[1] See *To Amend the Commodity Exchange Act,* Hearings before the Subcommittee on Domestic Marketing and Consumer Relations of the Committee on Agriculture, House of Representatives, on H.R. 11788, April 4, 5, and 6, 1966.

Congress, a useful purpose was, indeed, served. The either/or context tends to prevent the probing for weaknesses and small adjustments that make for progress.

Are futures markets good or bad? Some of both. They are here, they will remain for the foreseeable future, and they are growing. They will change and they can be improved.

Fun and Games

The first evaluative comment that seems to evolve out of our discussion of the use of futures is that they are large, exciting games that the participants enjoy. The markets have important economic functions but to facilitate this performance is not why people trade. Some firms—processors, warehousemen, etc.—use futures markets for serious business purposes but many tradespeople and speculators trade for the sport of it. Making and losing money is a serious matter but it is also a way of keeping score in a contest.

Professional football players compete to their utmost to win divisional championships so that they get into playoffs and Superbowls. They make a lot more money if they win than if they lose. What is the motivation? For some, football may be a grubby business in which they participate because it is the best way that they can make a living. But one doubts that money is the overriding motivation or that the sport exists for the sole benefit of the spectators and the people who make money from the spectators. The sport exists, in part, for the noneconomic benefits that the players, coaches, and owners derive. So it is with futures trading. It is not a spectator sport and so the players must pay the cost of operating the game. Whether this Simon pure amateurism is good or bad is for someone else to decide.

Our look at the history of futures trading with the major role played by speculation, the extent to which hedging in futures markets is speculative, the importance of speculation by commodity tradespeople, and speculation by the public all suggest that the basic orientation of futures trading is price speculation. The markets are about speculation and the economic functions performed are spun off from this central core.

How good are these markets as games that are open to the public? The entry fees, in terms of commissions paid, are large. How fair a shake does the participant get? This question is not posed in a bucket shop context of whether they should be prohibited to protect the public. The players are over 21 and members of a more or less free society. Whether or not they trade is quite their own affair and not a reasonable province of government, for if we prohibit people from losing money, we also deny them the opportunity to make money.

In Chapter 5 the markets were examined in the context of a model of pure competition with the conclusion that they are one of the closest approximations to the theoretical model to be found. The commercial reality of futures prices has been repeatedly mentioned. The price game is about the real world. The trader who is right about the course that prices will take inevitably makes money and the one who is wrong loses money. In this regard, it is an eminently fair game.

In connection with the fairness of the game, there are two sensitive spots, one is manipulation and price distortion and the other churning of accounts for commissions. Both of these are treated in the next two chapters. At this juncture we should only observe that he must know the game that he is playing and adjust his operations to it.

It is widely believed with reasonable ground that the technical conditions of markets sometimes result in short-term fluctuations that are not related to commercial market forces. If this is the case, such fluctuations are caused by unsophisticated trading by locals, by inadequate liquidity of markets, and the placement of orders dependent on market actions—stop losses, chart formations, etc. The basic notion is that markets grow on what they feed on; that a move in one direction triggers a further move in the same direction. An old belief is that markets always look strongest at the top and weakest at the bottom. But we noted earlier that day-to-day price variations are random. It is doubtful that traders are chopped up by technical conditions; it just seems like it. If technical moves in markets do exist, they present, not only a hazard to the outside trader, but an opportunity as well for they are distortions from real value and profiting from distortions is what speculation is about. If technical moves do occur, they are not relevant to the fairness of the game.

As we have seen, commissions are large; not large in relation to the value of the commodities traded but large in relation to the estimated profits and losses of traders. The earnings of commission houses and of most registered representatives are directly dependent on the volume of trading. We have also noted that an important aspect of speculation is the limitation of commissions. There is no doubt that some speculators get talked into making trades that are not contributions to their trading programs. This may be a market weakness but is not germane to the fairness of the game. The responsibility for prevention rests with the trader; he must control his own operations and if he gets hustled, it is his own fault.

Risk-Shifting Financing

Futures markets are devices for shifting price risks from people who are unwilling and/or unable to carry them to speculators, and through this process markets become devices for generating equity capital. In an expanding commodity economy and an increasingly commercial agriculture there is an expanding need for this combined risk-shifting financing function. The extent to which futures markets perform this function will determine the future growth and size of the markets.

Hedgers' Viewpoint. The most narrow ground on which markets can be tested for their effectiveness as risk shifting mediums is that of their usefulness to practicing hedgers. What a hedger wants of a market is that it be continuously available and that it be willing and able to absorb his sales and purchases of futures instantly without price concession.[2] To what extent do futures markets do this? The older, established, high volume markets do this very well. The corn warehouseman, the wheat exporter, the soybean processor, the feed manufacturer covering soybean meal requirements, or the cattle feeder can, if he exercises reasonable skill, get orders executed promptly without important, if any, price concession. These markets appear to be capable of absorbing all of the hedges that trade interests care to place. They are the liquid markets that are so extensively praised in the literature. They are the markets that have been so carefully examined for price bias and nonrandomness. There are minor imperfections that hedgers complain about so that rules and contract terms are continually changed, but, in general, they pass with high marks.

From the hedger's point of view, the successful markets work fine. But this is far from all of the active markets. This volume is not an appropriate place to grade the active futures markets for their effectiveness as hedging media. However, it is worthwhile to mention some hedging problems. Wheat futures are traded in Chicago, Kansas City, and Minneapolis. Minneapolis is a hard spring wheat market, Kansas City a hard winter wheat market, and Chicago a multiple kind of wheat market, both hard and soft wheats. Chicago trades, typically, with sufficient liquidity that the execution of hedging orders is possible without great difficulty. The Kansas City market is capable of absorbing a substantial volume of hedges but lacks liquidity so that hedges must be placed carefully and over a protracted period of time. The Minneapolis volume is small and the market appears incapable of absorbing much hedging.

To illustrate, on September 30, 1975 the positions in million bushels of reporting hedgers and volume of trading during September at the three markets were:

	Long	*Short*	*Volume*
Chicago	111.2	145.2	6,624.4
Kansas City	87.8	90.3	251.3
Minneapolis	27.9	30.2	122.2

The total open interest of reporting hedgers at Chicago was about 1.5 times as large as that at Kansas City but the volume of trading at Chicago was more

---

[2] It should also be noted that he would like for it to provide him with a profitable set of price relationships—carrying charges if he is hedging a stored inventory and inversions if he is covering a requirement. But he should realistically only ask that it provide him with an accurate reading of the going market price of storage; prices that are made by his and other hedgers' actions.

than 26 times that of Kansas City. The volume to total open hedges at Chicago was 25.8 to 1, that at Kansas City was 1.4 to 1 and Minneapolis 2.1 to 1. During the month of September the total open interest at Chicago increased 25.0 million bushels, that at Kansas City decreased 11.6 million, and that at Minneapolis increased 7.9 million. The volume to open interest change at Chicago was 265.0 to 1, at Kansas City 21.7 to 1, and at Minneapolis 15.5 to 1. One can reasonably ask the question of whether so much volume is necessary to change the open interest so little, but it should not be asked of a hedger. To him, volume is liquidity and ease of execution and the more the better.

Both the Chicago Board of Trade and Kansas City Board of Trade operated grain sorghums futures markets for years without success. In 1971 the Chicago Mercantile Exchange substantiated the commercial need for such a market and started trading in a carefully structured contract as a part of a cattle feeding futures program. After a good start with 8,155 contracts in 1971, trading fell to 1,354 in 1972. Even at its best, hedges were difficult to place and nearly impossible to remove without significant price concessions. Would-be commercial users of grain sorghums futures prefer to cross hedge in the liquid corn market in spite of the absence of precisely parallel price movement of the two cash commodities.

The soybean oil futures market is large, liquid, and an effective hedging medium but cottonseed oil futures trading dwindled to zero by summer, 1970. The hyper-active pork belly futures market can absorb any and all hedges incidental to the main activity of speculation but trading in skinned hams is so small that hedging is impossible.

How, then, do we grade the markets from the hedgers' viewpoint? Some are excellent and some, at times, are lacking in sufficient volume to effectively absorb hedges. *But this is only part of the story. A hedging market that is not satisfactory will not be used and will pass out of existence eventually. Thus, that which we see and can examine is generally satisfactory but it does not take into account the potential risk shifters in other commodity trades who are frustrated by the absence of liquid, unbiased markets.*

Aggregate Viewpoint. A second context within which markets might be appraised is the more general one of how well they fill the risk accommodation and equity financing roles described in Chapters 6 and 7. The general goal here is to maximize the economic efficiency of the commodity production and marketing processes. Specifically, the objective is to get the risks of price variability assumed and the equity capital for the financing of commodity value variations provided at a minimum cost. To achieve this objective the jobs should be turned over to speculators for they do it free.

The theory of normal backwardation—the existence of a risk premium—is not applicable to the developed, active futures markets. The theory does appear to be applicable to the informal forward contract markets that have generally preceded initiation of futures trading and to some of the low volume markets.[3] Our examination of the results of speculator operations and the generally accepted notion that speculators lose money suggest that speculators do not treat risk assumption as a disutility but rather are willing to assume risks at zero or a negative return in exchange for the opportunity to profit from risk assumption. This willingness of speculators may exist because they are, separately, so egotistical that they think they can beat a zero sum game (minus commissions), or may exist because they are willing to accept the probability of loss of an unimportant amount of money in exchange for the possibility of gaining an important amount, or may exist because they like the sport of trading, or may exist because their greed overpowers their better judgment. Probably all of these things enter in. But this is neither here nor there. The germane fact is that the willingness to assume and finance risks at no cost is present in the developed markets. This is a significant spin-off from the markets. It is difficult to improve on zero cost in the quest for economic efficiency.

A dramatic example of the reduction in the cost of risk assumption was provided by the development and demise of the onion futures market.[4] The market was active from 1949–58. The market died in 1958 when trading was banned by law. Gray computed the index of seasonal price variation for a period before futures trading was initiated, during the period of active trading, and for a four year period following futures trading. The before and after indexes were nearly identical and ranged from a harvest low of about 75 to a spring high of about 145. The index during trading had a harvest low of 87 and a spring high of 118. Seasonal variation in cash onion prices was greatly reduced during the period of futures trading and went back to the earlier levels when the market was killed. The seasonal variation in cash onion price during the period of active futures trading was approximately equal to the cost of storing onions from harvest to spring.

Farmers sell onions from the fields to dealers who store and merchandise them through the winter. During the first period their bids to farmers reflected their storage costs minus an allowance to cover the risks of price decline. During the period of futures trading their bids reflected the futures price minus the cost of storage. Following the demise of the speculators, they went back to their old, conservative bid policy that clearly included a risk premium. There was a substantial normal backwardation before and after futures trading that was totally absent during futures trading. These dealers reaped rewards for risk assumption and a return on the capital that it required. The speculators did not receive the reward or even a part of it but did the job free.

The literature of futures trading written by trade people in testimony before

---

[3] See earlier discussion of soybean product forward contracting and Gray, "The Characteristic Bias in Some Thin Futures Markets." Op. cit.

[4] Gray, Roger, "Onions Revisited" Journal of Farm Econmics, Vol. 45, No. 2, May 1963.

Congress and for assorted education symposia is replete with testimony that an allowance for risk assumption would be necessary in the absence of the opportunity to hedge in futures markets. The onion market is not an isolated example. It is a unique situation in which a before, during, and after comparison can be made. From these things it follows that the more of the risks that are assumed and financed by speculators, the lower will be the costs associated with the commodity processes.

How Large Are the Markets? The standard measure of the size of futures markets is the volume of trading and it is large. In 1974 there were 27,733,328 contracts traded on U.S. exchanges. The average value of each contract was on the general order of $16,750 so that the total dollar volume was approximately $465 billion. The only purpose that such a number can serve is to call attention to the fact that commodity futures trading is big business. As we have seen, it takes a lot of volume of trading to change the open interest very much and nearly all futures contracts are offset by opposite transactions so that few are finally consummated and result in change in ownership of cash commodities. Volume of trading is significant in that it relates to liquidity but it is not a meaningful measure of the size of markets.

The meaningful measure of the size of markets is the open interest. It represents the quantities and values that are at hazard; the amount of risks outstanding. Some are hedger to hedger (or, more accurately, trade interest to trade interest), some hedger to speculator, and some are speculator to speculator. In most markets a fairly high proportion of the open positions are opposite cash positions and thus represent actual commodities. The number of open contracts and their value for the regulated (under supervision of CFTC) commodities at the end of 1975 appears on the next page.

Trading in the regulated commodities is on the general order of 75 percent of all trading. The value of the regulated commodities traded was 350 billion, some 52 times the value of outstanding contracts. The amount of money at hazard was substantially less than the $6.7 billion value of open contracts. Margin requirements are on the general order of 5 to 10 percent of the value, say a 7.5 percent average. Both sides are margined so that the minimum capital investment is 15 percent or $1 billion. More money is carried in accounts than is required for margin and, as we noted in Chapter 13, losses are frequently greater than a margin requirement. Thus, the equity capital generated by the system is greater than $1 billion.

These are interesting numbers but are not meaningful unless they are compared to something. In the context of the effectiveness of the system in providing equity capital the germane comparison would seem to be with the total risk load.

Commodity	Open Contracts	Value (Mil Dollars)
Wheat	62,508	1,078.3
Corn	88,875	1,177.6
Oats	2,541	17.9
Soybeans	87,526	2,078.7
SBO	34,314	329.4
SBM	21,319	277.1
Eggs	1,780	20.0
Cattle, live	29,521	487.1
Cattle, feeder	1,311	21.1
Hogs	17,270	228.0
Frozen pork bellies	12,199	263.5
Coconut oil	25	4.5
Palm oil	15	1.7
Cotton	19,354	580.6
Orange juice	5,417	48.8
Maine potatoes	14,025	70.1
Idaho potatoes	250	2.0
Imported beef	202	3.6
Total	398,452	6,690.0

Production, average stock, and open interest for five commodities for 1975 were:

Commodity		Production	Ave. Stock	Open Int.
Wheat	(Mil. Bu.)	2,138	1,469	312
Corn	(Mil. Bu.)	5,767	3,334	444
Soybeans	(Mil. Bu.)	1,521	981	438
Cattle	(Thous. Head)	15,500	7,440	1,122
Hogs	(Thous. Head)	81,267	49,196	2,245

The size of the risk load is difficult to define. Producers are subject to price uncertainty on the entire crop so that the risk load might be defined as the crop size. But, as we have seen, for the grains they are also subject to production uncertainty and price and production variations are inversely related so that forward contracting the entire crop may not be the least risk program. Some 35 percent of corn production is consumed on the farms where it is grown so that price uncertainties really relate to livestock prices. The total of the risk load for grains is less than the total of production.

The three grains are the biggest volume futures markets and two are the oldest markets. Yet, only a small proportion of the risk of price variability is transferred to futures markets. Merchants and warehousemen transfer most risks of their risks of ownership of these grains to speculators. Converters and processors transfer a smaller but major proportion of their risks. But, as we compare the total risk load, as measured by either production or stocks, it is clear that only a small proportion of the total risks ever get involved with futures markets.

The live cattle market grew rapidly from 1964 onward and is one of the most successful of new futures markets. The best measure of the risk load is the number of cattle on feed (average stock). One of the strongest of all cases for the consistent use of futures markets for risk shifting and equity financing can be made in connection with cattle feeding. Yet, even if we assume the total of the open interest is hedger to speculator—which it obviously isn't—only 15 percent of outstanding risks were shifted in 1975.

The risk load for hogs is more difficult to define because it involves a production cycle some eighteen months long. A reasonable construction of the total amount at hazard might be $1\frac{1}{2}$ times the annual production. At a minimum the amount at risk is the average stock of butcher hogs. The definition of the risk load is not important; the average size of the open interest is but a trifle of the risk load, however defined.

Conclusion. Some conclusions about futures markets as risk-shifting financing institutions are warranted. First, those of them that work are quite good. A liquid, speculatively active futures market is a useful and effective tool that can be and is used extensively by people who have risk problems. The developed markets not only perform the risking functions effectively but do so at a cost so low as to defy measurement.

Second, many of the markets do not work well. They lack the liquidity and risk carrying capacity required of effective hedging media.

Third, the markets are large enough to be of major economic significance but are quite small in relation to the total risk load in the commodity trades.

From this it follows that the growth potential is fantastic. It is not surprising that the number of commodities traded and the volume is so large but rather that it is so small; not surprising that the volume doubled in the decade of the 1960's but that it only doubled. The key question is to account for their smallness and to determine means by which growth can be encouraged.

Price Variability

The speculative pricing function and the consequences of the quality with which it is performed were discussed in Chapter 8. We must now concern ourselves with some evaluation of the quality of the job done by speculators in futures markets. The goal of speculative discounting of events that lie in the future is complete price stability. If all things were foreseeable and their effects on prices perfectly discounted, the results would be unchanging prices at equilibrium levels and relationships. Thus, the extent to which prices fluctuate is a measure of market imperfection. So, the markets are less than perfect.

Much, if not most, of the controversy surrounding futures trading relates to the effects of speculation on price variability. The argument is made that speculation causes greater price variability than would otherwise exist and the counterargument says that high volume futures markets have a stabilizing influence and under-speculated markets have greater price variability than do those in which there is a large amount of speculation. For many years the anti-futures trading arguments tended to prevail so that speculation was treated as a necessary evil that accompanied the desirable hedging process. During the last decade the balance appears to have shifted so that a favorable view is more widely held. It is doubtful that the favorable view is yet in the majority but it is generally held by students of futures markets and increasingly held by members of Congress and by the CFTC.

The earlier view was typified in a statement by J. M. Mehl:[5] "It is recognized that in the commodity futures markets there is need for some speculation. Merchants and processors hedge their inventories by making short sales of futures against these inventories and holding the short futures contracts until the cash commodity is sold. Some of the short contracts of hedgers, of course, are offset by the long hedging contracts of other merchants or processors whose forward cash sales exceed their inventories. Under most conditions, however, members of the trade are net short in the futures markets. Speculators, by buying the offsetting contracts of hedgers, assume the risk of price changes, and merchants and processors thus obtain the equivalent of insurance against price risks, which in turn enables them to operate on smaller margins of cost. It is not believed that speculation is a basic factor in determining the general level of prices in the long run. It is believed, however, that an undue amount of speculation tends to make price fluctuations more erratic and at times accentuates price trends. We know from the number and character of traders entering the market that at times speculation does have a short-run effect upon prices."

A later comment on onions by CEA was in the same vein,[6] "After reaching its high of \$2.20 per 50 pound sack on February 4, the price of the March futures on the Chicago Mercantile Exchange registered a low of \$.85 on March 6. Since that date there has been a substantial recovery with the futures expiring on March 22 at \$1.58 to \$1.60. Price movements such as this cannot be justified by supply and demand factors and must be attributed either to manipulative activity, or, as appears to be the case in this instance, to a wave of excessive speculation." The main line of the argument was that uninformed traders, both large and small, made no real effort to evaluate supply and demand conditions but follow market trends and play the psychology of the market. Prices move and sharp moves catch the attention and imagination of the public who rush in and accentuate the move, pushing prices past their equilibrium level. When this wave of speculation is exhausted the inevitable decline occurs as some speculators take profits. The decline triggers stop losses and panic selling ensues, pushing prices well below equilibrium levels. It says price moves grow on what they feed on and so carry to excess.

[5] Mehl, J. M., Administrator, CEA, before the Joint Committee of the Economic Report, November 24, 1947.

[6] USDA, CEA, *Speculation in Onion Futures,* January–March, 1957.

The shift toward a more favorable view of the influence of speculation is primarily the result of the attempts to find the impacts of speculation that have failed. The evidence that price variations are random tends to refute the argument that markets grow on what they feed on. The clear evidence of backwardation in markets where there are no futures markets or where futures trading volume is small and the absence of backwardation in the high volume markets is strongly suggestive of a stabilizing influence. The Economic Research Service of the USDA examined the question "The nature of speculations in grains and their bearings on fluctuations in prices and whether minimum margin requirements by the CEA could be a feasible tool for controlling or helping to control excessive fluctuations"[7] and found that speculators' transactions often moderate rather than accentuate price volatility.

The question of the effects of speculation on price variability is difficult to measure. It really relates to whether there is more or less variation than if there were no futures markets. There cannot simultaneously be both futures markets and no futures markets for a given commodity. In its study, the ERS concluded, "The price effects can be measured quantitatively. But for the effects of speculation to be isolated from many other factors influencing price, it is necessary to have a reasonably complete model of price behavior." As yet, no one has devised such a model.

Level of Prices. It is fairly clear that the level of commodity prices is higher in the presence of active futures markets than it would be in their absence. We have seen that speculators, in the aggregate, are long most of the time. We have also seen that they not only fail to get paid for risk assumption but most lose money. We have seen testimony that hedgers would have to make an allowance for risk assumption if they could not hedge. Were there a cost of risk it would be borne by primary producers in the form of lower prices.

Seasonal Price Patterns. There is substantial evidence that there is no all-consistent seasonal variation in the prices of stored commodities for which there are developed futures markets, the cost of storage taken into account. We earlier discussed the absence of a consistent seasonal variation in corn and soybean futures prices. Gray has examined an assortment of futures markets for seasonal bias.[8] He found that those markets that are traded in volume and have large open interests do not have discernible seasonal patterns of prices, while those markets in which volume of trading and open interest are small have upward seasonal price patterns in futures prices from harvest to the end of the storage season.

The major grains are the clearest example of the effect of speculation on seasonal price patterns. Before, during, and immediately after harvest farmers

[7] ERS, USDA, *Margins, Speculation, and Prices in Grain Futures Markets,* December, 1967.

[8] Gray, Roger W. "The Characteristic Bias in Some Thin Futures Markets" Food Research Institute Studies, Vol. 1, No. 3, November, 1960.

sell larger quantities than move into consumption. These are bought by merchants and hedged in futures. As we have seen, merchants and warehousemen are somewhat flexible regarding hedging or standing open. When they hedge they do so because they elect not to stand open *at the prices that speculators are bidding*. Were there no futures markets they would still buy and store the grain that farmers offered for sale but only at lower prices. Speculators can assume ownership at harvest only because they are the highest bidders. That which they buy they subsequently sell. Therefore, their actions result in higher prices at harvest and lower prices later in the season than would otherwise exist. The interesting thing is that, at times, they are so exuberant about it that they foul their own nest *in the high volume markets*.

Interim Variation. As we move from the longer run effects to the short term variations we also move from agreement to controversy. The constructive influence of speculators in their seasonal risk-bearing behavior is widely recognized and the unsettling influence ascribed to them by many people is generally limited to the short run. Commodity Research Bureau, Inc. claims that their published studies indicate that there are definite seasonal price move tendencies. The question has not been explored enough that a final answer is possible.

The first point that we would make here is that to separate the long run and short run effects is difficult and to suggst that one is different from the other is inconsistent. For a given season, the open interest builds up gradually and is liquidated gradually. In most instances, its magnitude is a function of the hedges in the market. The open interest, not the volume of trading, is the appropriate measure of the amount of speculation. There are no short-term variations in the amount of speculation, rather there are seasonal and interseason variations. If there are no short-term variations, it is impossible to ascribe short-term price variations to variable speculation.

One buys and becomes long or one sells and becomes short. Gains and losses are the results of changes in price while positions are held; the result of taking a position, not of buying or selling. A buys and B sells. There is one open contract and the volume of trading is one. B buys and C sells. There is still one open contract but the volume has risen to two. B sells again and D buys. There are now two open ocntracts and the volume is three. B buys and E sells. There are still two open contracts and the volume is now four. The size of positions and the amount of money at hazard does not change as B trades in and out. Positions influence price as inventory is accumulated and liquidated and as money is put at hazard—one does not margin a trade, he margins a position.

The failure to associate the amount of speculation with the open interest rather than the volume of trading leads to interesting and troublesome errors. In the CEA study *Speculation in Onion Futures* the "excessive" price variation was attributed to excessive speculation. The volume of trading was quite large during the reference period but the open interest *gradually* declined from 3,260 contracts on January 31 to 636 contracts on March 6. There was not a wave of speculation, excessive or other.

Second, price variability is related to the frequency and the causes of speculator changes of mind about the future course of prices. The volume of trading is functionally related to the open interest. As two people want to take positions, one long and other short, they trade and there is volume. The line of causation between price variation and volume is the thing that is at issue. Does trading come into the market and cause prices to run up and down or do prices become variable because of increased uncertainty about production, stocks, uses, etc. and speculators react to the same uncertainty by frequently changing their minds and moving in and out? The answer to the question depends upon what makes speculators buy and sell when and as they do. Do they forecast price changes on the basis of new information and move prices by taking positions or are their actions determined by price variations? Do they control markets or are they controlled by markets? The answer is likely some of both. With such an extensive amount of the literature on how to trade based on chart, trend, and movement trading and the use of stops, both to enter and leave the market, there must be some trading based on market action. However, as we have seen, different chartists interpret the same price patterns differently and different number systems indicate different market positions. At least some of movement trading is offsetting.

Some of the regular traders described in the last chapter traded in a long list of commodities. They tended to go to those commodities for which prices were most variable, moving as price variability changed. They did not stay with positions for very long, tending to indicate an absence of fundamental convictions about prices. For example, one trader had a net profit of about $15,000 which was made up of 46 profitable trades and 41 loss trades. During the course of a year he traded in cocoa, sugar, cattle, bellies, silver, palladium, copper, corn, wheat, orange juice, eggs, potatoes, soybeans, and soybean oil. Obviously, no one can know enough about each of all those commodities to exert an intelligent influence on price. We do not know, however, whether he was trading market action or following commission house advice. There was some day trading. One speculator traded 130 contracts of bellies in one month without ever taking a position larger than 5 and most trades were one and two. (His net loss on that venture was almost exactly equal to the commissions paid.) There were speculators who were clearly trading with the direction of the price movement but there were others who were trading against the trend. The Blair Stewart study indicated about as much trading against price trends as with them. On the other hand, there were speculators who traded in one or two commodities indigenous to the area where they resided and who held positions for protracted periods. Their trading appeared to be based on firm convictions about longer term equilibrium values.

One line of argument that speculator behavior increases price variability relates to trading the psychology of markets. This point of view was well put by Keynes.[9] "Or to change the metaphor slightly, professional investment may be likened to those newspaper competitions in which the competitors have to pick out the six prettiest faces from 100 photographs, the prize being awarded to the competitor whose choice most nearly corresponds to the average preference of the competitors as a whole, so that each competitor has to pick not those faces which he himself finds prettiest but those he thinks likeliest to catch the fancies of the other competitors, all of whom are looking at the problem from the same point of view. It is not a case of choosing those which, to the best of one's judgment, are really the prettiest, nor even those which average opinion genuinely thinks the prettiest. We have reached the third degree, where we devote our intelligences to anticipating what average opinion expects average opinion to be." This line of reasoning loses some of its steam when we extend it to a fourth, fifth, etc. estate at which state of confused semantics some of the competitors decide to go back to the first estate and choose the six prettiest girls. In the case of commodities it loses more of its steam on first delivery day when commercial forces take over.

The case that markets generate their own volatility gets difficult to make when we consider that for every long there is a short, for everyone who thinks the price is going up there is someone who thinks it is going down, and for everyone who trades with the flow of the market, there is someone trading against it.

Again, we would point out that futures trading is a zero sum game in which speculators try to take money away from other speculators. The open interest is composed of short hedgers, long hedgers, long speculators, and short speculators. The hedged positions do not balance and are predominately short. Part of the speculative positions offset the imbalance of the hedge positions. In addition, there are speculator opposite speculator positions. In some markets this superstructure of speculation opposite speculation is quite small and in others, for example, pork bellies, it is quite large. As we have seen, hedgers hedge for a variety of reasons, only one of which is price expectations. The speculator standing opposite the hedger has a competitive edge because his actions are only influenced by price expectations. He is at the mercy of nothing save his own judgment. The speculator opposite another speculator is in a fully competitive position. From this it follows that markets in which there is a large superstructure of speculator opposite speculator are more competitive and unbiased in their aggregate price expectations than markets in which the speculative superstructure is small. We should expect the more competitive markets to do a better pricing job than the less competitive because on doing a better job rests the financial fate of the speculator.

[9] Keynes, J. M. *The General Theory of Employment, Money, and Interest.*

Three conclusions are warranted: (1) There is a lot of willy-nilly trading that may be unsettling or may be offsetting, (2) There is a lot of conviction trading in which positions are taken and held until forces in cash markets settle the question of the equilibrium price, and (3) when uncertainty is great, prices are volatile and vice versa, and when prices move from one level to another because of changes in supply-demand conditions, prices are volatile.

Price Forecasting

The pricing job that is undertaken by speculative or forward markets in seasonally produced commodities is to establish a price at the outset of trading that will finally turn out to have been the equilibrium price. Ideally, the price would remain constant throughout the production and marketing season. In the non-storage markets the objective is to establish and hold constant the price that will prevail during the delivery month. The skill with which markets do these things is the measure of their performance as pricing institutions. Prices do vary and there are frequently major changes. We must, therefore, conclude that the job is done somewhat less than perfectly. But how good are they? This question is countered with another: Compared to what? There is no standard by which to measure them. There is no four minute mile as in footracing or 400 batting average as in baseball. Accomplishment of the objectives would be the equivalent of batting 1000, all home runs.

How well markets perform should be evaluated on the basis of the difficulty of the forecasting job. This varies by commodities and from time to time for the same commodity. Prices of some commodities are inherently more volatile than those of others. Demand for some is more inelastic than for others. Inelastic demand contributes to price volatility. Prices of some commodities are influenced by many more factors than those of others and information is much more complete for some than for others. For example, soybean oil is but one of a dozen edible fats and oils that are more or less interchangeable so that the price of soybean oil is affected by the supplies of the others. These are produced all over the world and information is incomplete, late and much less than perfectly accurate. Substantial inventories are built up and liquidated. On the other hand, statistics about broilers are very complete, accurate, and immediate. Broilers compete with a limited number of products and demand is relatively elastic. It would seem to be easier to forecast broiler prices than soybean oil prices, thus the performance standards should be different.

Figures 8 through 11 show some price histories of markets in volatile situations. Figure 8 is the price history of the blight-stricken 1970 corn crop. The season was uneventful, save for a minor drought scare in late June, until the end of July. An unprecedented infection struck a high proportion of the corn. The extent of damage was not known until harvest in October and November. The

FIGURE 8. The Blight-Stricken 1970 Corn Crop

304

news spread as fast as the blight and prices rose rapidly. Within a week the price moved into a narrow range that lasted five months. The subsequent downward adjustment suggests the first adjustment was too much. However, there was an inadequate supply of blight resistant seed and it was not known how much blight vulnerable seed farmers would plant. Heroic measures increased the amount of good seed and farmers increased the acreage planted, hence the decline. The abortive run-up in June was a reasonably based blight scare. (The air was sampled and numerous spores found.) We should vote the performance excellent. The market quickly made the necessary adjustment in an unprecedented situation fraught with uncertainty.

Figure 9 is the 1974 corn crop. Land preparation went very well until late April. Then planting was delayed until quite late by excessive rainfall. There followed a very hot, dry summer and finally the late maturing crop was severely damaged by a record early and severe frost the third week of September. On October 4 some export sales were suspended by the federal government changing, arbitrarily, the rules of the game. It is doubtful that this action had a significant impact on what ultimately was to be the equilibrium price. The major reduction in use necessitated by the short crop was made in domestic utilization for feed; hog and broiler numbers were reduced and cattle were marketed without going through feed yards.

The price was at a rational level in May of 1974. It should have responded to the May rains sooner. The adjustment to drought and frost was quite rational if abnormal weather is really not predictable. The five month decline in price from October suggests that the market over-estimated the increase in price necessary to force reduction in domestic use; that the July, 1975 future should have gone to about $3.30 instead of $4.00. We must have some reservations about this conclusion of error. It may be necessary to overprice to get the attention of users sufficiently that adjustments are made promptly. On balance, it was a typical short crop pattern: quick adjustment to supply forces and underestimation of the impact of higher prices on use. There is an old adage, "Beware of the long tail of a short crop" that was certainly true in 1974–75. Actual information about the rate of use is only available quarterly as stocks are measured. Thus, it was not known that feeders were making sharp cuts until January 24, 1975, when most of the decline had already taken place. To have done better the market would have needed to forecast users' response to price and such forecasting is quite difficult. How should the performance be rated? Good? Fair? Poor? There is no standard. But it wasn't as good as 1970–71.

Figure 10 is the 1973 wheat crop. Russia had a small wheat crop in 1972 and bought heavily from the United States, pulling reserve stocks down to quite low levels. This was thought to be a non-repetitive event and world crops in 1973 were expected to be good, hence the $2.50 to $2.80 during much of June-July of 1973. World grain crops in 1973–74 were of record size and supplies were

FIGURE 9. The Short 1974 Corn Crop

FIGURE 10. The 1973 Wheat Crop

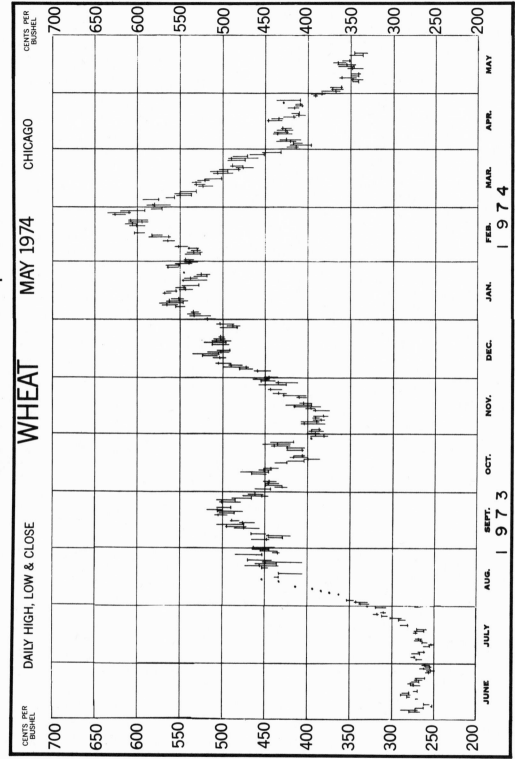

CENTS PER BUSHEL

WHEAT   MAY 1974   CHICAGO

DAILY HIGH, LOW & CLOSE

1973   1974

abundant by historical standards. The seven month rise from $2.50 to $6.25 was the result of increasing world demand. The demand increase was partly the result of worldwide prosperity and partly a flight from money associated with worldwide inflation. The March-May 1974 decline suggests that the long price increase was overdone. However, U.S. supplies were oversold; more wheat was committed for shipment before the 1974 harvest than there was wheat. It was necessary to go to buyers in destination countries and arrange postponement until after harvest. They were quite cooperative but might not have been had prices not been inverted. On February 25, 1974, Chicago wheat prices were: Cash $6.88, May $6.27, and September $5.67.

The market did a poor job anticipating the strength of world demand for wheat.[10] In the end, it took decisive action to solve a problem. People associated with the wheat trade were used to thinking in terms of $1.50 as a reasonable value prior to 1972 and in 1973 reasonably thought the effect of the short Russian crop was past and the world was back to a normal oversupply of wheat. Prices of $4 and $5 for abundant supplies were very difficult to believe. The rapid decrease in the value of money associated with petroleum price increases was not appreciated. How much of the error is forgiveable? It was a very difficult situation, but not done well.

Figure 11 is the April, 1974 cattle futures price with the current cash cattle price. The price started out about where it ended but followed a long route between; 1973–74 was a year of stress in cattle prices. The supply of beef was down, consumer demand was up, and the pricing process was badly disturbed by a period of governmentally imposed price ceilings. The April futures price was affected by cash prices, basing expectations about the future on today's reality. In addition, the market over-estimated the prices that would prevail in the future. With the benefit of hindsight, this appears to have been a failure of the market to accurately appraise the willingness of consumers to reduce consumption in response to price. How good a job? On the face of it, poor. But the situation was without precedent and consumer response is difficult to anticipate.

In general we should give the high volume futures market good marks for two reasons: First, when seasonal price patterns and price variability of the low volume and high volume markets are compared, the high volume markets appear to be with minimal seasonal bias and more stable. The actively speculated markets appear to bring all available information about supplies and uses to bear on prices. The larger the volume of trading, the greater are the resources devoted to the collection of information and price analysis. The process of speculation, with its rewards for being right about ultimate equilibrium prices and penalties for being wrong, must result in a greater sophistication in price analysis than would otherwise exist.

10 This is an excellent example of the kind of market error that can be exploited by a good trend-following system.

FIGURE 11 Cash and Futures Prices of Cattle

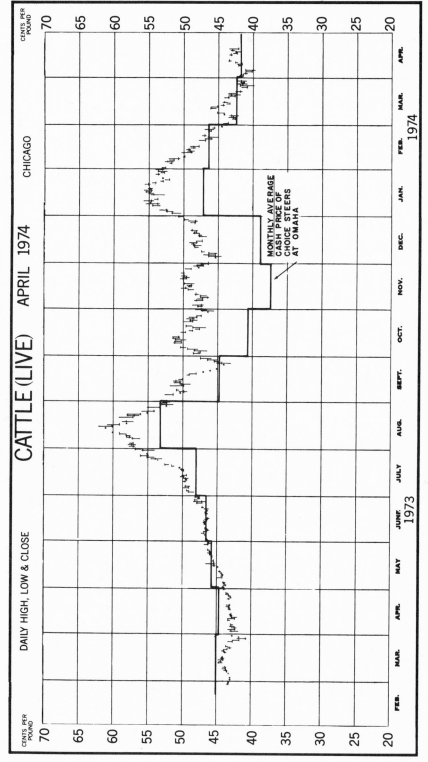

Second, these markets must be pretty good because they are so hard to beat. Many try but few succeed. If the markets performed as poorly in establishing prices as is frequently alleged, every ordinarily competent price analyst would be wealthy.

Commodity prices vary over wide ranges. They fail to fully foresee and accurately interpret events to come. There is a lot of uninformed speculation that cannot contribute to effective price formulation. Just as there is a need for more speculation to support more liquid, unbiased risk-shifting financing markets there is need for more speculation of greater sophistication to improve price establishment.

CHAPTER **15**

Market Regulation

This chapter is written at a time (January, 1976) that is either clumsy or opportune. The Commodity Futures Trading Act was signed into law in October, 1974 and became operative six months later. The law is an extensive revision of and addition to the Commodity Exchange Act of 1936. It is a very comprehensive piece of legislation and the process of implementation was only just begun in 1975. The full implementation will require, at a minimum, several years. There were numerous changes in the old areas of regulation and the Congress mandated numerous new areas for regulation. The writing of new rules and regulations is a lengthy and tedious task, fraught with controversy. The whole of the process will be tested in the courts for years to come. Thus, we cannot describe existing regulation because it is in a state of flux, but it presents an opportunity to draw attention to some things that may be central to decisions yet to be made.

There is a philosophic change in the law, the implications of which may have a major impact on regulation. For the first fifty years, federal regulation of futures trading had an anti-speculation bias that hampered market growth and development. This anti-speculation bias was not limited to governmental regulation alone but had, in part, to be laid at the doorstep of market self governance as well. The markets themselves tended to have a negativeness toward speculation. Part of it was the result of a public attitude that put the markets on the defensive. The easy thing to defend is risk shifting, and speculation has been easiest to defend by treating it as a necessary evil. Part is the result of a puritanical attitude toward speculation held by many members of exchanges who are not speculators. Part stems from members of exchanges and of the commodity trades who experience competition from speculators in their cash trading activities. Speculators are the natural enemies of hedgers and cash traders even though these people use futures markets and laud them as risk shifting institutions.

Everyone approves of competition—for the other guy. Speculators are a competitive force keeping the commodity trades people who do not use futures honest. Finally, part stems from the poor image that speculators project. There are greedy, vain, unskilled, and underfinanced people who speculate in commodities. People come in, lose money, let their losses run to unreasonable amounts, and some scream "foul." The competent ones are quiet and have a low profile. It is easy for exchange officials and commission house operators to form a negative impression of the speculating public. All of this carried over into legislation and regulation.

The anti-speculation bias gave way gradually as markets came to be more extensively used and understood. Legislation was introduced and hearings held in 1964 that would have strengthened anti-speculation regulation. These measures failed to get out of committee until 1968 when extensive changes in the Commodity Exchange Act were made. The anti-speculation elements were eliminated and, on balance, the law shifted toward a tolerant, if not favorable, attitude.

The 1974 Act was born out of the rapid price rises and great volatility of 1972 and 1973. Again, much of this was blamed on excessive speculation and several bills were introduced to increase regulation and curb speculation. Again, the legislative process was deliberate and the punitive aspects of proposals gave way to a constructive attitude toward the economic usefulness of futures markets and speculation. The CFTC has a mandate from the Congress to direct its activities toward the growth and development of futures markets. The future of regulation is uncertain. It may work out in a way that provides a climate within which competitive markets can grow and prosper. It may be that, under the stress of controversy regarding decisions about detailed issues, actions will be stifling. Or it may be that the best intended actions result in overprotection and regulation that prevent the forces of competition from surfacing and thus prevent growth and development. For, as we have seen, competition is not an orderly, benign process—a thing of beauty and of joy forever—but is disorderly, mean, and ruthless.

The bias of this chapter is toward the growth of speculation and the fostering of competition. It is a brief review of the history of regulation and the scope of the Act and a discussion of some of the issues that may be central as the CFTC develops.

Development of Regulation

The history of the regulation of futures trading is essentially as old as futures trading itself. Where there is an activity there must be rules about its conduct. The first seventy years of futures trading was a period of self regulation without significant governmental interference and there has now been more than a half century of regulation by the federal government.

Pre-1920. In Chapter 4 we looked at the history and development of futures trading prior to World War I. We found that one of the central themes was the development of rules and regulations. These were written as problems developed and were consistently in the direction of fostering competition. They were aimed at making prices representative of the commercial value of the commodities traded, at enabling all participants to have equal access to trading opportunities and information, and at the prevention of corners, squeezes, fictitious prices, false trades, and other forms of price distortion.

During the early development of futures markets as risk shifting-financing institutions little of the constructive aspects of trading was apparent to farmers. What appeared to them was a period of unbridled speculation, repeated market manipulations, and spectacular price fluctuations. From these apparent abuses stemmed repeated efforts of State legislatures, from the 1860's onward, to abolish futures trading. During the fifty years beginning with 1874 a long succession of bills to abolish futures trading was introduced in the Federal Congress. Bills levying a prohibitive tax on futures contracts in grains, cotton, and certain other commodities were passed by both houses of Congress in 1892–1893. This legislation failed only because a two-thirds approval was needed at one juncture of the House proceedings.

The general agricultural opposition to futures trading persisted but at a lower level as agricultural prices rose from about 1895 to 1920. During this period the development of improved regulation by exchanges and better grading methods and quality standards quieted much of the clamor and changed its direction from one of prohibition to improved regulation. The importance of futures trading to the development of a commercial agriculture and to international trade in grains and cotton was gradually becoming appreciated. The clamor for prohibition was by no means ended. As we have noted, a law prohibiting futures trading in onions was passed in the late 1950's. *The prohibition remains in the 1974 Act.* There were bills introduced to prohibit futures trading in potatoes in the late 1960's and early 1970's.

The Grain Futures Act. Following World War I grain prices fell sharply and speculative excesses were, as usual, blamed. The Futures Trading Act of 1921 was passed. It was based on the taxing power of the federal government and, on this basis, was declared unconstitutional. It was reintroduced in 1922 as the Grain Futures Act, based on the interstate commerce clause and held constitutional.

The Grain Futures Act of 1922 enabled the government to deal with exchanges themselves rather than with individual traders. The exchanges had to be licensed and designated. A condition of designation was that the exchanges effectively prevent price manipulation by their members. There was a weakness in the effectiveness of this in that the only recourse was suspension which was correctly considered overkill. There were provisions against manipulation and some legal actions were taken. These proved ineffective because of limitations in the law.

The most effective point of the 1922 law was the provision for continuous fact-finding and supply of continuous trading information. The Grain Futures Administration made several major studies that provided information and analysis of market operation. Some of these identified sources and patterns of what was thought to be excessive speculation and manipulation. In 1927 the United States Department of Agriculture began submitting recommendations to the Congress for changes in the law. Hearings were held in 1934–36, resulting in major changes, including renaming to the Commodity Exchange Act of 1936. It is worth noting that this occurred during a period of continuing commodity price distress.

The principal contributions of the Grain Futures Act were the development of greatly increased knowledge about futures trading and the movement of control of trading to the public sector. The exchanges were put on notice that the effects of futures trading were of public concern and therefore subject to regulation as a part of interstate commerce.

The Commodity Exchange Act of 1936. Under this act authority was granted to deal with market abuses by traders generally as well as exchange members, to prosecute price manipulation as a criminal offense, to limit the scope of operations by large scale speculators, and to extend regulation to the field of Futures Commission Merchants to suppress cheating, fraud, and fictitious transactions in futures.

Futures trading in designated commodities was prohibited on other than designated, licensed exchanges. Futures Commission Merchants had to be registered, as did brokers. Funds deposited by customers of commission houses had to be segregated and there was provision for audits to assure compliance. There were extensive provisions for the submission of information and power to make investigations into apparent or alleged market abuses.

Between 1936 and 1968 there were several amendments to the Act which brought additional commodities under regulation and enabled better information and tightened control of individual trader actions. During this period there were numerous charges of manipulation and other violations brought against individuals and firms and a substantial amount of case law was developed. The Congress did not specifically define manipulation and other forms of price distortion but left the matter for the courts to develop.

The Commodity Exchange Act of 1936 provided, in the main, for administration by the Commodity Exchange Authority which was a part of the United States Department of Agriculture. Administration of some provisions of the Act was reserved to the Commodity Exchange Commission which was composed of the Secretary of Agriculture, the Secretary of Commerce, and the Attorney General. Most notable among these was the establishment of limits on speculative transactions and positions.

The 1968 Amendments. The several bills introduced between 1964 and 1968 culminated in several significant changes. These were: (1) it required that Futures Commission Merchants meet certain minimum financial standards, (2) increased the penalties for certain law violations such as manipulation and embezzlement, (3) authorized the issuance of cease and desist orders when violations of the law were established, (4) required contract markets to enforce their trading rules and contract terms—put teeth in the self regulation requirements, and (5) brought livestock, livestock products, and frozen concentrated orange juice under regulation.

Thus matters stood in April 1975 at the time of effectiveness of the CFTC Act of 1974. The Commodity Exchange Act was predicated in findings and conclusions of the Congress that (1) transactions in commodity futures are carried on in large volume by the public as well as by persons engaged in the business of buying and selling agricultural commodities in interstate commerce, and (2) such transactions and prices are susceptible to speculation, manipulation and control, and sudden and unreasonable price fluctuations, and such fluctuations are an unreasonable burden upon interstate commerce and make regulations essential in the public interest. This remained as the legal basis for the CFTC Act.

In broadest outline, regulation under the Commodity Exchange Act was designed to (1) assure that the exchange rules force competition in commodity trading, (2) prevent price distortion, and (3) protect the public from fraud and noncompetitive prices.

The Commodity Futures Trading Act of 1974. The Act is in the form of an amendment to the Commodity Exchange Act as amended. It consists of 27 pages of fine print such as "Sec. 216. The Commodity Exchange Act, as amended, is amended by inserting the following new section immediately after section 8 b (7.4.S.C.12b). . . ." The Act as it stands in its entirety with the new amendments included and the appropriate deletions made is 45 pages of small type. What is attempted here is a brief statement of the principal changes. The Act consists of four titles:

Title I. Creates an independent regulatory Commission called the Commodity Futures Trading Commission consisting of a Chairman and four other Commissioners. They are appointed by the President with the advice and consent of the Senate. The President is to seek a balanced Commission including persons of demonstrated knowledge in futures trading or its regulation and persons of demonstrated knowledge in the production, merchandising, processing, or distribution of commodities.

1. Not more than three of the members of the Commission shall be of the same political party and are appointed for staggered five year terms.

2. The Commission shall have a general counsel and an Executive Director with the executive director subject to Senate confirmation.

3. The Secretary of Agriculture shall appoint a liaison officer to be housed with the Commission and have the right to attend and observe all deliberations and proceedings of the Commission. There is an opposite liaison officer appointed by the Commission and housed in the U.S.D.A.

4. All existing authority under the Commodity Exchange Act and the Commodity Exchange Commission was transferred to the CFTC as were existing personnel.

5. A reparation procedure before the Commission is authorized for handling complaints which arise from violations of the Act. A reparative order by the Commission is subject to judicial review in the Court of Appeals. The reparations procedure is not to become effective until one year after the date of the bill.

6. The Commission—in issuing any order, rule, or regulation of a contract market—is to take into consideration the public interest to be protected by the antitrust laws and to endeavor to take the least anticompetitive means of achieving the objectives of the Act.

Title II. Provides broad authority to the Commission to regulate futures trading and exchange activities.

1. All goods, articles, services, rights, and interest traded for future delivery are brought under Federal regulation.

2. Commodity Trading Advisors and Commodity Pool Operators are required to register with the Commission. In addition, the existing registration and examination for futures requirements applicable to futures commission merchants and floor brokers are expanded to include all individuals handling customers' accounts.

3. The Commission will determine whether trading by floor brokers and futures commission merchants for their own account and at the same time trading for their customers will be permitted. The Commission shall further determine the circumstances under which it will be conducted. The Commission may make separate determinations for different contract markets.

4. Contract markets are required to demonstrate that futures contracts for which they seek designation will not be contrary to the public interest.

5. The Commission may establish additional points for the delivery of a commodity in order to diminish price manipulation, market congestion, or abnormal movement of the commodity.

6. Contract markets must submit for Commission approval bylaws, rules, regulations, and resolutions which relate to the terms and conditions of futures contracts or other trading instruments. In addition, the Commission may require a contract market to make changes in its rules and practices which are necessary or appropriate for the protection of the public interest.

7. The Commission has the authority to go directly into court to enjoin any contract market or other person from violating the Act or restraining trading

in any commodity for future delivery. However, no restraining under injunction, or writ of mandamus will be issued ex parte.

8. The Commission has authority to act in emergency situations and direct a contract market to take such action as is necessary to maintain or restore orderly trading.

9. Penalties in amounts up to $100,000 can be imposed in both administrative and criminal proceedings in violation of the Act.

10. The Commission has authority to regulate transactions for delivery of silver bullion, gold bullion, or bulk silver coins or bulk gold coins persuant to standardized margin or leverage account contracts.

Title III. Provides enabling authority at the discretion of the Commission for persons registered under the Act and in the commodity trading business to establish voluntary futures associations for regulating the practices of members.

Title IV. Provides for several miscellaneous things, mainly relating to the establishment of the Commission operation.

1. It is a felony for Commissioners, employees, or agents of the Commmission to participate directly or indirectly in any transactions in commodity futures or commodity options or in actual cash commodities. It is also a felony to transmit confidential information.

2. The ban on trading in options in commodities under regulations at the time of the passage of the Act is continued. Options trading with respect to all other commodity futures is also banned if contrary to Commission rules or regulations prohibiting or allowing such trading. The Commission is to prescribe the regulations governing such trading within one year after the effective date of the bill unless the Commission notifies the Senate Committee on Agriculture and Forestry that it is unable to do so within one year.

3. The Commission, in fixing trading and position limits, is authorized to exempt transactions known to the trade as "arbitrage." "Arbitrage" in domestic markets is defined as being the same as a "spread" or "straddle." The Commission is authorized to define the term "international arbitrage."

4. The Commission is authorized to define bona fide hedging transactions or positions. Certain transactions are required to be included in the definition.

5. The Commission is authorized to conduct regular investigations of the markets and furnish reports of its findings to the public on a regular basis.

6. Every clearing house and contract market must maintain daily trading records.

7. The Commission is to establish research and information programs to investigate the feasibility of trading by computer and the expanded use of modern information systems technology.

It is readily apparent that the scope of regulation of trading was greatly increased, that the degree of control of the Federal government over the actions of people in the futures trading industry other than actual trading was increased and extended to more kinds of people, that regulation was extended to include redress of grievances of public users of markets, and there are numerous questions that must be answered and numerous regulations that must be formulated by the commission. It is to some of the questions and issues that we will next turn.

Issues: Market Operation

As is shown by the above summary of changes in the law, there are several facets of regulation of market operations that require fairly early decisions by the Commission. There are other matters stemming from the law as it stood before amendment and from legislative proposals that were not included that will be under consideration during the years ahead.

Regulation of Cash Commodity Trading. The Act provides broad authority to deter price manipulation of "any commodity in interstate commerce, or for future delivery. . . ." (Section 6 b, 6 c, and 9 b). The CEA exercised authority over cash-price manipulation only in conjunction with the regulation of futures markets or spot markets operated by designated contract markets. This limited the intrusion of government into cash market activities to those cash markets for which there were futures markets and to cash transactions associated with suspected manipulation of futures prices. The CEA construed its mission in matters of price manipulation as limited to futures price manipulation.

The question, "Should the Commission undertake a program to prevent manipulation in *all* cash transactions in *all* commodities or should it adapt a policy limiting its authority to preventing manipulation in situations related to transactions on futures markets, cash markets operated by futures markets, or leverage contract markets?" arose during the early deliberations of the Commission. This question opens a Pandora's Box that should be promptly closed. The name of the Act and its entire thrust is toward futures markets and trading. There are not futures markets in either goose eggs or cabbages and the CFTC would certainly seem to be going quite far afield were it to inquire into possible manipulation of the price of either. The question serves the useful purposes of illustrating the broad scope of the Act and the possible scope of the activities of CFTC should it, at some future time, run out of something to do in relation to existing futures markets.

The mandate to do at least some regulation of cash markets raises some interesting questions about where the authority of the CFTC should stop. Suppose an individual acquires a dominant position in frozen pork bellies, takes delivery of the total supply of bellies, and extracts a monopoly price, both cash and futures. It would appear clear that the cash operation is a part of a manipulation. But suppose that the same individual simply buys all of the bellies that other people take on delivery until he has a dominant position and can extract a monopoly revenue without ever participating in the futures market himself. Has he now done something more or less manipulative than had he cornered the market in goose eggs? Likely, he would be a part of a conspiracy, else he wouldn't try it, but suppose he is not? Lines of authority will need to be drawn.

Margin Requirements. One of the more interesting aspects of the CFTC Act is that it does not include direct authority for control over margin requirements. There is indirect authority through the power to disapprove of exchange rules but direct authority is conspicuously absent. There was a long campaign on the part of the Commodity Exchange Authority to gain control over margin requirements. There were numerous proposals to amend the Act to include margin control. For example, such a provision was included in the Defense Production Act of 1950 and defeated in Congress. The 1966 amendments included margin control but this was taken out in committee. It was argued that low margins contribute to excessive speculation that results in excessive price variation. Some of the principal examples cited included the collapse of the cotton market in October, 1946, the boom in grain prices in 1947, the successive market breaks in February, 1948 and February, 1949, and the soybean boom in 1950. The arguments were made at length and the examples were examined in detail. In most instances speculative accumulation was described in rising markets and speculation liquidation cited in declining markets. The arguments were persuasive until the circumstances of the cash commodity markets were examined. The boom in grain prices in 1947 was the result of a real shortage of grain induced by government buying for war relief. The collapse in 1948 was the result of oncoming large crops following a short crop year. The break in 1949 was associated with general economic stagnation that caused a decline in the demand for grain. The 1950 soybean boom was partly the result of short supplies relative to requirements, partly the outbreak of the Korean war, and had manipulative overtones relative to large positions held by a group of Chinese.

The argument was made that small margins enable speculators to pyramid positions in rising markets so that prices are forced to much higher levels than would otherwise exist and that thinly margined speculators are forced to liquidate when prices decline slightly with the result that markets collapse instead of correct.

There are several arguments against granting authority to establish margins to the government. The presumption is that there would be, at least on occasion, higher margins than would otherwise exist. CEA officials stated in testimony that the authority would be used sparingly—only when they had reason to believe that there was danger of sudden or unreasonable fluctuations in prices. However, the result would be higher margins and the use of margins to attempt to control price variations.

The minimum margins that exchanges set for commission house customers tend to be as small as the exchanges judge is consistent with the guarantee of contracts. The purpose of margins is to assure the financial integrity of the contracts. As we have seen, the system works very well; the contracts are valid.

One point that has caused confusion in margin discussions needs to be cleared up: Commodity margins are in no way comparable to margins on securities. The commodity margin is a guarantee of performance; earnest money. It is not a down payment on a purchase as is so often suggested. A futures contract is an agreement to later buy and sell; title does not change. When delivery is made and taken, payment is made in full with no credit involved between the clearing house as the deliverer and the member as the recipient. Both the short and long sides are margined. Security markets are spot markets in which title changes. The security margin of, say, 65 percent is not a margin in the commodity sense but, rather, is a part payment for property received. The balance is a loan made to the purchaser on which he pays interest. The extension of credit in the purchase of securities can be inflationary, can lead to inflated values in proportion to the credit extended. Such is not the case in commodity margins because commodity margins are a two way street. For every long, there is a short, and both post margins. If small margins posted by longs are construed as inflationary then small margins posted by shorts must be construed as equally deflationary.

An increase in margin requirements would increase hedgers' cost of doing business and reduce economic efficiency. The high proportion of the value of commodities that can be borrowed at banks and the low interest rates paid by merchants and processors result from the price certainty afforded by hedges. The cost of this certainty is lower as margin requirements are lower. If margin requirements were higher interest costs would be greater as would marketing costs.

If margin requirements were greatly increased some hedgers would find it advantageous to carry their own risks. As we have seen, there are a lot of "sometimes" hedgers. A major increase in margins could result in a sufficient decrease in hedging to destroy markets. With firms forced to finance their own risks, business would migrate to the largest, best financed companies and competition would be reduced.

An increase in margin requirements would reduce equity capital availability and increase its cost. As we have seen—whatever the motivation—the equity capital furnished hedgers by speculators has no measurable cost in the high volume, heavily speculated markets. It has a substantial cost in the thin, underspeculated markets and in informal forward contracting markets. The negligible cost of the equity capital that is raised in futures markets is probably the result of the existence of the great leverage that low margins make possible; the possibility to turn an unimportant amount of money into an important amount.

There is a multiplier effect in margin increase because both sides—short and long—are margined. To illustrate, suppose that margin requirements were raised to 100 percent. The capital for commodity ownership must be provided by the banking system. Hedgers would similarly provide the full capital for margin, perhaps obtainable from the banking system, and speculators a like amount for a total capital of 300 percent. No system can endure such an absurdity and any system is weakened by some part of such an absurdity.

An important reason for not granting margin control for the purpose of preventing price excesses is that it would not work. Suppose that a speculative boom gets started and grows on what it feeds on and that the controlling authority recognizes the rise as a price excess. He imposes higher margins. The longs will not have any trouble; they already have profits and experience no difficulty. The shorts will have difficulty since they have losses; it is their capital position that is extended. An increase in margin requirements would force them to buy in short positions, lending further upward impetus to prices. Long speculators do not mind larger margins in rising markets; the shorts do. The thinking of the people who proposed governmental control of margin requirements has long since been intriguing.

We noted that variations in securities prices appear to be greater than variations in commodity prices (Chapter 13). One of the reasons for this is the low speculative margins on commodities. Low margins provide incentive to do the careful analysis that results in finely tuned markets. A five percent price move is a 50 percent return (gain or loss) on a ten percent margin but only 16 percent on a 30 percent margin. A five percent price move on a security is 7.7. percent on capital when "margin" is 65 percent. There is not so great an incentive to fine tune.

The most offensive thing about the margin proposal and proposals that grant government officials power to issue cease and desist orders when they judge price aberrations are incipient is that they would supplant the wisdom of the market with the judgment of the officials and convey the power to manipulate prices. They would permit an official to compel traders to comply with his notions of what price behavior should be. They presuppose that the official could recognize incipient cases of price distortion. This goes back to the difficulty of anticipating price changes. Seemingly erroneous courses of prices often, if not usually, turn out to be quite correct when we gain the advantage of hindsight. The wisdom of the market is greater than that of government officials; this is a basic tenet of a competitive system. Were authority to control margin granted to government, it would be for the purpose of enabling government to cause prices to be something other than they would have been; for the purpose of manipulation. This is the antithesis of competition.

Manipulation

Historic Corners. The question of manipulation is both old and complicated. In Chapter 4 we referred to the endless allegations of corners and manipulations that occurred throughout the first half century of futures trading. Because these were so important in generating and shaping legislation, they deserve a further look. The detail of the activities of the giants of the era, the record of the other activities in the markets, and, most importantly, the commercial circumstances relating to cash commodity values were never chronicled. The records that exist have to do with who was long and who was short and who made and who lost and contain little of cash supply, demand, and price. More is known of the "Three Big Corners" of the era, Hutchinson, Leiter, and Patten that occurred in 1888, 1898, and 1909.[1] In May of 1888, the Hutchinson year, the government crop report forecast a shortage of wheat and the price rose moderately. Hutchinson started buying September futures in August and was estimated to be long 5 million bushels. There was serious frost damage reported; the price rose sharply. In late August, European prices rose because of European crop shortages. Hutchinson received and paid for large quantities of wheat in September and started buying December wheat. The price rose to $1.00 on September 22. Hutchinson sold one million bushels without checking the price advance. It became clear that the Northwest had suffered a major crop disaster. The price rose to $1.28 on September 27, $1.50 on September 28, and $2.00 on September 29. December wheat was $1.04 on October 1 and rose to $1.08 on a further reduction in the crop estimate. The market turned dull and variations were narrow for the balance of the year. Hutchinson was again very active in 1890 but with no appreciable fireworks. The stocks of wheat at Chicago reached the comparatively low level of 3.6 million on September 1, 1888. The cash price of wheat rose from about $.80 in the spring to $.94 in late May, declined to $.85 in August, was $.92 September 1, $.91 on September 15, $.96 on September 22, $1.45 to $2.00 September 29, $1.14 on October 6 and $1.15 on October 27.

Hutchinson apparently foresaw a shortage of wheat developing and profited from the rise from $.80 to the $1.00 level. He saw the relatively small stocks in Chicago and acquired them by both cash purchases and taking delivery. The shorts apparently did not discover the identity of the ownership until too late in September to buy elsewhere to fill contracts. Hutchinson controlled the limited stock of wheat in Chicago for long enough to extract a monopoly revenue of something up to $1.00 per bushel from the shorts. He, by no means, controlled a significant proportion of the total wheat in the U.S. The price of wheat at Chicago was clearly distorted for a few days. Some giants played a game and one of them won. Neither farmer nor consumer prices were significantly affected nor the wheat and flour industries disturbed.

The Leiter corner occurred in 1897–98. Joseph Leiter, a young man, came out from the East, apparently backed with his father's money, and started buying wheat futures. He accumulated a large long line through the early spring. The cash wheat price was $.81 in January and drifted down to $.69 by early July.

[1] See Boyle, James Ernest, "Speculation and The Chicago Board of Trade," Macmillan Co., N.Y., 1920.

There were rumors of a corner in July and the price rose to $.79 on July 26. Deliveries were made and these were taken by Leiter and shipped to Europe. The European crop was short. The price continued to rise and reached $1.07 at the end of August. The rise was credited to the short European and Indian crops. Stocks of wheat in Chicago declined from 10 million bushels in late April to 1.7 million at the end of August. The price declined moderately in October and November and attention switched to December when the climax was expected. Leiter was long a lot more wheat futures than there was cash wheat in Chicago.

The main short was Philip Armour of the Armour Elevator Company and Armour & Co., the meat packers. He had been a dominant factor in both cash and futures trade at Chicago for years and was immensely wealthy and successful. He had been in most of the futures contests of the preceding decade. Finding himself caught short without deliverable stocks, he started putting wheat in deliverable positions. Some of his efforts were heroic, including running tugs continuously and using dynamite to keep the frozen waterways open from Duluth. Stocks of wheat at Chicago increased from 1.7 million at the end of August to 9.7 million at the end of December. Armour filled all of his contracts and the price of spring wheat fell to $.90 at the end of December.

Wheat continued to arrive at Chicago throughout the first half of 1898. Leiter held the operation together until June 10 with wheat prices rising from $.90 in January to $1.83 in May. The government crop report on June 10 forecast a record crop and the price collapsed to $.80 to $.87 on June 17. Leiter also collapsed, lost several million dollars, failed to settle in full, and was indefinitely suspended from the Board.

Leiter moved into a basically strong wheat market and made money. It appears that he tried to create and take advantage of a technically short deliverable supply at Chicago late in the year and was defeated by an astute and resourceful merchant. How much Leiter lost moving wheat out of Chicago and how much Armour lost moving wheat into deliverable positions is not known. Perhaps the movement at Chicago was forced out of line by the long positions so that Leiter and his followers had to not only "corner" the deliverable supply at Chicago but absorb all of the wheat west of Chicago. They could not do this and the effort failed. 1897–98 was a year of real shortage and price strength. If the price was distorted it was only during May, 1898. But stocks at Chicago declined from over 10 million bushels in January to less than 400 thousand ahead of the new crop harvest. Perhaps wheat at Chicago was really worth more than $1.50 in late May and would have sold that high had there not been a contest in futures.

The Patten corner culminated in May, 1909. Patten accumulated wheat from July, 1907 onward, staying long in a situation of successive short crops and large export demand. The price of cash wheat rose from $.85 to $.90 in July 1908 to $1.44 at the beginning of May, 1909, to $1.50 on May 25. On June 1, the cash price was $1.51½ and ranged upward to $1.55 to $1.60 in the middle of June. It declined to $1.24 when the new crop came in. The top price for May futures was $1.35½ and the trading expired at $1.34. Because the cash price was above the May futures and continued even higher after the May was settled and because prices at other markets were in line with Chicago, the alleged corner could not have existed. Patten was blamed for the rising cost of wheat and he replied that he had kept wheat in America and the high prices were due to fundamental supply-demand forces. The price was not distorted; the seasonal variation would doubtless have been greater without Patten's actions. This was the corner that was not a corner at all.

Such was the fabric from which the original legislation was cut. There were contests among giants. The so-called corners worked when the economic fundamentals favored rising prices and then failed when they did not. There were short-term price distortions that resulted from inadequate supplies in delivery positions. These worked when the shorts were caught unaware and when the longs had enough money to absorb selling. They failed when the longs could not absorb the stocks or some of the longs deserted the operation to avoid absorbing the over-priced deliverable supply.

As time passed, the frequency of the distortions decreased and the number of successes declined. The shorts became more prudent, the merchants became more sophisticated in making delivery preparations, and the would-be manipulators became the target of other speculators who saw distortions as profit opportunities. The rules were gradually changed to allow the shorts greater opportunity to make delivery and to reduce the congestion at the expiration of the delivery month. The problems of extreme power plays had been mainly cured by competitive forces and adjustments in the rules to establish competitive balance by the time the first legislation was passed. The last of the big power plays was the alleged Patten corner. A strong man did an economically sound thing and made money. The shorts, who were fundamentally wrong about the value of wheat cried "damn the evil speculators" and in this climate legislation was passed.

The Modern Era. Section 9 b of the CFTC Act provides "It shall be a felony punishable by a fine of not more than $100,000 or imprisonment of not more than five years, or both, together with the costs of prosecution for any person to manipulate or attempt to manipulate the price of any commodity in interstate commerce, or for future delivery on or subject to the rules of any commodity market, or corner or attempt to corner any such commodity. . . ." At no place in the act or in preceding legislation is there a definition of manipulation. The Congress discussed, in hearings and debate various definitions but deliberately left definition to the courts. Through decisions in a succession of cases, the courts have arrived at a succession of implied definitions. In one of the more recent cases that has been concluded, *Volkart Bros., Inc. v. Freeman,* 31F 2nd and 52

(5th Cir. 1962) the court accepted a definition offered by Arthur B. March, President of the New York Cotton Exchange before a Senate Committee in 1929: "Manipulation is any and every operation or transaction or practice . . . calculated to produce a price distortion of any kind in any market either in itself or in relation to other markets. If a firm is engaged in a manipulation using devices by which the prices of contracts for some one month in some one market may be higher than they would be if only the forces of supply and demand were in operation. . . . Any and every operation, transaction or device, employed to produce these abnormalities of price relationship in the futures market, is manipulation." The most prevalent forms of alleged manipulations that have been tried under the CEA have involved: 1. A dominant or controlling futures position, 2. A dominant or controlling position in deliverable supplies, 3. An artificial price, and 4. Manipulative intent. Most cases have also included elements of false information, concealment of records, concealment of positions, and collusion. In short, manipulation is causing with intent, the price to be something other than it would have been under the "ordinary" forces of supply and demand.

A manipulation may be either a long side or short side operation. In the long manipulation, the operator buys futures in excess of the immediately deliverable supply, accepts the delivery that is made, and exacts an artificially high price from the shorts. The price at the delivery market is forced abnormally high in relation to other markets or in relation to the price immediately following the liquidation of the outstanding futures contracts. Most of the cases that have reached the courts have involved long side operations.

In the short manipulation the operator puts an inordinate quantity in deliverable position, sells more futures contracts than the quantity of the cash commodity owned and hammers the price down with delivery. The deliveries fall into weak, unsuspecting hands who must not only redeliver but must sell long positions as well, adding to the debacle. Rarely are such accusations made.

Formal charges of manipulation are infrequently brought. The suggestive power of government is very great. In addition, the exchanges are sensitive in the matter of manipulation. A manipulation case is bad publicity and they have quite enough image problems without them.

Manipulation Is Difficult. The manipulation of a futures market is a difficult and hazardous undertaking. In the long side operations, the first problem is the corpse. If the price at the delivery point is distorted the manipulator gets ownership of all of the readily deliverable supply. He may dispose of it as he gets it by shipping it out of the market at a loss. The supplies that he ends up with must be eventually sold. Because the only time at which effective control of the deliverable supply can be gained is at the end of a season, he ends up merchandising old crop supplies into lower new crop markets. If the distortion is large enough to be very profitable the corpse is most likely to be very large.

The shorts are sometimes vindictive enough to pull supplies in for delivery when they could buy their way out of the short futures positions cheaper. The cost of the funeral tends to be at least as great as the profits on futures.

The short side operations run the risk of having the supply taken away. An inordinately depressed futures price is the cheapest source of supply and there are always smart merchants around to take delivery. In addition, speculators can recognize real cash bargins. A bear raid of much magnitude is essentially impossible in markets where large scale, well financed speculators are present.

It Takes Two to Tango. An interesting thing about alleged manipulation is that it is always the winners who are guilty. When a price is apparently distorted upward it is the longs who draw the charges. But futures trading is a zero sum game—for every long there is a short. For every long who stands for delivery when delivery supplies are very small or owned by the longs, there is a short who cannot readily make delivery. Who is responsible for the distortion? In May, 1971 there was a very small quantity of wheat available for delivery in Chicago. Most of it was owned by speculators who had earlier taken delivery. At the outset of trading on the last day, a substantial share of the open interest was held by two speculators. Wheat had been trading quietly with little movement in price except that the May futures had been weak in relation to the July future. On the last day the May price rose 9⅝ cents, slightly less than the limit, when the longs sold. Accusations of manipulation were made against the longs. There was one major short who appeared to be capable of moving wheat into delivery position before the end of May. Instead of taking such steps he elected to pay the price and get out. Leaving aside the question of whether a minor aberration of this sort should be identified as an artificial or manipulated price we pose the question of who was to blame. The longs had held their position for a long period of time and it was widely rumored that there was concentration in the May open interest. The longs simply stood in the pit with their hands in their pockets. It was the shorts who bid the price up at the close. The longs contended that wheat was really worth more and they only got out because they had been urged to see that there was an orderly market. The short imprudently got himself into a position in which he preferred to pay up rather than take the steps required to fill his contracts. Doubtless he was lulled into a sense of security by the expectation that the longs would not stand their ground. Among the reasons for thinking this was the belief that if the longs stayed, they would be accused of manipulation. The longs were pushing the shorts but the shorts were also pushing the longs. The effect of the law in this instance was to say "Go ahead and play the game but don't win."

The court recognized the joint responsibility for price change in *Volkart Bros., Inc. v. Freeman,* 31F. 2nd and 52 (5th Cir. 1962). The case related to a runup in the price of cotton. There were adequate deliverable supplies of cotton but only a small quantity had been certificated for delivery. Enough could have been certificated but the shorts didn't bother. The court found that control of the certificated supply was not effective control of the supply so long as other stocks could have been certificated in time to make delivery.

Let the Market Trade Out. What all of this says is that the original legislation prohibiting manipulation was based on the belief that much greater market abuses existed than was truly the case; that accusations and prosecutions of manipulation under the law have been directed at market events that were of minor general economic significance; that price distortions due to futures trading are extremely difficult to identify because it is not possible to determine what the price would have done under the "ordinary" forces of supply and demand; that there are fewer instances of real distortion than is generally thought; and that responsibility for price distortions must be placed on the losers as well as the winners. None of this should be construed as condoning market performance that results in a futures price that fails to accurately reflect real economic value.

Futures trading is a contact sport played by competitive people who place a high value on winning. A futures market is not a scholarly seminar in which learned men debate what is, and arrive at, an equilibrium price; it is a game in which businessmen compete, with money at hazard, to establish a market price that works. Competition is sometimes a vicious business but it works well.

A distorted futures price is the result of inadequate delivery rules or inadequate speculation or both. In earlier chapters we placed the primary responsibility for price during the delivery month on the people in position to make or take delivery and counseled commission house customers—the speculating public—to stay out of the delivery month unless they are on very firm ground and prepared to accept the consequences of their actions. Market officials should continually examine price behavior, particularly near the expiration of contracts. When aberrations appear to have existed, the rules should be carefully examined for possible weaknesses that may have made the aberration possible.

Exchanges, with the government continually looking over their shoulders, are too sensitive to the contests that sometimes occur near the expiration of contracts. When they note congested situations—those in which there is a large open interest and small deliverable supply or in which a large proportion of the open interest is held by one or a few interests—they sometimes take steps to assure an "orderly" liquidation. Orderly is construed as without much price variation. Their powers of moral suasion are great. Some have rules under which they can direct that trading be for liquidation only or even suspend trading and fix settlement prices. These have been used sparingly but the threat is always present. This process reduces the extent to which the full forces of competition are allowed to work themselves out in price formulation. Any directed settlement reduces the strength of one side or the other and is thus, in itself, a manipulation. The objective in operating a market is to develop situations in which power is equally met with countervailing power. To achieve this markets must be allowed to trade out. Such "leaning" that has been done has tended to come down hard on speculators. In the 50 year effort to curb "speculative excesses" the weight of control has weakened the position of speculators and tended to reduce speculation. This reduces the ability of markets to establish fully competitive prices.

Manipulation is its own best cure. To manipulate a price is to put it where it doesn't belong. The over-priced inventory or the under-priced commitment invariably leads to losses. Space does not permit making the argument but a strong case can be made that most alleged manipulations get started defensively. The long who is thought to finally squeeze the market gets his inventory position started by defending a long position from what he thinks is overzealous delivery with manipulative overtones. It is when he finally gets control and hits back that he gets accused. The cost of carrying the inventory and the cost of burying the corpse costs him more than he gains from the punishment that he metes out to the shorts.

In the actively speculated markets the forces of countervailing power effectively prevent manipulation. It is only in the thin markets that power plays cause minor distortions which are profitable. A speculator of moderate scale commented, "Show me a market that someone has distorted and I will show you a way to make money, both with him and against him." The greater the level of speculation, the less is the amount of hanky-panky. Let them trade out.

Definition of Hedging

Section 4 a of the CFTC Act provides for the fixing of limits on the size of positions that speculators may hold. Section 4 a (3) states "No order issued under paragraph (1) of this section shall apply to transactions or positions which are known to be bona fide hedging transactions or positions as such term shall be defined by the Commission. . . ." Thus the Commission must define hedging in a way that identifies the kinds of transactions that are exempt from speculative limits.

The definition of hedging in the context of the CFTC Act is extraordinarily difficult, if not impossible. It assumes that "hedging" and "speculation" are at least different, if not opposite. They are not. All hedges are more or less speculative and all speculative positions are more or less hedged. There is not a simple solution to the problem of establishing a process for granting exceptions from speculative position and trading limits.

Hedging. Hedging can and is defined in various ways, depending on the purpose. In earlier chapters we defined hedging as: (1) to hedge is to assume a position in futures equal and opposite to an already existing or immediately anticipated cash position, and (2) to hedge is to shift the risks of price level change while retaining the opportunity to speculate in changes in price relationships. For purposes of granting exemptions from speculative limits we should add: To hedge is to use futures contracts in managing risk exposure associated with commodity ownership and commitment and with variable price relationships among commodities and related commodity products to levels consistent with profit maximization and/or profit regularization and with capital preservation and expansion. The first definition is descriptive of a process of risk aversion. The second is descriptive of a process of highly selective risk assumption. The third is descriptive of commercial uses of futures in a broad spectrum of activities in which capital and earnings are subject to risk exposure resulting from variation in commodity prices and price relationships. It opens the door to a long list of legitimate exemptions to speculative limits.

One thing is common to the three definitions: They all imply a reduction in risk exposure from levels that would otherwise exist or the maximization of profits from variations in cash commodity or commodity product prices or price relationships. The test, then, of whether a specific futures activity is a hedge is: Does it reduce risk exposure? Or, does it contribute to an attempt to maximize profits from business activities associated with cash commodities? On the other hand, if an activity in futures contracts is designed to obtain earnings from price or price relationship changes in futures, it is speculation. Or, if it increases risk exposure, it is speculation.

Development of Exemptions. When the law providing for speculative limits was originally passed in 1936, the list of exemptions was quite short and was strictly equal and opposite in the same commodity, plus one year's production of a farmer. By 1968, it was expanded to include product hedging and the accumulation of up to one year's production requirement. In 1975 the list was expanded to include wheat against prospective flour requirements, corn against prospective production of dry milling products, corn against sales of seed and sweet corn, and product futures against raw material positions. With this we were on a middle ground with the door open for a long list of equally valid cases for other exemptions. It would seem that there would be no stopping-point so long as a trader had some cash commodity base for his operations.

In looking at the broad definition of hedging, it was clear that more kinds of futures activities should be added to the exemptions list. It also seemed that some things were included in the list that need not meet the criterion of risk reduction. As it stood, there were opportunities for taking large positions not offset by cash commitments.

Several kinds of futures activities warrant special comment.

Anticipatory Hedging. By this is meant the purchase of futures against expected sales of products or the sale of futures against the expected requirement of raw material. Whether the purchase of futures against anticipated sales of the cash commodity or products from the cash commodity is risk reducing depends upon the relationship of buying and selling prices. When raw material and product prices move up and down togther, purchases without offsetting priced sales add to risk exposure and so are not hedges. But, if product and raw material prices do not move together, anticipatory purchases may be risk minimizing. Flour and wheat prices move together. Thus, wheat purchased in anticipation of eventual flour sales is not risk-reducing. But behavior within an industry is not uniform. Proprietary brands of margarine have quite sticky prices, so that advance purchases of soybean oil to the amount of stickiness of prices are risk-minimizing. When to cover is a speculative decision that cannot be avoided. In this instance, the decision that now is the time to fix raw material cost is speculative, but it is also a hedge. On the other hand, prices of private label brands of margarine relate closely to soybean oil prices. To take forward cover is to speculate rather than hedge.

In the corn wet milling industry there is a saying, "If you are not long, you are short." Corn starch prices are sticky and do not relate closely to corn prices in the short run. A wet miller once calculated his automatic position; the size of the long corn position that he needed to minimize his risk exposure. It was three months corn requirement in a rising corn market and one month in a declining market. How large a position was a hedging one depended on whether the price of corn was going up or down.

The 1975 exemption list appeared to permit the purchase of a full year's raw material requirement. It is doubtful that very many firms avail themselves of the opportunity. For virtually all commodity users it would be the grossest kind of increased risk exposure. For example, no meat packer in his right mind would buy enough cattle futures to cover a year's kill. The anticipatory hedging exemption appears to include a lot of room for speculation.

Partial Hedging. Partial hedging is the use of futures to cover part of an existing cash position. A better term is selective hedging. One hedges when and to the extent that he elects not to speculate. Selective hedging is also selective speculation.

Partial hedging is a legitimate risk management practice. In some circumstances, to be partially hedged results in less risk exposure than being fully hedged. It also enables the hedger to reach a balancing point between risk avoidance and profit maximization.

A farmer is a good example in making the case for partial hedging. One construction of his least risk program is to space sales at frequent intervals across the whole time spectrum of a crop season. If he does this, he takes the average price for the season. At the other extreme, he may attempt to maximize his return by attempting to select the single best time (highest price) to sell. By the same construction this is his highest risk policy. He usually makes a compromise. If he is short futures, it is usually in an amount less than his total production.

Partial hedgers can reasonably change the size of their futures positions. If the price offered by futures is a highly profitable one and there appears to be substantial risk of adverse price change, he may elect to be fully hedged. But, if the price changes substantially so that it is unprofitable and there is little risk of further adversity, he may elect to remove all or part of his hedges. Trading-in-and-out is a legitimate activity and should be permitted.

There are no rules that require hedging. A firm can speculate with cash commodity inventories or obligations to whatever extent that it elects. A soybean processor may carry a five year inventory of crush if he wants to and can arrange the financing. But this election of hedging or not is fraught with problems in futures market regulation. Suppose that a soybean processor accumulates an inventory of six months crush of soybeans. He thinks prices are low so he doesn't hedge. Prices rise to what he judges to be dangerous levels so he hedges. They decline, so he unhedges, etc. If he has a large enough commercial base, as many processors and exporters do, he can trade in and out of futures market in large amounts at will. This activity can conceivably be disruptive of prices. It would appear that the only way to prevent such disruptive activity with position and trading limits would be to require that firms that are granted exemptions follow policies of being fully hedged or hedged to some fixed proportion of risk exposure. This is hardly an acceptable suggestion, but regulations regarding exemption from limits should recognize and cope with problems associated with partial or selective hedging.

Cross Hedging. The concept of cross hedging was not brought into the exemptions list in 1975. It should be. To cross hedge is to assume a position in futures opposite to an existing cash position in a different but price related commodity. This may be done because there is no futures market in the commodity on which market risks are outstanding or because existing futures markets are not sufficiently liquid, or because the use of futures in a different commodity is judged to be a better hedge than one in the same commodity.

In the matter of using futures in a different commodity, a good example is hedging soybean meal inventories by selling soybean and buying soybean oil futures. Price relationships are sometimes such that a soybean oil hedge involves less risk or greater profit opportunity than a direct meal hedge. It is equal and opposite and risk-reducing, hence, a hedge.

There are no futures markets for many commodities. When a wheat miller buys wheat and books flour at firm prices, he is long millfeeds. Millfeeds prices fluctuate and there is not a futures market. Prices fluctuate in relation to other feed prices such as corn, oats, and soybean meal and risks can be hedged. By the same token, cottonseed oil can be reasonably hedged in soybean oil futures, corn gluten feed in a combination of corn and soybean meal futures, and pork inventories in live hog futures.

The problem in the matter of cross hedging exemption from speculative limits is how far afield the hedger may be allowed to go. Some degree of co-variation of prices is essential for a cross hedge to be legitimate. How close the relationship need be is related to the degree of risk. When prices of the commodity to be hedged are fairly stable, the co-variation needs to be fairly close else the operation may be risk-increasing rather than risk-reducing. But when prices are highly volatile and risks of adverse price changes are great, co-variation can be very much less—any old port in a storm.

Legitimate cross hedges go far afield. Bakery wastes are collected and processed into animal feeds. They are bought on long term contracts—up to several years—at firm prices. The product is priced date-of-shipment on the basis of the current price of corn. The sale of corn futures is a nearly precise hedge. The hedging of bakery wastes in corn futures should be exempt from speculative limits.

Every position is a hedge against something. A long position in a commodity future is opposite a long position in money just as the ownership of real estate is a hedge against a decrease in the value of money. And a short position in commodity futures is a hedge against an increase in the value of money. Some commodities, such as gold, are widely judged to be storehouses of value. If a holder of an inventory of money is apprehensive about inflation, he can trade it for gold in an attempt to preserve its value in real terms. But, he may judge that gold has been already bid up to levels that make it a poor hedge for money; but that wheat is very cheap relative to gold. He thus hedges money in wheat.

Bonds can be hedged in silver spreads. Bond prices go down as interest rates go up, and vice versa. Silver spreads widen as interest rates increase. Thus, if one is long bonds and fears an increase in interest rates, he can buy distant and sell less distant silver futures as a hedge against his bond position. The gain from the silver spread should offset his bond loss if interest rates increase, and the gain in bonds offset his silver spread loss if interest rates decrease.

The point of all this is that cross hedges are a bona fide hedging use of futures; but it is difficult to draw a line between what-is and what-is-not a cross hedge, and it appears virtually impossible to specifically list all exemptible cross hedges.

Raw Material and Product Spreads. The soybean complex is unique in that there are active futures markets in a raw material and its products, and that raw material and product prices are closely related. Processors can sell cash products against cash soybean inventories, sell product futures against cash soybean inventories, sell cash products forward against soybean futures positions, and sell product futures against soybean futures positions. Soybean processors are in the business of selling the service of processing soybeans into meal and oil. They do this at a margin described by the difference between soybean and product prices. Margins are variable and only rarely are they as wide as the cost of processing. These are highly developed and highly speculated markets. The objective of the processor is to sell his services at as wide an average margin as possible. The industry has had a history of operating below cost profitably. They do this with trading skills. It is skill in the timing of putting on and taking off of crush and by skill in basis—cash to futures—operations. The whole operation is a remarkable tribute to the efficiencies forced by a fully competitive pricing system. Fully competitive is essentially synonymus with highly speculative.

If soybean processors are to continue to operate at such remarkable efficiency, they must be allowed to have a full range of opportunities to use their skills.

This should include not only the putting on of crush by buying soybeans and selling products, but the taking off of crush by selling soybeans and buying products. In their operations, processors are opposed by speculators who have long since learned to trade in processing margins.

The cattle feeding complex is as complete as soybean processing with futures markets in feeder cattle, feedstuffs, and fat cattle. However, trading is less highly developed and used, and price relationships are not as closely related. But it is developing.

Approaching these two are the hog and broiler production activities in which there are futures markets in feeds and finished products. These markets, too, are developing and expanding as producers make increased use of them.

The use of futures on both sides of these several processing activities are risk-reduction operations, hence, bona fide hedging. They should certainly be exempt from speculative position limits. It is to be hoped in the interest of productive efficiency that these kinds of fore and aft futures operations with full speculative participation can be extended to many more parts of the economic system. The only reasonable restrictions would be related to production capacity.

Toward a Solution. From this, three things stand out, (1) to qualify as a hedge a position, or set of positions, should be risk-reducing, (2) in anticipatory hedging and partial or selective hedging there are opportunities for abusive practices if large positions do, indeed, enable abuses, and (3) it appears to be virtually impossible to specifically enumerate the kinds of positions that exemptions from speculative limits will be automatically granted. There will be risk-reducing activities left out and there will be included room for the taking of positions that are risk-increasing rather than risk-reducing or that permit the trading in and out of markets on a large scale.

A reasonable solution to the problem is twofold. First, to exempt strictly equal and opposite cash-to-futures offsets in the same commodity, with the promise that all cash transactions be kept essentially fully hedged. Second, to broadly define hedging in the context of risk-reduction and require that firms seeking exemption apply for it. The application should include justification in terms of the general definition, a statement of policy, a description of proposed operational practices and proposed position sizes. Each application would then be judged on its merit and the allowable practices and positions described. It would be necessary to establish a system of auditing to assure compliance.

Position Limits

The rather long foregoing discussion of a hedging definition is by way of preface for advancing the notion that speculative position limits should be eliminated. This is not to say that there should not be some system of monitoring and, in some instances, restricting position size to avoid market dominance.

Perhaps there should be, but the distinction between hedger and speculator should be eliminated.

Section 4a of the CFTC Act states: "Excessive speculation . . . causing sudden or unreasonable fluctuations or unwarranted changes in price is an undue and unnecessary burden on interstate commerce. . . . For the purpose of diminishing, eliminating, or preventing such burdens, the Commission shall, from time to time . . . proclaim and fix such limits on the amount of trading which may be done or positions which may be held. . . ."

In 1938 speculative position limits of two million bushels of grain (wheat, corn, oats, barley, flaxseed, rye) either long or short, were fixed. In June, 1971 these limits were increased to three million bushels of corn and soybean futures.

Position limits on cotton were fixed at 30,000 bales in 1940. The same position limits as grain were fixed for soybeans in 1951. Maximum positions of 150 carlots of eggs (with lesser positions for certain delivery months) were fixed in 1951. Potato limits of 150 carlots were added in 1964. In 1953, position limits of 3.6 million pounds of cottonseed oil, 3.0 million pounds of soybean oil, and 1.6 million pounds of lard were fixed. However, following vigorous opposition by market interests, this order was suspended and, finally, revoked in 1968.

Limits on speculative positions have met with a high degree of trade acceptance and only recently has the size of some of the limits begun to be called into question. The general notion is that no one person should be allowed to have such a position or trade in such volume that he could push the price around with his sheer bulk.

Basis for Limits. In looking at the question of position limits it is again necessary to go back to the beginning. The legislative history of the CEA of 1936 establishes three studies made in the 1920's as the basis for the law and the amounts of 2 million bushels of the grains. These were Senate Document No. 135, "Fluctuations in Wheat Futures," USDA Bulletin 1479, "Speculative Transactions in the 1926 May Wheat Future," and USDA Technical Bulletin No. 79, "Major Transactions in the 1926 December Wheat Future." The last of these was the most influential. These three reports taken together covered a period of two years, the first extending from January 2 to April 18, 1925; the second from April 19, 1925, to May 29, 1926, and the third from June 1 to December 31, 1926. The results of the third study were said to confirm and strengthen the earlier conclusions. A summarization of the summary follows.

In the third study three groups of traders were analyzed. The first group consisted of the 42 largest speculators operating on the Chicago Board of Trade. They comprised all of the speculators whose market position reached 500,000 bushels or over in any one future at any time during the period.

The second group consisted of the customers of 15 clearing firms. The business of these 15 judged to be representative of the small and medium sized speculative traders. The customers of these firms carried an average of 39 percent of the total open contracts on the long side of the market and 30 percent of the total of all contracts open on the short side.

The third group included all of the hedging accounts on the Chicago Board of Trade which at any time during the period reached a position of 500,000 bushels or more. There were 22 of these accounts representing milling companies, elevator companies, and grain shippers.

The trading operations of each of the three groups were compared with the price for the 1926 December wheat future and for all futures combined. This consisted of comparing the combined net position of each group at the close of the market each day with the closing price of the appropriate future. This comparison revealed a pronounced direct relationship between the trading of the group of large speculators and the price. This relationship when measured statistically showed a direct correlation of +0.71.

The second group, consisting of the small trader customers, when compared with price revealed an equally striking relationship, but inverse in character, the correlation coefficient being −0.83. On days on which the price advanced, this group sold more than it brought; and on days on which the price declined, it bought more than it sold. The group of 22 hedging accounts also showed an inverse relationship, although not as pronounced as the small traders.

Further analysis of the trading of the 42 large speculators was made. It was found that five of the 42 each accumulated a long or short position in the market of over 2,000,000 bushels at some time during the period June 1 to December 31, 1926. One of the five reached a maximum position of over 12,000,000 bushels short and another a position of over 10,000,000 short. It was further found that the combined trading of these 5 largest speculators accounted almost entirely for changes in the position of the 42, the transactions of the 5 being directly related to price to the extent of a correlation of +0.72. The individuals comprising the remaining 37 of this group traded at irregular intervals, but as a class their trading showed no significant relation to price movements.

By uniting the trading of these five leading speculators, a single figure representing the combined net trade for the group of five was obtained for each day. There were, in all, 94 days of a total of 176 on which this group traded a net amount of 500,000 bushels or more. On 64 of these 94 days, or 68 percent, the price moved in the same directions as the net trade of the group. The net trading of the five amounted to 1,000,000 bushels or more on 56 days; on 44 of these days, or 79 percent, the price moved in the same direction as the net trades. There were 28 days on which the net amount traded was 2,000,000 bushels or over and on 24 of these days, or 86 percent, the price moved in the same direction as the net trade. There were five days on which trades exceeded 5,000,000 bushels and in each case the futures price moved in the same direction as the net trade.

From these findings it was concluded that without the accumulation of long or short lines of millions of bushels by a very few leading speculators, the major swings in price would not have been so large. And so originated the 2,000,000 bushel limit (raised to 3,000,000 bushels for corn and soybeans in 1971).

These were interesting pieces of pioneering work that contributed a great deal to the knowledge about how various groups of traders behaved. Unfortunately, they were not critically reviewed and the conclusion that large scale traders could and did cause excessive and unwanted variations in prices, was held valid. A closer look at the evidence does not completely back up the conclusions reached above. For example, during the period May through December of 1926, the price of the nearby wheat futures followed an erratic pattern, centering on $1.38 per bushel. It declined from $1.43 in early May to $1.34 the third week of May, then rose to $1.42 the second week of June, but then declined to $1.32 on the first of July. It rose to its season's high on July 19, declined to $1.33 September 4, rose to $1.45 October 2 and traded between $1.38 and $1.42 for the balance of the season. The range during the period was almost exactly 10 percent of the median value. There were frequent reversals in direction. The period from pre-harvest on was one in which the size of the crop was uncertain and flour book-ings were heavy and erratic. We would question whether there were excessive and unwarranted changes in prices. Would not a reasonable man judge the speculative performance of the market as respectable?

The aggregate positions of the 5 leading speculators were net short during nearly all of the period studied. They were net short about 10 million bushels during May, got even during June, went net long up to 8 million bushels during the peak of the July harvest, gradually switched to a net short position of nearly 24 million bushels the first week of September, gradually liquidated this net short position until they were net long on October 20. They went short again immediately and were net short 8 to 16 million during November and December. They were short an average of about 8 million bushels from May to December. They were short when the price rose and they were short when it went down. It appears that, on balance they about broke even. They were not making money coming and going as the conclusions of the study imply.

The correlation values are impressive but they relate only to the relationship of direction of change in price and change in net position. No analysis of the relationship of *size of change* in price to *size of change* in net positions was made. Inspection of the data suggests that the relationship was not close. There were days of substantial change in price on which there was little change in net position of the large traders and vice versa. Did a major change in net position sometimes cause a change in price but fail to cause a change in price at others? Or did both price and speculators respond to the same outside forces? The question was not examined.

The large scale speculators accommodated the market. There were both long and short hedges in the market throughout the period. The hedgers were net about even during May and June. There was fairly large hedge buying during early July so that the hedgers became net long. This was at the time that the price rose to its seasonal high. Hedgers were net short about two million bushels at the end of July. The amount of long hedges increased and the short hedges decreased during August so that the hedgers were net long 12 million bushels in early September. This net long position gradually decreased to about 4 million bushels at the end of the year.

The commission house customers—the speculating public—maintained net long positions throughout most of the period. They were about even at mid July and built up a net long position of 15 million bushels in early September. They liquidated down to a net long position of 5 million in late October. They maintained a net long position of 14 million for the balance of the period.

The maximum net long position of hedgers and one of the larger net long positions of the public coincided with the maximum net short position of the five leading speculators in early September. The hedgers were net long because flour bookings and other hedge purchases exceeded sales by farmers. The large scale speculators offset the positions of hedgers and, in part the speculating public. They supplied the market with the wheat it wanted and could not get from farmers.

What would have been the price pattern of wheat had the large scale speculators not been in the market? The price would probably have been higher during July and August when millers and small scale speculators were buying and lower later as the price fell back to its equilibrium. Did the large traders cause excessive price variations or did they prevent excessive price variation? A definitive answer cannot be made at this late date but we should note that a 10 percent variation about the median is not a swinging market.

From all of this we must conclude that the legislation authorizing position limits and the 2,000,000 bushel limits that lasted all of those years was on shaky ground. The most recent increase for corn and soybeans may be partial recognition of this view.

The Case for Review. Two things suggest that the matter of volume of trading and position limits should be reviewed. First, they are very old. It seems unlikely that what was appropriate for the wheat markets of the 1920's is also appropriate for the broader spectrum of commodity markets of the 1970's. (The position limit for wheat has since been raised to 3,000,000 bushels.)

Second, the studies that led to the imposition of limits were limited to actions in futures markets, failing completely to take into account the commercial factors relating to cash commodities that influence prices and price patterns. As we have said repeatedly, futures markets are a part of the real commercial world of the commodities traded. The study of futures markets should not be conducted in a vacuum.

The Case for Large Speculators. A strong case can be made that large scale speculators are not the evil musclemen they were described as a half century ago but, instead, are an asset to the market and should be encouraged.

Large scale operators carefully avoid influencing prices. They stay out of situations in which they are apt to hold a large share of the open contracts, particularly in an expiring future. A speculator with a large share of the open interest is his own worst enemy. He loses his liquidity and cannot change positions on the basis of changed market factors but must wait until the holders of the other side of the contracts change their minds and let him loose. He is their man rather than his own. The smart speculator maintains his liquidity unless he decides that he can gain control of and influence the equilibrium price of the total of a cash commodity. This reluctance to try to dominate a market should not be attributed to a higher motive of accurate price establishment or to business morality but, rather, to a humility born of the lessons learned while becoming a large scale speculator.

Large scale speculators relieve hedging pressure during periods of peak supplies. Invariably, they are found in net long positions when short hedges, reflecting cash sales, are large.

Large scale speculators contribute to the fine tuning of the price structure. In large measure, hedgers are nulls in the market, taking positions when they make purchases or sales. The speculating public appears to have a long side bias and to trade with less sophistication than the large traders. Large traders are more pliable in their position directions and sizes, are better informed, and respond quicker to changed market circumstances. Almost by definition, the large speculators are the smartest traders; they are professionals because they are good, not good because they are professionals.

The markets are in need of more and better skilled speculation. It is indeed strange that the expression of their skills should be arbitrarily cut off at levels established many years ago.

Large speculators are the strongest defense that markets can have against the predatory behavior of large hedgers. As we have seen, it is the large scale speculators who stand ready to take delivery, keeping hedgers from forcing wider carrying charges, and holding the price of storage at its market value. Again, as we have seen they arbitrage between raw materials and product values, helping to keep processing margins competitive.

Some of the commercial interests in commodity markets are large—large merchandising and warehouse firms, processors, exporters, etc. They can, if they elect, take very large positions in cash markets and hedge in and out of futures markets at will. Cash interests are the forces that have the muscle required to force futures markets out of line. This is not to suggest that they do but rather to suggest that the temptation would be greatly reduced if they knew there were no limits on the countervailing power permitted speculators.

Toward a Solution. Should it be found desirable to fix and maintain position and trading limits to avoid market dominance by one or a few firms or individuals it should be recognized that the matter is more complex than casting certain bushelages or tonnages in stone and leaving them for all time as has been the case in the past. The objective of limits should be to prevent the exercise of market power to the extent of distorting price. Exercise of market power is the essence of the definition of manipulation which is in violation of the law and the rules of all exchanges. The concept of limits is redundant and at most they should be considered only a tool to assist in the prevention of price artificiality. There are other tools: prosecution and punishment of manipulation and cease and desist injunctive power in congested situations.

If position limits are to be employed they should apply equally to all classes of traders, commercials and speculators alike. As we have repeatedly noted, the possibilities of distorting a price are greatly enhanced by the existence of an associated cash position. The history of the development of regulation shows an anti-speculation bias that is not justified in the light of the way that markets really work. Much of this bias was eliminated from the CFTC Act of 1974. This philosophy should be implemented by equal treatment of commercials and speculators.

If position limits are to be employed they should be flexible and kept appropriate to the circumstance at hand. A position limit appropriate to the last delivery month of a crop year is quite different than one appropriate to the far out months covering the whole of a crop year. For example, a 10 million bushel position in August soybeans in a year of a small carry-over might be dominating but by no stretch of the imagination could it be considered dominant if held in November soybeans in a year of a 1,500 million bushel production. A position of a given size is much more of a factor on the last trading day of the delivery month than on the first delivery day as, in turn, is the same position more significant on the first delivery day than two or six months before first delivery.

What all of this says is that there is no simple solution to the problem of fixing position limits save by fixing them at infinity. To fix and administer positions limits is a complex matter and would require great effort.

Delivery Points

If the CFTC finds that the delivery terms for a commodity are inadequate to prevent or diminish price manipulation, market congestion, or abnormal movement, it is empowered to change delivery terms, particularly by designating additional delivery points. This is a power of the Commission that will have to be exercised with great care for there is in it a danger of the destruction of markets. As we have seen in earlier chapters futures markets are fragile things; many are started and fail, many more fail to grow to viable size, and even the best are small in comparison to the jobs that need to be done.

One of the most difficult tasks in starting and operating a futures market is establishing the terms for delivery. A futures contract is a temporary substitute for an eventual cash transaction. In markets that work, delivery is rarely made and taken; futures contracts are entered into for reasons other than exchange of title. Markets where there is a large amount of delivery fail and go out of existence because extensive delivery is an indication of an out of balance contract, one that favors either the longs or the shorts. When a contract is out of balance the disadvantaged side ceases trading and the contract disappears.

The objective in writing a futures contract is to obtain such even balance that only an amount to test the price—to keep it honest—is delivered; to make the contract so readily deliverable and receivable that there is no incentive to make or take delivery. The terms of the contract must be precisely representative of the commercial trading practices of the commodity. When contracts are written their terms are as closely descriptive of existing practices as a committee of knowledgeable people can make them. The commercial circumstances surrounding a commodity change as the production, marketing, processing, and consumption change. The delivery terms appropriate at one time are not appropriate at another so that changes, sometimes frequent ones, are necessary.

As we noted in Chapter 3 there are several terms of futures contracts: commodity, amounts, price, quality, place of delivery, time of delivery, terms of payment, and provision for default. All of these except price are standardized. The terms are simple to write except quality and place of delivery. Both have been the source of continuous problems for exchanges but quality issues have remained out of the public sector.

For the first century of futures trading deliveries were almost entirely at the central markets where the futures markets are located. Nearly all trade was in raw agricultural commodities and a large proportion of each moved to central markets for storage and processing and then into distributive channels. The amounts that flowed naturally to and stored at central markets were large enough to be fully representative of value and to prevent congestion in delivery months. Following World War II the marketing system was decentralized as the results of numerous changes in the commerce of commodities. A high proportion of wheat now moves from areas of production to export points. Livestock slaughter moved from central markets as Chicago to the interior. Trading in new commodities developed and many of these have never moved through central markets. The soybean processing industry developed in the interior near points of production and oil and meal moved from the dispersed processing plants to equally dispersed points for further processing. It was thus necessary to designate multiple delivery points at interior locations. The questions continually at issue are not single versus multiple delivery points but one of how many points at what locations.

Commodity exchanges are great democratic institutions and they make changes slowly. It is a clumsy matter to change delivery terms. It takes a lot of committee work and consultation with all affected parties. Contracts for which trading has started must be continued with the old terms until they expire. It either takes a year to implement a change or there is overlapping so that there is trading in, say, "Old March Wheat" and "New March Wheat." Exchanges have had a record of changing slowly, sometimes too late. Trading in rye futures expired. One reason doubtless was the failure to recognize that Chicago was no longer a viable delivery point. Trading in oats futures nearly stopped before Minneapolis was made an alternate delivery point.

Delivery on futures contracts is a sampling of value process. The objective is to get a representative sample. There must be a sufficient amount of the commodity move to and through the delivery points that no one can control and distort the price. The amount must be large enough that the price is representative of the value of the commodity generally so that the relationship with prices at other points of commerce are rational. These are minimum requirements and the minimums should be maximums. The delivery process must be kept as simple as possible. Speculators will not participate in markets in which delivery is complex and great merchandising skill is required to know what market value is and to dispose of the commodity received on delivery.

Proliferation of delivery points results in distortion of price relationships over space. Delivery will be made at the point of lowest value and cash prices at other points are above this by commercial value differences. Delivery goes to the least common denominator. As we noted in Chapter 9, the identity of the least common denominator is continually changing. When delivery hops from point to point cash to futures price differences at all other locations become erratic. This makes hedging difficult if not impossible. There is not only danger of losing the speculators but of losing the hedgers as well. Primary producers and interior merchants have a tendency to want delivery points close to their operations so they can make delivery when they cannot readily merchandise the commodity. It is a simplistic notion that has appeal—delivery at the entry point to the marketing system. But speculators are not merchants and to force them to become merchants is impossible; they will simply go away.

An incident in the corn market in July, 1973 was of major influence in getting attention focused on the delivery point question and inclusion of the delivery point legislation in the law. Exports of all grains were extremely large that summer. Movement of wheat to the Gulf tied up rail cars so that movement of corn among interior points and to the Gulf for export was difficult and limited. Where there was transportation to move it, corn was valuable and where there was not transportation the price was unusually low in relation to other markets. In early July the cash price at interior Iowa points was unusually low relative to Chicago, the interior Illinois points price was above Chicago rather than a usual 10 cent discount and the Gulf price was much higher than usual in relation to

Chicago. The cash price at Chicago was above the futures. It was an abnormal spatial price structure caused by a huge export movement and limited transportation. The price of July futures rose from $2.33 on July 12 to $2.49½ on the 17th, $2.59½ bid on July 19. Trading limits were removed and the price spiked up to close at $3.70 to $3.90 on July 20 which was the last day. It appears that the primary shorts were out of position hedgers and the primary longs were exporters who were counting on corn from Chicago for Great Lakes shipment. Until the last day of trading the July futures price lagged the cash prices at Chicago, interior Illinois and Indiana, southeastern U.S., and Gulf prices. Cash prices continued strong and relationships distorted following the expiration of the July futures.

The hedgers not only went into the delivery month without foreseeable means of making delivery but they stayed until the end. The abnormality was basically caused by transportation problems rather than inadequacy of delivery points. Had interior Iowa and Minnesota points been deliverable the futures price would have gone to the Iowa level and all of the other points would have gone to huge premiums over the future. The spatial disequilibrium would not have been corrected. That which would have been a good deal for some hedgers would have created a very difficult situation for others. Most importantly, the predicability of basis would have been reduced, hence the usability of the market by hedgers.

What all of this says is that the designation of delivery points is a delicate matter that should be approached carefully by knowledgeable people. Markets can be destroyed by the wrong delivery terms.

Dual Trading

The Commission must determine whether trading by floor brokers and futures commission merchants for their own account and for their customers will be permitted. The more delicate and urgent of the two is trading by floor brokers. There is an almost automatic presumption of conflict of interest. The question was discussed in Chapter 3 in describing the activities of the various pit traders. A marked tendency to specialize was noted. In high volume markets trading tends to hamper the operations of specialized brokers and brokerage gets in the way of good trading.

The rules of the big exchanges provide that customer orders get preference and good brokerage practice helps enforce the rules. The same kinds of rules should and likely will be required of other exchanges.

At a minimum, one kind of dual trade must and will be permitted. This has to do with an error account. Brokers do make mistakes in both price and number of contracts and, in high volume pits, the error accounts are sometimes large. It is necessary that brokers be held responsible for their mistakes.

Attention has been focused on the possibilities of brokers exploiting their knowledge of orders and gaining from offsetting customer orders at prices profitable to brokers. This is the wrong focus. Attention should be addressed to the effect of dual trading on the quality of fills of customer orders. Whether dual trading results in better or worse execution of outside customer orders than would exist were it prohibited is the germane question.

Central to the question of quality of fills is liquidity. In low volume markets (which includes a majority of markets) the amount of brokerage is insufficient to attract enough high quality brokers. Similarly, the volume of trading is insufficient to attract scalpers and pit traders whose presence is essential to liquidity. It is only dual trading with earnings from both sources that attracts members to many markets. If dual trading is prohibited in low volume markets there will be a reduction in liquidity, outside traders may cease trading, and trade dwindle to nothing. When there is a low level of liquidity outside customers must either wait a long time for fills at the risk of missing opportunities or make price concessions to get orders filled. To prosper, a market must be liquid.

There is doubtless some cheating that goes on in some, if not most, pits. How extensive it is is unknown as is its effect on the quality of fills. The Comptroller General[1] identified some trades that appeared to be in violation of the rules. The number was not large. Most of the violations involved the broker taking the other side of customer trades. In no instance was a resulting profit to the broker positively identified. What was the effect on the customer price? Did the selling customer receive a lower price than the broker would have gotten by trading with someone else? Or did he receive a higher price than he would have gotten had the broker sold to someone else? It is possible that brokers cheat in the interests of improving customer fills more often than in the interests of wrongful gain. A broker's success rests in his reputation for obtaining good fills. Also, they are ethical men who are attuned to the best interests of their customers. It is possible that rules for low volume markets should be changed to permit the offset of customer orders by brokers!

Outside customers have protection from mistreatment by brokers. First, the rules of most exchanges give precedence to customer orders; they must go ahead of any trades for the broker's own account. This is policed, not only by the exchanges, but by other pit traders. A violation that is advantageous to the violator is disadvantageous to at least one other trader. They not only complain to exchange officials but they can and do retaliate. There are numerous and subtle ways that this can be accomplished.

Second, many commission houses employ floor managers whose job it is to see that customer orders are filled at the best possible prices. They are quick to

---

[1] Comptroller General of the United States, *Improvements Needed in Regulation of Commodity Futures Trading*, June 24, 1975. See especially pages 23-26.

question doubtful fills and they have powerful influence on the success of brokers in the way that they distribute orders.

Finally, the customer always has the opportunity of placing limited orders. He need not put himself at the mercy of a broker but may trade only at his price or not trade.

Issues: Protection of the Public

There is another set of issues that are raised by new amendments that relate to the protection of the public. The 1974 Act has a flavor of fostering the growth and development of markets and of recognition that the public, speculators in particular, is essential to the prosperity of markets. Several provisions concern the behavior of the people who are in contact with traders—Commission Futures Merchants, Registered Representatives, Pool Operators, and Commodity Advisors.

Registration of Registered Representatives. Under the old law there was provision for registration and examination for fitness of futures commission merchants and floor brokers. This was extended to include persons handling customers' accounts. All of these will be registered so that the employment history of individuals can be traced. The industry has been troubled in the past by a few people who have a record of hard selling, churning accounts, and moving on. Identification is made easier.

In due course the Commission will have to face the question of fitness. Several questions are readily apparent: What examinations should be passed? What educational background qualifies? What is a necessary experience record? Should there be financial requirements? Should evaluation of performance be a part of fitness? Decisions by the Commission will have an impact on the growth and development of the industry.

Pool Operators and Commodity Advisors. During the early 1970s there was a substantial increase in commodity trading pools and the selling of trading advice, usually based on computerized trend following systems. This growth raised questions about the desirability of its impact on prices and about the appropriateness of selling such operations to the public. Pool operators and advisors are required to be registered with the Commission but no guidelines regarding their behavior are included in the Act. Questions of fitness for registration will doubtless arise.

One set of questions relates to market impact. The extent of system trading is not known and its impact has not been studied. Careful study would seem to be appropriate before regulation is undertaken.

A second set relates to the extent that the government should undertake to protect the public from its own gullibility and greed. Should there be performance standards? Advertising standards? Financial standards for the entry of customers?

Again, decisions by the Commission will have an impact on growth and development of the industry.

Research, Publication, and Educational Efforts. The Act includes authorization of research into the operation of markets and for publication of results. This authorization is aimed at obtaining the research base for improved regulation and at improved use and performance of markets. It is an important development tool.

As we noted, there was a substantial amount of research done by the Grain Futures Administration which was influential in shaping the Commodity Exchange Act of 1936. The Commodity Exchange Authority did numerous special market surveys and regularly published some information but did little analysis of market operations and performance.

The regulatory agency is in a unique position to conduct market research because of its access to otherwise confidential information. Effective use of the authorization and opportunity is essential to enlightened regulation. Hopefully, the Commission will proceed into new areas of regulation only after a sufficient research base is developed.

Regulatory Philosophy

The Commodity Futures Trading Commission is an established fact. If precedent established by other governmental Commissions is observed the fact will not go away; it is here to stay and the chances are that it will grow and there will be amendments to the Act. It, thus, is important that a regulatory philosophy be developed during the formative stages of the Commission. What should be the philosophy with regard to the economic performance of futures markets? The question is best presented as a dichotomy. One extreme would be based on the belief that futures trading is an evolutionary and pragmatic activity and that initiative for change should rest with exchanges and the users of markets. The role of the Commission would be negative. It would review and approve or disapprove of industry proposals, assuming that experimentation and change are desirable and only ask whether it was necessary to disapprove because the proposal was contrary to the public interest. At the other extreme the Commission would view its role as positive or activist. It should initiate changes when, after investigation, it finds such changes desirable and set standards of performance that would result in uniform applications of the changes. It would evaluate existing economic performance levels of markets in terms of potential performance and seek changes designed to increase the economic utility of markets.

It is easy to look at existing markets as we did in Chapter 14 and be seduced by the appeal of the activist role. It is easy for students of markets to look at performance in relation to potential and get annoyed by and impatient with the actions of exchanges, members, commission houses, and users of markets. To advocate an activist role for the Commission would be to fly in the face of most of all that has been said in the foregoing chapters. For markets are the closest approximation to the model of pure competition that has yet evolved and one must have faith in the wisdom of competitive forces.

To suggest the central planning of competitive markets is a contradiction of terms. Competition is decentralized, disorganized, and messy. That it works at all is surprising and that it works so extraordinarily well is amazing. In view of the track records of government and competitive forces the Commission will be well advised to make its role the negative one of policeman and to regulate with as loose a control system as is permitted by the law.

CHAPTER 16

Market Development

Expansion of futures markets toward their full potential in the commodity world can be accelerated by making changes in the operation and development of the markets. The key to expansion is increased and improved speculation. Growth is dependent on the inflow of new equity capital and equity capital is synonymous with speculative capital. The expansion of speculation to greater direction of commodity production and inventory use is necessarily a move toward a closer approximation of the model of perfect competition. An increase in speculation results in an increase in competition and vice versa. The road to attainment of perfect competition is a rocky one because everyone involved, consciously or otherwise, seeks a noncompetitive shelter. The problem is to probe for weaknesses in the system and suggest changes that will increase speculation.

The moving force must be the markets themselves. They are the only neutrals in the contest. And they are only neutral to the extent that they include, in equal balance, all of the diverse elements of the commodity trade. There are fairly strong tendencies toward noncompetitiveness on the part of exchanges themselves. They have done a remarkably good job of maintaining balance of representation of the diverse interests of their members—democratic governance does work effectively in maintaining competitive balance. But exchanges tend to look inward and, in extreme cases, act as if they were private clubs. Exchanges must be operated in the best interests of the long run efficiency of the industries they serve. In the very long run, this goal is compatible with the self-interests of the exchange membership. The achievement of the semi-public utility role places a heavy burden of responsibility on the exchanges.

Why Markets Fail

The history of markets is replete with instances in which trade has dwindled to zero and in which the trade is so small that it is not significant to the commodity that it is designed to serve. The reasons for failure of markets are not readily apparent if they are at all ascertainable. The broad brush answer is that markets are not used when their use is not more profitable to existing and potential users than some other method of coping with financing and pricing problems. Markets in which there is a consistent upward bias so that short hedgers chronically lose money soon discourage hedgers. Markets with a chronic downward bias eventually get too expensive for longs to use whether the longs are commercials or speculators. Only the markets without discernible bias trade in large volume. In addition to chronic price bias is a lack of liquidity. If the prompt execution of orders requires appreciable price concession, up or down, use is soon judged to be too expensive. As the outside trade of commercials and speculators decreases, the attractiveness of the markets to the locals—the liquidity suppliers—decreases and the liquidity problem is further aggravated. Those markets that work, work well, but those that don't work dwindle and disappear. Successful futures markets are zero sum games, equally attractive to longs and shorts. Five principal reasons for the dwindling and demise of markets can be pulled out of the history of market failure.

First, one market failed because it was legislated out of existence—onions. The Maine potato market has had some close calls from this kind of death.

Second, markets have lost their economic basis for existence. While there are instances of markets, pork bellies in particular, prospering without a large commercial or hedging base, we should continue to accept the general concept that the markets originate out of a need to shift risks and their size is determined by the amount of hedging use. When the need for use by hedgers decreases the markets decline and disappear. An outstanding example is the storage egg futures market. It developed and grew out of a need to shift price risks associated with inventory ownership. In time, technological developments in egg production resulted in the virtual elimination of the seasonality of production so that inventories were not built up. Year by year the size of inventory decreased and the build-up of open interest in futures almost exactly paralleled it. The market nearly went out of existence as the need for it declined toward zero. The storage egg contract was not suitable for hedging fresh eggs. The Chicago Mercantile Exchange gradually shifted to a fresh egg contract and this market has grown rapidly as the changing structure of the egg production industry has created an increasing need for the forward pricing of egg production.

A second example is the cotton futures market. For many years, the cotton futures market was one of the most active commodity markets. From 1955 on, trade in cotton futures declined to the point of vanishing at New Orleans in 1964. With the exception of a brief flurry in 1968, trade at New York was very small until 1971. The overall decrease in trading was the direct consequence of the entry of the Federal Government into cotton merchandising. The cotton price program was operated in such a way that the Commodity Credit Corporation bought and sold most of the U.S. cotton at a very narrow range of prices, eliminating the need for hedging by cotton merchants. Until 1971, trading went the way of economic basis for merchant hedging. The unusual situation that developed in 1971 was a combination of a sharply reduced supply, a small prospective production and a crop scare. This stimulated great speculative and trade interest since it potentially removed the dominance of the Government in regulating prices.

When the general upheavals in commodities occurred in 1972, the cotton price, too, was ripped loose from its anchor in the government support system. There was an immediate and very large increase in the volume of trading and the size of the open interest.

Much of the increase in futures trading in the grain complex from 1972 onwards was the result of the disappearance of the government as a price making force. Should government programs again dominate argicultural prices there will be a decline in the need for, hence the amount of, futures trading.

Third, markets have failed because of weakness in contract terms that gave an advantage to either the buyers or sellers. If the contract terms are out of balance they enable either the buyer or the seller to squeeze the other so that one side chronically profits at the expense of the other. This is discouraging to the losers and, in due course, they refuse to play. A futures contract is a temporary substitute for a cash transaction that will eventually be made and it must reflect commercial standards and movement closely enough to avoid price distortion.

A turkey futures market was quite active in 1962 and 1963 but then dwindled rapidly. The terms of the contract permitted delivery of packaged and branded turkeys that were difficult for someone other than the packer to merchandise. It became a dumping ground for the surplus production of turkey packers, to the disadvantage of the longs.

Fourth, markets fail because they are boycotted by commercial interests. As we have seen, the development of an active futures market represents an increase in competition; it puts the commercials in a more competitive position. There is a marked and understandable tendency for the commercial interests in a commodity to oppose futures trading at its outset. After markets are developed the strongest supporters are the commercial users but they have to be forced into use by the superior risking and pricing efficiencies of the markets.

We should not want to suggest that the political hue and cry that resulted in the execution of the onion futures market was generated by onion dealers but we could not blame them had they been responsible. Their advantageous monopolistic position was wrecked by the development of the market and restored with its demise.

Cottonseed oil futures trading was of major importance until 1963 but has since died out. The reasons are not clear and there are likely several but one important one seems to be a boycott by cottonseed oil producers and users. They can cover the bulk of their price level risks in soybean oil futures and work the differences between cottonseed and soybean oil prices to their own advantage. If they are to return they will have to be forced back by competition from speculators.

Fifth, markets fail to attract speculation. The short and long positions taken by hedging firms are almost never evenly balanced. Speculation is essential to the balancing of hedging positions and to liquidity. Hedgers are predominantly short. If sufficient speculative buying is not attracted, futures prices are unduly depressed, hedgers lose money, and discontinue use of the markets. Markets may be built on the need to shift risks and raise equity capital but it is certain that they cannot successfully exist without an adequate speculative interest.

These several reasons for failure of markets suggest that for a futures market to succeed there must be an economic need, the contract terms must be right, hedgers must be either attracted or forced in by competition, and there must be an active speculative interest. But the problem is not that simple: markets are built on commercial use and speculation is attracted but markets will not be used by commercials unless speculation is present. It is difficult to get markets off of dead center.

The Exchanges

What steps should markets take to accelerate expansion? As a general proposition they need to recognize their role as semi-public utilities whose purpose is to serve their outside trade—speculators and commercials. To the extent that exchange governance is weak in this recognition, the faults seem to lie with too much control by the locals who are present every day and too little by the members who represent the outside trade. There are many members of the exchanges who belong only to get reduced commission rates and who never go near the markets nor participate in the affairs of the exchanges. Some improvement might result from a change in the commission structure so that it would be less favorable to members. The exchanges should consider having more than one class of membership with different voting rights for each. Some would benefit from turning more control over to paid administrators. But in the main, improvement must come from enlightened membership and is a slow process.

Contract Terms. The purposes of futures trading are other than exchange of title. In instances in which delivery has been extensively made and taken markets have failed. In broad context, the purpose of futures trading is to enable specialized speculation; to separate the speculative functions from production, processing, storing, merchandising, etc. Thus, the theoretically perfect futures market is one on which delivery is neither made nor taken. The market must protect the speculator from having to procure and make delivery and from having to accept and merchandise delivery. At the same time the contract must be commercially real, representing and pricing actual commodities as they exist and are used in ordinary commercial activity. The rights and obligations of delivery must be inviolate. The contract must be so readily deliverable and so easily takable that neither party has reluctance to make or take and, thus, no desire to make or take delivery. Delivery is made and demanded to test markets and to force price relationships into line but the better the contract, the less this occurs. When it is possible to distort prices or price relationships by making or taking delivery, there is a fault in the contract that is in need of correction.

The existence of a futures market with its obligation to make and take delivery should not distort the flow of the commodity in its ordinary marketing channels. The pricing system, of which futures trading is a part, must adapt itself to the physical marketing problems, not vice versa. The objective of contract delivery terms should be to sample the flow of the commodity, test it for its value in exchange, and return it to stream.

The writing of futures contracts is difficult and the terms of the contracts need to be continually revised to maintain balance between buyers and sellers. Changing the terms of contracts is not simple. It takes agreement on the details by the committee of diverse interests that is appointed by the exchange. A soybean meal committee properly includes processors, feed manufacturers, merchants, and exporters. Each member is torn between loyalty to his company's advantage and service to the industry. As a result, changes are difficult to bring about. Once trading in a delivery month is authorized the terms of the contract cannot be changed for that delivery. Thus, there is always a lengthy transition often involving two different contracts for a particular month. The existence of two contracts in a commodity at one time is confusing to speculators and makes basis operations difficult for commercial users. It is avoided as much as possible.

Exchanges must have supervisory control of delivery. The clearing house is finally responsible for the fulfillment of delivery terms—that payments is made, that quality is appropriate, that delivery is made on time, and that warehouse receipts or ownership certificates are bona fide. This results in a tendency for delivery on contracts to be restricted to locations and to firms that can be supervised with a minimum danger of fraud, default, or contract violation. The supervisory requirement also makes contract change difficult.

Contract terms must be kept as simple as possible in the interest of the position of speculators. The speculators are not merchants and so are at a disadvantage when they must make or take delivery. From the individual speculator's point of view the solution is simple—stay out of the delivery month. However, this does not solve the problem of contract balance. Except as contract terms are kept simple and delivery restricted, speculators are put at a disadvantage and the long side of the market is weakened.

With this set of thoughts we have set up a contradiction. In the interest of representativeness we have argued for wide open delivery but in the interest of balance between speculators and commercials, we have argued for restricted delivery. Given this choice we will side with restricted delivery, for delivery terms have been too long modified and watered down to prevent market congestion. The futures contract, hence the futures price, should represent the top quality commercial commodities that are traded in substantial volume. If the standard trading grade of soybeans is U.S. No. 1 the futures contract should require U.S. No. 1. If the premium location and the place of the largest volume movement of soybeans is Gulf Ports, the Gulf should be the delivery point. If the standard item of commerce is strictly fresh eggs, the contract should specify strictly fresh eggs. The key consideration is that a readily merchantable commodity be placed in the hands of longs on delivery.

The long term preoccupation of the markets and of the government in connection with delivery terms has been the prevention of corners, squeezes, and price distortion associated with limited deliverable quantities and qualities at delivery points. The rules have been repeatedly relaxed to permit delivery of less than contract quality at approximate market discounts, delivery in high-rate warehouses, furnishing of minimum freight billing on delivery, and the suspension of trading before the end of the delivery month. Nearly every modification has been made in the direction of strengthening the position of the shorts versus the longs—the position of the commercials versus the speculating public.

Too restricted delivery terms can lead to congestion and price distortion although, as we saw in the last chapter, the danger of this tends to be exaggerated. The solution is simple: allow off grade, out of position delivery at punitive discounts. If the usual cash market discount of No. 3 corn is 2 cents under No. 2 let it be delivered at a 4 cent discount, etc.

That these suggestions for tightening up delivery are designed to strengthen the position of speculators does not mean that they are disadvantageous to normal hedging operations. They would be useful in preventing the putting of off grade commodities out of position for the purpose of creating an abnormally wide basis or distorting futures prices downward. This goes back to the notion that a short side distortion is easier to engineer and profit from than a long side distortion. A tightening up of delivery terms would tend to regularize price relationships, both over space and over time because it would make contracts more concisely representative of commodities traded. Normal price relationships are essential to out of delivery position hedging.

Promotion. During most of their existence the main objectives of the exchanges in their relationships with the public has been to keep a low profile.

The general negativeness toward futures trading led exchanges to feel that any image was bound to be bad and so the less image the better. They fought their political battles in smoke-filled rooms. A marked change occurred immediately following World War II when some of the exchanges, particularly the Chicago Board of Trade, began to develop educational programs. The Board celebrated its centennial in 1948 with a big bash, including extensive publicity. It took the position that if it had survived 100 years, it was a useful institution and the story should be told. It, and other of the exchanges, have continually sponsored symposia, seminars, research fellowships, educational films, and tours since that time. In addition the exchanges publish informational booklets and classroom materials. Most of this effort has been directed toward the educational system, particularly colleges. The objective is to introduce the subject matter into curricula and have it presented in a favorable light. Interestingly, the primary motivation appears more image building than promotion of new business. Exchange members truly believe that futures trading is a very useful institution and feel badly about the generally unfavorable image that it has so long had. The extent of success and direct effects of these programs is not measurable but the extent of general knowledge about futures trading is greater and the image is more favorable than it was in 1948. There remains a long way to go.

Beginning about 1960 some exchanges undertook more direct promotional programs. These were aimed at commercial interests, primarily smaller processors, country elevators, and, more recently, livestock producers. As new commodities are introduced, the exchanges make major efforts to acquaint the relevant trades with the nature and uses of futures markets. The objective is to teach firms how to use futures in connection with their businesses. This effort is useful in the introductory phases but the job is far greater than the resources of the exchanges permit; the bulk of the work must be done by the people who get revenue from trade—the commission houses.

So far so good; the efforts relate to general education and trade use. In the 1960's the more touchy area of promotion of speculation was introduced. This has been done on a modest scale with documentary type films and newspaper and magazine advertisement. It has been circumspect, not suggesting speculation but only inviting further inquiry. This development raises two questions: To what extent should the exchanges promote commodity speculation by the public? And what are the obligations to the public in teaching them to speculate in a way that will give them a reasonable chance of success? A lot more speculation than existed in 1976 is needed and its quality needs to be improved. Exchanges should not be reticent in calling attention to the merits of commodity speculation. Their only guideline should be the fact that futures trading is a zero sum game minus commission. Again the size of the task is beyond the resources of the exchanges and should be mainly left to the people who collect commissions. The main role of the exchange should be the development of educational materials for the use of others in teaching the public how to speculate.

Control of Commission Houses. The bulk of the job of promotion, development, and improvement of speculation is and will continue to be done by commission houses. It is important that their behavior be especially circumspect. All of the exchanges need to review their rules as they apply to commission house customers, particularly speculators, and develop sets of rules and supervisory procedures that will assure high professional standards of performance by commission houses.

The control of the activities of commission houses vis-à-vis their customers is difficult. When a small commission house holds membership in only one exchange or concentrates its activities in the commodities of one exchange it is easy to control. Large exchanges are able to control the behavior of commission houses because of the importance of trading on the large exchanges to the houses. But much of the match-up is small exchange and large, multi-exchange commission houses. Here, the ability of the exchanges to control is inherently weak. Exchanges are dependent on commission houses for volume. Commission house customers go to the exchanges and commodities that the houses recommend. A boycott of or failure to support an exchange by several major houses can be ruinous to an exchange. It is sometimes thought that large commission houses have more than optimum power in the governance of small exchanges.

High Cost of Overhead

Prior to 1973 all commodity exchanges prescribed minimum commission rates that commission houses had to charge customers. They did not establish maximum rates but this was not of consequence because the minimum was invariably the maximum. They prescribed nonmember rates, member rates which were usually one half of nonmember rates, floor rates which were about 10 to 15 percent as large as member rates, and scratch rates for trades made in pits at one price by scalpers that were but a fraction of the floor rates. In addition they prescribed the fees that brokers were paid. In 1972 the Department of Justice brought action against the Chicago Board of Trade under Anti-Trust law for price fixing. There followed class action suits against numerous exchanges and commission houses. In 1973 an agreement was reached by which fixed commissions would be gradually phased out by early 1978. The first step was to make commissions on trades of 25 contracts or more negotiable, then six months later, trades of 20 contracts or more become negotiable, etc.

The change is not complete at the time of this writing nor is the effect on commission houses to date known. In general, commissions have been increased with inflation. The increase has not been uniform. Houses that provide a minimum of services for customers or that specialize in larger accounts have tended to forego increases in the rates charged. Full service houses that handle smaller accounts have increased the most.

The fixed commission charge per contract was not economically rational—no fixed price ever is, else it would not be fixed. The charge for a two contract trade was $60 and $300 for a ten contract trade, but the cost was not five times as great. Brokerage and clearing fees were greater and the order transmission and accounting costs were greater if the larger transaction was offset in installments but there was no way for the cost difference to be $240. Inactive accounts that trade in one or two contracts per year are much more expensive per contract than active accounts. Some accounts call registered representatives incessantly and request large amounts of information, publications, etc., while others only use the commission house to take and execute orders and keep accounts. There is a tremendous range in profitability of accounts.

We can only speculate about the eventual impact of decontrolling commission rates. Some combination of several things will likely occur. First, the per contract rate will be reduced for large trades and increased for small trades. Competitive rates will become cost rational.

Second, commission rates may eventually be tied to some concept of annual volume of business done. Most of the cost of an account is fixed. The accounting procedure, the rendering of monthly statements, the furnishing of market letters, the research overhead are not directly proportionate to the volume of business done. The time that a registered representative must spend in opening and servicing an account is not directly proportional to volume. Small accounts often take more time than large accounts. One problem that commission houses encounter is that customers sometimes trade with more than one house to get a variety of opinions and move from house to house frequently. A system of charging one amount for the first 100 contracts in a given year, and a lesser amount for succeeding trades on a scale down may evolve. It would be cost and reward rational.

Third, there will be an unbundling of services. Clients that want only execution and accounting will be able to obtain it at lower rates. Clients that want, in addition, market letters and advice will pay more, and clients that want full service including business operational programs will be able to get it but will pay more.

Fourth, commissions will be related to customer success. This can take different forms. One could be quite indirect in that houses who can show good results obtained by customers can command higher commissions than others. Some houses may go directly to relating commissions to results.

Fifth, there probably will be an increase in nonmember Futures Commission Merchants. With fixed commisssion rates, the only incentive that many members had for owning memberships was reduced rates. With fully negotiated rates some merchants will not have incentive to belong to exchanges. This will raise problems that exchanges have in exercising control over the way that commission house customers are handled.

Commissions Can Be Costly. One lesson learned from the look at trading results in Chapter 13 is that commission charges are large in relation to the total amount of money that changes hands—the slot in the table drains a lot of money out of the game. If the objective is to maximize the amount of speculation and the amount of equity capital generated by the system, the cost of operating the game must be held at a minimum.

When compared to the total value of the commodity represented by the contract, commissions are small; $40 per contract when corn is $2.50 per bushel is .3 of one percent and $40 per contract of soybeans worth $5.00 is only .16 of one percent—impressively small numbers. They are much larger numbers when compared to minimum margin requirements. When the commission is $40 and the margin requirement for corn is $1000 and for soybeans $2000, the commission charge is 4 and 2 percent respectively—much less impressive.

Commission charges are small when compared to the size of price changes that regularly occur in commodities. A ¾ of a cent change in the price of a bushel of corn covers the cost of commission as does .06 cents per pound of soybean oil, etc. Speculators show little concern about the cost of commissions and the volume of their trading does not seem to be affected by commission rates. But, as we saw, they should be concerned. They cannot afford to trade for small price moves because commission charges tip the profit—loss odds against them. A one cent profit on 50,000 bushels of corn is a net profit of $100 while a one cent loss is a net loss of $900. Prospective moves have to be fairly large before a speculator who pays full commission can intelligently participate; the fine tuning of the market is left to the people whose cost of trading is small.

In our cursory look at the results of speculation in Chapter 13 we noted that the difference between profit and loss for the regular traders was commission paid. Other studies have shown much the same thing. Commissions are a large cost in a zero sum game. It grinds up a lot of speculative capital. There would be more speculative capital available if the cost of commissions were less. This does not mean that profits are inordinately large—they are not. It does mean that commodity speculation can be increased more readily if the cost of commission can be reduced. It can be done in two ways. First, by reducing the frequency of turnover of positions held by speculators. They would choose positions more judiciously and hold on to them longer. Were this to be accomplished they would probably be more successful, not only because of lower commission costs, but because one of the most serious faults that speculators have is over-trading. They tend to continually trade, which puts them in competition with professional locals and, in that game, they have little chance of success.

Second, by increasing the size of the capital units controlled by one person whether an individual trader, a registered representative, or a commodity trading pool. The arithmetic of being a registered representative is illustrative of the principle. Registered representatives typically get one third of the commissions they generate. If the average account generates one dollar of commision for each dollar of average value—which is not far from the current industry standard— the RR must control an average of $90,000 to have an income of $30,000. But if he controls $360,000 he can have the same income by trading the accounts only one fourth as actively. To reduce the activity would not mean that the money would be kept less fully invested but only that it would be turned over less often.

There are two powerful forces that work against a reduction of turnover. RR's are predominantly paid by the contract. This is a strong incentive to encourage activity. Commission houses have the same incentive.

Second, commission house customers have a built-in bias toward over-trading. They are unhappy if they do not have a position. They tend to want to grab a quick profit rather than wait for the whole of a situation to develop. They take larger positions than their available capital justifies and so are forced to take numerous small losses.

The operation of commodity pools is relatively new and the best methods of operation are not known. One thing that seems to be evolving is that they are more successful, as they hold a large proportion of their capital in reserve and as they are able to filter out the price static that surrounds markets as they make major moves.

Commission House Operation

The rudiments of commission house operation were discussed in Chapter 3. The objective here is to explore some ways in which improvements in commission house operations can contribute to increased and improved participation in futures trading. The remarks are necessarily critical because they deal with changes. This should not be construed as a negative attitude toward the commission house industry as it now operates; they do a generally conscientious and competent job.

The commission houses are the primary instruments for expansion and improvement for they are the firms that gain revenue from growth. They are the ones who have the money needed for promotion of trading and the training of traders. They must bear a heavy burden of responsibility for achievement of the aggregate goal of market growth. This requires far-sighted operation and willingness to forego short-term gains in the interest of long-term gains and the general welfare of the industry.

The basic objective of commission houses must be to get traders to succeed; if the "how to" chapters in Part III of this volume are correct, to get traders to operate as recommended there. The primary emphasis is on speculators, not on the larger and successful speculators but on the smaller and unsuccessful speculators. It is a challenging task because futures trading is a zero sum game in which traders try to take each other's money; the rate of failure must, by the terms of the game, be high.

Commission houses must play a major role in the development of new markets and the expansion of undertraded markets by seeking out the best speculative opportunities and guiding speculators to them.

Speculators tend to be vain and greedy. They enter markets because they have heard of someone who has made a lot of money from a little very quickly. They are after a fast buck, fail to understand what the game is about, and are not aware of the work, discipline, and patience that is required for a reasonable chance of success.

Speculators fail to grasp the basic concept that speculation is about forecasting prices of commodities that move in commercial channels. They depend too much on the advice of other people and, as a result, fail to make progress in developing forecasting skills. In their quest for action they frequently go outside their own areas of competence and trade in commodities they know nothing about. Few speculators appear to have any concept of money management. They trade for quick returns from soybean or cocoa price changes rather than for returns on invested capital with objectives that are established in relation to the risks they are willing to take.

Finally, few speculators understand how to admit error and take their losses before they are put out of the game. Part of the reason for this is that account executives are loath to say, "I blew it; take your lumps and let's try again.", part stems from the natural optimism that is required if one is to enter the game, and part from the misguided notion that losses are only "paper" until a trade is closed.

This is the assortment of errors and suicidal tendencies that commission houses must cope with if they are to develop a new breed of improved speculators.

Training Registered Representatives. The registered representative is the place where the system meets its lifeblood—the commission house customers. The success of markets is dependent on outside trade. Commission house earnings depend on the generation of commissions by RR's. The long run growth and development of futures trading will depend on the effectiveness with which RR's perform. Being an RR is a complex job requiring skill and a good working relationship with the house. As the futures trading industry expands there will be need for an increasing number of RR's. The structure of the commission house industry and the method of compensation has not been conducive to the development of effective RR's. In the mid 1960s a centralized examination was developed that one must pass to solicit business for commodities traded on major exchanges. But it does not require much knowledge or training. Some commission houses have established training programs but they are usually fairly brief. In the main, all that is required is that one be willing to undertake a job that is compensated on a piece work basis.

Training programs need to be developed that will adequately prepare people for securing and handling customer accounts. Ideally, these should be based on the curricula of universities. Cooperation between the commission house industry and the colleges is necessary in development of such curricula, for the knowledge and teaching of commodities and futures trading is limited. A training program should be broad, including not just the specifics of actual trading, order transmission, and contract terms but also the study of commodity price behavior, investment portfolio management, and psychology.

Compensation of RR's. Alterations or changes in the compensation system should be considered. Football coaches get fired when teams lose too often and get raises and new automobiles when teams win. Perhaps this should be the system for RR's; pay them bonuses when their assigned or recruited customers win and fine them when their customers lose. "But where are the customers' yachts?" is an old joke in the securities brokerage industry. One commodity house has a Yacht Club to which the RR's whose customers have been the most successful are admitted. There is special compensation to the members.

There needs to be incentive for performance and performance is the generation of commissions. But there is need for the industry to take a longer view. It needs a compensation system that does not put undue short run financial pressure on its employees. RR's must have time to develop a clientele that has a reasonable chance of success.

Selection and Control of Customers. Houses vary in the standards that they apply in accepting customers. Some only want to know if the prospect has an initial margin although even the most nondiscriminating try to see that the man is not playing with the rent money. At the other extreme, some houses require complete financial and income statements and limit the amount that can be put into commodities to the amount that they judge the prospect can afford to lose. There are all gradations. Note that these standards are based on the cynical attitude that the customer is probably going to lose money.

What is needed is a more positive approach. Commission houses should aggressively seek out people who need but are not currently using futures in connection with cash commodity businesses and people who have a reasonable probability of success as speculators. They need to do some serious study of the factors affecting customer success and methods of identification of speculative talent. Even the best of football coaches lose if they don't have the horses and most spend more time recruiting than coaching.

Control of customers is both important and difficult. The two worst faults that speculators have is letting losses get too large and letting success go to their heads so that they overtrade. It is difficult to stop a man from letting his losses run as long as he produces adequate margin money. Houses can watch closely and advise, and they can put teeth in their advice by raising margins for individual customers. This latter course is apt to cost the house a customer but no customer is better than a losing customer. Forcing customers to accept losses is also dangerous because the house doesn't know what is going to happen to the price. They may succeed in forcing a loser out just at the time that the price turns around. There is no weapon other than moral suasion to slow down a customer who holds a hot hand. The best course is to try to prevent his getting really clobbered when his hand turns cold.

Training Customers. More resources need to be put into the training and management of customers. The houses should get to know customers well, evaluate their forecasting skills, and help establish their investment objectives. This requires not only a flow of information and advice about positions but a continuous flow of the rationale behind the advice. The goal must be the development of competent, specialized, commodity analysts.

Finally, the name of the game is money. Customers need to be taught how to establish investment objectives and how to manage money in the ever changing profit-loss picture so that they have the best shot at success.

The Problem of Taxes. Under Internal Revenue Service regulations commodity futures contracts are capital assets. When traded in connection with a cash commodity business, gains and losses are treated as ordinary income. When traded by speculators they get capital gain and loss treatment. Gains on long positions held less than six months are taxable at ordinary income rates. Gains on long positions held for more than six months are long term so that only half of them are taxed. All gains on short positions are taxable as ordinary income, regardless of the length of time held. Only $1,000 of losses are deductible from ordinary income. This set of rules reduces the available speculative capital and results in some modifications of trading activity that may not be economically productive.

Suppose that two speculators, whose marginal income tax rates are 50 percent, take opposite market positions; one long, the other short. Suppose that the price goes down so that one loses $20,000 and the other makes $20,000. Suppose further that these are the only transactions that each makes in the year. The winner will pay $10,360 in taxes and the loser will have his income tax reduced by $480. $9,880 is taken out of the game by the government when there is no real gain or loss. The government is an interesting partner in commodity speculation, taking an increasing share of winnings and refusing to participate beyond the most niggardly way in losses. It is a "heads I win, tails you lose" game.

It is doubtful that many people are discouraged from speculating in commodities out of tax considerations, but tax treatment lends incentive to trading in ways that will postpone taxes and sometimes provide long term rather than short term gain. Tax modification can be accomplished by spreading, and the most popular spreading vehicle at this time (1976) is silver futures. Tax spreading may turn out to be the primary economic use of gold futures trading. The silver market has never been cross-sectioned but a cross section of the open interest would doubtless reveal a high proportion of spreads. The open interest typically declines sharply each January.

When an individual makes some money trading commodities his first objective is to spread it into the next year. He takes offsetting positions in futures deliverable in the next tax year with the long positions more than six months forward, say short June and long August silver. If the price goes up, so that short side loss equals his previous gain, he realizes the loss by buying June and offsets his long August position with a short position in October. He now has no taxable income in the current year but a locked in position value that can be realized the next year. If the price stays up long enough the gain becomes long term, only half is taxable. If a long term doesn't work out the whole process can be repeated the next year, etc., until it does. Careful operators can carry gains forward for quite long periods.

Experienced speculators try to carry gains forward because of the ever present possibility of loss. Suppose that one year a trader in a marginal 50 percent bracket makes $20,000 of short term gain. He pays $10,360 in taxes. The next year he loses $20,000 but from this he can recover only $480 from savings in taxes on other income. He can carry the loss forward to be used in the third or fourth year when he again wins but in the meantime his trading is handicapped by a capital shortage. Better to pay taxes later than sooner.

Traders often lose money trying to extend gains from short-term to long-term. Tax considerations bias traders toward the long side. They result in trading that would not otherwise occur, some of which is not productive in rationalizing commodity price.

This tax structure does not make sense and should be modified *in the interest of preserving speculative capital*. The whole futures trading industry supports long term capital treatment. But such treatment is questionable. No futures contract is a long term capital asset in the sense that a farm or factory is a capital asset. Commodities aren't capital; they are goods. If this is the case, then losses on positions should not have capital treatment but should be permitted to be offset by income from other sources.

A change from capital asset to ordinary income treatment would still result in capital loss because of the graduated tax structure but the loss would be much less. A trade of the long term treatment on long positions held over six months for other income offset of losses would be a net gain for the industry, both of the amount of speculative capital and rationality of trading. This is a loophole, through which good speculative money is drained into government, that should be closed.

Index